Critical Essays on
SHAKESPEARE'S
Richard III

CRITICAL ESSAYS
ON
BRITISH LITERATURE

Zack Bowen, General Editor
University of Miami

Critical Essays on
SHAKESPEARE'S
Richard III

edited by

HUGH MACRAE RICHMOND

G. K. Hall & Co.
New York

G. K. Hall & Co.
1633 Broadway
New York, NY 10019

Library of Congress Cataloging-in-Publication Data

Critical essays on Shakespeare's Richard III / edited by Hugh Macrae Richmond
    p.   cm. — (Critical essays on British literature)
    Includes bibliographical references and index.
    ISBN 0-7838-0449-0 (alk. paper)
    1. Shakespeare, William, 1564–1616. King Richard III. 2. Richard III, King of England, 1452–1485—In literature. I. Richmond, Hugh M. II. Series.
    PR2821.C75   1999
    822'.3'3—dc21   99-33428
                                           CIP

This paper meets the requirements of ANSI/NISO Z3948-1992 (Permanence of Paper).

10 9 8 7 6 5 4 3 2 1

Printed in the United States of America

For Elizabeth and Claire, with love.

Contents

◆

General Editor's Note

◆

The Critical Essays on British Literature series provides a variety of approaches to both classical and contemporary writers of Britain and Ireland. The formats of the volumes in the series vary with the thematic designs of individual editors and with the amount and nature of existing reviews and criticism, augmented, where appropriate, by original essays by recognized authorities. It is hoped that each volume will be unique in developing a new overall perspective on its particular subject.

Hugh Richmond's introduction begins with a well-argued account of audience fascination with the character of Richard, tortured and abetted by physical deformity and his own intimate knowledge of human psychopathology, yielding a character study of the greatness of a villain who totally involves the actors, producers, critics, and audiences both before and after Shakespeare's original version, revealing "the theatrical perfection of a theme with proven fascination." For many, the play proved the danger of immoral delight in evil, but according to Richmond there are other reasons for the veneration of Richard: his self-knowledge, his individualism, and his acceptance of himself, for better or worse.

The selection of essays is divided into four groups, each section separately introduced by Richmond. The first deals with original contexts—historiographical, literary, and theatrical—and the second with revisions and rewritings of the play, particularly the one by Colley Cibber, which dramatically shifts the emphasis to melodrama. The third section details the reevaluation of the play in the late twentieth century, and the final section contains three contemporary essays: a review of the most recent staged versions, a feminist interpretation, and an essay about Richard's deformities. Richmond's own essay on contemporary productions is a witty bonus to this collection of major Shakespearean scholars.

ZACK BOWEN
University of Miami

Publisher's Note

◆

Producing a volume that contains both newly commissioned and reprinted material presents the publisher with the challenge of balancing the desire to achieve stylistic consistency with the need to preserve the integrity of works first published elsewhere. In the Critical Essays series, essays commissioned especially for a particular volume are edited to be consistent with G. K. Hall's house style; reprinted essays appear in the style in which they were first published, with only typographical errors corrected. Consequently, shifts in style from one essay to another are the result of our efforts to be faithful to each text as it was originally published.

Introduction: Richard III *Restored*

♦

HUGH MACRAE RICHMOND

Around the time of the appearance of *Richard III* William Shakespeare had all the characteristics of a successful commercial dramatist: his *Henry VI* plays were generally regarded as secure popular successes, *The Comedy of Errors* marked a happy assimilation of Terentian comedy, and *Titus Andronicus* showed him willing to compete with Kyd in the horror feature stakes. However, *Richard III* marked his breakthrough to a new level of significance beyond professional competence that transcended conventional interest. Soon Francis Meres would claim that Shakespeare had achieved the status of being the English Seneca, the "most excellent" writer of tragedies, as shown by his *Richard III*.[1] The comparison is of more than casual significance, for much of modern criticism has noted how closely Shakespeare's play follows classical conventions in general and the patterns of Senecan rhetoric in particular, as shown by Wolfgang Clemen's survey of Senecan echoes in the play's opening (64–72) and by Roy Battenhouse's application of Aristotelian criteria to the play's audience impact (170–175).

By 1606, Barnabe Barnes could take note of the play's topic, "which is yet fresh in our late chronicles; and hath been many times represented unto the vulgar upon our English theatres, of Richard Plantagenet, third son to Richard, Duke of York" (Ingleby, Toulmin Smith, and Furnivall, 1:162). The relevance of the earlier historical accounts of popular chroniclers to the play is documented by Peter Saccio's recapitulation (17–36) of the various accounts on which Shakespeare depended. But by 1616 or so, Richard Corbet records that Burbage's performance of Shakespeare's Richard had preempted such written histories, for a local tour guide "could tell where Richmond stood, and Richard fell," but when the guide "would have said, 'King Richard died, and called "A horse, a horse!"' " he 'Burbage' cried" (Ingleby, Toulmin Smith, and Furnivall, 1:271). Already in 1600, historians such as Sir William Cornwallis were upset by misjudgments of Richard, because "malicious

1

credulity rather embraceth the partial writings of indiscreet chroniclers, and witty play-makers, than his laws and actions" (Ingleby, Toulmin Smith, and Furnivall, 1:85). By 1684, William Winstanley was even more exercised about the distortions: "so hath that worthy prince's fame been blasted by malicious traducers, who like Shakespeare in his play of him, render him dreadfully black in his actions, a monster of nature, rather than a man of admirable parts" (Ingleby, Toulmin Smith, and Furnivall, 1:305). The play's popularity has depended to a large degree on this legendary scale of its hero's wickedness, aided by the resulting controversies generated by Richard's defenders, including members of the present day's Richard III Society, which is dedicated to his defense. Such concerns are illustrated in Josephine Tey's effort in *The Daughter of Time* to transpose guilt for the death of the Princes in the Tower to Richard's supplanter, the Tudor King Henry VII. Antony Sher pursued these studies in preparation for his Royal Shakespeare Company (RSC) performance of Richard in 1984, as we shall see (258).

Because of its vindication of the Tudor succession, the play was frequently performed at court, and Milton found it expedient to prove the viciousness of Charles I by arguing that his posthumously published meditation, *Eikon Basilike,* had been corrupted by "the closet companion of these his solitudes, William Shakespeare: who introduces the person of Richard III, speaking in as high a strain of piety, and mortification, as is uttered in any passage of this book" (Ingleby, Toulmin Smith, and Furnivall, 1:523). Just how ominous a figure Richard had become in Shakespeare's rendering can be gathered from the anonymous prologue provided for a revival of the play in 1661, which cautioned the audience about "how you crowd to join with a usurper" but hopes to remedy this affinity when, "from the rage of Richard's tyranny, Richmond himself will come and set you free" (Ingleby, Toulmin Smith, and Furnivall, 1:103).

From the start actors and audiences of the play knew that they were witnessing a work of obsessional fascination, capable of driving both sexes into compulsive behavior, such as the female spectator whose assignation with Burbage after his performance as Richard was supposedly preempted by the greater claims of his creator with the words: "William the Conqueror was before Richard III" (Ingleby, Toulmin Smith, and Furnivall, 1:98). A student actor auditioned by Richard Burbage in *The Return from Parnassus* is sardonically encouraged by the star: "I like your face, and the proportion of your body for Richard the Third. I pray you, Mr. Philomusus, let me see you act a little of it." Completely familiar with so celebrated a text, the neophite immediately launches into Richard's opening soliloquy: "Now is the winter of our discontent" (Ingleby, Toulmin Smith, and Furnivall, 1:102). The play's dominance on the stage in subsequent centuries ensured that success with Richard marked the triumph of theatrical superstars in every age, whether that of Burbage, Garrick, Kean, Olivier, or even McKellen. Indeed, well before Garrick's time, the role acquired a momentum of its own distinct from Shakespeare's script, so that performance of Richard had flowered into a version of the text designed to flatter the egomania of its players and the morbid delight of its audiences, as described by Scott Colley (75–94), who shares the surprising persistence of a preference for Cibber's careful rewrite over Shakespeare's more provocative version.

However, the romantics gave their own reinterpretation of the text, favoring the role of Richard not so much as the blend of melodrama and didacticism as defined by Cibber but validated as more psychologically perceptive. Their interest in aberrant psychology found an anticipatory hint even in Samuel Johnson, who found parts of the play "trifling, others shocking, and some improbable," but who also notes that "Shakespeare very diligently inculcates that the wickedness of Richard proceeded from his own deformity, from the envy that rose at the comparison of his own person with others, and what incited him to disturb the pleasures that he could not partake."[2] Such more psychological approaches appear in Whately's association of *Richard III* with the more profound characterization of *Macbeth* (95–102), even though the juxtaposition differentiates the heroes. By the time of Charles Lamb, that critic can write "I am possessed with an admiration of the genuine Richard, his genius, and his mounting spirit, which no consideration of his cruelties can depress" (Scott and Williamson, 8:159). For example, Lamb admonishes us: "read his most exquisite address to the Widowed Queen to court her daughter for him, the topics of maternal feeling, of a deep knowledge of the heart, are such as no monster could have supplied. Richard must have felt, before he could feign so well." The German romantic Augustus William Schlegel was able to show (103–105) how Richard's role in the three parts of *Henry VI* provided just such a rich realm of experience from which the role of Richard might plausibly evolve. Coleridge follows these precedents when he argues that Richard's "character is drawn with the greatest fulness and perfection; and the poet has not only given us that character, grown up and completed, but he has shown us its very source and generation. The inferiority of his person made the hero seek consolation and compensation in the superiority of his intellect; he thus endeavoured to counterbalance his deficiency" (Scott and Williamson, 8:161). Once the psychological credibility of the character was validated, it became clearer why actors of all ages found the part so rewarding and compelling. Hazlitt shows how such empathetic interpretations were realized on the stage by Edmund Kean (106–111).

In this willful apotheosis, Richard's role achieved the reversal of interest achieved by Milton's Satan, seen as the true hero of *Paradise Lost* in the same period by revolutionaries such as Shelley, a parallel noted by Nathan Drake (112–114). By the time G. B. Shaw was writing about productions of *Richard III*, he could assert that "nobody now alive has seen what can be done with Richard," arguing that to treat him as "a really brilliant Nietzschean would be fresh and delightful" (Scott and Williamson, 8:182). This assertive reading of Shakespeare's characterization persists to the present, reflected in the suppression of anti-Richard roles such as Margaret's in Olivier's Oscar-winning film, which uses several of Cibber's rewrites, and in the yet greater extravagances of McKellen's film, which is nearer to a James Bond thriller than a true tragedy. In view of such popular hit versions, Al Pacino could hardly be more wrong in his film *Looking For Richard* than when he talks of the story's impenetrability, for its hero has always enjoyed the same popularity as the Herod figure in medieval biblical plays, or the demon king of pantomime, or the modern villains who are James Bond's intransigent opponents, not to mention uses of the Punch and Judy stereotype of which "most popular of dramatic entertainments" G. B. Shaw finds "*Richard III* is the best" (Scott and Williamson, 8:181).

Modern criticism has been more thoughtful and sympathetic than Shaw's, implicitly rejecting Pacino's misrepresentation of the role's impenetrability. Bernard Spivack has shown (50–57) how Shakespeare's Richard was consciously modeled on the medieval versions of just such popular figures. Indeed, Richard explicitly identifies himself with "the formal Vice, Iniquity" (3.1.82).[3] Biographers of the historical Richard such as Paul Kendall have noted that both as duke of Gloucester and as king he enjoyed medieval drama of the kind favored in the city of York, his principal base of support. These medieval precedents have been recognized as norms against which to measure Shakespeare's distinctive rendering of the character by many of the critics in this collection, such as Rossiter's detection of a profound dualism in the portrait of Richard; many others, such as Nicholas Brooke, agree with Rossiter, and find the treatment nearer to the tragic subtlety of that in *Macbeth,* as is perceived by such an early critic as Thomas Whately.

Nevertheless, systematic modern exaggeration of Richard's self-conscious dominance in Cibber's vein has overshadowed Shakespeare's more balanced treatment of evil. This distortion may have encouraged T. S. Eliot's censure of "the self-consciousness and self-dramatization of the Shakespearean hero," which he accepts as "new" but does not find "very agreeable."[4] However, Eliot's experience of Richard's role would necessarily be unfair to Shakespeare; indeed he admits that "I rebel against most performances of Shakespeare" (96). From the end of the seventeenth century to at least the middle of the twentieth century, Shakespeare's work was refracted by forces that reflected the obsessional nature of the theme Shakespeare had epitomized in *Richard III,* but that he had himself honorably worked to contain, in the progressive alienation of the audience from Richard, which Eliot almost necessarily ignored. For Richard's decline has been minimized by theater professionals down to our own age, who protracted their own delight in Richard's black humor, proving less morally and aesthetically scrupulous than Shakespeare. As appears in the last section of this anthology, the Rustaveli version of *Richard III* favored by Antony Sher and his cohorts shows that the Restoration period's pattern of confident "improvement" of Shakespeare is returning to favor in our own era's postmodern contempt for authorial and textual integrity. Such reactionary modifications can objectively be described as "medieval" in their bold moralizing. They revert to a pre-Shakespearean treatment of the topic.

For, as modern scholarship has documented, Shakespeare did not himself invent the provocative role or even the initially moralistic treatment of Richard: characteristically, he merely consolidated and heightened the inventions of his predecessors, after the high impact of these precedents was established. The first of these historical reconstructions was solicited by Richard III's overthrower himself, King Henry VII. Himself guilty of later authorizing the assassination of the earl of Warwick, a young princely rival to the throne imprisoned in the Tower, Henry found it expedient to represent Richard as equally callous. Bullough registers (37–49) the precedents provided when, with the aid of propagandists such as Polydore Vergil, an early spin doctor, Henry created the image of a literally as well as allegorically monstrous Richard, whose necessary overthrow was a legitimizing prerequisite for Tudor subversion. This expedient reading was confirmed by Sir Thomas More, when he sought to ingratiate himself with his own Tudor nemesis, Henry VIII, who had imprisoned him in the Tower for resisting the king's divorce from Katherine of Aragon. More created a black pendant to the positivist natives of his *Utopia,* providing a chiaroscuro effect of contrasting human villainy with their rational virtue, in the form of a diabolic Richard III.

Motivated by a desire to investigate the "Englishness" (at the time under threat by World War II), Tillyard shows (117–128) how this myth validated Tudor usurpation and also proved expedient to later, patriotic Elizabethan historians subject to a Tudor monarch, such as Hall and Holinshed, and to dramatists following them, such as Thomas Legge. In his Latin tragedy *Richardus Tertius* Legge presented a dramatization of the Ricardian legend to flatter Queen Elizabeth, granddaughter of Henry VII, for the University of Cambridge. The unnatural wickednesses of Legge's theatrical caricature inherited all the thrilling excitement that had made the clergy so nervous about the popularity of the Devils and Vices of late medieval drama. Indeed, in his *Worthies,* Fuller notes that the material already showed the possibility of compulsive identification with its principal role maintained by Shakespeare's version. The actor who played Legge's Richard, John Palmer, entered theatrical legend because he "had his head so possessed with a Prince-like humor that ever after he did what he acted" as Richard, ending in prison, despite having been master of Magdalen College and dean of Peterborough cathedral.[5] Legge's Richard is also shown associating with the delicious seductress Mistress Shore, and Richard himself attempts to seduce his own niece, Princess Elizabeth. Bernard Spivack shows how such scenes modulate from medieval conventions to Shakespeare's script. For Legge's provocative scenes match the reenactment of the medieval dramas' temptation of Eve through the machinations of Satan, matched later in Shakespeare's own Richard of Gloucester's more successful seduction of Lady Anne. Legge's play survives in numerous versions, establishing the kind of distinctive theatrical precedents by the university wits that Shakespeare characteristically followed so adeptly and perfected for the public stage. Robert Greene bitterly noted this indebtedness in his *Groatsworth of Wit*, with his warning to his fellow dramatists against this "upstart crow, beautified with our feathers" (Ingleby, Toulmin Smith, and Furnivall, 1:2–3). At least one other Richard III play follows Legge's in anticipating Shakespeare's grasp of the theme's potentialities. Many of Shakespeare's best effects in *Richard III* are thus highly traditional, as perceived by Irving Ribner (58–63) and Marjorie Garber (194–202).

So, as Geoffrey Bullough makes clear in his study of these direct sources and close analogues of the play (37–49), what we have in Shakespeare's *Richard III* is not the radical invention of wholly fresh material but the theatrical perfection of a theme with proven fascination. The self-conscious villain derived from the biblical Satan, as enacted in the medieval cycle plays. He was reincarnated in the guise of the Machiavel into which Protestant polemic had distorted Machiavelli's *The Prince*. Marlowe had sustained this misrepresentation by bringing Machiavelli onto the Elizabethan stage as Chorus to *The Jew of Malta*, taking at face value the sardonic (perhaps even ironic) advice the exiled Machiavelli had offered to the usurping Medici prince (who had imprisoned and tortured him, as a supporter of a once democratic Florence). In the third part of *Henry VI*, Shakespeare added his own anachronistic twist to the Tudor myth of Richard's wickedness by making his cynical manipulations the expression of a rivalry with Machiavelli a whole generation before *The Prince* was written.

Moreover, as an alienated younger brother of the Yorkist monarch, Edward IV, Shakespeare's Richard synchronized with the malcontent role that Elizabethans found fascinating for its mordant social criticism, whether in the form of Jaques's contributions to the comedy of *As You Like It* or Hamlet's more profound disruption of the political expediencies of Denmark. In all three cases Shakespeare showed himself a master of the black humor that allowed such ominous figures to seduce Renaissance audiences. However, as Madonne Miner shows, in *Richard III* Shakespeare had balanced the fascination of his virtuoso villain by another anachronistic device: the resurrection of Margaret of Anjou, widow of King Henry VI, exiled and ultimately dead in the time covered by the play. She becomes the fury figure who expresses Richard's own doom, joined with other mothers whose children are Richard's victims, to correspond to the choric force of the Eumenides in the *Oresteia* of Aeschylus. The curses of these women neutralize the charm of Richard's wit by driving home its costliness in terms of human suffering. It is ironic that this most sustained of Shakespeare's female roles (appearing throughout the whole first tetralogy), and one Peggy Ashcroft considered one of his greatest female parts,[6] has seemed less inspiring to many feminist critics, as we can see with Jean Howard and Phyllis Rackin. Actresses have been more appreciative, as Henry Fenwick notes (232–240) in recalling production of the British Broadcasting Corporation (BBC) version.

But, just as cynical modern sociology has accepted too absolutely the patriotic Machiavelli's Swiftian irony about cynical "modern" politics, so many male theatrical practitioners have decided that they want the pure villainy of the early Richard without the constraints of any counterbalance to explain his ultimate fall. Shakespeare wrote as inheritor of the medieval biblical and morality plays, and he carefully showed the progressive constriction of Richard's villainy by individual and social forces mustered implicitly by Providence and most explicitly in the female roles, which are among Shakespeare's most assertive (see Madonne Miner, 241–254, and Jean Howard and Phyllis Rackin, 267–272). These women on stage are explicitly buttressed by the off-stage historical roles of Henry VII's mother, the countess of Derby, and of his future wife, Elizabeth of York. Female resentments increasingly lattice Richard's initiatives in the net of moral, political, and military constraints from which he struggles in vain to break free. As Shakespeare's version of the Eumenides, these figures are reinforced by similar divine sanctions, which validate their curses.

However, from the time of Colley Cibber, this inhibiting framework was dismantled, the female roles diminished or suppressed, so that the megalomaniac delights of Richard's sadism flourished unconstrainedly, to the self-indulgent satisfaction of actors and audiences, creating the prototype for modern horror movies. Nevertheless, the same process of excision continues: it was reflected in the removal of Queen Margaret from the cast of the touring version of Antony Sher's *Richard III* just a few years ago, despite his protests about the centrality of the female components of the play, as registered in his *The Year of the King,* which takes a formally Freudian view of Richard's resentment of rejection by his mother (258–259). A less doctrinaire psychoanalytic approach by Murray Krieger (146–160) proves the superiority of the script to mere conceptual readings. Modern attempts to minimize the significance of these women's roles as merely rhetorical conform to the macho reading of the play's exceptionally numerous female characters that has flourished since 1700. Such readings seem more to be symptoms of an epidemic obsession with violent assertion of the male self than accurate responses to the complex structure of the original script (see M. M. Mahood, 208–31), which is rejected in favor of a stress on the fascination with unconstrained evil, ornamented by witty cynicism, as preferred by postmodern Shakespeare revisionists such as Charles Marowitz.

Before these simplifications can be diagnosed and rectified, it seems necessary to establish the original nature of Shakespeare's distinctive formulation of his largely inherited material. That there is a compulsive interest in Richard's witty perversity for many audiences is confirmed by consistent reactions over four centuries, by means of which the play has survived as a popular work of art whereas interest in analogous but less humorous texts such as *Tamburlaine* or *The Jew of Malta* has remained largely confined to scholarly audiences. Since the time of Edward Alleyn no actor has ridden to public acclaim as Tamburlaine or Barabas. Shakespeare achieved something more archetypal than a portrait of mere uninhibited ambition. Popular approval remains an essential factor in evaluating the success of a play, which cannot flourish on academic interest alone.

Drama differs from most other art forms in that it is a communal—even a community—experience. Unlike paintings, or novels, or sonnets, it needs a team of performers and an actively participating audience of more than one. In the first instance one source of audience involvement depends on a basic theme of all popular literature: the triumph of the seemingly inferior, of the outsider, over his supposed betters. Because most readers and playgoers, being human, tend to competitiveness and anxiety, any audience instinctively empathizes with Richard's opening confidences: that as a youngest son, and a cripple to boot, he is alienated, and frustrated, and excluded from power, not to mention sexual satisfaction. Most of us, even if we are quite successful, have felt similarly frustrated by our superiors at times. Consequently, we delight in his unexpected triumphs over stupid people who seem more attractive and powerful than he: his brother the king, his other older brother, Clarence, the hostile Queen Elizabeth, and her rampant Woodville faction, ex-Lancastrian supporters who threaten the Yorkists after Edward IV's death. Last, and by no means least, Richard is challenged by the seemingly inaccessible and wealthy Lady Anne. She is the seductive widow of a major rival to the Yorkist succession, the Lancastrian Prince of Wales, in whose murder, like that of his father, King Henry VI, Richard was supposed to be directly involved.

The crucial scene of that seduction is one of Shakespeare's most brilliant reversals of expectation: Richard achieves the ultimate male escapist dream of being able to seduce even the most inaccessible woman: the wife whom he has widowed. By contrast Anne's situation provides a subtler temptation to the female audience, the desire to attract the most unruly yet most dynamic and talented male in society: a fascinatingly outlandish figure who will reappear in later centuries as Richardson's Lovelace and Byronic heroes, such as Brontë's Heathcliff. As we can see in Hazlitt's account of Edmund Kean's interpretation, the popularity of Richard's role during the romantic period confirms the age's interest in the farouche male. This reflexive desire to conquer the most unaccommodating male available may lie behind all those unlikely female infatuations with convicted criminals on death row of which we hear recurrently. And if this choice of a feminine motivation is held to be too selective, we can always fall back on the more ancient ground rule that power is the ultimate aphrodisiac, and the successful murderer of one's husband and father-in-law is surely the dominant male. To reform such a monster through his flattering passion for oneself would be a triumph indeed.

The play cleverly emancipates us from serious guilt in our connivance with Richard by stressing that most of the victims of Richard early in the play are themselves at least as guilty as he is (and as Henry VII or Henry VIII will prove). Thus, in some ways, Richard merely acts as God's agent in punishing evil, as Tillyard argues in his pivotal essay that establishes the credibility of *Richard III* as a serious statement of Tudor ideology. Moreover, Richard's victims are stupid: they mishear his ironic confessions of responsibility for their downfalls, and they do not perceive their own criminality until it is too late to escape its penalties. In this condition, they are morally inferior to Richard, who at least always knows that he is culpable and is thus one stage closer to redemption: you cannot repent of a crime of which you are not conscious. So the first two acts of the play invite audiences to share Richard's bravura and mastery, to enjoy his black humor without serious qualm. It is an exhilarating sensation to observe this histrionic mastery and an even greater one to perform it, which is why Cibber rewrote the second half of the play to sustain exactly the same affirmation of Richard's initial dominance until the very last moment, when history is allowed summarily to redeem morality, as in most melodramas. But Shakespeare's text denies us much continuation of the initial euphoria from the moment that the deaths of the innocent young princes show us that Richard is no longer punishing the guilty but murdering indiscriminately and unnecessarily. From that point, we begin to share the feelings of affronted motherhood and to realize to what a leader and what values we have committed ourselves. The stress of this realization and the guilt of sharing Richard's amusement, which we now increasingly perceive as reflecting his sadism and lack of an inner self, constitutes the unique catharsis of the play. An element of his reevaluation is the appreciation of how dangerous Richard's fluency and plausibility are. To the extent that these qualities invested in Richard are Shakespeare's own talents, we can clear him of Eliot's accusation of empathy with a "disagreeable" cunning, as the play calls in question the very fluency that is Shakespeare's own greatest professional resource.

Granted this underlying rhythm, it is clear that for the principal actor the obligation is progressively to deny himself the dominance and assurance that make the part initially so seductive, and for the director there is a need to enhance the authority of the female opponents to Richard, whose concerns afford little occasion for fun or humor (which is why so many of their later scenes are cut or dropped altogether). This concern bears particularly on the scene in which Richard tries to repeat the seduction of Lady Anne by winning Queen Elizabeth's acceptance of his incestuous marriage to her daughter, his niece—which we know Richard ultimately failed to accomplish and for which he seems ultimately to struggle more desperately than convincingly. Emrys Jones evokes thoughtfully how far our modern awareness can approximate to Elizabethans' immediate application of Tudor history to the staging of *Richard III*. By the end of the play, both the actor who plays Richard and his audience must assent to a rueful reevaluation of the bravura mood of the opening as no more sustainable artistically than historically.

Colley Cibber's rewriting of the play largely averts this reevaluation of Richard's fascination. It sustains the opening vivacity of evil in the play to its end, at the expense of systematically turning the script into an emotionally exploitive melodrama. It was such proto-Byronic extravagance that led to Kean's romantic readings of the role, followed by Irving, Olivier, and even McKellen—at least, in his filmed version of the play, which outbids Cibber in presenting the gleefulness of Richard's last moments. In such versions the play serves as a vast Rorschach test, a protracted inkblot to be misread in terms of the principal actor's aberrations or those of his director. If such self-indulgence is true of most performances, it may also be a factor in many critics' responses. We must ask whether they are offering objective insights into the text or merely betraying their own predispositions. Unfortunately, the frequent censure of the text for immoral delight in evil is most likely to suggest repressed anxiety about critics' own affinities with Richard's initial stance, which also inhibits their confident acceptance of the Shakespearean script's ultimate repudiation of it. Many of the critics cited here, such as Rossiter (129–145), Brooke (161–169), and Charnes (273–281), seem openly resentful that Richard cannot somehow be made to escape the determinism of recorded history. In the following pages it is instructive to watch the dawning realization of the serious artistic intentions of the history plays in general and *Richard III* especially, particularly in those that follow from Tillyard's deeper awareness of their serious modern interest, spurred on by his patriotic exposition of English historical identity elicited by World War II. After Hitler, Richard no longer seems an artificial monster, and it becomes possible to treat *Richard III* as a serious artifact. In this awareness Tillyard is followed by such self-consciously "English" critics as M. M. Reese, but these deeper insights often coexist with remnants in other critics from earlier contemptuous misrepresentations of the play as mere melodrama (which I have mostly excluded here).

Having so questioned the detachment of some critics, I must probably abide by their reciprocation of my censure, because I too feel an obsessive interest in *Richard III* beyond detached appreciation. Even while the play may be properly vindicated in the more objective terms proposed earlier, because they are shared by many of the essays in this volume, this consensus does not penetrate to the heart of the play's interest for me, nor does it fully define Shakespeare's own subjective relationship to the text, as highlighted by the relevance to it of many of his sonnets from the same period. Eliot has asserted that "In Elizabethan England . . . any emotional attitude which seems to give a man something firm, even if it be only the attitude of 'I am myself alone.' is eagerly taken up" (112). As an example of this kind of self-affirmation, we can see that, in his own persona, Shakespeare matches Richard's egotism when he writes in Sonnet 121:

> 'Tis better to be vile than vile esteemed
> When not to be receives reproach of being, . . .
> For why should others false adulterate eyes
> Give salutation to my sportive blood? . . .
> No, I am that I am, . . .

In his final crisis of self-recognition, Richard asserts that "Richard loves Richard; that is, I am I" (5.3.183). The same entrenched self-awareness recurs in another, less monstrous villain, Parolles, of whom a stunned observer of his confession of cowardice exclaims: "Is it possible that he should know what he is, and be what he is?" (*All's Well,* 4.1.44). The power to live with a Pauline self-awareness of one's own wickedness is what Reformation psychology aspired to but rarely attained, despite Shakespeare's Calvinistic hint in concluding this sonnet that "All men are bad."

Similarly, the specious amatory relationship between Richard and Anne seems ominously close to that between Shakespeare and his Dark Lady in Sonnet 138:

> When my love swears that she is made of truth,
> I do believe her though I know she lies, . . .
> Simply I credit her false speaking tongue;
> On both sides thus is simple truth suppressed. . . .
> O, love's best habit is in seeming trust . . .
> And in our faults by lies we flattered be.

Each partner is flattered by the supposed but unvalidated surrender of the other, yet neither openly admits to the doubt each may plausibly feel. Richard shares with the sonnet writer the knowledge that society survives on suppression of sincere feelings, but Lady Anne seemingly remains as yet less conscious of the mere expediency of her alliance with Richard. For Shakespeare the apparent arbitrariness of Anne's surrender to Richard is intrinsic to his autobiographical sense of the artificiality of sexual relationships, which most readers detect in the *Sonnets* and which makes lovers' girations in such plays as *The Two Gentlemen of Verona* and *A Midsummer Night's Dream* so disconcerting.

Lastly and most disturbingly, the persona of Richard bears a surprising resemblance to the manipulative model of excellence offered in Sonnet 94, which looks forward to a whole sequence of dominant Shakespearean rulers:

> They that have power to hurt and will do none,
> That do not do the thing they most do show,
> Who, moving others, are themselves as stone,
> Unmoved, cold, and to temptation slow,
> They rightly do inherit heaven's graces
> And husband nature's riches from expense;
> They are the lords and owners of their faces,
> Others but stewards of their excellence.

Critics (such as my colleague Stephen Booth, in his edition of the *Sonnets*[7]) find the values in this sonnet painfully paradoxical and unresolved, but the sonnet clarifies a quality Richard shares with such other characters as Falstaff and Hamlet of transcending their particular contexts and specific attributes. In an impressive way both Richard and Falstaff are shown to know and to accept who they are and to live similarly at ease with others whose vices they know with almost equal precision: as Richard says, "'Tis death to me to be at enmity" (2.1.61). This mind-set is one Hamlet painfully comes to share, albeit too late for the plot to save him. The capacity to achieve this calm awareness and detached performance will allow humanity to elude that accusation of being "passion's slave" that Hamlet levels at the majority (3.2.72) but that also all too well describes the heroic roles that entrap romantic critics into admiration of a Romeo, an Othello, or an Antony.

The only problem in this deliberately reconstituted human nature lies in its susceptibility to powerful misuse by hypocrites, and this kind of misapplication matches Richard's tragic failure to the "festering lilies" of Sonnet 94. As Richard Wheeler accurately observes (176–193), Richard is not truly Machiavellian. Ultimately Machiavelli was a patriot, and an irrevocably committed public servant. Richard fails to achieve adequate goals for his talents and they are wasted on offsetting his private morbidities. In this his tragedy is like the Macbeths', because they all underestimate their own deepest potentialities. Macbeth's tragically neglected talent is for being modestly loyal, whereas Richard's is for being cleverly unconstrained by adverse circumstances: he need not be a victim, or even seek victims. His ingenuity can set him beyond the law, but it could equally mean that he need not be set against the law. We shall see that later Shakespearean heroes begin to approach this realization of omnipotence: Henry V's less brutal triumphs in the last act of his play, Duke Vicentio's wry solution of the problems in *Measure for Measure,* Octavius Caesar's first steps to creation of the Roman empire in the face of civil war in *Julius Caesar* and an international one in *Antony and Cleopatra* and *Cymbeline,* and Prospero's pacification of his own vengeful fury in *The Tempest.*

We may not like such manipulators, but they prove more successful servants of society than charismatic heroes if they feel no need to oppose the public good. In this capacity, but not in its application, Richard illustrates Shakespeare's first discovery of the transcendent potentialities of such a personality. The character opens up a feeling of potential freedom from conventional restraints that is exhilarating without necessarily having to be as destructive or selfish as Richard proves. This choice of a more positive option is made by many of Shakespeare's manipulative comic heroines, including Portia, Rosalind, and Helena. While suppressing their own compulsions to the point of surrendering their very identities, they can neutralize destructive forces in society and individuals—often in ways we find disconcerting if not shocking. In comedies written at the same time as *Richard III,* Shakespeare may already have been making preliminary attempts at more constructive male versions of Richard, in Petruchio and Berowne. Each seeks to use manipulation to broader social advantage than Richard, although Richard remains the archetypal manipulator with whom the dramatist himself must be equated insofar as he drives his plots forward.

As seen in the concluding essay of this anthology, by Linda Charnes, many recent commentators are driven by Shakespeare's final endorsement of the Tudor establishment in *Richard III* to a more negative view of individual and social potentialities than this broader interpretation affords. She shares the empathy with subversion of the new historicists but also their pessimistic view of society's susceptibility to conscious change. This determinism is matched by the Freudian determinism of C. L. Barber's static view of the world of Shakespeare's comedies, which he feels (incorrectly, I believe) merely return to the previously established order after a momentary escape into the festival world. Among new historicists, the political failure of left-wing ideologies has apparently encouraged stoic disbelief in an individual character's capacity for plausible and significant achievement. This conviction of the hero's inevitable defeat governs how Linda Charnes interprets the character of Richard's doomed attempt to elude the predetermined persona imposed on him by history and theatrical convention.

For such critics, the only way to break this vision of Shakespeare's obligatory paternalism as master dramatist seems to be the radical dismemberment of his texts, as illustrated by the Marowitz rewrite of *The Taming of the Shrew* or the drastically reconstructed *Richard III* of the Rustaveli Company so admired by actors such as Antony Sher (not to mention the enforced suicidal self-hatred of the Shakespeare presented in Edward Bond's *Bingo*). These "adjustments" make Cibber's revisions seem minor; but, like them, modern reconstructions permit Shakespeare to remain current even amidst postmodern interpretational anarchy. As Eliot says, "The last conventional Shakespeare is banished from the scene, and a variety of unconventional Shakespeares take his place" (107). The question remains whether such dramatic reconstructions can survive the inevitable reaction, and their revised Shakespeares with them, because so few earlier reinventions have done so. However, the next millennium's exact responses to *Richard III* are happily unpredictable, though they are likely to remain as obsessive as those of the previous one.

Notes

1.   C. M. Ingleby, L. Toulmin Smith, and F. J. Furnivall, *The Shakespeare Allusion-Book: A Collection of Allusions to Shakespeare from 1591 to 1700,* 2 vols, edited by John Munro, and reedited by E. K. Chambers (1909; reprint, Freeport, N.Y.: Books for Libraries, 1970), here 1: 48. Hereafter cited in the text.

2.   Mark W. Scott and Sandra L. Williamson, eds., *Shakespearean Criticism,* vol. 8 (Detroit: Gale Research, 1989), 145–46. Hereafter cited in the text.

3. Shakespeare references are cued to *The Riverside Shakespeare,* 2d ed., edited by G. Blakemore Evans et al. (Boston: Houghton Mifflin, 1997). References are to act, scene, and line.

4. T. S. Eliot, *Selected Essays* (New York: Harcourt Brace, 1950), here 119. Hereafter cited in the text.

5. Emrys Jones, *The Origins of Shakespeare* (Oxford: Oxford University Press, 1977), 280–81.

6. Peggy Ashcroft, "Margaret of Anjou," *Shakespeare Jahrbuch* 109 (1973): 7–9.

7. *Shakespeare's Sonnets,* ed. Stephen Booth (New Haven: Yale University Press, 1977), 305–9.

RICHARD III CONTEXTUALIZED

◆

The following excerpts place *Richard III* in its various original contexts: historiographic, literary, and theatrical. Notably, the commentaries all belong to the same 20-year period, reflecting the serious scholarship that resulted from the revised estimate of the importance of the history plays. This enhancement derived in part from Tillyard's previous assertion that the history plays provided an epic repository of English political values, then under challenge by Nazi threats to Britain's survival in World War II.

Peter Saccio summarizes the historical data available in such chronicles as Hall's, on which Shakespeare drew largely for his plots, characters, and ideology in *Richard III*. Geoffrey Bullough reviews and excerpts the most directly relevant literary and theatrical sources and precedents for *Richard III*. Bernard Spivack identifies the principal conventions of medieval drama from which history plays such as *Richard III* emerged and demonstrates the continuing relevance of these precedents to the play's detailed character. Irving Ribner investigates the character of the Elizabethan history play as a distinct dramatic genre, memorably realized in *Richard III*. Finally, Wolfgang H. Clemen surveys the exact rhetorical procedures, developed from classical times onward, that Shakespeare used to heighten the individual scenes of *Richard III*.

The overall result of these investigations is a precise account of the origins and character of *Richard III*, seen as a worthy goal in itself, without a need to demonstrate modern "relevance." The aesthetic value of the English historical plays was assumed, and this assumption of their viability was corroborated simultaneously by the sustained authority of such high drama as the RSC's performances in 1964 of the two English tetralogies in sequence, in celebration of the fourth centenary of Shakespeare's birth. The goal of the scholarly texts excerpted in this section is the accurate description of objective phenomena, providing a full account of derivations and aesthetic categories, not a critical reevaluation or reinterpretation by fresh modern criteria. The outcome is a series of definitive examples of what Spivack's preface (in the book from which his essay is drawn) calls "dramatic archeology," which he claims can enhance understanding and authentic enjoyment because it is not "subverted by its aesthetic preconceptions" (p. viii).

Richard III: The Last Plantagenet

PETER SACCIO

What heir of York is there alive but we?
And who is England's king but great York's heir?

1. EDWARD IV, 1471–1483

The Tudor imagination revelled in Richard III. Archvillain and devil incarnate, he supposedly started his infamous career by lingering sullenly in the womb for two years, finally coming to term with teeth and shoulder-length hair. Having thus discommoded his mother, he murdered his way through the royal house, slaughtering his cousin the last Lancastrian king Henry VI, Henry's son Prince Edward, his own brother the duke of Clarence, his nephews the child-king Edward V and Richard duke of York, and finally his wife Anne. He was the bane of his brother Edward IV's wife Elizabeth Woodville and of her relatives; he contrived the judicial murder of Edward's loyal chamberlain Lord Hastings; and he spun his plots whilst seated in a privy. He was the final embodiment of the wrath of God visited upon England for the crimes of the Plantagenets since Richard II's deposition in 1399. He was a criminal so appalling that his own death was not a further crime requiring still more retribution, but a purgation of all England. After his defeat at Bosworth, the kingdom could rest united and secure under the Tudor dynasty that had conquered him.

This lurid king, hunchbacked, clad in blood-spattered black velvet, forever gnawing his nether lip or grasping for his dagger, has an enduring place in English mythology. He owes something to the facts about the historical Richard III. He owes far more to rumor and to the political bias, credulity, and especially the literary talent of Tudor writers. A Warwickshire antiquary of Henry VII's time started the tale about Richard's prolonged prenatal life. Polydore Vergil, the Italian humanist hired by Henry VII to write the history of England, placed Richard in the framework of God's providential scheme

From SHAKESPEARE'S ENGLISH KINGS, 2ND EDITION by Peter Saccio. Copyright © 1977 by Peter Saccio. Used by permission of Oxford University Press, Inc.

for the fifteenth century. Early in the reign of Henry VIII, St. Thomas More started a history of Richard III, a gem of ironic narration that established the popular image of the king (the crooked shoulders, the withered arm, the gnawed lip) and the popular account of the fate of his nephews. More reported many details as mere rumor, but his readers tended to accept them as fact. The chronicler Edward Hall, completing a corrupt text of More's tale and fitting it within his own elaboration of Polydore's providential scheme, fused the two to form the climax of his *Union of the Two Noble and Illustre Houses of Lancaster and York*. Raphael Holinshed, in his *Chronicles of England*, stole from Hall, and out of them Shakespeare created his *Richard III*. In Shakespeare the providential scheme is articulated by Henry VI's widow Queen Margaret (who was in fact dead at the time of Richard's accession): cursing the Yorkists, she predicts the punishments they will receive for their crimes in destroying the Lancastrians. Richard himself appears as a monster, More's villain endowed with superb dramatic exuberance and a rich vein of sardonic humor:

> March on, join bravely, let us to it pell-mell!
> If not to heaven, then hand in hand to hell!

As myth, the Tudor Richard is indestructible, nor should one try to destroy him. This demonic jester and archetypal wicked uncle is far too satisfying a creation, and the works of More and Shakespeare are far too vigorous, for us to wish them otherwise. As history, however, the Tudor Richard is unacceptable. Some of the legend is incredible, some is known to be false, and much is uncertain or unproved. The physical deformity, for example, is quite unlikely. No contemporary document or portrait attests to it, and the fact that he permitted himself to be stripped to the waist for anointing at his own coronation suggests that his torso could bear public inspection. Concerning Richard's character and career as a whole, much controversy has raged. Richard has had ardent defenders in modern times, some of whom have described a king as virtuous as the Tudor villain is monstrous. This Richard commits no crimes; his claim to the crown is altogether just; he is unwaveringly loyal to his family; and his conqueror Henry VII is the real villain, responsible first for the murder of the princes and then for the murder of Richard's reputation. This chapter cannot change the minds of readers who happen already to be partisans of either Richard the Monster or Richard the Good. It can perhaps set forth briefly what is known of Richard and relate that to Shakespeare's play.

Richard III begins where *3 Henry VI* left off, with the restoration in 1471 of the first Yorkist king, Edward IV. Compressing selected events of a dozen years into half a dozen scenes, it rapidly proceeds to Edward's death in April 1483. It then dramatizes more carefully the three-month interregnum, the nominal reign of the twelve-year-old Edward V that ended with Richard's accession in late June. The last two acts deal with Richard's own reign, cut short in August 1485 by Henry Tudor's victory at Bosworth. Richard, however, dominates the whole play. His brother Edward IV, indeed, appears only in one scene, on his deathbed. The first historical injustice that Shakespeare commits victimizes, not Richard, but Edward IV.

Of all the English kings in Shakespeare's double tetralogy, Edward IV is most neglected by the playwright. Shakespeare's telescoping of time so elides Edward's twenty-two years on the throne that he does not even have a play named after him. Yet the reign was prosperous. Aside from Henry V, he was the most successful of the later Plantagenets.

In justice to Edward then, and by way of supplying background frequently alluded to by the characters of *Richard III,* the history of the house of York prior to Richard's accession must be recounted here. As readers of the previous chapter will recall, throughout the 1450s Richard duke of York repeatedly attempted to gain control over the government of his pious but disastrously incompetent cousin Henry VI. In December 1460, an army gathered by Henry's fierce queen, Margaret of Anjou, defeated and killed Duke Richard at Wakefield. Also perishing in this battle was the second of York's sons by his duchess, Cecily Neville: the seventeen-year-old earl of Rutland. (Following the Tudor historians, Shakespeare made Rutland a child at the time of his death. The cruelty of Rutland's slaughter, compounded when Margaret flourished in York's face a handkerchief dipped in Rutland's blood, is an outrage many times recalled by the Yorkist characters in *Richard III.*) The Yorkist cause then descended to the duke's three surviving sons, Edward, George, and Richard, aged eighteen, eleven, and eight respectively. In March 1461, three months after Wakefield, Edward was proclaimed king by a faction of Yorkist lords, of whom the most powerful was the Duchess Cecily's nephew, Richard Neville earl of Warwick. A few weeks later, Edward and Warwick inflicted a decisive defeat upon the Lancastrians at Towton, driving Henry and Margaret into flight and securing the Yorkist hold on the crown.

Edward then settled down to rule England, and his young brothers George and Richard became dukes of Clarence and Gloucester respectively. He married a beautiful widow, Elizabeth Lady Grey, née Woodville. He also alienated his chief supporter Warwick. The king's marriage embarrassed Warwick: he had been negotiating a diplomatic betrothal between Edward and the French king's sister-in-law when Edward secretly wed Elizabeth. The results of the marriage also annoyed Warwick: led by the queen, numerous Greys and Woodvilles began to secure influence at Edward's court. Most significantly, Edward ignored Warwick's advice in matters of foreign policy. Finally, in 1469–1470, Warwick the kingmaker revolted against the king he had made. Seducing Clarence to his side and marrying him to his eldest daughter Isabel, Warwick allied himself with Queen Margaret and drove Edward into exile. He then put back on the throne poor Henry VI, who had spent most of the previous decade in the Tower. The so-called re-adeption of

Henry VI was, however, a short-lived affair based on a strained alliance. Edward, vigorously supported by his loyal brother Richard of Gloucester and eventually regaining the allegiance of his turncoat brother George of Clarence, returned to England in 1471 and seized the kingdom once again. Warwick was defeated and killed in the battle of Barnet (14 April). Margaret was defeated and captured in the battle of Tewkesbury (4 May). During the latter battle, the only son of Henry and Margaret, Prince Edward of Lancaster, fell. (As with Rutland, the Tudor writers converted this death of a young prince in battle into an atrocity. In *3 Henry VI,* Shakespeare has the three York brothers, Richard in the van, savagely cut young Edward down after he has surrendered. This outrage is also extensively recalled in *Richard III:* old Margaret curses each of the Yorkists for his role in the destruction of her "sweet son.") Some days after Tewkesbury, the final extinction of the house of Lancaster was achieved by the assassination of Henry VI, once again a prisoner in the Tower. Edward, or Edward and his council, presumably ordered the deed. Thomas More, however, reported the dubious tale that Richard of Gloucester personally slew Henry on his own initiative. The Tudor Richard now had two crimes to his credit.

Thus by late May 1471 Edward reigned secure, without a rival dynasty or an overmighty subject to harass him. During the next twelve years he enjoyed himself thoroughly. It may have been a stroke resulting from self-indulgence that killed him at forty. Certainly he grew rather fat from the pleasures of feasting, and he thoroughly earned a reputation for lechery unrivalled by any other English king except Charles II. (His most famous mistress, Jane Shore, is often mentioned in *Richard III.* The wife of a London merchant and supposedly the merriest harlot in the realm, she long outlived her royal lover, surviving well into the next century.) But lust and gluttony did not so preoccupy Edward that he failed to rule well. Despite his pleasures, his chief concern was the business of government. Under his guidance the kingdom prospered. He may have lacked the kind of overmastering will and single-minded devotion by which Henry V bent all his own and his subject's energies to clearly conceived goals: Edward was more pragmatic, less forethoughtful. Yet during his reign England recovered from the Wars of the Roses, and Edward managed to cure some of the disorders that had led to those wars.

He restored to the monarchy the prestige it had lost during Henry VI's long and wretched reign. Unlike the shabby, vacant-faced Henry, he looked like a king. He was over six feet tall, remarkably handsome, and fond of magnificent clothes: his personal appearance fixed in his subjects' minds the power and glory of the crown. Although he had the unattractive habit of handing over to his friends the women whose charms he had wearied of, his rampant sexuality seems to have enhanced rather than detracted from his reputation. Of greater significance was his firm rule. The orders of the king, or the king and his council, were obeyed in a way they never had been under

Henry VI. He qualified his firmness with a leniency designed to heal past wounds. By a practice of judicious mercy, he allowed the surviving Lancastrian lords or their heirs to secure reversals of their attainders for treason, and thus to regain their titles and at least some of their lands. His handling of financial matters was particularly notable. He introduced into the administration of the royal estates financial reforms that enabled him to garner the true wealth of the crown. The commons had long complained to Henry VI (and to his two predecessors) that crown income was thriftlessly managed. By reinvigorating the methods of accounting, by replacing some of the cumbersome exchequer machinery with simpler arrangements, by entering into trade on his own behalf, and above all by securing a hefty pension from Louis XI in return for cancelling an invasion of France, Edward contrived to pay off crown debts, achieve solvency, and even to establish a comfortable surplus. Between 1475 and 1482, for the first time in the fifteenth century, the king was able to do what the commons had always begged the king to do: namely, to "live of his own," to pay all the expenses of his household and his government out of the regular crown income without asking parliament for taxes. That he was fighting no war, civil or foreign, naturally assisted him. Here Edward IV may deserve credit even above Henry V. During his reign, partly because of his own good sense and partly because of developments in continental politics, the English set aside the old dream of conquering France and thus saved the price in blood and treasure attached to that dream. Finally, he even managed to make some inroads upon the disorders and feuds that had long prevailed in the remoter parts of the kingdom. Here his achievement was less spectacular than it was in finance. The Welsh and the northerners could not quickly unlearn obstreperousness. But a good start was made. Edward made his brother Richard a kind of viceroy in the north by giving him extensive authority and estates on the Scottish marches and in Yorkshire, Cumberland, and Westmorland. To rule Wales he established a council at Ludlow in the Welsh marches. This body, nominally headed by his eldest son the prince of Wales, was directed by the queen's brother Earl Rivers. Rivers and Richard exercised their power effectively, suppressing the sort of treason and insurrection that had led to the civil wars.

Had Edward lived until his sons were grown, there would have been little after 1471 to mar his record as a king. Except for his brother Clarence (of whom more later), the great lords were loyal to him, and he was able to cope with the jealousies that sprang up among them. His coping, however, was entirely ad hoc. He made no lasting arrangement to ease or defuse court rivalries and thus to ensure a smooth succession in case he died betimes. These rivalries were the more dangerous because his policies had made Richard, Rivers, and others so powerful. They arose chiefly from Edward's startling and imprudent marriage.

Insofar as the marriage was fruitful, it was a success. Edward's dynasty was apparently secured by the birth of two sons, Edward prince of Wales (b.

1470) and Richard duke of York (b. 1473). Five daughters also survived infancy, of whom the most important was the eldest, Elizabeth (b. 1466). But Queen Elizabeth Woodville also brought to her husband a throng of relatives: a flock of brothers and sisters as well as two sons by her previous marriage. The Woodville clan, deeply responsive to the dictates of self-interest, swiftly capitalized upon their new royal connection by cornering the aristocratic marriage market and securing for themselves various titles and court offices. Now the Woodvilles were not complete upstarts. The queen's father had been made a baron long before she married Edward. Her first husband had had connections among the nobility. Her mother had been Jaquetta of Luxembourg, widow of Henry V's brother the duke of Bedford and daughter to the count of St. Pol, a distinguished European nobleman. Nor was the advantage the Woodvilles took of their new position unprecedented: other families had risen in comparable ways during the previous century. The extraordinary swiftness and success of the Woodvilles' rise, however, together with the irresponsible behavior of some of them and their previous participation on the Lancastrian side of the civil war, caused them to be *regarded* as upstarts by the older nobility and those who had shared the Yorkist struggle for the throne. At the time of Edward's death they were both powerful and unpopular. Aside from the queen herself, four of these Woodvilles crucially enter the story of Richard III. Elizabeth's eldest brother Anthony, who became Earl Rivers in 1469, was governor to the prince of Wales. The most interesting member of the family, he was a polished, educated, pious, rather nonpolitical peer, famous for chivalric jousting. Another brother, Sir Edward Woodville, served as a military commander. The queen's first-marriage sons, Thomas Grey marquess of Dorset and Lord Richard Grey, were playboy courtiers. Their chief occupation seems to have been debauchery, an activity in which they sometimes joined their stepfather.

Four important men were at odds with the Woodvilles: the king's brothers Richard and Clarence, the king's chamberlain Lord Hastings, and the most eminent peer outside the house of York, the duke of Buckingham. In the veins of Henry Stafford duke of Buckingham ran Plantagenet blood: he was great-great-grandson to Thomas of Woodstock. He had succeeded to his duchy at the age of five, after his grandfather's death at the battle of Northampton (1460). A royal ward until 1473, he had been married off to the queen's sister Katharine at about the age of ten. Youthful marriages were common practice among the aristocracy, but Buckingham came to resent being thus saddled with a comparatively humbly born wife. Perhaps because of this, he took very little part in public events during Edward's reign despite his rank and descent. By contrast, William Lord Hastings was at the center of the court. Having shared all Edward's perils since 1460, he was the king's closest friend and most trusted councillor. Rivers resented Hastings for gaining a post both had wanted, the captaincy of Calais. Dorset and Hastings maintained a private quarrel, probably arising from rivalry over mistresses.

The entire Woodville clan was jealous of Hasting's intimacy and influence with the king. In 1482 they contrived to get him into serious, although temporary trouble with Edward, an incident mentioned several times early in Shakespeare's play.

Richard seldom came to court. For a dozen years he served Edward as his deputy in the north, occasionally travelling to London when the king's business required it. There is no evidence whatever that during this time he was anything but loyal to his brother. The Tudor story of Richard's early schemes for the crown is entirely unfounded. He could not in any case have anticipated that Edward would die at forty, leaving a minority that would afford him the opportunity to seize the throne. In the north he earned a reputation as an able administrator, a successful general in several forays against the Scots, and an upright man. He dwelt chiefly at Middleham in Yorkshire, with his wife Anne Neville. Anne's father Warwick had previously married her, or at least betrothed her, to Prince Edward of Lancaster as the seal on his alliance with Queen Margaret. She married Richard in 1472, a year after the death of her first husband. In Shakespeare their courtship forms a macabre scene: the murderer of Anne's husband and father-in-law zestfully woos the poor widow over the corpse of the father-in-law. No such melodramatic episode took place. Recent defenders of Richard have claimed that the marriage was a love-match, but there is little more evidence for this rosy view than for Shakespeare's grim one. It is more to the point that Anne and her sister Isabel (Clarence's wife) were the greatest heiresses in the kingdom. Richard, like most lords of his time, presumably wanted to marry well, and Anne may have wanted a husband who could prevent Clarence from swallowing her half of the Warwick estates. Clarence did indeed try to prevent the match: he thrust her, disguised as a kitchen-maid, into a friend's house, whence Richard rescued her; and then he challenged the division of the Warwick properties. Aided by the moderation of Richard's demands, King Edward settled the quarrel over the inheritance after it had gone on for three years. This awkward dispute, however, did not create lasting resentment in Richard. Apparently he tried to prevent Clarence's execution in 1478. Certainly he held the Woodvilles responsible for Clarence's death. His lasting resentment was directed toward them.

Clarence was very unlike Richard. Where Richard was stable, reliable, and faithful to the king, Clarence was an ambitious will-o'-the-wisp. He had already betrayed Edward once by joining Warwick's revolt: he was lucky to be alive, free, and rich after Edward's restoration. Yet this skittish prince continually hatched plans for self-aggrandizement, indulging finally in behavior so foolish that one may doubt his sanity. Clarence was a royal nuisance. In the early 1470s he not only upset the family by quarrelling with Richard, he also seems to have dabbled in trivial Lancastrian plots. In 1477 his activities became a scandal. In that year, after the death of Isabel, he schemed to marry the heiress of the duchy of Burgundy. Edward firmly scotched that plan, which would have dragged the English into a continental war. Next, entirely on his own authority, he tried and executed a servant on the ridiculous charge that the unfortunate woman had poisoned Isabel. (The poison, according to Clarence, was administered two months before Isabel died. No such slow-acting poison was then known.) Clarence thus not only committed a reasonless judicial murder, but took the king's justice into his own hands to do it. The offense to Edward was all the greater since Edward had been trying to reestablish the probity of the law courts after the abuses they had suffered in Henry VI's time. Next Clarence protested Edward's execution of another servant of his, a man convicted of witchcraft: with truly remarkable folly, he chose as his spokesman a friar who had publicly expounded the Lancastrian right to the throne during the re-adeption of Henry VI. Finally, he stirred up a small, ineffective rising in Cambridgeshire. The king's patience broke. Arresting Clarence, he introduced into parliament a bill of attainder of treason against him. Clarence was charged with perverting the king's justice, with trying to alienate the king's subjects, and with spreading rumors that the king was illegitimate. He was also charged with preserving a copy of an act of the re-adeption parliament, an act that declared Clarence himself heir to the crown should Henry VI and his son die without issue. (The last charge is dubious: there is no other evidence that such an act was passed. Clarence may have forged the thing in a wild dream of securing the throne, or Edward may have invented it to seal Clarence's fate.) Clarence had been many times forgiven. Now he was officially found "incorrigible." In February 1478 he was condemned. Ten days later he was privately executed in the Tower. Surprisingly enough, the story (used by Shakespeare) that he was drowned in malmsey may be true.

The responsibility for Clarence's death has been debated. In Tudor times Richard was blamed. In Shakespeare, Richard contrives both the arrest and the execution in order to remove an obstacle in his path to the throne. This he certainly did not do. Contemporary reports suggest that he was grief-stricken at the whole affair. He held the Woodvilles responsible and thereafter came to court even less frequently than before. The Woodvilles *may* have encouraged the king in the deed. Any threat to the king threatened their power and position. They disliked Clarence anyway because of his participation in the re-adeption, during which several Woodvilles had died. Many did hold them guilty during the next few years. But the chief responsibility for Clarence's death must lie with Edward. He initiated proceedings. He took the very unusual step of acting as Clarence's prosecutor in parliament—normally kings arranged for someone else to do this. It was his power that Clarence's schemes and follies threatened. The death of Clarence demonstrates Edward's authority in England and the length to which he would go to maintain that authority. He would have no subject opposed to him, not even his own brother. His own strength, the legality of the procedure, and Clarence's manifest guilt enabled him to escape the retribution that Richard II had suffered eighty years earlier for taking similar measures against a close royal relative.

2. THE ACCESSION OF RICHARD III

Edward IV died on 9 April 1483. Two days later his eldest son was proclaimed king. On 26 June, however, Richard of Gloucester was proclaimed in his stead, and on 6 July he and his wife were crowned King Richard III and Queen Anne at Westminster Abbey. The intervening three months were busy with plots and counterplots, not all of which can be clearly discerned now.

April saw a struggle for possession of the prince. Edward had made the obvious appointment of Richard as protector during the minority. Richard was, after all, the only surviving adult male in the house of York, a loyal, long-tested prop of the Yorkist throne, and the most powerful man in the realm. Edward had also, however, left the prince himself in the hands of Richard's enemies the Woodvilles. The struggle was the more acute because the persons concerned were geographically scattered. Richard was in the north. Buckingham was on his own estates at Brecon (Brecknock) in southern Wales. The twelve-year-old prince, together with his governor Rivers, was at Ludlow in the Welsh marches. The rest of the Woodvilles, the little duke of York, and Hastings were in London where the king died. (Shakespeare does not adhere to this geographical scattering. For dramatic convenience, all his characters except the prince are in London.) Those in London, moreover, were deeply suspicious of one another. Despite Edward IV's deathbed attempt to reconcile them, the Woodvilles glowered at Hastings and his friends across the council table as they tried to make arrangements for the succession. Each party bid for the support of moderate members of the council: John Russell bishop of Lincoln, John Morton bishop of Ely, Thomas Lord Stanley.

The Woodvilles wanted no protectorate. They feared Richard and could only perpetuate their power through young Edward. They therefore sought to terminate the protectorate by crowning the prince as soon as possible. Gaining the support of the moderates, they scheduled a coronation for early May and directed Rivers to bring Edward to London posthaste. They also strengthened their military position. Dorset was made constable of the Tower; Sir Edward Woodville put to sea with a fleet. Apparently the royal treasure was split up among Dorset, Sir Edward, and the queen. In all this they governed in disregard of the protectorate and over the opposition of Hastings. The best Hastings could do was to persuade them to limit the prince's escort from Ludlow to 2000 men (the Woodvilles wanted Rivers to bring a large army) and to send frantic messages to Richard. It was only through Hastings that Richard learned of his brother's death and his own appointment as protector. No official message came to him from the pro-Woodville chancellor (Thomas Rotherham archbishop of York) or the Woodville-dominated council. Hastings urged Richard to come quickly to London, taking charge of the prince on the way.

Richard, having publicly sworn fealty to his nephew and written to reassure the queen, started south in late April with 300 Yorkshiremen. Simultaneously Buckingham, who had also been in touch with Richard, came from Wales with a small force. The two dukes met at Northampton on 29 April. By this time the Ludlow party had arrived at Stony Stratford, fourteen miles nearer London, but Rivers rode back to Northampton to greet the dukes and spend the night there. Early the next morning he found himself under arrest. Richard and Buckingham rode hastily to Stony Stratford and offered homage to young Edward. They then disbanded the Ludlow escort and, to Edward's dismay, arrested Sir Thomas Vaughan (the prince's elderly chamberlain) and Richard Grey (the prince's half-brother, who had come out from London the day before). The dukes had neatly severed the prince from the Woodvilles. Accused of plotting to ambush Richard and of dark designs against the prince, Rivers, Vaughan, and Grey were sent as prisoners to Richard's castles in Yorkshire. When news of Richard's coup reached London the next day, the remaining Woodvilles were thrown into confusion. After several lords refused to grant her further military support, the queen, together with her daughters and little York, rushed into sanctuary at Westminster Abbey. Hastings, jubilant, ruled the city until Richard and the prince arrived on 4 May.

During the next month Richard solidified his position as protector. The council recognized his authority and issued writs in the name of Edward V for a parliament in late June. Archbishop Rotherham was replaced in the chancellorship by Bishop Russell. (When the queen fled into sanctuary, Rotherham may have given her the great seal of the realm, to which she had no right whatever. More, at any rate, reports such an incident, and Shakespeare uses it.) Grants of authority were bestowed upon Richard's supporters Buckingham and John Lord Howard. (The latter became duke of Norfolk at the end of June.) Most of Sir Edward Woodville's fleet was induced to return to London, although Sir Edward himself fled to Brittany with several ships. In only one significant action that we know of did the council overrule Richard: they refused to entertain treason charges against Rivers, Vaughan, and Grey on the grounds that, even if the three men had in fact planned any move against Richard at Northampton, Richard at that time held no office that would make an attack upon him treasonable. No new date for the coronation was announced. Although Richard arranged for more oaths of loyalty to be sworn to Edward V, he seems to have planned an indefinite postponement of the coronation and a confirmation of his protectorate by parliament.

Except possibly for the attempt to condemn Rivers, Vaughan, and Grey, Richard's actions in May demonstrate no design on his part to seize the crown. The Woodvilles had attempted to exclude him altogether from power:

he had responded with the coup at Northampton and Stony Stratford and then proceeded to shore up his authority. London and the prince were in his hands; he was reasonably popular with the citizens and backed by Buckingham and the council; parliament would meet to seal the status quo. The realm might go comfortably on, ruled by Richard until the prince came of age, by which time Richard might have weaned him away from the influence of his maternal relatives. His failure to crown Edward immediately is no reliable indication that he intended to depose him: the child Henry VI had been king in name for seven years before his council decided to crown him. Unfortunately for Richard, the queen remained hostile. Her refusal to emerge from sanctuary, and especially her refusal to allow little York to join his brother under Richard's care, constituted a loud statement of distrust in Richard and provided a focus for any discontent with his government.

According to the Tudor myth, Richard had long dreamed of the crown and, once Edward IV was dead, deviously and cannily plotted to obtain it. The actual events of April–May 1483 show a less masterful and far less wicked Richard. Thrust into an unexpected situation and openly antagonized by an upstart party he already had reason to distrust, he moved, sometimes skillfully as at Northampton, sometimes awkwardly as with the treason charge, to secure the authority his brother had bequeathed him and to neutralize the threat of Woodville rule. He may have been more the victim of events than their master. Sometime in June, however, whether through ambition or through fear for his own safety, he decided that the protectorate was not enough.

Early in June the council scheduled Edward's coronation for the 22nd. Richard had evidently decided that only under such circumstances would the queen release her younger son. On 10 June, Richard despatched a letter to the city of York, telling his friends there that the Woodvilles were plotting the destruction of Buckingham and himself, and begging them to send troops. Since Richard could hardly have expected these troops to arrive until late in the month, he cannot have foreseen an immediate crisis. Perhaps he wanted them on hand when parliament met. Hastings, however, took fright, perhaps because of Richard's move to reinforce himself. He began to conspire with his former enemies the Woodvilles against his former ally Richard. His plot included the ex-chancellor Rotherham, Bishop Morton, and, oddly enough, Jane Shore. (After her king's death, Jane seems to have become Hastings's mistress or Dorset's, perhaps both. She may have been the go-between in the Hastings plot.) Richard, perhaps equally alarmed, struck hard. On 13 June he suddenly arrested Hastings's fellow conspirators and had Hastings himself executed without trial. On 16 June the queen, persuaded by the arguments of cardinal-archbishop Bourchier of Canterbury that little York should attend his brother's coronation, or perhaps more persuaded by the presence of soldiers around the abbey, at last surrendered York. In the next few days, Richard cancelled both the coronation and the parliament (far too late to prevent people from coming to London for these events) and issued death warrants for Rivers, Vaughan, and Grey. By 22 June he was openly preparing his own accession.

In More and Shakespeare, the order of two crucial events is reversed: the queen releases York before the death of Hastings. This sequence has the merit of making better sense of the queen's behavior: why, unless she was absolutely forced, would she have given York up if Richard had already started high-handedly killing people? Indeed, a historian has recently argued that the Shakespearean order is correct, but, after a flurry of controversy in the historical journals, it seems that the Hastings plot and execution did in fact come first. Also in More and Shakespeare, the Hastings plot is a mere fabrication designed by Richard to destroy Hastings after Hastings has made it clear that he will not help Richard to the crown. It seems more likely, from Richard's startled response and his hasty illegal procedure, that Richard was gravely frightened by a genuine conspiracy. With Hastings and the moderates on the council joining the Woodvilles, his support was rapidly collapsing. The fate of royal uncles to young kings in the past century (including two previous dukes of Gloucester, Richard II's uncle Woodstock and Henry VI's uncle Humphrey) furnished little hope that he could live to a hale old age. He arrived at the decision to take the crown, I think, after he had dealt with the immediate threat of Hastings and had gotten hold of York. More and Shakespeare, as previously mentioned, suppose that Richard was governed by long-range ambition. It looks much more likely that he was governed by fear, that he was anxiously trying to cut through a difficult and dangerous impasse. Indeed, it looks as if all the persons concerned were governed by fear.

Starting on 22 June, Buckingham and a popular preacher named Ralph Shaa (brother to the lord mayor of London) delivered public addresses claiming that Richard was the true heir to the crown. The reasoning behind the claim was shoddy and inconsistent. Shaa apparently charged that Edward IV was illegitimate. Since that would disinherit the princes, and since Clarence's attainder disqualified his children, Richard was the only available heir of the house of York. Edward's bastardy was an old and feeble story (Warwick and Clarence had both bandied it about) and a peculiarly embarrassing one: the Duchess Cecily, at whose London house Richard had been living in May and early June, cannot have enjoyed a public accusation of adultery. Two days later, it seems, Buckingham charged that it was Edward's children—not Edward himself—who were illegitimate. They were supposedly the fruit of a bigamous union: at the time of his marriage to Elizabeth Woodville, Edward IV had allegedly been contracted to a foreign princess. This story could stand up a little longer, although it too was eventually changed. When circumstances obliged Richard to ask the parliament of the following January for confirmation of his title, Edward's supposed precontract turned out to involve, not a foreign lady, but one Eleanor Butler, who had died in 1468. The foreign betrothal could be disproved, but a secret betrothal, to which both parties were now dead, could not be. Even this third story has flaws, however. Edward's marriage to Elizabeth Woodville had long been recognized by the clergy and people of England; the secular court of parliament had no authority to pronounce on matters touching the sacraments; and the legitimacy of a prince born in 1470 probably could not be affected by his father's betrothal to a woman who had died two years earlier. In short, Richard had grave trouble devising a suitable hereditary claim to the crown. Yet a hereditary claim was essential. In law, the Yorkist crown was based entirely upon the contention that the Yorkists were the true heirs to Edward III whereas the Lancastrians had been usurpers. Moreover, unlike the deposed Edward II and Richard II, the child-king Edward V could not be plausibly charged with bad government. Richard had to maintain that Edward V had never had any right to the throne. The flimsiness of his declarations was not amended by the peculiar constitutional arrangements he was forced to adopt. Richard was acclaimed king on 26 June by "the lords spiritual and temporal and the commons of this realm." That phrase was intended to suggest parliament, but the persons who had been summoned for parliament under the writs of Edward V could not constitute a legal parliament if the king who had summoned them was no king. That is one of the reasons why Richard needed a further act of parliament the next January. In short, Richard was legally as well as morally the usurper of his nephew's crown. On that point, the Tudor legend is correct.

Richard's usurpation, despite its moments of legal muddle, was in one way the most efficient and least costly of the many irregular seizures of power in medieval England. No lives were lost in battle or riot. Only a handful of men were executed. The dangers of another long minority, with royal relatives squabbling over the government, were averted. A selfish and unpopular faction was removed. An experienced administrator became king, and his proven abilities suggest that, had he ruled longer, England would have enjoyed a reasonably enlightened and strong reign. In another way, however, Richard's usurpation was a startling act of tyranny barely clothed in the rags of legal process. There was no real justification for the execution of Rivers, Vaughan, and Grey. There was no justification for the execution of Hastings without formal trial. The flimsy bastardization of the princes was a flagrant violation of a cherished medieval principle, the right of inheritance. Although Queen Elizabeth Woodville certainly helped to make Richard an enemy and a usurper by behaving as if he already were one, Richard finally acted with no more political finesse or understanding than she had. He certainly alienated many former supporters by his drastic solution to the problem of the minority. Reflecting upon all the experiences of the house of York since the 1450s, he may have thought that taking the crown in one swift and decisive gesture would settle matters, but in his case the cost of the deed was too high. One problem not experienced by earlier Plantagenet princes who had seized the crown dogged him particularly. Although Henry IV and Edward IV almost certainly caused the deaths of the kings they replaced and thus can be held guilty of murder, they replaced adults with a long history of misrule. They could not be accused of slaughtering innocent children.

Did Richard III murder his nephews? It is the master-crime attributed to him in the Tudor legend. More provides the famous account. According to this curious tale, Richard, while on progress through the west country after his coronation, despatched an agent with a letter ordering the constable of the Tower, Sir Robert Brackenbury, to murder the princes. Brackenbury refused. Thereupon Richard, introduced by a "secret page" to the ambitious and unscrupulous Sir James Tyrell, sent Brackenbury orders to surrender his keys to Tyrell for a night. Brackenbury complied. Two ruffians hired by Tyrell smothered the boys and buried them. All this, More claims, Tyrell confessed before he was executed for treason (on a different charge) nineteen years later. Shakespeare dramatizes a large portion of this tale. Its errors and impossibilities have long been exploded, most recently in P. M. Kendall's biography of Richard. Not the least among them concern Tyrell and Brackenbury. Tyrell was hardly unknown to Richard: he had been a Yorkist knight since Tewkesbury, and in the summer of 1483 was Master of the King's Horse. Brackenbury, whose behavior in surrendering the keys after refusing to commit murder appears incredible, neither lost his post for his failure to cooperate nor turned against Richard for a crime he must have known of. Two years later he fought and died for Richard at Bosworth.

Defenders of Richard have passionately argued that Richard was not guilty. Many have pointed out that he had no need to kill the princes since he had already bastardized them. Some have suggested that Buckingham was the culprit. Some have argued that the princes survived Richard only to be killed by Henry VII, who did need to get them out of the way since he had relegitimated them in order to marry their sister. This is also difficult to believe: there is no contemporary accusation of Henry and no evidence that the princes survived the summer of 1483.

The existing historical evidence does not permit a firm conclusion on the fate of the princes. There is really no courtroom evidence upon which to convict anyone. We must rest content with a probability, and the probability points toward Richard. An Italian visitor to London who left England shortly after Richard's coronation in July wrote later that year that many Englishmen (including Edward V himself) feared that they would soon die. In the fall of that year, an alliance against Richard was undertaken by Elizabeth Woodville, Dorset, Bishop Morton, Buckingham, and Henry Tudor. This unlikely quintet sought to place Henry Tudor on the throne. They could hardly have joined in such an aim unless they believed that the princes were dead. Neither of these arguments proves that the princes were indeed dead by late 1483, or if they were that Richard killed them, but they contribute to the likelihood. One overwhelming fact stands out: the princes were not seen after the summer of 1483, when, of course, they were in Richard's hands. Although he was ever after plagued by the rumor of their death, he never produced them to disprove the damaging charge. If he did murder them, it is strange that he did not follow the usual practice in such matters, namely to still the clamor by exhibiting their bodies with some beguiling tale of death from natural causes. Yet the responsibility for their death must touch him most nearly. It was he who had taken their throne. In all other cases of displaced English kings down to the mid-seventeenth century, deposition led to death. To others may belong some of the guilt for the deposition: Edward IV perhaps, for having made no better arrangements for the succession of his son; Elizabeth Woodville perhaps, for treating Richard with such unmitigated hostility; Buckingham perhaps, for urging Richard on. Nonetheless, Richard brought about the deposition, and thereby in some sense signed the princes' death warrant.

3. BOSWORTH AND THE TUDORS

The cat, the rat, and Lovell our dog
Ruleth all England under the hog.

The cat was Sir William Catesby, a lawyer, Hastings's estate-manager, and afterwards councillor and squire of the body to Richard III. In Shakespeare he serves as a valuable agent for the usurpation. The rat was Sir Richard Ratcliffe, another close advisor, who had fought for Richard at Tewkesbury and against the Scots. Shakespeare accurately depicts him as supervising the execution of Rivers, Vaughan, and Grey. Francis Lovell, whose crest included a dog, was a viscount, Richard's lord chamberlain, and another fellow-soldier against the Scots. The hog was Richard himself, whose personal emblem was a white boar. Hence in Shakespeare Richard is frequently reviled as boar, hog, and hedgehog. The whole scurrilous jingle sums up the disaffection of many Englishmen for their new king. Although the rhyme dates only from 1484, public restiveness under Richard broke into open revolt in the fall of 1483. Dorset appeared with rebel soldiers in Yorkshire; the family of Guilford rose in Kent; the Courtenays (one of whom was bishop of Exeter) did likewise in Devon. Some of these people initially sought to rescue the princes, but, with the rumor of the princes' death, all eventually proclaimed the cause of Henry Tudor. They were ill coordinated and easily crushed, but they represented a widespread threat. The threat was all the greater because the rebels included Richard's most powerful ally, the duke of Buckingham.

Buckingham's motives throughout 1483 remain a matter of conjecture. We do not know why this peer, formerly inactive in politics, suddenly leapt forward and helped Richard to the throne; we do not know why he turned on Richard within three months of the coronation. In June he may have sought vengeance on the Woodvilles, but it is harder to see what he sought in October. Many have supposed that the puzzle of Buckingham's breach with Richard would be solved if we knew more about the princes' death. Perhaps he briefly dreamed of a crown for himself; if so, he soon espoused the Tudor claim. Thomas More has him lured into rebellion by the wily tongue of Bishop Morton, whom Richard had committed to Buckingham's charge. Hall offers several explanations, one of which Shakespeare dramatizes: that Richard welshed on a promise to give Buckingham the earldom of Hereford. This is simply not true. In July Richard signed letters patent giving Buckingham the crown's portion of the earldom (the rest Buckingham had already). Whatever the cause, Buckingham marched from Brecon against Richard. He was hampered by rains and floods until his troops deserted him. He was then captured, denied the favor of a final interview with Richard, and executed at Salisbury on All Souls' Day, 2 November.

The October rebellion made Henry Tudor, hitherto an obscure offshoot of the house of Lancaster, a major figure in English politics. Fifty or more years earlier, his grandfather Owen Tudor, a Welsh squire of no particular standing, had consoled, wooed, and married Queen Catherine, widow of Henry V. This striking misalliance was revealed only at Catherine's death in 1437. The sons of the union, Edmund and Jasper, were acknowledged and made earls of Richmond and Pembroke respectively by their half-brother Henry VI. Edmund died, probably of natural causes, in 1456, a year after marrying Lady Margaret Beaufort, Margaret's ancestry was less obscure. She was the only child of John Beaufort duke of Somerset (d. 1444), who was in turn son to the eldest of John of Gaunt's bastard offspring (later legitimated) by Catherine Swynford. Several months after Edmund's death, Margaret gave birth to Henry Tudor. Since both the main Lancastrian line and all the male Beauforts had been exterminated by 1471, any hope of a Lancastrian revival lay in this hybrid red rose. Henry was reared in Wales by his uncle Jasper, officially losing his father's earldom of Richmond during the Yorkist years, visiting London perhaps once during the re-adeption of Henry VI. (On this occasion, according to Tudor legend and Shakespeare, Henry VI prophesied that the lad would eventually rule England.) After the Yorkist triumph of 1471, Henry fled with Jasper to Brittany. His mother, however, remained in England. She married Thomas Lord Stanley, councillor and steward of the household to both Edward IV and Richard III. (Stanley is a secondary character in *Richard III,* also anachronistically called earl of Derby, a title he received from Henry VII after Richard's death. Margaret Beaufort does not appear in the play, but is alluded to as countess of Richmond). It seems to have been Margaret and Bishop Morton, assisted by such confidential agents as the priest Christopher Urswick, who spun the plots of October 1483, attempting to bring together the Woodville interest, the Beaufort-Tudor interest, and those simply disaffected with Richard. Margaret won Queen Elizabeth Woodville's support by proposing that, if Henry won, he should marry the queen's eldest daughter. Henry himself attempted to join the October revolt, crossing from Brittany with a small fleet. His ships were scattered by adverse winds and he found the English coast too heavily guarded to risk a landing. He sailed back to Brittany to await a better day.

Shakespeare, compressing the time sequence, converts Henry's return to Brittany into a false report, and arranges for Henry's successful landing of 1485 to follow directly upon the defeat of Buckingham. Thus most of Richard's two-year reign is abolished. During that time parliament confirmed his title as king (supposedly "quieting men's minds") and attainted many persons associated with the October rising. Margaret Beaufort, however, was generously treated. Richard punished her merely by handing her estates over to her husband Stanley. The generosity was not uncharacteristic of the king. He persuaded Elizabeth Woodville and her daughters to emerge from sanctuary and treated them honorably at court. His policies with respect to trade, finance, the administration of justice, and the promotion of learning were beneficent and salutary. Unfortunately, he soon encountered a dynastic problem. His only legitimate son (not mentioned in the play) died in April 1484. For a time he seems to have declared Clarence's son heir presumptive. (He did not, as Shakespeare asserts, imprison the boy, nor did he meanly match Clarence's daughter in marriage. It was left to Henry VII to do both those things and eventually to execute the boy on a trumped-up charge of treason. The daughter lived into her late sixties, becoming the last surviving grandchild of the old duke of York. For this offense Henry VIII chopped off her head in 1541.) Clarence's son, however, may have been feeble-minded; certainly his position was complicated by his father's attainder. Richard eventually designated as his heir another nephew, his sister's son John earl of Lincoln. These arrangements for the succession were the more necessary because Queen Anne was ill and Richard could not expect to have more children by her. She died in March 1485. Upon her death, two damaging rumors circulated: that Richard had poisoned her, and that he intended to marry his niece Elizabeth, sister to the missing princes, in order to secure his tottering throne. There is no reason to believe the first of these exciting stories: in the Middle Ages, suspicions of poison far too commonly accompany the death of the great. The second story presumes a strange streak of illogic in Richard. His claim to the throne hinged on the declared illegitimacy of Edward IV's children: even if he had managed to obtain papal dispensation for an incestuous union, marriage with a bastard could not have strengthened his hereditary right. Nonetheless, the rumor vexed Richard enough to force him into public denials of such an intention, denials that some historians take as evidence of the rumor's truth. Shakespeare uses both stories, suggesting with deliberate murkiness that Richard has done away with Anne, and expanding the marriage project into a striking scene in which Richard woos Queen Elizabeth Woodville for the hand of her daughter.

Meanwhile, refugees from England gathered around Henry Tudor. Bishop Morton fled to the Low Countries, kept in touch with Henry, and helped him escape from Brittany into France at a moment when Richard had persuaded the Bretons to hand Henry over. Dorset joined Henry, although he came to be considered an unreliable ally. Most significantly, Henry gained the services of an experienced general, John de Vere earl of Oxford. Oxford was one of the few surviving unrepentant Lancastrian lords. He had fled after the Lancastrian defeat at Barnet in 1471, led an attack on the southwest coast of England in 1473, and been imprisoned at Hammes Castle near Calais since 1474. In 1484 he escaped and joined Henry, bringing with him the captain of Hammes, James Blunt. Lord Stanley also wrote to assure Henry of his support.

On 7 August 1485 Henry landed at Milford Haven in Wales. As he marched up the Welsh coast and across to Shrewsbury, his following swelled. Sir Walter Herbert of Pembroke, Sir Gilbert Talbot uncle to the earl of Shrewsbury, and Rhys ap Thomas the leading figure in central Wales, joined his cause. Richard called up his nobles. The two armies met on 22 August in the heart of England, near Market Bosworth in Leicestershire.

Among the crucial battles in English history, Bosworth affords a notable peculiarity: the victory was determined, not by those who fought, but by those who delayed fighting until they were sure of being on the winning side. The calculation of his supposed supporters cost Richard the day, the kingdom, and his life. By all military judgment he should have won. Since the age of eighteen (he was now thirty-two) he had been a skillful and successful general. Henry, who was twenty-eight, had never fought in a battle before. Richard also had the larger army. But part of it was under the Percy earl of Northumberland (Richard's only rival as a northern power during Edward IV's reign), who did not strike a blow. Part was under the Stanleys—Henry's stepfather Lord Thomas and the latter's brother Sir William. Richard had tried to secure Lord Stanley's allegiance by holding his son George hostage, but the Stanleys sat on hilltops, awaiting a sign of the outcome. (They may have concerted strategy with Henry beforehand, but this is disputed.)

The main fighting was done by the vans of the two armies, Henry's under Oxford, Richard's under the duke of Norfolk and his son the earl of Surrey. After Norfolk was killed, the royal forces began to waver. Then Richard adopted one last time the strategy of the quick stroke that would, if successful, settle all. He led his household knights around the main battle in a charge at Henry Tudor on the opposite rise. If Henry fell, his troops would have nothing to fight for. The charge was very nearly successful, Richard himself cutting down Henry's standard and its bearer Sir William Brandon. At this point one Stanley joined the battle: Sir William led his cavalry upon Richard's flank. Richard's knights were killed around him. He himself fought to the last in the thickest press of his enemies: even the most hostile Tudor accounts pay tribute to his courage. His battle crown was found among the spoils and placed on Henry's head by Lord Stanley.

Of Richard's followers, Ratcliffe and Brackenbury as well as Norfolk fell at Bosworth. Catesby was executed during the next few days. Lovell escaped and, together with Richard's designated heir the earl of Lincoln, died in a rising against Henry two years later. Northumberland made his peace with Henry and was murdered while collecting taxes four years later. Tyrell served Henry at the fortress of Guisnes, near Calais, until 1502, when he was called home and executed for treason. Surrey, after a period of disgrace, became a loyal servant of the Tudors and regained his father's duchy of Norfolk.

Henry, of course, became Henry VII, first Tudor monarch. He married Elizabeth of York, ruled for twenty-four years, and founded a dynasty that lasted until 1603. Bishop Morton became his chancellor, archbishop of Canterbury, a cardinal, and the patron of Thomas More. The Tudor myth depicts Henry as a savior figure, an angel rescuing England from the turbulent Plantagenets. In Shakespeare he is God's "minister of chastisement." It is difficult now to see anything angelic about Henry VII. Indeed, he was a man far subtler and craftier than the historical Richard, which is why, with the help of luck, he ruled far longer than Richard did. He had good reason to be a careful, scheming, suspicious man: he had become king of England while having no experience of government and knowing practically no one in the country. He had spent half his life in exile, needing all his wits to stay alive. He again needed all his wits to rule England, maintain the new dynasty, become a respected European power, and amass wealth. (In pursuit of the last aim he gained notoriety for avarice and extortion.) He did not differ greatly from the Yorkist kings in his methods of government. He took over and made even more efficient the techniques developed by the Yorkists: Edward IV's accounting methods and his Welsh council, the council of the north that Richard instituted. The great change from medieval to modern government in England came under Henry VIII, during the Reformation in the 1530s. Before that, the chief difference between Tudor rule and the rule of the later Plantagenets was the success of the Tudor kings in keeping the crown on their heads. In part this difference arose from the relative infertility of the Tudors. Only one of Henry VII's sons survived to adulthood. None of Henry VIII's did. Thus the Tudors were not harrassed by a plethora of royal dukes who might claim the crown. Indeed, their dynastic problem was exactly the opposite: Henry VIII spent the first twenty-eight years of his reign trying to beget a legitimate son who would live more than a few days. In many other respects it made no difference whether England was governed by a Plantagenet or a Tudor.

It did, of course, make a difference to the Plantagenets. Henry VII was for a time pestered by risings in favor of surviving members of the house of York and by pretenders who impersonated them. Henry VIII in turn feared displacement by the last buds of the white rose. Accordingly, the first two Tudors exterminated the remaining Plantagenets. The fates of Lincoln and of Clarence's children have already been noted. Most of Lincoln's younger brothers (that is, the younger sons of Richard III's sister) were hounded to death. Even Buckingham's son, the last representative of the line of Thomas of Woodstock, was executed on a flimsy treason charge in 1521. Henry VIII himself was of course half a Plantagenet through his mother, but, aside from that strain, the blood of the Plantagenets, once kings of England and France and lords of Ireland, had become a death sentence to those who carried it in their veins.

The Literary Background of *Richard III*

Geoffrey Bullough

Literary Background

The legend of Richard III's wickedness began during his lifetime and spread during the sixteenth century not only because every supporter of the Tudor régime wished to attack him but also because the circumstantial details given by the chroniclers provided interesting stories about him, his friends and his enemies.

The Song of Lady Bessy survives in many MSS and may have been printed in the century.[1] Written by Humphrey Brereton, servant of Lord Thomas Stanley, Earl of Derby, this immensely long ballad tells how Princess Elizabeth, daughter of Edward IV, organized the conspiracy which brought Richmond over to destroy Richard and to marry her. She begs Lord Stanley's help because the tyrant is wooing her, promising to poison his Queen and his son if she will marry him, and threatening also to slay all Stanleys and Talbots. After long demur Stanley agrees; they send money and Bessy's ring to Henry, who invades England; whereupon Richard orders Stanley to send troops in his support, otherwise his son Lord Strange must die. At Bosworth Stanley joins Richmond, and Strange is saved by the collapse of Richard's army.

> When King Richard that sight did see,
> In his heart hee was never soe woe.
> "I pray you, my merry men, be not sory
> For upon this field will I like a man dye:
> For I had rather dye this day
> Than with the Standley prisoner to be."

He refuses to mount on horseback and flee:

> "Give me my battle axe in my hand;
> I make a vow to myld Mary that is so bright,
> I will dye the King of merry England."

From *Narrative and Dramatic Sources of Shakespeare* by Geoffrey Bullough. © 1979 Columbia University Press. Reprinted with the permission of the publisher.

He fights until his brains are beaten out. Bessy marries the victor. Shakespeare did not use this piece, but he may have known it. Another, shorter and better, ballad about the part played by the Stanleys in bringing back Henry Tudor, is the anonymous *Rose of England.* This pleasant allegorical poem makes much use of heraldic family devices, and its garden-imagery anticipates that in *Richard II.*

The first edition of *The Mirror for Magistrates* (1559) contained three complaints taken from the period of the play: Baldwin's *Henry VI*[2] and *George Duke of Clarence,* and Skelton's *Edward IV.* The 1563 edition included six more tragedies relevant to our purpose: *Sir Anthony Woodvile, Lord Rivers,* by Baldwin; *The Lord Hastings,* by John Dolman; *The Complaint of Henrie, Duke of Buckingham,* by Thomas Sackville; *Collingbourne,* by Baldwin; *Richard Plantagenet, Duke of Gloucester,* by Francis Seager; and *Shore's Wife,* by Thomas Churchyard.

In his complaint Clarence explains his changes of allegiance, how Edward IV, on attaining the throne, "forgot his frendes, dispisde his kin,/Of oth or office passing not a pinne": how Warwick took advantage of this, marrying Clarence to his daughter, "Thus karnall love did quench the love of kind"; how after Barnet Field Clarence was imprisoned and then murdered because

> A prophecy was found, which sayd a G
> Of Edwardes children should destruccion be.

Clarence discusses at some length the value of "such doubtfull riddles" with reference to the prophecies of Merlin[3] and the lore of his own servant who warned him that

> "my brother Richard was the Bore
> Whose tuskes should teare my brothers boyes and me."

He tells briefly how "like a wolfe the tirant Richard came" and having failed to strangle him "with a prepared string," threw him into a butt of Malmsey wine and

> "New Christned me, because I should not crie."

Skelton's *Complaint of Edward IV* is a *memento mori,* describing how he "through his surfeting and untemperate life, sodainly died in the mids of his prosperity."

In his story of Anthony Lord Rivers Baldwin preaches prosily against the perversion of marriage by those who

> For gayne, for frendshyp, landes or honours wed,
> And these pollute the undefyled bed.

Rivers and his brother John were married to wealthy brides by Edward IV, which brought them the enmity of Warwick, Clarence and Richard of Gloucester. He tells how he was treacherously seized by Richard, Buckingham and Hastings at Stony Stratford; of the dream he had of the river

> Where through a Swan, a Bull and Bore dyd passe.

The Boar killed the others, and Rivers saw an ugly toad crawling towards him ere he waked. Lastly he describes the executions at Pomfret ordered by "that incarned devyll" Gloucester.

Dolman's account of Hasting's betrayal through "trustyng too much to his evyl counsayler Catesby" treats Hastings as the Pandarus of Edward IV, and describes their adventures together, e.g. their escape from Lynn. He represents himself as "For bloudy warre too feete [apt]/A Tyger was I, all for peace unmeete." He confesses that he helped slay Henry VI's heir at Tewkesbury, and aided "the Boare and Buck" to take Rivers. In condemning them he condemned himself. Derby urged him to flee, telling him of a dream he had:

> Methought a Boare with tuske so rasd our throate
> That both our shoulders of the bloud dyd smoake.

The other ominous incidents from Hall are related, Richard's sudden change of mood, the charge of treason and Hastings' speedy beheading, the donning by Richard and his helpers of "rusty armoure as in extreme shift" to announce Hastings' treachery, and the fact that the public proclamation was penned before the accusation was made.

As Baldwin declares, the *Mirror* poems were mostly based on Hall, with references to Fabyan and others. They were written for the learned ("for such as Magistrates are, or should be"), hence "it cannot be too hard, so long as it is sound and learnedly wrytten."

Sackville's *Induction* to the Complaint of the Duke of Buckingham is well known still, and admired for its splendid opening, its Dantesque imagery, its evocation of Sorrow, and the portrait of Hell, with Remorse, Dread, Revenge, Misery, and all the

> Prynces of renowne
> That whilom sat on top of Fortunes wheele
> Nowe layed ful lowe, like wretches whirled downe.

Buckingham himself uses the same cumulative method of recalling historical parallels—Cyrus, Cambyses, "bluddy Brutus"—to Gloucester and himself. He turned against Richard partly in anger at his disdain and partly to avenge the deaths of the two Princes. Banister, his betrayer, is described as

> "one whom earst I had upbrought
> Even from his youth, and loved and liked best
> To gentrye state avauncing him from nought."

In the Collingbourne verses the ancient liberties of poets are defended, and it is claimed that no treason was intended in the rhyme for which he suffered.

Richard III's Complaint, one of the dullest, starts with his ambitious desire, being Protector, to seize the throne. The murder of the Princes, narrated in detail, turns his followers against him,

> For cruell murdering unnaturally my kyn,
> Not only kyn, but kyng the truth to saye.

The rest is briefly told, with no mention of his dream before Bosworth, and the conclusion is:

> Loe here you may beholde the due and just rewarde
> Of tirany and treason which God doth most detest,
> For if unto my duety I had taken regarde,
> I myght have lived stil in honour with the best . . .

The prose comment on this tragedy shows that some contributors to *The Mirror* thought Seager's work, in very rough "rhyme royal," hardly up to standard. It was "not vehement ynough for so violent a man as kyng Rychard had beene. The mater was wel ynough lyked of sum, but the meeter was mysliked almost of all." However, "seying then that kyng Rychard never kept measure in any of his doings, . . . it were agaynst the *decorum* of his personage, to use eyther good Meter or order."

In compensation for this crabbedness, Churchyard's more regular *Shore's Wife* was included. Her early spousals are used to protest against "forced maryage," and her benevolent use of her power is stressed. She curses Richard because he exposed her publicly not for moral reasons but to despoil her of her goods. She describes herself finally as begging from door to door (like Henryson's *Cressid*). This completed the volume, for says Baldwin, "here endeth the cruel reigne of kyng Rychard the thyrd"; he hoped to make another book about events up to the reign of Queen Mary.

Shakespeare read *The Mirror* but his particular debts to it in *Richard III* were not great. He accepted the general contemporary notions of kingship which it embodied, believing that "whosoever rebelleth agaynst any ruler either good or bad, rebelleth against God, and shall be sure of a wretched end: for God cannot but maintain his deputie"[4]; yet his treatment of Richmond's revolt is in line with the qualification of this doctrine suggested elsewhere:

"Whatsoever man, woman or childe, is by the consent of the whole realme established in the royall seat, so it have not bene injuriously procured by rigour of sword and open force, but quietlye by title eyther of enherytaunce, succession, lawful bequest, common consent, or eleccion, is undoubtedlye chosen by God to be his deputie."[5]

Henry IV was a usurper by this standard. Richard III, having "injuriously procured" his throne was so likewise, and could justly be unseated. Shakespeare did not imitate the laboured moralising of *The Mirror,* but he shared its moral attitudes, and showed that the downfall of great men was often due either to divine justice working against them or to other men's evil desires which would finally bring an evil reward. *Richard III* is heavily loaded with this sense of moral retribution, and study of *The Mirror* may have deepened an impression which the dramatist got elsewhere, from Hall, and possibly from *Richardus Tertius.*

The *Mirror* was the first work to make Richard personally responsible for Clarence's death, and though Shakespeare could have found statements that Richard killed his brother George in the *True Tragedy* and Legge's Latin tragedy, he probably took from *The Mirror* the idea for I.1.144–51 and the use of the wine-butt when other means failed the murderers (I.4.274–80). The closeness of the prophecy in I.1.31–40 to the "G" prophecy in Baldwin also suggests reminiscence, and the pun at I.1.49–50.

> O! belike his majesty hath some intent
> That you should be new-christen'd in the Tower,

is obviously a jesting allusion to Baldwin's

> And in a butte of Malmesey standing by
> Newe Christned me, because I should not crie.

The dream of Rivers in *The Mirror* may have suggested Clarence's dream, but, as J. D. Wilson points out, Clarence's matter is nearer to elements in Sackville's visionary journey to Hell in his Induction, e.g.

> We passed on so far furth tyl we sawe
> Rude Acheron, a lothsome lake to tell
> That boyles and bubs up swelth as blacke as hell,
> Where grisly Charon at theyr fixed tide
> Stil ferries ghostes unto the farder side.

Wilson concludes "that Shakespeare consulted *The Mirror* for *Richard III* alone of his Histories, and that the only 'tragedy' he made use of was Clarence." (*Camb* xxvii). This I believe understates the general position. Text II gives a long excerpt from the "tragedy" of Clarence.

The Latin tragedy *Richardus Tertius* by Thomas Legge (1535–1607), Cambridge Professor of Civil Law and Master of Caius College, was probably written in 1579—the date given in a MS in the Cambridge University Library. That it was quite well known is proved by its survival in at least nine MSS. Legge's aim, assisted by Grafton, Hall or Holinshed, was to write a Senecan drama in which Nemesis brought the downfall of a tyrant. The play was divided into three "Actiones," each Actio containing five Acts and intended to be presented on a different evening. The Unities are not kept; there are many characters and a broad sweep of events.

The first Actio extends from the death of Edward IV to the execution of Hastings and the condemnation of Shore's wife in June, 1483; the second to Richard's coronation; the third to his death. The classical Chorus is not used, but a Choric song ends each Actio, and there are tableaux, e.g. the first Actio shows "Shore's wife in her peticote, havinge a taper burning in her hande" doing her penance.

Legge shows considerable skill in making drama out of a close rendering of Hall's narrative. He reduces Richard in stature by making him cowardly and dependent on confidants, but he provides excellent spectacle, and he uses Senecan rhetoric with some force, often introducing phrases or lines from Seneca's plays. In the third Actio the Argument is an impassioned speech in which Furor urges Richard and Buckingham on to destruction. The whole play is conceived in terms of vaulting ambition overreaching itself. The murder of the Princes is performed with abundant detail after a long debate between Brackenbury and Tyrrell whether Richard's command should be obeyed, in which Tyrrell gives a horrific account of Richard's wrath at Brackenbury's reluctance. On the night before the Battle of Bosworth, Richmond meets Stanley, who explains that if he helps Henry his son's life will be forfeit. Richard relates the dream in which he saw himself torn by a troop of Furies. The Orations of both leaders are summarized from Hall. Richard's death is told by a Nuntius who (like Hall) balances the good he might have done against the evil he chose to do. The play ends when Lord Strange brings prisoners to the victor, who is crowned.

The Epilogue celebrates the happy uniting of both houses, and traces its results down to Elizabeth, the daughter worthy of her great father.

Inevitably, since Legge followed More and Hall, his play contains scenes parallel to Shakespeare's, but as Churchill shows, the variations which they share from the common sources are few, and may be coincidental; e.g. in both plays Norfolk obtains the postponement of Lord Strange's execution. An interview between Richmond and Stanley occurs in both, but it is also found in the *True Tragedy of Richard III,* and Shakespeare may have got the idea from that play. Legge's second Actio has a scene in which a Citizen discusses with a stranger to London the sad condition of England, while they are waiting for Richard's coronation. This momentarily resembles *Richard III* II.2 but this scarcely proves that Shakespeare imitated Legge.

Richard III gives bigger parts to women characters than do Shakespeare's earlier Histories; and there are four major women characters in the play as against three in each of the *Henry VI* plays. Legge also takes every advantage afforded by the chronicles to introduce scenes with female participants. Queen Elizabeth opens his first Actio with grief for her husband and forebodings about her elder son as he comes from Ludlow to be crowned. She speaks of the evil wrought by Fate on her and her family in terms taken from Seneca's *Hercules Furens* and *Octavia* (Churchill, 281–5). Soon the Queen learns of the arrest of her kinsmen in a scene modelled on Phaedra's frenzy in the *Hippolytus;* she utters a curse against Hastings. When the Duke of York is taken from sanctuary her parting words are expanded to over forty lines. The first Actio ends with the mingled morality and pathos of Shore's wife's penance. In the third Actio we hear through the Queen's maidservant how she learnt of her sons' murder, of her ominous dream (like that of Stanley in Hall). She swoons and laments with many classical allusions. Lewis the physician confers with her about a marriage between her daughter Elizabeth and Henry Richmond. Later Lovell (now Richard's bad adviser) persuades her, after she has cursed the King for his crimes against her, to give up her daughters. Richard welcomes his two nieces. Queen Anne complains to him about his neglect of her and the rumours of her death; he promises to tend her. Soon we learn of her death, and at once follows Richard's wooing of the Princess Elizabeth.

If Shakespeare knew *Richardus Tertius* he may have been affected by the use made of women to prove Richard's persuasive villainy, to look back over the past, and to shower curses on the tyrant. Legge drew heavily on Seneca in such scenes. Maybe Shakespeare did so too, and went direct, either to the Latin, or to translations such as Jasper Heywood's *Troas* (1559), *Thyestes* (1560), and *Hercules Furens* (1561), and Thomas Newton's *Seneca His Tenne Tragedies* (1581). Legge has no counterparts to the Duchess of York and Queen Margaret, neither of whom plays any part in the chronicles of this reign. *Richardus Tertius* has been described as the first play to show the possibility of combining Senecanism with English chronicle. But Senecanism and a more centrally focused use of English history had been combined already in *Gorboduc* (1561/2) and the Senecan drama in English had produced other examples before 1592. Shakespeare's use of his women characters in formalized scenes of lament, woeful rivalry, retrospection and prophetic combination, is quite unlike Legge's. But his introduction of three generations, each with its memories and griefs, recalls Seneca's *Troades.*

Legge has two "wooing" scenes. In one Lovell persuades Queen Elizabeth to surrender her daughters; in the other Richard woos Princess Elizabeth unsuccessfully. Shakespeare has two similar scenes, more widely separated. In I.2 Richard successfully woos Anne. There was no basis in the chronicles for this scene except that Richard actually married Anne. It is possible that these scenes were suggested by *Richardus Tertius,* and that Shakespeare substituted the wooing of Anne for that of Elizabeth in order to avoid having the two scenes close together, and because Anne's marriage to the man who had killed her husband and his father was a mystery which challenged the dramatist's skill. Shakespeare uses the two incidents to give astonishing proof of Richard's diabolical power over women in two phases of his career. But it is again possible that, having decided to include Senecan elements in his tragedy, Shakespeare went as Legge did, to the *Hercules Furens,* where a similar, but unsuccessful, wooing occurs when the usurper Lycus who has murdered her father and two brothers, tries to win over Megaera, wife of the absent Hercules. Shakespeare *may* have taken some hints from Legge, but he organized his play on different lines, reducing the chronicle element, conceiving both Richard and Richmond as stronger characters than Legge drew them, and increasing the importance of his women so as to provide links with the Henry VI plays and to serve as a substitute for the Senecan chorus.

The relationship between *Richard III* and the anonymous *True Tragedy of Richard III* (entered in *S.R.* 19 June, 1594, and published in that year but written probably 1590–2) is likewise not clear. As printed, the *True Tragedy* was a botched version of its drama. G. B. Churchill believed it to have been written after the three parts of *Henry VI.* Possibly, or gobbets of *Henry VI* may have been introduced when the Quarto text was patched up for printing. "As a history play," writes Churchill, "the *True Tragedy* is undoubtedly the first in which the interest is fixed upon one central and dominating figure" (p. 398). This is not quite correct, and there is an important subsidiary centre in the downfall of Shore's wife, which is given more importance—as an instance of man's ingratitude—than its lack of political results would demand. Nevertheless, Richard is the main focus, and the chronicle material is organized to reveal his nature. The *True Tragedy* is crude in construction and confused in its use of Hall or Grafton's *Continuation* of Hardyng; nevertheless it provides an interesting attempt to fuse the Senecan Revenge play with the English History play. Richard here is a more complex character than in Legge. He has something of Marlowe's Tamburlaine, something too of Dr Faustus; for while insisting that Might is Right and his Will justifies any means, he is not merely a brutal tyrant but also a man with a conscience. As soon as he has gained the throne he begins to fear that his reign will not endure, and he becomes the prey of wild alarms. He worships Fortune, whereas his rival Richmond is a pious Christian; the opposition between the Senecan and the Christian ideas of tragedy is thus embodied in this play.[6] The Ghost of Clarence sets the play in motion with his demand for Revenge; but the ghosts seen by Richard appear only in his imagination; they are not shown on the stage. He is a brave, energetic, credible creation; but he entirely lacks the sense of humour, the ingenuity and eloquence of Shakespeare's Richard.

Critical opinions differ on whether Shakespeare used the play. I agree with Churchill and Dover Wilson that he did.[7] Both plays anticipate by some time the appointment of Richard as Protector. Both have a scene immediately after Edward IV's death in which a Citizen represents what More called "Mutterynge among the people, as though al should not long be well." Both ascribe to Buckingham the suggestion that the Princes should be removed from the Queen's friends; and make Rivers refer to the reconciliation between the rival parties as "but green" when the dismissal of the young king's train is discussed. The boy himself shows a similar regality and forwardness in both, complains of his kinsmen's arrest and is told by Richard that he is but a child and is therefore treated as such.

Resemblances in the scenes between Richard and Stanley go beyond what might be expected from the chronicles. In both plays Richmond is seen encouraging his comrades "not at landing, as in Legge, but after he has proceeded some way into England" (Churchill, 513). The conversations between Richmond and Stanley are alike. In the *True Tragedy* Richard tells us of the ghosts which afflict his mind; in *Richard III* they appear to him and to Richmond in a vision. In both plays Richard in battle cries for a horse, and refuses to flee. A similar incident occurs in *The Battle of Alcazar,* which may have imitated the *True Tragedy* and was performed before *Richard III;* but that Shakespeare recalled the *True Tragedy* here is proved by the fact that immediately afterwards in both plays Richard refers to the gloomy day, the ominous absence of the sun.

That Shakespeare knew the play is proved by his making Hamlet refer to a line from it

> The screeking Raven sits croking for revenge
> (1892)

in the Play scene (III.2.257) where he is urging the Player to hasten with his inset play of murder and usurpation:

> Come: the croaking raven doth bellow for revenge.

Some of the above parallels may be coincidences, but the plays depart from the chronicles in the same way so often that one is justified in concluding that Shakespeare took some hints from the *True Tragedy,* no doubt from the authentic version of which the 1594 text is a debasement. If so, some other features of *Richard III* may be accounted for. Shakespeare's play rather strangely omits several elements present in the chronicles and literary analogues. He barely mentions Jane Shore, whose downfall was of considerable interest for the student of Edward IV's, Hastings' and Richard's characters. The capture of the Queen's kinsmen at Northampton is not represented; nor is the Archbishop's persuasion of the Queen to give up the Duke of York. More remarkable still, Shakespeare avoids showing the murder of the two Princes, but transfers material from the historical accounts of this to the murder of Clarence, which is shown in great detail. This cannot have been through squeamishness or through dislike of repeating effects, since repetition with variation was a common feature of his technique at this time and in this play. Nor do we see the death of Richard. In a Senecan drama narration of important incidents might be expected; but it seems likely that Shakespeare was also consciously avoiding the use of materials recently dramatized in *The True Tragedy,* perhaps because he had recently been accused of plagiarism by Robert Greene,[8] and because he wished to prove his independence. Shakespeare's attitude to his sources was not as "contrasuggestible" as Bernard Shaw's (though *Othello* might make us think so), but a resolve to make *Richard III* different from either *Richardus Tertius* or the *True Tragedy* may have been in part responsible for some features of the play's *ordonnance,* and for the subtilizing of Richard's character by infusing so much humour and intelligence into a figure in danger of becoming a stock theatrical tyrant.

In the main the play took the form it did because Shakespeare wished not only to present the personal and national tragedy of Richard III but also to show his career as the climax of the great dramatic movement which began with the death of Henry V. Accordingly the period it covers extends from the death of Henry VI (May, 1471) to the Battle of Bosworth (22 August, 1485), and the dramatist's problem was to select from the varied material offered by the chronicles the incidents which would most cogently link the machinations and usurpation of Richard with what had gone before in *3 Henry VI.* In the first Act therefore he picks out three important events: the burial of Henry, the marriage of Richard of Gloucester to Prince Edward's widow, Warwick's daughter Anne (1472), and the execution of Clarence (1477). The chronology of these is purposely confused so that Clarence's arrest occurs before the late King's funeral; and the wooing of Anne takes place during the funeral procession, while the quarrels between the nobles, which might have happened any time after King Edward's marriage to Elizabeth Woodville, coincide with Clarence's imprisonment and the King's illness. [This did not occur until 1482, and his final sickness lasted only a few days after Easter, 1483.] The return of Queen Margaret, who never came back to England after she was ransomed, is another means of recalling the past. So the first Act is at once a link clasping the new play to the previous trilogy, a Prologue to the main action, and an indication of Richard's special villainy. The remainder of the play covers the same period as the *True Tragedy*—from Edward's last sickness onwards. A detailed analysis of the action is not possible here,[9] but a few notes may be useful.

In I.1 Richard's soliloquy takes up his self-revelation in *3H6* V.6, referring to his plots against Clarence. The audience is prepared for a play of audacious Machiavellianism. Two striking instances of his cleverness are introduced successively in the arrest of Clarence and the wooing of Prince Edward's widow over the bier of her father-in-law. The (fictitious) imprisonment of Hastings is referred to (I.1.66–80) so as to prepare for the latter's conversation with the Pursuivant in III.2. The second scene also links the play with *3H6* in time. It proves that Shakespeare used Holinshed, not Hall, for the statement that the King's corpse bled during its last progress. Anne could not have been there.[10] The scene with its many changes of mood proves how far Shakespeare had advanced in technical mastery since *3 Henry VI*. . . .

I.4 in which Clarence is murdered draws material from Hall's account of the Princes' murder, which is not to be shown. The two murderers and Brackenbury come from there (*inf.* 278–9), and the hiding of the body "in some hole, Till that the duke give order for his burial," comes from the burial of the boys "at the stayre foote" and then secretly elsewhere. . . .

The time scheme of IV.3 extends from about July, 1483, to September, when Buckingham's rising began. Richard's reaction to the news of this is characteristically rapid.

Next comes a great scene of recapitulation when Queen Margaret, lurking in London, gloats over the grief of Queen Elizabeth and the Duchess of York (not dead after all), as she points out the accuracy of her vengeful prophecies. She looks forward to Richard's end (IV.4.61–78). The Duchess and Queen Elizabeth assail Richard with complaints which he takes ill; but he seizes the occasion to woo the latter on behalf of her daughter. In Hall he persuades the Queen by secret emissaries to hand over her daughters, meaning to marry Elizabeth should his wife die. Here the Queen suspects (probably rightly) that Anne has been removed, but Richard repeats the *tour de force* of I.2 as he turns her from vituperation to close attention and then to agreement though she knows the quasi-incestuous nature of his desire (as pointed out by Hall).

Richard's triumph is short lived, and history is compressed to show the fluctuations of two years. At news of Richmond's first approach (Oct. 1483) he becomes confused (IV.4.434–57) and suspicious of Stanley. Risings in Devonshire and Kent enrage him so that he will scarcely let the Messenger tell of Buckingham's dispersal (507–14). Good news of Richmond's withdrawal (*inf.* p. 285) and Buckingham's capture is succeeded by word of Richmond's landing at Milford (1485). Act IV ends with news that Stanley's son is a hostage and that Queen Elizabeth will agree to Richmond's marrying her daughter. In Hall she had agreed to this before Richard sent his startling proposal, and her turning to him was proof of her "mutable mind" (*inf.* 282–7). Shakespeare makes no comment on the contradictory decisions, but he puts the "right" one second. Perhaps we are to imagine that she tricked Richard, or that she reverted to good.

Act V moves rapidly towards the climax. Buckingham goes to execution without being permitted to speak to the King (cf. *inf.* p. 284 for a suggestion that he meant to assassinate Richard). He notes that it is All Souls' Day, that the oath he made to Edward IV in II.1.32–40 has turned against him, and "Margaret's curse falls heavy on my neck" (i.e. her warning, I. 3.297–301).

The avenger marching to meet the "usurping boar" near Leicester shows in V.2 none of the despondency in which Hall says he "dragged behind his host" at Tamworth (*inf.* p. 290). Instead of wondering whether Stanley could be relied on he mentions the "Lines of fair comfort and encouragement" received from his stepfather.

At Bosworth Field in V.3 the movement of the chronicles between the two sides is turned into a formalized moral and theatrical antithesis, with the rival tents set up, the nervous Richard threatening Stanley's son, Stanley coming secretly to encourage Richmond, who prays before sleeping; the rising of Ghosts to afflict Richard and bless his adversary; Richard's awaking to self-realization and despair (178–207), Richmond with his heart "very jocund" (228–34); the two orations. There are significant modifications of the sources. In Hall Stanley's behaviour seems dubious to Richmond until the last moment; Shakespeare clarifies his position during his interview with Richmond. Instead of the dream which Hall gives Richard, of "diverse ymages, lyke terrible develles whiche pulled and haled hym," Shakespeare takes from *The Mirror for Magistrates* or *True Tragedy* Richard's dream of

> All those murderd Ghostes whome I
> By death had sent to their untimely grave (*Mirror*),

and uses them to display the moral contrast between the two leaders before giving a more subtle analysis of Richard's mental state as he realizes the evil end of his "I am I" philosophy (178–207) in a soliloquy which embodies Hall's comment, "this was no dreame, but a punccion and pricke of his synfull conscience"; but Richard cannot repent, and declares, "Conscience is but a word that cowards use." . . . The order of the orations is reversed, possibly to disgust the hearer with Richard's base appeal. Richmond's prayer may be compared with Henry V's before Agincourt. In keeping with the play's theme, it has more sense of mission: "Make us thy ministers of chastisement" (114). His speech begins religiously, like Hall's, but then, leaving egoism and euphuism aside, becomes more manly, direct and persuasive.

Features of Hall's vivid account of the battle appear in the play. There are references to archers, staves, helms. The report "the enemy is pass'd the marsh" (used as a defence on Richmond's right flank) reaches the King opportunely to save George Stanley's life (346–7). Richard goes seeking Richmond in the fray (V. 4.4–11). In Hall he does not lose his horse but is brought "a swyfte and a light horse to convey hym away" when things go badly. Perhaps for theatrical convenience *The True Tragedy* showed him dismounted and crying out for a horse. Shakespeare uses the device. When Richard has been killed offstage no details of the abuses performed to his corpse are given. Richmond's final speech is a fitting close to the tetralogy as he directs attention away from the mad domestic strife of the past years to the union of the white rose and red symbolized in his marriage with Elizabeth, and to the "smiling plenty and fair prosperous days" which peace should bring.

Notes

1. Thomas Percy, *Bishop Percy's Folio MS.* ed. F. J. Furnivall and J. W. Hales, London: N. Truebner, 1910. iv.

2. See William Baldwin, ed. *A Myrroure for Magistrates.* London: Thomas Marsh, 1563. Reedited John Higgins, 1574. Modern edition: Lily B. Campbell, ed., *The Mirror for Magistrates,* Cambridge: Cambridge University Press, 1938, pp. 182–90.

3. Shakespeare may have remembered this in *1H4* III.i.

4. *Mirror,* 178.

5. *ibid.,* 420–1.

6. I. Ribner, *The English History Play in the Age of Shakespeare,* Princeton: Princeton University Press, 1957, p. 89.

7. George B. Churchill, *Richard III up to Shakespeare, Palaestra X,* Berlin, 1900, 497 ff., and John Dover Wilson, "Shakespeare's *Richard III* and *The True Tragedy of Richard III,* 1594." *Shakespeare Quarterly* III. 299–306, 1953.

8. J. D. Wilson suggests this (*Camb* xxxi). I came to think it independently before reading his Introduction. J. D. Wilson, ed. Shakespeare, *RICHARD III,* Cambridge: Cambridge University Press, 1954. Corrected, 1961,

9. The reader should consult the notes on *Material* given scene by scene by J. D. Wilson (*Camb*) 165ff).

10. *Camb.* 227.

Richard III and the Vice Tradition

BERNARD SPIVACK

Whatever the lapse of time between the completion of *3 Henry VI* and the writing of *Richard III*—it cannot have been long—the shape of affairs in the later play derives immediately from the earlier one and is closely knit up with it. The speech of Edward which ends *Henry VI*—

> And now what rests but that we spend the time
> With stately triumphs, mirthful comic shows,
> Such as befits the pleasure of the court?
> Sound drums and trumpets! Farewell sour annoy!
> For here I hope begins our lasting joy.

—is exactly caught up by Richard in the first words of *Richard III:* his description of the "merry meetings" and "delightful measures," the gallantry and amorous sport, that have replaced "the winter of our discontent" with its war and rigor. His advance to the throne likewise proceeds in unbroken movement from his poised footfall at the end of *Henry VI,* where he announced, "Clarence, thy turn is next." For the turn of George of Clarence is indeed next in *Richard III,* in the first scene of which we see taking effect those prophecies respecting him and the letter "G" that Richard was just about to "buzz abroad" at the close of the earlier play. In every other way as well, including the whole complex of political circumstances, *Richard III* follows in tight sequence to the last part of *Henry VI.*

The moral portrait of Richard is no less continuous from one play to the other, if we disregard for the moment the intervention in both of the veteran dramatic image which is not, in fact, an aspect of his character, but rather the stock performance of our acquaintance, with its highly stylized homiletic bravura, that his character and stigmata invite. Disregarding this part of him, we discover that in his last play he is of a piece with what he has been before. He maintains his regal ambition, his enormous energy and sovereign force, his bonhomie and craft, to the end of his career. But after he reaches the throne events begin to harden against him. If he declines at intervals there-

From *Shakespeare and the Allegory of Evil,* by Bernard Spivack. © 1958 Columbia University Press. Reprinted with the permission of the publisher.

after into a tyrant at bay, nervous and irascible, fearful, with good reason, of treachery, and on the night before Bosworth ghost-ridden and conscience-stricken—such or similar alterations in the heart are perfectly in keeping with Richard's mortal frailty.[1] They are, in fact, the common formula of intimation with which Shakespeare usually darkens the eve of disaster—as with the French before Agincourt, Macbeth before Dunsinane, Brutus before Philippi, and even Antony before Alexandria. If he confesses to the loss of "that alacrity of spirit" and "cheer of mind that I was wont to have," he acknowledges simply the turn in his life—he is fey; and Napoleon, dramatized by Shakespeare, might have made the same confession before Waterloo. And although he suffers the tyrant's destiny of having now everything to lose and nothing more to gain, Richard is Richard still in his last course. On the morning of battle he recovers completely from his trepidation of the night before and marshals his troops with his old dispatch and burly confidence: "A thousand hearts are great within my bosom." The formula of his life and character remains clearly discernible even when he thrashes about, with animal fury, in the toils:

> I have set my life upon a cast
> And I will stand the hazard of the die.
> I think there be six Richmonds in the field;
> Five have I slain to-day instead of him.
> A horse! a horse! my kingdom for a horse.
> [V.iv.9–13]

What we see so far is something of the character of Richard as it maintains itself through all three plays in which he lives: the moral image of a formidable, if depraved, human nature, drawn from history and dramatized by the method of naturalistic art. What we have yet to see in combination with this image is another whose plastic stress transmutes the role, just as it does, in greater or less degree, all the others that have already come under review. For the playwright not only follows history, he *dramatizes* it for the theater; and he does so by the techniques native to his stage and unerring in their popular effect. The portrait of Richard in the chronicles, with its emphasis on his guile and depravity, invites and gets a dramatization in several notable scenes that reproduces once more the pungent *theatrical* image with which homiletic allegory endowed the popular stage. Shakespeare's rendition of Richard does not recast the historical figure, but from time to time it abrogates him entirely. It abrogates him because it applies to him the method of a performance designed originally for a timeless personification in a staged homily, not for a literal person in the moral dimension of human history.

Richard himself supplies the reference that documents this theatrical side of his lineage. Subjecting the young Prince Edward to the trick of verbal equivocation that identifies beyond peradventure the vested performance he imitates, he confirms the imitation by his comment immediately following and unmistakably directed to the audience:

> RICH: So wise so young, they say do never live long.
>
> PRINCE: What say you, uncle?
>
> RICH: I say, without characters fame lives long.
>
> [Aside] Thus, like the formal vice, Iniquity,
>
> I moralize two meanings in one word.
>
> [III.i.79–83]

To moralize two meanings in one word is, as we saw, a commonplace in the Vice's repertory of deceit, and Richard does not refer to any one version of the Vice. He refers rather to the composite role, for which *Iniquity,* a moral designation equally composite, became the common name after precise homiletic distinction between one Vice and another dissolved into the generalized figure who became a fixture of the stage. Thus one of the characters in Dekker's *Old Fortunatus,* evoking a recollection of the Vice, is addressed as "my little leane Iniquity."[2] Falstaff's affinity with the role is fortified by the description he gets as "that reverend vice, that grey iniquity."[3] It is the undiscriminated Vice of the moralities with the typical name of Iniquity who actually appears in Jonson's *The Devil Is an Ass,* before he is dismissed by the Devil as too old fashioned and ineffectual for the times:

> We must therefore ayme
> At extraordinary subtill ones now,
> When we doe send, to keep vs vp in credit,
> Not old Iniquities.
>
> [I.i.115–18]

And in the quotation from *The Staple of News* which begins the previous chapter the Vice is once more generalized as "Iniquity [who] came in like Hokos Pokos."[4]

It is not, therefore, the proper noun that carries the burden of Richard's meaning, but the adjective. In one of its common Elizabethan senses, "formal" means *conventional* or *regular,* and applies to anything which is unmistakable because it retains, to use Dr. Johnson's definition, "the proper and essential characteristic" of its informing nature, as in Cleopatra's advice to the messenger who brings her bad news:

> Thou shouldst come like a Fury crown'd with snakes,
> Not like a formal man.
>
> [*Antony and Cleopatra* II.v.39–40]

Richard uses the word to explain that, although he appears something different from the conventional and obvious Vice of the popular stage, he is imitating the method of that role. His words tell us even more. Directed as they are to the audience, their demonstrative force explicit in "thus," they proclaim also the homiletic demonstration and its nature. He is inviting the appreciation of the audience for his dexterity in deceit, for his skill in that kind of exhibition which evolved out of the moral metaphor of the Vice. He has become for the nonce the artist, his ornate duplicity an end in itself. The historical figure who ruled England dissolves into the theatrical figure who ruled the English stage.

Although these two realities enclosed by the single name of Richard are as implicated with each other as the chequered features of a topographical map, we are able to mark the turn from one to the other. As his role rears itself out of the welter of historical incident in the last part of the *Henry VI* plays, it begins at the same time to shift from its previously recessed naturalism into a different perspective. The change is signaled at the end of the soliloquy already quoted in part, five sixths of which is a passionate debate inside the heart of the aspiring cripple who identifies his life's joy with the crown. Upon this passion intrudes, however, a very different note, for the long speech concludes with a piece of stylized rhetoric that is neither more nor less than another version of the *moral pedigree* of the Vice, although we notice a naturalistic modification. The catalogue of aggression which creates the background of allegorical meaning for the behavior of Barabas, Edricus, and Aaron, becomes in Richard's case potential rather than preterit—a catalogue of what *he can do*:

> Why, I can smile, and murther whiles I smile,
> And cry "Content!" to that which grieves my heart,
> And wet my cheeks with artificial tears,
> And frame my face to all occasions.
> I'll drown more sailors than the mermaid shall;
> I'll slay more gazers than the basilisk;
> I'll play the orator as well as Nestor,
> Deceive more slily than Ulysses could,
> And, like a Sinon, take another Troy.
> I can add colours to the chameleon,
> Change shapes with Proteus for advantages,
> And set the murtherous Machiavel to school.
> [III.ii.182–93][5]

This is exposition in the homiletic dimension of the morality drama, as we have seen it before when the Vice comes forward to announce his moral identity and the nature of his timeless activity in the world; and we notice that all of Richard's self-comparisons converge upon a single theme: his mastery of the art of aggression through deceit. In the last two scenes of *Henry VI* the dramatic method thus introduced begins to control the role. His monologue in the Tower, after he murders King Henry, moves unmistakably into the audience: "*See* how my sword weeps for the poor King's death!" and "Had I not reason, *think ye,* to make haste?"[6] In the very end of the play, Edward, now undisputed king and mellow with prosperity, sets up a target for the Vice to shoot at when he intones a hymn to the transcendent values of love and peace, invoking love from his brothers to his queen, his son, himself:

> Clarence and Gloucester, love my lovely queen,
> And kiss your princely nephew, brothers both.
> . . . .
> Now am I seated as my soul delights,
> Having my country's peace and brothers' loves.
> [V.vii.26–36]

The Vice is ready and rises to his cue. Richard in this scene becomes a creature of asides, an histrionic homilist who puts on a show of love and honesty and turns away with a grin to share his jest and register his art with the audience. The kiss of love and fealty he gives the young heir apparent, and his accompanying words, directed half one way and half another, are his last action in *Henry VI* and announces the bravura role to follow in the play that bears his name:

> And that I love the tree from whence thou sprang'st
> Witness the loving kiss I give the fruit.
> [Aside] To say the truth, so Judas kiss'd his master
> And cried "All hail!" when as he meant all harm.

The traditional image thus initiated in the earlier play expands in *Richard III* in equal measure with the expansion of the figure to whom it is assimilated. By the end of *Henry VI* Richard has only begun to emerge from the press of men and events which diversifies that trilogy, although we become aware that already he has magnetized a change in dramatic perspective: the mural of national history in a succession of panels, its large population crowding through multiple phases of war and politics, by degrees surrenders foreground and focus to his looming portrait. In *Richard III* this portrait monopolizes the canvas, and its archaic features show a corresponding proliferation. They are enriched, moreover, by a consummate artistry such as the moralities never knew. No "formal Vice" weeps more fluently than Richard, or uses that gaudy device to better effect upon his victims. None enjoys a happier intimacy with the audience, or titillates them more exquisitely in the ways prescribed by the old role's homiletic bravura. By none is the art of deceit so lavishly cultivated, so merrily held up for exhibition, or so richly organized around the paired antinomies of essential enmity and pretended love, essential turpitude and pretended virtue, essential villainy and pretended honesty. And in none of Richard's hybrid fellows in the secular drama does the ancient aggression show so plainly the twofold method that governed it originally; for the emphasis in his achievements, as often in his hyphenated role as he wears the mantle of Vicehood, is not on his progress toward the crown—that is the naturalistic Richard—but on his ability to create dissension in the place of unity and love, and on his cognate ability to seduce his victims from their virtuous allegiance and bend them to his will. In all these features of his role, but especially in the homiletic principle that binds them into demonstrative intimacy with the audience and supplies them with an impetus that has nothing to do with ambition, we recognize the arch-metaphor that fathered them in the morality drama. The metaphor itself has been abolished by the literal play, but the dramaturgic personality of its chief exponent still flourishes in the role of Richard.

This hereditary pattern in his performance is so emphatic and stylized as to be unmistakable. Already humid with the weeping of its unhappy women, the play welters in the tears of Richard. Either as they are shed on stage or as they are reported they lubricate his fraud perpetually as he moves in episodic demonstration from one victim to another. . . . Of these episodes the most memorable is Richard's florid manipulation of Lady Anne, so far neglected. She stimulates his most brilliant achievement in this kind because she is his most difficult undertaking, the immaculate intensity of her abhorrence for the murderer of her husband and her royal father-in-law corresponding to the more abstract enmity of virtue to vice that puts the Vice of the moralities on his mettle when faced with the equivalent situation. Shakespeare exploits this traditional crux to the uttermost by allowing Richard to intrude upon her at a moment the most hopelessly inauspicious for his enterprise, when she is following the corpse of murdered King Henry to its burial, her grief mingled with curses against the author of it. So contrived to extend his skill, the scene is Richard's masterpiece, its quality and method matched by only one other in Shakespeare—the great seduction scene in *Othello;* and both are amplifications of the typical beguilement effected by the Vice upon his victim in the pivotal scene of the moralities. At the end Anne has made the same moral reversal that marked the career of Mankind and all his descendants: she has thrown over her alliance with virtue and united herself to evil. And Richard at the end is left alone with the audience to share with them the homiletic jest and the familiar laughter, the latter diffused through all his words and explicit in the triumphant syllable of the last line:

> What? I that kill'd her husband and his father
> To take her in her heart's extremest hate,
> With curses in her mouth, tears in her eyes,
> The bleeding witness of my hatred by,
> Having God, her conscience, and these bars against me,
> And I no friends to back my suit withal
> But the plain devil and dissembling looks?
> And yet to win her—all the world to nothing?
> Ha!
>
> [I.ii.230–38][7]

Although dyed on its surface by the naturalistic colors of the historical play, the whole scene readily discloses its nuclear difference. Its grain is homiletic, not naturalistic, and we feel it as bravura because that is exactly what it is by hereditary principle—homiletic bravura in the dimension of display. Richard is putting on his happiest exhibition of villainous deceit in its most conventional masquerade, the pretense of love, in this instance romantic love: "I'll have her, but I will not keep her long." The ancient virtuosity is here wonderfully enhanced by the poet's finesse and power. Shakespeare's abundance crams the old image with dramatic wealth without defacing its familiar features. Anne succumbs, not because she is especially frail but because she is human, to a tempter who gets from Christian homiletics a prescriptive victory over her astonished heart; but the formula is now surcharged with great vitality and acuteness. Richard exerts upon her every artifice of moral and physical deceit, exploiting her human and feminine frailty with enormous effrontery and assurance, until he mesmerizes her out of her passionate loathing and into a fascinated creature subdued to his will. She submits to an imperious skill that thrusts against her mood at its fiercest, engages it with flexible pressure while it struggles, and grasps it with careless, rough control when it melts. She is wooed out of her will by impassioned periods, impudent stichomythia, uninhibited flattery, outrageous sophistry, suicidal despair—by calculation so inspired and ironic it summons up the murder of the husband she mourns for testimony to the love of the murderer. Nothing, however, dissolves her more effectively than Richard's tears, for they rain on her incessantly:

> Thine eyes, sweet lady, have infected mine.
> . . . .
> Those eyes of thine from mine have drawn salt tears,
> Sham'd their aspects with store of childish drops—
> [I.ii.149–54]

He who never wept before, not even for the piteous deaths of his father York and his brother Rutland, now offers her this humid proof of his desperate, honest love:

> In that sad time
> My manly eyes did scorn a humble tear;
> And what these sorrows could not thence exhale,
> Thy beauty hath, and made them blind with weeping.
> [I.ii.163–66]

On these buoyant waters he soon sails from the port of love into the port of conscience, and she, now won over, hears with pleasure that he will take Henry's burial off her hands and "wet his grave with my repentant tears." So prosperous is the old device that in his merry privacy with the audience he promises to continue it:

> But first I'll turn yon fellow in his grave,
> And then return lamenting to my love.
> [I.ii.260–61]

His weeping and laughter do not by themselves establish the archaic source of Richard's performance, but they confirm it, alongside his other unmistakable tricks of language and behavior. The dominant trait in his descent appears in the unnaturalistic dimension of his role, in the repetitious and gratuitous deceit surviving out of the old Christian metaphor, in the homiletic method of the timeless personification. It is the inspirational force of the method itself that gives birth to Richard's wooing of Lady Anne, for which there is no hint in the chronicles. That scene has its origin in theatrical convention, not in history, and its dramatic caliber sufficiently explains the playwright's recourse to the old dramaturgy. *His* caliber explains the great energy and brilliance we discover in this flashing version of the transformed Vice.

Notes

1. Richard's words after he awakens from his dream (V.iii.178–200), though frequently misunderstood, are precisely in the tradition of the morality drama. They are a dialogue between himself and his half-personified Conscience. Cf. *Appius and Virginia,* II. 501–508, for which see p. 271.

2. *Old Fortunatus* II.ii.

3. *1 Henry IV* II.iv.498.

4. See also *Club Law,* ed. G. C. Moore Smith (Cambridge, 1907), 1. 1916; and Ben Jonson's Epigram (CXV) "On the Townes Honest Man," 1. 27.

5. Richard's reference to "murtherous Machiavel" is dealt with on pp. 377–78 [of Spivack's book].

6. *3 Henry VI* V.vi.63–72. The italics are mine.

7. The resemblance between Richard's wooing of Lady Anne and an episode in the morality *The Three Lords and Three Ladies of London* (1589) in which Lady Love is wooed by Dissimulation (Dodsley, VI, 420–21) has been noted by Sidney Thomas, *The Antic Hamlet and Richard III* (New York, 1943), pp. 28–30. To Dr. Thomas's work the present treatment of Richard is generally, sometimes specifically, indebted.

Richard III as an English History Play

IRVING RIBNER

With the three *Henry VI* plays must be grouped *Richard III*, for the four plays make a consistent and meaningful tetralogy, of which *Richard III* is the culminating and perhaps most significant unit. Although the disintegrators have been almost as busy with this play as with *Henry VI*, there are few scholars who would today deny that it is by Shakespeare and entirely by him. Since the play must have followed hard upon *3 Henry VI*, it is usually dated in late 1592 or 1593,[1] although some writers who are inclined to push back the beginnings of Shakespeare's writing career would date it in 1591 or earlier.[2] The play was entered in the Stationers' Register by Andrew Wise on October 20, 1597, and printed by him in quarto in the same year. David L. Patrick has conclusively demonstrated that this first quarto was a memorial reconstruction prepared by some of the Lord Chamberlain's men, including the prompter, for a performance during a tour of the provinces in 1597.[3] *Richard III* must have been extremely popular, for six quartos had been printed by 1622. The folio text was prepared from a collation of the sixth quarto with a theatre manuscript, thus giving us a better text than any of the earlier printings.

When *Richard III* was written, the character of Richard of Gloucester had already assumed a conventional Senecan cast, and Shakespeare treated the subject along the lines laid out for him by his predecessors. Although it is unlikely that he knew Legge's *Richardus Tertius,* and is impossible to establish a debt to *The True Tragedy of Richard III,* largely because of the corrupt state of that text,[4] Shakespeare used the same sources which had shaped those plays. He used Holinshed and Hall,[5] both of which drew their material from Polydore Vergil's *Anglica Historia* and More's *History of King Richard III,* the two works which, more than any others, had helped to shape the tradition of Richard III as a Senecan villain.[6] *Richard III* thus continues along the Senecan lines we have noted in the *Henry VI* plays, and in this respect it goes considerably beyond them. The play is dominated by the single figure of Richard of Gloucester. In his great soliloquy in the preceding play,[7] he had already

Ribner, Irving: THE ENGLISH HISTORY PLAY IN THE AGE OF SHAKESPEARE: Copyright © 1957 by Princeton University Press. Reprinted by permission of Princeton University Press.

established himself as the cynical villain-hero who would "set the murderous Machiavel to school," advancing through villainy after villainy until he seized the crown. The Senecan elements in *Richard III* have been amply commented upon: the villain-hero with his self-revealing soliloquies, the revenge motif, the ghosts, the stichomythic dialogue, and not least, the abundant echoes of Seneca's own plays. The dominating figure of the Senecan villain-hero gives to *Richard III* a unity which the *Henry VI* plays had lacked. Every episode in the play serves to advance the cause of Richard up to a climatic point, after which every episode serves to hasten his destruction.

But *Richard III* is more than a Senecan tragedy; it draws upon other dramatic traditions as well. The play, in large measure, continues the line of Marlowe's *Tamburlaine*, for the theme of *Richard III* as of *Tamburlaine* is that of the steady rise of a dominant personality. In Marlowe's play the expanding hero embodies a philosophy of life of which the author approves; in Shakespeare's it is a force of evil which he allows the audience to view with a horrified fascination. Marlowe's hero is triumphant, but Shakespeare's must be cut off and destroyed by the divine providence which inevitably brings to wickedness its just reward. Richard has been called a symbol of Renaissance aspiring will in opposition to the medieval world of order; and thus he must inevitably be destroyed by fortune and punished for his crimes.[8]

In spite of its high degree of Senecan formalism, *Richard III* continues also in the morality play tradition which is an important shaping force upon the entire tetralogy. Despite the prominence of its titular hero, the primary purpose of the play, as Tillyard[9] (p. 199) has indicated, is to "display the working out of God's plan to restore England to prosperity." England continues as a kind of morality hero torn between good and evil forces; in *Richard III* she suffers the depths of degradation, and finally through God's grace she is allowed to win salvation by a proper choice: the acceptance of Henry of Richmond as king. The morality element in the play is particularly evident in the scene in Richard's tent on the eve of the Battle of Bosworth Field. This Tillyard (p. 108) has acutely described:

> The scene of the ghosts of those Richard has murdered follows immediately on Richmond's solemn prayer. . . . It is essentially of the Morality pattern. Respublica or England is the hero, invisible yet present, contended for by the forces of heaven represented by Richmond and of hell represented by Richard. Each ghost as it were gives his vote for heaven, Lancaster and York being at last unanimous. And God is above surveying the event. The medieval strain is continued when Richard, awaking in terror, rants like Judas in the Miracle Plays about to hang himself.

The morality tradition is carried on in the ritual technique with which *Richard III* abounds. The most basic dramatic device in the play is a ritualistic portrayal of the futility of Richard's philosophy of individual self-sufficiency and of the triumph of divinely instituted degree and order.[10] The otherwise incredible scene in which Richard woos and wins Anne Neville (I, ii) becomes meaningful when seen as a ritual act designed to repeat the theme of Edward IV's earlier wooing of Lady Grey, rather than as a depiction of historical fact to be taken at face value.[11] The great choral scene of lamentation in which Queen Margaret, Queen Elizabeth, and the Duchess of York sit upon the ground and give themselves up to despair (IV, iv) is a ritual scene whose effect has been compared to that of the choric odes of Greek tragedy and whose function is very similar. The murder of Clarence is handled in ritual fashion: his dream and his penitential lament (I, iv, 43–64) emphasize the divine retribution for sin which his coming murder will illustrate. In the penitent murderer with his Christ image:

> How fain, like Pilate would I wash my hands
> Of this most grievous murder!
>
> (I, iv, 279–80)

we have a ritual gesture to underscore the horror of the act. The parallel orations of Richmond and Richard before the final battle, serve also a ritualistic function; they relate Richard to the side of evil and emphasize that Richmond comes as the champion of God. That Richmond is the executor of God's purposes is made evident in his prayer:

> O Thou, whose captain I account myself,
> Look on my forces with a gracious eye;
> Put in their hands thy bruising irons of wrath,
> That they may crush down with a heavy fall
> The usurping helmets of our adversaries!
> Make us thy ministers of chastisement,
> That we may praise thee in the victory!
> To thee I do commend my watchful soul,
> Ere I let fall the windows of mine eyes:
> Sleeping and waking, O, defend me still!
>
> (V, iii, 108–17)

We have thus in *Richard III* a highly unified tragedy centring about one demonic figure, and, in the manner of *Tamburlaine*, concerned with his ruthless and steady advance to a climax. This figure is the Senecan villain-hero which literary tradition had already made of him before Shakespeare approached the subject, and the play is rich in formal Senecan stylization. But in spite of the prominence of Gloucester and his domination of the action, the primary purpose of the play is to terminate a tetralogy in which he, hitherto, had had but a small part, to emphasize the role of providence in history, and to show how God's grace enabled England to rise out of the chaos of the Wars of the Roses. To do this most effectively, Shakespeare used a highly ritualistic technique which came down to him as part of the morality play tradition, and whose effectiveness he had already begun to explore in the preceding plays.

There is one important respect in which the political doctrine in *Richard III* goes beyond that in the *Henry VI* plays, for in *Richard III* Shakespeare introduces a new political notion which he is to further develop in his second tetralogy. We have noted in the *Henry VI* plays a strong emphasis upon divine right and passive obedience, and the implicit doctrine that the *de facto* king, no matter what his merits and no matter how he attained the crown, must be obeyed, for rebellion against him is a sin against God which inevitably must bring destruction to a nation. But in *Richard III* this doctrine had to be somewhat modified, for the rebellion against Richard had to be justified. Henry of Richmond was the ancestor of Elizabeth, and his victory had ushered in the great age which God had granted to England after her atonement for her sins. Tillyard (p. 212) holds, in explanation, that Richard III, "was so clearly both a usurper and a murderer that he had qualified as a tyrant; and against an authentic tyrant it was lawful to rebel." But orthodox Tudor doctrine had never endorsed rebellion against a tyrant. Archbishop Cranmer had written very clearly: "Though the magistrates be evil, and very enemies to Christ's religion, yet the subjects must obey in all worldly things."[12] And the 1571 *Homily Against Disobedience and Wilful Rebellion* said just as clearly:

> What shall we then do to an evil, to an unkind Prince, an enemy to us, hated of God, hurtful to the Common-wealth! Lay no violent hand upon him, saith good David, but let live until God appoint, and work his end, either by natural death, or in war by lawful enemies, not by traitorous subjects.[13]

Henry IV also is a usurper and the murderer of Richard II, but the rebellions against him in the later plays Shakespeare unequivocally condemns.

The notion that rebellion against a tyrant may be justified is not an orthodox one, but it is nevertheless implicit in *Richard III*. Although there is no sign of it in *Henry VI*, in *Richard III* we have an important distinction between lawful king and tyrant, and the implicit doctrine that a tyrant—a usurper who rules for his own aggrandizement rather than the good of his people and who is destructive of the commonwealth—is not entitled to the rights and privileges of a lawful king. This doctrine, as we shall see, Shakespeare was to develop further in *Macbeth*.

The tacit exception of Henry Tudor from their general doctrine of passive obedience was one which Elizabethans almost universally must have made; it was thus easy and natural for Shakespeare to favour Richmond's campaign against Richard III without appearing to challenge Tudor absolutist doctrine. Shakespeare did not wish to brand Henry VII as a rebel, no matter how great a tyrant Richard III may have been. Shakespeare was thus forced deliberately to play down the rebellion motif in his play, and to do this he used several dramatic devices. In the first place he carefully characterized

Richard of Gloucester as an instrument in a great scheme by which England was punished for her sins before she could win salvation. Richard is made to serve as a "scourge of God," an evil instrument used by God in order to execute divine vengeance. All of those murdered by Richard, except for the young princes, are murdered in retribution for their own sins. When God's purposes have been served, the evil scourge must himself be destroyed, and for this purpose God chooses another agent through whom he may operate.

Shakespeare thus uses every dramatic device he can to portray Richard's death as caused by God rather than by any man. Richmond is God's agent. We have seen this stressed in his prayer before battle. His personality is deliberately underdeveloped, and his role in the play is a passive one; he is instrument rather than actor. On the symbolic, ritual level, we do not have a king killed by a rebellious subject; we have rather a "scourge of God" destroyed by his creator as soon as he has fulfilled the purpose for which he was created. A similar symbolic means of toning down his rebellion theme Shakespeare later was to use in *Richard II*.

Full of evil as *Richard III* may be, the crimes of its villain-hero are perpetrated within a profoundly moral universe in which evil must inevitably be punished. It is a stern morality which combines a Senecan notion of *Nemesis* with a Christian faith in providence, for the evil path of Richard is a cleansing operation which roots evil out of society and restores the world at last to the God-ordained goodness embodied in the new rule of Henry VII. But the cold, humourless scourge of the chronicles has in Shakespeare's play been transformed into a comic villain, and in this there is a key to Shakespeare's supreme achievement in *Richard III*. We delight in the antics of Richard himself, and in his comic posturing and play-acting he becomes a comic commentary upon the stern moral world of whose inexorable justice he is an instrument. Shakespeare thus for a moment exposes the historical myth of Polydore Vergil and Edward Hall to ridicule, and we wonder at the nature of a providence which must destroy even the young princes for nothing more than the sins of their father. This dramatic exposure of a moral postulate to the test of its antithesis is a characteristic Shakespearian device, but it must not here be emphasized out of proportion. Before the end of the play Richard has lost most of the comic attributes with which we can sympathize, and any imaginative participation we may have felt in his quest for power has been dissipated before the opening of the final act. We see his death at last as the lifting of God's curse from England, and in the humourless figure of Richmond there is the fulfilment of a divine promise.

It seems evident that Shakespeare intended his first tetralogy to be taken seriously as history, that he probably saw himself as continuing in the line of Polydore Vergil and Edward Hall. Taken together the four plays embody a significant philosophy of history, they enunciate important political lessons, and they offer parallels from which the immediate age of Elizabeth might draw much profit. They are not great plays, although they give promise of the greatness which is to come, and *Richard III* must rank among the most impressive productions of its day. As history plays, however, they are of great significance, for they show us a dramatist seriously attempting and accomplishing the political and philosophical purposes of the historian.

Notes

1. E. K. Chambers, *William Shakespeare* (Oxford: Clarendon Press, 1930), I, 270; Dover Wilson, ed. *Richard III* (Cambridge: Cambridge University Press, 1954), pp. ix–x, holds that it was probably written some time between June 28, 1592 and the end of 1593, during which time the theatres were closed because of the plague, and Shakespeare would have had much time for composition.

2. E. A. J. Honigmann, "Shakespeare's 'Lost Source Plays,' " *Modern Language Review,* XLIX (1954), 305, who would thus place it before *The True Tragedy of Richard III,* which he considers a bad quarto of a play written in imitation of Shakespeare's *Richard III.*

3. David L. Patrick, *The Textual History of "Richard III"* (Palo Alto: Stanford University Press, 1936).

4. Chambers, *William Shakespeare,* I, 304. G. B. Churchill, *Richard III up to Shakespeare,* (Berlin: *Palaestra,* X, 1900), p. 497, argues for Shakespeare's use of *The True Tragedy,* as does Dover Wilson, "Shakespeare's *Richard III* and *The True Tragedy of Richard the Third,*" *Shakespeare Quarterly* III (1952), 299–306.

5. See Edleen Begg, "Shakespeare's Debt to Hall and Holinshed in *Richard III,*" *Studies in Philology,* XXXII (1935), 189–96.

6. See Chapter 3.

7. *3 Henry VI,* III, ii, 124–95.

8. A. P. Rossiter, "The Structure of *Richard III,*" *Durham University Journal,* XXXI (1938), 72.

9. E. M. W. Tillyard, *Shakespeare's History Plays* (New York: Macmillan, 1947).

10. Rossiter, *op. cit.,* p. 72.

11. Whitaker, *Shakespeare's Use of Learning* (San Marino: Huntington Library, 1969), p. 69, would read the scene literally and explain it in the light of the courtly love tradition. Since Richard pleads that Anne's beauty has led him to commit his crimes, she by the courtly love code becomes equally guilty of them and thus must submit to him. For S. C. Sen Gupta, *Shakespeare's Historical Plays,* (Oxford: Oxford University Press, 1972), pp. 91–2, it is an extraordinary alteration of historical fact by a dramatist concerned only with character delineation, designed to show Richard's ability to manipulate other people by having him undertake and accomplish a seemingly impossible task.

12. *Miscellaneous Writings of Thomas Cranmer,* ed. John Edmund Cox (Cambridge: Parker Society, 1846), p. 188.

13. Cited by Alfred Hart, *Shakespeare and the Homilies* (Melbourne: Melbourne University Press, 1934), p. 46.

Richard III: Act I, Scene One

WOLFGANG H. CLEMEN

GENERAL STRUCTURE

This first scene—and indeed the whole play—is dominated by the figure of Richard.[1] He opens and closes the scene with a soliloquy, and keeps a constant steering hand on the direction of the dialogue. These two soliloquies make a frame for Richard's encounters with Clarence and Hastings, which are separated from each other by yet another short monologue. The central episodes (Clarence going to prison and Hastings leaving it) are also similar in content: in both Richard meets a future, unsuspecting victim; in both he dissembles, then explains the purpose of his deceit in the soliloquy that follows. Thus the first scene with its symmetrical construction introduces a technique used in various forms throughout the play and indeed throughout Shakespeare's early work. In *Richard III* this symmetry is still very obvious, almost obtrusive: Richard's twice-repeated show of hypocrisy before two of his future victims has an artificial flavour about it. Yet at the same time, the careful construction of this scene suggests the work of a highly conscious author unwilling to admit any fortuitous element into his plot, preparing well in advance for future developments. Themes and characters introduced here will not remain unutilized in future scenes.

THE OPENING SOLILOQUY (1–41)

The great opening soliloquy, delivered in prologue-like fashion by Richard alone on the stage, falls into three distinct parts: in lines 1–13 he surveys the situation; in 14–27 he describes his own appearance and character; and in 28–40 he tells us of his future plans. What is here presented in one speech furnished in pre-Shakespearian drama the subject-matter for three: the prologue revealed the opening situation; the monologue of exposition and self-introduction presented the main character; and the "planning monologue"

From Wolfgang H. Clemen, *A Commentary on Shakespeare's "Richard III,"* trans. Jean Bonheim (London: Methuen, 1968). Reprinted with permission of the publisher.

(the soliloquy in which the speaker announces his future plans) prepared for future events. These three motifs did not normally follow one upon the other. It is something new for *one* monologue of moderate length to fulfil these three functions.

The soliloquy (and the play) begins in the same tone with which *3 Henry VI* had ended. King Edward, in the concluding lines of the earlier play (V, vii, 42 ff.), had spoken of the *stately triumphs* and the *mirthful comic shows* in which the court would spend its days now that the Lancastrians had fallen: a season of *lasting joy* was about to open. And now Richard contrasts this joyful time with the period of war which has just ended. Richard's opening references to a season of sunny peace—ironic in the light of his later actions—remind the audience that England is actually enjoying an unclouded prospect free from civil and foreign wars. In other plays the opening situation provides grounds for the hero's subsequent action;[2] but nothing in the external world serves to explain Richard's aggressive behaviour.[3] The motive for his actions must be sought solely in his character, his will.

That Richard's sympathies are in fact for war is emphasized in: "this weak piping time of peace" (24), and in his admission: "And hate the idle pleasures of these days" (31). Lines 10–13 contain a disdainful criticism of the warrior's unmanly peace-time behaviour (the *he* in line 12 surely refers to this hypothetical soldier, with a possible hint at Edward IV[4]); the choice of the word *capers* for what the warrior does in a lady's chamber (12)[5] underlines Richard's low opinion of this particular amusement. But, more important, the striking and concrete description following the more conventional lines on the passing of war and coming of peace infuses the passage with movement and vivacity.

These first thirteen lines differ from the usual passages of introductory exposition in sixteenth-century drama[6] in that they contain hardly any names or historico-political detail; instead, images of war are juxtaposed with images of peace in an extended contrast. The ponderous chronicling of facts which burdens so many opening scenes is replaced by evocative description incorporating a number of conventional expressions common in Elizabethan drama.[7] These first thirteen lines, rich in rhetorical devices[8] are marked by a stately, ceremonious tone in striking contrast with what follows. The *gravità, maestà,* and *dignità*[9] which, according to Castelvetro, should characterize tragedy, lend their weight to Richard's opening words. But here style is suited to content; elevated rhetoric appears only where it is appropriate. As soon as the soliloquy takes on a more personal note (14 ff.), the diction too grows more personal; tempo and language adjust themselves to the new tone.[10]

And yet a personal note emerges even in these first thirteen lines. When Richard speaks of the "glorious summer" which has been ushered in by "this sun of York," the *this* (referring to his brother, Edward) has a disparaging ring. In any case, the pun on *sun = son* (suggested by the Yorkist badge, the sun-in-splendour[11]) is ironic, for Edward, the sun of York, is fast fading and near death; moreover, Richard lacks belief in both the radiance of this sun and the present *glorious summer.* It is typical of Richard, too, that these lofty images of sunrise, of summer's victory, of clouds *in the deep bosom of the ocean buried,* are evoked not by feelings of contentment, but by dissatisfaction. Thus Richard's feelings are the opposite of the sentiments seemingly expressed in these resounding opening lines. Nor is the subjective description of the warrior's antics what we should expect from an impersonal prologue. It has even been suggested that the high rhetoric of the opening lines is Richard's particular way of mocking the sentiments expressed.[12]

The second section of the soliloquy opens with Richard's *But I,* which stresses his isolation while it detaches him from the *our* which had linked the earlier lines on conditions at court and in the country.[13] It also forms a natural bridge (both syntactically and logically) from the more general survey of the situation to the picture he then draws of himself. In pre-Shakespearian drama the various sections of the monologue had usually followed one another without any connecting link.

The seven-fold repetition of the word *I* in the second section, like the repeated use of *our* in the first section, lends the pronoun a special emphasis;[14] moreover, four of the *I's* occur in the stressed position at the beginning of a line. In the first section the sentences were relatively short, but this section consists of one extended sentence, in which three relative clauses precede the eventual appearance of the verb. The third of these clauses, with its agglomeration of past participles all conveying a negative image of Richard (*curtail'd, cheated of feature, deform'd, unfinish'd, scarce half made up*), accelerates the pace of the speech and increases the bitterness of tone. For Richard, self-observation is clearly a fascinating activity.

The scornful way in which Richard makes fun of the lover's rôle[15] is striking. This particular tone—mocking and sarcastic, indeed spiteful—will make itself felt in many later passages. Here and elsewhere in the play he describes himself as though he were looking in a mirror: he enumerates individual imperfections (19–21) and dramatizes his disabled state in his account of the dogs barking at his approach (22–23). "Deform'd" from birth, he feels "cheated" by *nature*[16]—the same nature that had, as he says in the next scene, endowed Anne's murdered husband, Edward, with such "prodigality" (1, ii, 243), whereas he himself is later addressed by Margaret as the "slave of nature and the son of hell" (I, iii, 30).

Critics have been rather too ready to treat this second section of the soliloquy as though it were a modern exploration of the psychological roots of Richard's misanthropic attitude; line 19 ("Cheated of feature by dissembling nature") and Richard's subsequent statements on the reasons for his villainy are interpreted by such psychologically oriented critics somewhat as follows: Richard's physical deformities, which exclude him from the enjoyment of love, cause him to seek compensation in his villainous undertakings; not Richard himself, therefore, but the twisted body foisted upon him by nature, must be held responsible for his criminal behaviour. In fact, however, the main purpose of these lines is to make clear that the leading character *is* a villain, and, moreover, that he freely *chooses* to be a villain ("I am determined to prove a villain" 30).[17] His decision leads inevitably to his tragic end. These lines, then, introduce the theme of guilt and expiation that is to pervade the play. In Shakespeare's main source, Holinshed—More, and in Bacon's *Essay* 44[18] (cited by Wright in his discussion of these lines) an evil disposition is taken to result from a deformed body; but the connection is not seen to be inevitable and does not prohibit the exercise of the free will. These writers do not, then, suggest that a twisted body absolves its owner from the moral responsibility for his evil acts; this is a modern, not an Elizabethan,[19] concept. However appealing modern psychological interpretations of Richard's motivation may be, it is the content of the play itself that proves most helpful in interpreting difficult passages. Thus to view Richard's choice of evil as "compensation," ignoring both his freedom of will and his subsequent guilt, is to view the play from an alien standpoint—and this notwithstanding the fact that modern psychoanalysis is particularly familiar with the psychological state hinted at by Richard.

If Richard's motives for his villainy fail to convince us that the passage is as Freudian as Freud suggests,[20] they are nevertheless a thoroughly convincing expression of Richard's own character. Just as later he is never at a loss for an explanation, brazenly and cynically justifying each of his crimes in turn, so here at the very outset he finds an apparently logical reason for being what he is.[21]

The last section of the soliloquy (32–40)[22] discloses the speaker's designs in the manner usual for a planning monologue (see below). Richard's methods of intrigue become immediately apparent: instead of openly confronting his enemies, he covertly seeks to divide them and sow dissension among them. His self-portrayal (37)—intended for the audience's ear—and his objective description of King Edward[23] as *true and just* are carefully balanced in intentionally contrasting phrases (*if he be . . . As I am . . .*) so that the self-portrayal is less direct than, for instance, that in Marlowe's *Tamburlaine.* The key-word *hate,* heard twice in this section, frequently recurs later in the play contrasted to *love.*

The soliloquy closes with the traditional address to the speaker's own thoughts, "Dive, thoughts, down to my soul. Here Clarence comes"—a reminder that Richard's secret thoughts, though revealed to us, must remain unknown to the other characters in the play. In his early plays Shakespeare made frequent use of this obvious and unrealistic device from pre-Shakespearian drama. Equally primitive and unrealistic is the way in which a character mentioned in the dialogue (in this case, Clarence) promptly appears on stage. It is true that in later plays characters continue to appear at precisely the right moment, but the wires by which they are drawn are more decently obscured than in *Richard III,* where the identity of each new arrival is carefully announced ("But who comes here? The new-delivered Hastings?" 121) in phrases which vary little from case to case.[24]

Never again after *Richard III* did Shakespeare choose to open a play in so direct a manner—with a soliloquy in which the hero introduces himself and provides necessary information for the audience. And yet the conventional aspects of this soliloquy[25] are not intrusive. On the contrary, it seems entirely appropriate that Richard, whose experience has been that of isolation and whose personality dominates the play, should step forward on an empty stage to address us. Moreover, the image of Richard which emerges from this monologue is in no way blurred by the interwoven factual and expository detail.

Such a subtle and convincing portrait at the very outset of *Richard III* would hardly have been possible without the foundations provided by the careful preliminary sketch in *3 Henry VI*.[26] The audience, who may be assumed to know the earlier plays in the tetralogy, thus re-encounter Richard in an opening soliloquy where traits merely suggested before are now revealed as parts of a sharply defined, fully realized character.

THE PRE-SHAKESPEARIAN OPENING SOLILOQUY

In morality plays and in certain Elizabethan dramas,[27] and even in *Romeo and Juliet, 2 Henry IV,* and *Henry V,* the prologue was spoken by a figure not taking part in the action itself. Such prologues, by conveying necessary facts and preparing the audience for the opening situation, simplify the otherwise overburdened opening scene. But even in older plays a soliloquy rather than a prologue often opened the proceedings or introduced a new stage in the action;[28] in many other cases (right up to Marlowe's *Faustus* and *The Jew of Malta*) the play begins with both a prologue *and* an opening soliloquy, the soliloquy spoken by one of the characters but designed primarily to convey information. The opening soliloquy also has roots in the naïve self-introductions of characters in medieval drama (*Deus sum*). In some of the earlier pre-Shakespearian comedies—for instance Nicholas Udall's *Ralph Roister Doister*—the opening soliloquy serves to characterize its speaker and to describe other characters. The interludes and farces often begin with a monologue in which the speaker introduces himself, provides necessary background material, and discloses future plans.[29] Villains in pre-Shakespearian drama[30] always reveal themselves in a planning-monologue at the outset of the play or at the end of the first scene in which they appear.[31]

Critics have pointed to the long introductory soliloquies spoken by the leading characters in many of Seneca's plays (*Medea, Octavia, Oedipus, Hercules Oetaeus*) as the model for Richard's first soliloquy.[32] It is true that in *Richard*

III the device of the Senecan opening soliloquy (also incorporated in English classical drama)[33] has been retained; and, indeed, *Richard III* may be said to belong to the tradition of tragedy rather than to that of the chronicle play, where an opening soliloquy by a leading character was not the rule. But in style and content Richard's soliloquy bears little resemblance to those of Seneca. Richard's cool and objective description of his own state of mind, his appearance, and his present situation is at the same time a complex character study, whereas the tumultuous Senecan outbursts of feeling convey only a general impression of an agitated personality. The Senecan soliloquies occasionally contain factual information on past events and future plans (*Hercul. Fur., Medea*), but such passages remain subordinate to the extended rhetorical outbursts of emotion; moreover, the expository material itself often turns out to be irrelevant, whereas in Richard's monologue every detail has its importance in the light of later events, and the monologue is an actual part of the opening scene, rather than the separate preface found in so many Senecan dramas. Seneca, then, cannot be said to have influenced either the content or the method of composition of Richard's opening monologue.[34]

There are also important differences between Marlowe's and Shakespeare's treatment of the opening soliloquy. Thus Guise in his opening speech in Marlowe's *The Massacre at Paris* puts all his cards on the table (whereas Richard only partly reveals his dark designs). But save for one quality—ambition—Guise remains a hazy figure; his soliloquy abounds in abstract reflection, in contrast to Shakespeare's concrete portrayal of a human situation.

Barabas's opening speech in Marlowe's *The Jew of Malta* is, on the other hand, an unusually vivid, if less pure, example of the monologue of self-introduction. Barabas is portrayed, not through the primitive method of self-description, but dramatically through his actions: counting his money, looking over his treasures, watching his weathervane and thinking of his argosies. The world in which he lives and the values by which he lives are thus depicted with economy and verve. There is none of the usual dull recounting of related material. The language[35] is fully as dramatic and vigorous as that of Richard's soliloquy—indeed the mid-phrase opening is more dramatic than Richard's studied and prologue-like lines. The monologue possesses a dramatic intensity and, in some respects, a modernity greater than that of Richard's more formal utterance.

Marlowe's 47 lines (which in fact put before us a short countinghouse scene) all treat the same theme—the world of Barabas; Shakespeare's 41 lines, on the other hand, cover a much wider field—the political situation at court with its emotional overtones, Richard's personality in relation to this background, and his plans and intentions. Richard's soliloquy thus prepares for and is carefully linked to future events, whereas that of Barabas lacks any such precise connections; Marlowe is carried forward by his own sonorous and richly allusive diction.

Notes

1. Throughout this commentary Richard of Gloucester is called *Richard*. In the play he is called *Gloucester* up to IV, i, and *Richard* only after his coronation (IV, ii).

2. e.g. *The Spanish Tragedy, The Jew of Malta.*

3. Cf. Frank W. Cady, "Motivation of the Inciting Force in Shakespeare's Tragedies," *Elizabethan Studies and other Essays in Honor of George F. Reynolds* (University of Colorado Studies. Series B. Studies in the Humanities, vol. II, No. 4, 1945).

4. In the relevant line annotation in W. A. Wright ed., *Shakespeare* (Cambridge: Cambridge University Press, 9 vols. 1891–3), Wright believes this *he* to refer to "War, still personified as a rough soldier." But J. D. Wilson believed that, in spite of the antecedent *war* (*War*), the *he* refers to the notoriously lascivious king, Edward IV. Cf. J. D. Wilson ed., William Shakespeare, *Richard III.* (Cambridge: Cambridge University Press, 1961), p. 168.

5. Cf. the use of *caper* in *2 Henry VI*, III, i, 365, *L.L.L.*, V, ii, 113.

6. Cf. for instance *Locrine*, I, i; *Misfortunes of Arthur*, I, i; *The Spanish Tragedy*, I, i.

7. Cf. "winter of our discontent" with "winter of my miserie," Sidney, *Astrophel and Stella* (annotation in George Steevens, ed., *The Dramatic Works of William Shakespeare*, 9 vols., London: J. Boydell, 1802). With "grimvisag'd war" cf. Sackville's *Induction*, 386 f. (J. D. Wilson's edition) and with "bruised arms," cf. *Rape of Lucrece*, 110 (in Edward Malone, ed., *The Plays and Poems of William Shakespeare*, 10 vols., London: H. Baldwin, 1790). For the contrast between "marches" and "measures" cf. Lyly's *Campaspe*, IV, iii, 32 ff (in W. A. Wright, ed., *Shakespeare*, Cambridge: Cambridge University Press, 9 vols., 1891–3) and for the contrast between war and the "delicate tunes and amorous glances" of peace, see II, ii, 35 ff. of the same work (in Samuel Johnson and George Steevens, eds., revised by Isaac Reed, *The Plays of William Shakespeare*, 21 vols., London: J. Johnson, 1803). A. H. Krappe suggests that the metaphor "winter of our discontent" goes back originally to Claudian's *De Bello Gothico* (151 f.) (*Anglia*, LII, 1928, p. 174 f.).

8. Cf. the anaphora, the alliteration (2, 4–5, 7–8, 11, 12–13), the balanced lines with their contrasting pairs of words (7, 8). Cf. the parallel grammatical construction of the line endings (adjective followed by noun, 5, 7–11).

9. Cf. M. J. Wolff, "Die Theorie der italienischen Tragödie im 16. Jahrhundert" *Archiv*, CXXVIII (1912), pp. 161 ff., 339 ff.

10. J. W. Draper's work on tempo in Shakespeare's plays is largely based on the proportion of "slurrings of words or phrases" to the expressions uttered without slurring; he too concludes that lines 13–32 show a marked increase in tempo ("Patterns of Tempo in *Richard III*" *Neuphil. Mitteilungen*, L, 1949).

11. Cf. A. Venezky, *Pageantry on the Shakespearean Stage* (New York: Twayne, 1951), p. 181: "In the opening passage of the play, Richard employs a favorite device of the royal entry pageant when he rejoices that the recently crowned sun-king has dispersed . . . all the clouds that lowr'd upon our house." Cf. also the same image used in *Battle of Alcazar*, II, i. And similarly, *Mirror, Richard Duke of Gloucester* (*The Mirror for Magistrates*, ed. Lily B. Campbell, Cambridge: Cambridge University Press, 1938), 238. On the heraldic significance of the badge cf. C. W. Scott-Giles, *Shakespeare's Heraldry* (London: Dent, 1950), p. 172 f. The "sun emerging from a cloud" was Richard II's special badge. Cf. *Richard II*, ed. J. D. Wilson (Cambridge: Cambridge University Press, 1939), p. xii.

12. Cf. J. Palmer on the opening of the soliloquy: ". . . while, across the play of intellect restfully aware of itself, runs a vein of mockery which, with a precise and amusing exaggeration, flouts the easy rhetoric as it marches to a conclusion. All those preliminary adjectives have, as it were, an elfin smile in their delivery—*glorious, victorious, dreadful, delightful*" (*Political Characters of Shakespeare* London: Macmillan, 1945, p. 77 f.).

13. Cf. H. Glunz, *Shakespeare und Morus* Bochum-Langendreer: H. Poppinghaus, (1938), p. 150; Theodore Spencer, *Shakespeare and the Nature of Man* (London: Macmillan, 1942/49), p. 72.

14. At the same time these lines extend Richard's "I am myself alone" (*3 Henry VI*, V, vi, 83).

15. Cf. *3 Henry VI*, III, ii, 146 ff.

16. This conception of nature as creating men and imparting certain gifts and a certain outward shape to them is recurrent in Shakespeare, see Alexander Schmidt, *Shakespeare Lexicon* (Berlin: G. Reiner, 1874), *nature*, sense 1. In his *Faerie Queene* (VII, vii, 5–6), Spenser had shown that nature can be double-faced and is fundamentally ambivalent. Cf. also John F. Danby, *Shakespeare's Doctrine of Nature: A Study of "King Lear"* (London: Faber and Faber, 1949). On *Richard III* specifically, see pp. 58–67, though this particular passage is not cited. J. D. Wilson (cf. also Warburton, Malone, etc.) understands "dissembling nature" to suggest "hiding my real greatness under a deceptive appearance"; thus, keeping in mind the Renaissance insistence on the dual rôle of nature (cf. Danby), "dissembling nature" may mean: hypocritical, perfidious, treacherous, deceitful, false. See Schmidt, sense 1a, and editions of S. Johnson, W. A. Wright, H. H. Furness. On the Goddess Natura in the classical period, the Middle Ages, and the Renaissance, cf. E. R. Curtius, *European Literature and the Latin Middle Ages* (New York: Pantheon, 1953), ch. 6.

17. For a divergent interpretation of *determined* see: D. S. Berkeley, " 'Determined' in *Richard III*, I, i, 30" *SQ*, XIV (1963), pp. 483–484.

18. "Deformed persons are commonly even with Nature. For as Nature hath done ill by them; so doe they by Nature: Being for the most part, (as the Scripture saith) *void of Naturall Affection;* And so they have their Revenge of Nature" (*Of Deformity*).

19. Cf. R. L. Anderson, *Elizabethan Psychology and Shakespeare's Plays*, Univ. of Iowa, Humanistic Studies, III, 4 (1928), pp. 146–147. Cf. also M. C. Bradbrook, *Themes and Conventions of Elizabethan Tragedy* (Cambridge: Cambridge University Press, 1935), p. 57: "Most of the villains are given some kind of defect which embitters them and cuts them off from humanity. This is no justification for their behaviour, for the Elizabethan mind was not accustomed to distinguish between crimes which were the result of choice and those which were the result of heredity." Cf. also A. Harbage: "Nearly always the physical trait is also a moral symbol—in extreme cases a stigma like Richard the Third's hump" (*As They Liked It. An Essay on Shakespeare and Morality* New York: Macmillan, 1947, p. 20). Hardin Craig (*An Interpretation of Shakespeare* New York: Dryden Press, 1948, p. 70) mentions in connection with this soliloquy the Platonic doctrine "a fair soul in a fair body," and its opposite application, "a crooked and evil soul in a deformed and crooked body."

20. Sigmund Freud is one of the many who have commented on this monologue: "I think, therefore, that Richard's soliloquy does not say everything; it merely gives a hint, and leaves us to fill in what it hints at. When we do so, however, the appearance of frivolity [imparted by Richard's explanation of his motive for doing evil] vanishes, the bitterness and minuteness with which Richard has depicted his deformity make their full effect, and we clearly perceive the fellow feeling which compels our sympathy even with a villain like him. What the soliloquy thus means is: Nature has done me a grievous wrong in denying me the beauty of form which wins human love. Life owes me reparation for this, and I will see that I get it . . . I may do wrong myself, since wrong has been done to me . . ." (S. Freud, *Imago, Zeitschrift für Anwendung der Psychoanalyse auf die Geisteswissenschaften* IV, 6, 1916, p. 320).

21. Towards the end of *3 Henry VI* Richard makes a similar choice of villainy, and gives the same reason for his attitude:

> "Then, since the heavens have shap'd my body so,
> Let hell make crook'd my mind to answer it."
>
> (V, vi, 78 f.)

22.   A change of stress at the beginning of line 32 marks the opening of the new section: "Plots have I laid . . . ."

23.   On the villain's self-revelation in his monologues and on his objective assessment of heroic figures, cf. L. L. Schücking, *Character Problems in Shakespeare's Plays* (London: George G. Harrap, 1922), pp. 59 ff.

24.   Cf. I, iii, 17; I, iii, 339; II, i, 45; II, iv, 38; III, i, 24; III, i, 95; III, iv, 22; III, v, 13; III, v, 21; III, vii, 55; III, vii, 82; IV, i, 1, IV, i, 12; IV, ii, 46; IV, ii, 68; IV, iv, 456.

25.   S. L. Bethell has discussed, with reference to this soliloquy, the convention of "informing the audience" (*Shakespeare and the Popular Dramatic Tradition,* Durham, N.C.: Duke University Press, 1944, pp. 71–73). A new interpretation of this matter is given by Nicholas Brooke, "Reflecting Gems and Dead Bones. Tragedy versus History in *Richard III." The Critical Quarterly* VII (1965), p. 129.

26.   Cf. in particular *3 Henry VI,* I, ii, 22–34; III, ii, 124–195; V, vi, 61–93. And cf. *2 Henry VI,* V, i, 213–214, 216. Cf. too the characterization in J. Palmer, *Political Characters of Shakespeare* (1945), p. 66 ff., and Hardin Craig, *An Interpretation of Shakespeare* (1948), p. 68 ff. Craig reminds us that there is little in the Richard of *2 Henry VI* to suggest his later character, which took shape in *3 Henry VI,* III, ii. Indeed (as A. Leschtsch has pointed out in *Richard III, eine Charakterstudie,* (Berlin: H. Paetel, 1908), the Richard of *Henry VI,* Parts 2 and 3 is in some respects the opposite of the Richard in our play. Certainly the character is not developed along altogether consistent lines.

27.   e.g. *Conflict of Conscience, Locrine, Gismond of Salerne, Battle of Alcazar.*

28.   e.g. Bale, *King John.*

29.   e.g. *Thersytes, The Play of the Wether, Johan Johan, The Foure PP.*

30.   Cf. C. V. Boyer, *The Villain as Hero in Elizabethan Tragedy* (New York: E. P. Dutton 1914).

31.   *Selimus,* 231 ff.; *Edward II,* 1 ff. For further examples cf. note 3, p. 18. Another example from Shakespeare's early works is York's monologue at the end of I, i in *2 Henry VI.* Cf. M. C. Bradbrook, *Themes and Conventions of Elizabethan Tragedy* (1935), p. 115.

32.   Cf. Hardin Craig, "Shakespeare and the History Play," *Joseph Quincy Adams Memorial Studies* (1948), p. 57 f.

33.   e.g. *Gismond of Salerne; Misfortunes of Arthur.*

34.   Howard Baker (*Induction to Tragedy: A Study in a Development of Form in "Gorboduc,"* New York: Russell and Russell, 1939) discusses the overestimate of Senecan influence on pre-Shakespearian drama.

35.   Cf. F. P. Wilson's discussion of it in his *Marlowe and the Early Shakespeare* (Oxford: Clarendon Press, 1953), p. 58 ff.

RICHARD III REINVENTED

◆

One of the ironies of editorial investigation into the earliest published versions of *Richard III* is that it shows that the text was subject to substantial modifications from the start. The earlier, single-play editions of *Richard III*, the Quartos, seem to be based originally on some reconstructed version of yet earlier texts, perhaps derived from actors' recollections of their parts in previous performances. Compared with the fuller edition published later in the Folio collection of Shakespeare's plays, the Quarto versions seem to be shortened, perhaps initially for a provincial touring production, since several speeches and minor characters have been cut. While the longer Folio version seems still to have partly depended on these earlier Quartos, they were probably amplified from some even earlier authorial draft. However, this latest synthesis was in turn purged of various religious allusions, curses, oaths, and profanities still found in the earlier versions, material that had become unacceptable by the Folio's date of publication. So, from the start, there is a tradition of modifying the text to suit particular conditions of performance and taste.

After the closure of the theaters during the Commonwealth period, shifts to a more fashionable European taste invited the managers of the theaters, newly reopened on the restoration of King Charles II, to accommodate Shakespeare's scripts to new theater designs based on French and Italian models and to the neoclassical conventions of drama that matched them. Shakespeare was cut, unified, and generally made more consistent, sentimental, and narrowly focused, as we can see in the revisions made to *Richard III* by Colley Cibber as described by Scott Colley. This more theatrically consistent version, focused on an even more dominant Richard, remained popular until the twentieth century, and some of its more picturesque strokes persist in such modern versions as Olivier's film of the play. Some modern critics, such as Scott Colley, share the approval for Cibber's version, which he finds in Norman Rabkin's *Shakespeare and the Problem of Meaning*.[1] Both critics still seem to favor Cibber's tidier, narrower, and more consistent script to Shake-speare's less focused and less predictable treatment.

Throughout the later eighteenth and nineteenth centuries critics had already made the first sustained attempts to define the revised play's place in the Shakespearean tradition, as we can see in the efforts of Thomas Whately to contextualize the work in Shakespeare's *oeuvre* by comparing it with *Macbeth*. Similarly, Augustus William Schlegel's work stresses *Richard III's* function as the climax of the first English tetralogy, and Nathan Drake's attempts to locate Richard's relationship to Milton's creation of Satan. As a result of the powerful performances of *Richard III* by such leading actors as David Garrick and Edmund Kean, the play emerged as an icon for the evolving romanticism that found in Richard a prototype for the Byronic hero. The psychologizing of Richard fostered by both critics and actors reflected an intensification of the interest in the nuances of his character, as we can see in William Hazlitt's comments on Kean and other actors in the lead role. The romantics thus initiated a revised estimate of the play's importance, no less keyed to their own aesthetic values than the neoclassical one of Cibber and his contemporaries but more sympathetic to Shakespeare's aesthetic and thus proving of more lasting interest to later periods. However, despite increasing critical resistance to "improved" Shakespeare texts, the preferred script of *Richard III* was usually Cibber's version of Shakespeare, with its exploitation of a more consistent bravura role for Richard than the original text and with far fewer constraints on his wickedness.

To a surprising degree, this rather facile interpretation held the stage and the critical foreground until a reaffirmation of English identity was provoked by World War II, occasioned by a demonic Hitler who matched the legendary Richard's monstrosity. These circumstances led E. M. W. Tillyard to treat the history plays as more than picturesque theatrical artifacts and to find in them a kind of national epic meriting serious political investigation of the plays' original context and character. This shift has already been reflected in the extracts in the previous section of this book, all of which postdate Tillyard's redefinition of the play as something more significant than romantic melodrama.

Notes

    1.   Notmas Rabkin, *Shakespeare and the Problem of Meaning* (Chicago: University of Chicago Press, 1981), 97–101.

Colley Cibber's *Richard III*

SCOTT COLLEY

In writing about the period during which he composed his revision of *Richard III,* Cibber at several points compares himself to the crookback villain of Shakespeare's play. That is, Cibber explains how his own physical limitations forced him, like Gloucester, to play the villain: "snubb'd, by the Insufficiency of my Voice; to which, might be added, an uninform'd meagre Person . . . I had but a melancholy Prospect of ever playing a Lover" (*Apology* 102). Thus he was forced, early in his career, to turn to "particular Characters in Tragedy, as *Iago, Wolsey, Syphax, Richard* the *Third &c*" (213). As a gloss upon his physical limitations, Cibber tells the parallel story of Samuel Sandford, who was a major player at the Theatre Royal when Cibber joined the company: "poor *Sandford* was not the Stage-Villain by Choice, but from Necessity; for having a low and crooked Person, such bodily Defects were too strong to be admitted into great, or amiable Characters; so that whenever, in any new or reviv'd Play, there was a hateful or mischievous Person, *Sandford* was sure to have no Competitor for it" (77). Sandford, like Cibber himself, was denied "that Applause, which I saw much inferior Actors met with, merely because they stood in more laudable Characters" (78).

In 1690, the year that Cibber joined the Theatre Royal, Sandford played the lead role in Shakespeare's *Richard III* (see Wilson [1968] xlviii for a discussion of that performance). Cibber was so struck by Sandford's power in the role that he later described him as if he embodied the essential characteristics of Shakespeare's Richard:

> Had *Sandford* liv'd in *Shakespear's* Time, I am confident [Shakespeare] must have chose him, above all other Actors, to have play'd his *Richard the Third.* . . . [H]e had sometimes an uncouth Stateliness in his Motion, a harsh and sullen Pride of Speech, a meditating Brow, a stern Aspect, occasionally changing into an almost ludicrous Triumph over all Goodness and Virtue: From thence falling into the most asswasive Gentleness, and soothing Candour of a designing

Originally published in Colley, *Richard's Himself Again: A Stage History of "Richard III"* (Greenwood Press, Westport, CT, 1992). Copyright © 1992 by Scott Colley. Reprinted with permission of Greenwood Publishing Group, Inc.

Heart. Those . . . would have been Colours so essentially shining in that Character, that . . . *Sandford* must have shewn so many masterly Strokes in it . . . as are visible in the Writing it. (81)

When Cibber composed his adaptation of Shakespeare's play, he tried to employ Sandford in the main role, but the great villain was engaged elsewhere. Therefore Cibber himself performed the role in imitation of Sandford: "I imagin'd I knew how *Sandford* would have spoken every Line of it: If . . . I succeeded, let the Merit be given to him" (81). Sir John Vanbrugh, who knew Sandford well, is supposed to have told Cibber that his imitation was a success: "*You have,* said he, *his very Look, Gesture, Gait, Speech, and every Motion of him, and have borrow'd them all, only to serve you in that Character*" (*Apology* 82).

Cibber thus played the part of his own Richard in imitation of an actor whose connections to Richard III were both personal and professional. Sandford, of course, was not literally deformed and unfinished like Shakespeare's Gloucester. Nor indeed was Cibber. But Cibber chose to think of both Sandford and himself as cursed by nature in voice and form, and thus denied the fame and fortune that heroic actors could command.

Cibber also compared himself unfavorably to William Mountfort, who had played Richmond in the 1690 production in which Sandford had played Richard III. After Mountfort's sudden death, Cibber took on some of his roles:

Had he been remember'd, when I first attempted them, my Defects would have been more easily discover'd . . . If it could have been remember'd how much he had the Advantage of me in Voice and Person. . . . For he . . . had a melodious, warbling Throat; [while] I alas! could only struggle . . . under the Imperfection of a feign'd, and screaming Trebble, which at best could only shew you what I would have done, had Nature been more favourable to me. (76)

Cursed by nature, Cibber felt he had to follow the path of the villainous Crookback rather than the heroic Richmond.

Cibber thus embarked upon his quest for the golden prize of applause by adapting and acting in his version of Shakespeare's *Richard III*. When he rewrote Richard's opening soliloquy, it is the theme of driving ambition that dominates the speech. Indeed, Cibber adds ten new lines in which Richard says he seeks the crown as compensation for having been cheated of fair proportion. Shakespeare's original Richard hates the "idle pleasures" of this time of peace; Cibber's crippled Richard seeks solace in his voracious appetite for power and control:

> —*Then since this Earth affords no joy to me,*
> *But to Command, to Check, and to Orebear such,*
> 'As are of Happier Person than my self,

'Why then to me this restless World's but Hell,
Till this mishapen trunks aspiring head
'Be circled in a glorious Diadem. . . .
                                    (Cibber, I.ii.19–24)

Cibber thought he would win a glorious theatrical diadem by playing a heroic, Macbeth-like Richard III. The prize was not easily won.

Indeed, too many harsh critics agreed with Cibber's ruthlessly candid self-portrait as an actor. His Richard was strongly criticized for his "screaming Trebble." The anonymous author of *The Laureat; or the Right Side of CC* (1740), doubtless with some touches of truth, observes:

> he screamed thro' four Acts without Dignity or Decency. The Audience, ill-pleas'd with the Farce, accompanied him with a Smile of Contempt; but in the fifth Act, he degenerated all at once into Sir *Novelty;* and . . . in the Heat of the Battle . . . our Comic-Tragedian came on the Stage, really breathless, and in a seeming Panick, screaming out this Line thus—"A *Harse,* a *Harse, my Kingdom for a Harse."* This highly delighted some, and disgusted others of his Auditors; and when he was kill'd by *Richmond,* one might plainly perceive that the good People were not better pleas'd, that so *execrable a Tyrant* was destroy'd, than that so *execrable an Actor* was silent. (35)

A few years earlier, a critic in the *Grubb Street Journal* observed: "[When he] makes love to Lady Anne, he looks like a pickpocket, with his shrugs and grimaces, that has more a design on her purse than her heart; and his utterance is in the same cast with his action. In Bosworth Field he appears no more like King Richard than King Richard was like Falstaff; he foams, struts, and bellows with the voice and cadence of a watchman rather than a hero and prince" (31 October 1734).

These critical views are extreme, but they do accord with some of Cibber's own reflections. A writer in *The Prompter* went to the heart of the matter: "Nature herself limits parts to a player by voice, the figure, and conception. In every one of these three she meant Mr. Cibber for a COMEDIAN" (19 November 1734, Hill 6). When he played Richard III, "instead of . . . disturbed reflection we see a succession of comic shruggings, and in place of menaces and majestic transports the distorted heavings of an unjointed caterpillar" (ibid). It would have been such objections that moved Cibber to descant at such length upon his deformities in the *Apology.*

Some commentators liked Cibber in the role. Thomas Davies says Cibber had his good moments (*Life* I, 19–20). Richard Steele thought his early scenes were excellent (*The Tatler* 182 [8 June 1710]). John Downes suggested in *Roscius Anglicanus* (1708) that Cibber would have been nearly as good a tragedian as the actor Mountfort, "had Nature given him Lungs strenuous to his finisht Judgment" (107). These scattered words of praise give some balance to the chorus of near-hysterical attacks upon the would-be heroic actor.

Certainly Cibber's earliest audiences were not taken with him. In a preface to the printed version of his play *Ximena* (1719), Cibber ruefully notes that *Richard III* "did not raise me £5 on the third day."

Business picked up as the years went by. George Winchester Stone observes that before Garrick had his great success with Cibber's play, Cibber, Ryan, Roberts, Hulett, Quin, Crispe, Delane, Hyde, and Turbutt all played the part. Of these, Cibber, Ryan, Delane, and Quin had some success in the role. Cibber's tragedy was put on eighty-four times in the first forty years of the eighteenth century, three times in performances for the King. During most of the period, it was played nearly every season, and sometimes by as many as two or three different houses. While it was not what anyone would call a smash hit, the play commanded a continuing place in the repertory during the pre-Garrick years (Stone [1968] 15).

Cibber thought his own slow start was due to official meddling. The Master of the Revels made him cut the entire first act, "without sparing a Line of it," because the murder of Henry VI "would put weak People too much in mind of King *James,* then living in *France.*" By 1715, Cibber was able to present his play whole, but not before "it was robb'd of, at least, a fifth part of that Favour, it afterwards met with" (*Apology* 152).

While relatively popular as the century went on, the revision did meet with some critical reservations. Charles Gildon (1710) argued that adapters such as "Mr. C—b—r . . . shou'd never meddle . . . unless they cou'd . . . give us the *Manners, Sentiments, Passions,* and *Diction* finer and more perfect than they find in the original" (Vickers II, 228). Nearly half a century later, "Shakespeare's Ghost" writes in the *London Magazine:*

> Nor yield me up to Cibber and Tate:
> Retrieve the scenes already snatched away,
> Yet, take them back, nor let me fall their prey.
> (Vickers III, 382)

However, at the end of the eighteenth century, the textual editor George Steevens put the matter in terms that explain the remarkable success (and longevity) of the revision:

> Mr. Cibber's reformation . . . is judicious: for what modern audience would patiently listen to the narrative of Clarence's Dream, his subsequent expostulation with the murderers, the prattle of his children, the soliloquy of the Scrivener, the tedious dialogue of the citizens, the ravings of Margaret, the gross terms thrown out by the Duchess of York on Richard, the repeated progress to execution, the superfluous train of spectres, and other undramatick incumbrances which must have prevented the more valuable parts of the play from rising into their present effect and consequence? (Vickers VI, 594–95)

While extreme, Steevens' comments are insightful: none of the dramatic encumbrances he praises Cibber for removing has escaped heavy cutting or excision in modern productions of Shakespeare's play.

A modern theater historian, George Odell, lauds Cibber's text, claiming "it is probably a more effective acting vehicle than Shakespeare's" (Odell [1920] I, 75). While observing that Cibber's Richard is more of a melodramatic monomaniac than is Shakespeare's crafty tyrant, Odell, with some overstatement, insists that Cibber's play "is nervous, unified, compact, where the original is sprawling, diffuse, and aimless" (II, 153). Arthur Colby Sprague agrees that Cibber manages to retain the most memorable episodes of the original, while probably making them stand out in bolder relief than did Shakespeare: "But Margaret is gone and Clarence and Hastings and Edward: the price paid for compactness was high." What remains for Sprague is a version "which does best when it keeps to surfaces and shallows; an opportunist version, cunning, prosaic and vulgar" (Sprague [1964] 124).

Cibber's version invites adjectives like "prosaic and vulgar" in part because it clarifies matters that Shakespeare leaves unexplained. Cibber has given us Shakespeare-made-easier. In *Shakespeare and the Problem of Meaning* (1981), Norman Rabkin comments upon such eighteenth-century attempts to clarify Shakespearean conundrums. In the dramatic worlds of *Richard III* and *Macbeth* "human behavior is governed by unknown and unknowable forces from within and without." Attempts to make these forces more easily comprehensible by reference to later moral and aesthetic formulations naturally distort the original. Indeed, such attempts to rewrite the plays in ways that skirt stubborn ambiguities in Shakespeare's text merely demonstrate that the unconscious figures more in Shakespeare's view of character than the revisers were prepared to acknowledge. Such revisions remind us that "the ultimate ineffability of human motivation is close to the meaning of Shakespearean tragedy" (110). Cibber's revision was probably more successful than others because it supplied linkages, transitions, and motivations that Shakespeare seemed at times almost perversely unwilling to supply. *Richard III* is less complete than *Macbeth, Lear,* and other tragedies that were rewritten in the seventeenth and eighteenth centuries. It is a tragedy that begs more questions than Shakespeare's later works. In making this play "complete," Cibber made a play that audiences could comprehend. In simple terms, audiences needed more help with *Richard III* than with most other plays in the Shakespearean canon: "To his final breath [Cibber's] Richard is torn between mounting ambition and agonizing conscience; at the last he recognizes he has lost the fruits of both. The scheme is far more rational than Shakespeare's, not entertaining for a moment the possibility that the character is really motivated not by neat polarities but rather by the impulse to destruction and self-destruction that makes Shakespeare's Richard both painful to contemplate and human" (101).

Cibber's Richard is more like "his own materialistic father" the Duke of York, or perhaps he resembles "the ambitious Claudius." Shakespeare's Richard is more like Macbeth and other later tragic heroes in that his central motivation is not easily grasped: "Neither ambition nor the more modern explanation of Richard's behavior as his response to his physical deformity carries adequate conviction. The pleasure of Richard's crimes lies in the acting out of deep intrapsychic motives, in the annihilation of the hero's family and his world. So far has Shakespeare come at the very beginning of his theatrical career" (ibid.). One might wish to question Rabkin's formulation of Richard's tragic dilemma: the impulse toward self-destruction might be as much a symptom as a cause of Richard's psychic condition.

But Rabkin's broader critical point seems valid: Richard's ambition, his deformity, even his wicked cleverness do not entirely explain the fascination audiences have had with a play that otherwise hardly approaches the poetic and tragic stature of *Macbeth* or *King Lear. Richard III* has held the stage (as well as held the imaginations of readers) largely because Richard's tragedy, paradoxically, is as compelling as the tragedies of Macbeth and Lear. Actors have continually made this character come to life, and readers have continually perceived the life within him, despite the sprawling, diffuse nature of the text. The play, by all accounts, should not be as fascinating as it is.

The character of Shakespeare's Richard is a problem because he embodies mysteries as complex as those embodied by Hamlet or Macbeth while remaining remarkably unreflective about his condition. In making Richard reflective, however, Cibber changed the focus of the play. Most of the added lines make it clear that Richard's quest is purely political, and that he suffers from the stings of remorse for his deeds. Shakespeare's Richard does not reassure us that his actions are based on such explicable grounds. Indeed, Shakespeare's Richard is resolutely silent at moments when we most would like him to explain himself.

When he began his revision, Cibber apparently read widely in English history, finding new materials particularly in Holinshed (1587) and John Speed's *History of Great Britain* (1650). Albert Kalson has shown that many of Cibber's additions are based upon these two historical works, with smaller debts to others. Cibber might have been led to the chronicles by the prologue to John Caryl's *The English Princess, or the Death of Richard III* (1667), a retelling of the narrative as a royal romance in which Richmond wins Elizabeth's heart as well as the crown. Caryl straightforwardly acknowledges that "to plain Holinshed and down right Stowe/We the course web of our Contrivance owe" (Prologue, cited by Kalson 256). Cibber used both Caryl and Caryl's sources as materials for his own *Richard III.*

Kalson observes that Cibber's "original" additions to the play were in fact recounted in historical sources, and were details Shakespeare for some reason chose to ignore: (1) In Cibber, I.i.107–08, King Henry recalls his compassionate order to remove the bodies of traitors from the city walls; (2) Tressel relates in I.i.177–79 that King Edward struck the prince with his gaunt-let; (3) Richard tells his wife in III.ii that he no longer loves her; (4) the princes have a tender scene with their mother in the Tower in IV.i; (5) Richard is given certain details of the princes' burial in IV.iii; (6) Richmond comments upon his victory over Richard, who lies dead at his feet in the last scene; and (7) Stanley implies at V.ix.35 that Richmond has won the crown not merely by conquest but also by popular choice. As Kalson notes, the only two new scenes that had been thought original with Cibber—Richard's rejection of his wife Ann (*sic*), and the episode between Queen Elizabeth and her sons in the Tower—in fact must be credited to the chronicles: "No adaptable dramatic situation escaped his notice" (263).

At the beginning of the play, Shakespeare's Richard, of course, enters an empty stage and in a soliloquy promises a series of plots which begin almost immediately to unfold. Cibber delays this entrance with an original 240-line scene which depicts the prison life of Henry VI and his sorrow at the news of his son's death. For this new scene, Cibber borrows some lines from *Henry IV* (Northumberland's grief at Hotspur's death) and *Richard II* (Bolingbroke's thoughts at his banishment). Yet the borrowed lines do not account for the genesis of this introductory interlude. Cibber's first scene owes more than a little to Richard II's farewell to his wife and the subsequent soliloquy in his Pomfret Castle prison cell (*Richard II*, V.i and V.v), and to Clarence's reflec-tions in the Tower in Shakespeare's version of *Richard III* (I.iv). Cibber's open-ing imposes a symmetry upon events: Stanley appears in I.i with King Henry VI; and naturally, it is Stanley who hands the crown to Richmond in V.ix. Richard murders one Henry at the start of the play, and is vanquished by another at the end. The opening also provides some historical background, and offers Richard a regal antagonist in his first plot. Of course, the murder of Henry VI in Cibber's third scene is based almost entirely upon *3 Henry VI*, V.vi.1–93. Shakespeare himself had depicted Richard's murder of the saintly Henry, but of course, Shakespeare did not choose to include this killing in *Richard III*. Cibber's major accomplishment in his first act is to turn the focus from a national drama of crime and punishment to a chronicle of Gloucester's villainies. Evil is located within one person, and is no longer a condition which embraces most of the participants of the drama. On the other hand, Shakespeare makes it apparent from the beginning that Richard's tragedy must be understood in the larger tragedy of a nation that has long been at civil war. By beginning the play with the murder of the king, Cibber person-alizes the violence which in Shakespeare's tragedy had been a communal vio-lence, enacted by many of the noble characters in the play who figure vari-ously in the *Henry VI* plays and in *Richard III*.

Cibber's Richard enters after Henry's initial appearance, and begins his soliloquy with "*Now are our Brows bound with Victorious wreaths.*" Gone are "the winter of our discontent" and Richard's observation that he lacks "love's majesty." He will harp on that theme in a soliloquy just before his wooing of

Lady Ann. To the initial soliloquy Cibber adds lines from *3 Henry VI* (III.ii.165–71) which testify to Richard's vaulting ambition:

> —*Then since this Earth affords no joy to me,*
> *But to Command, to Check, and to Orebear such,*
> 'As are of Happier Person than my self,
> 'Why then to me this restless World's but Hell,
> Till this mishapen trunks aspiring head
> 'Be circled in a glorious Diadem.
>
> (Cibber I.ii.19–24)

Shakespeare, just as easily as Cibber, could have dramatized in *Richard III* the motives Gloucester expresses in *3 Henry VI*. Lines such as *"I have no Brother, am like no Brother"* (Cibber I.iii.78; Shakespeare *3 Henry VI*, V.vi.80) offered dramatic opportunities that Shakespeare for some reason chose to avoid in his own tragedy of Richard. While Shakespeare wrote the tragedy early in his career, inexperience or clumsiness alone cannot serve as explanations of the ambiguity with which he cloaks Richard. For reasons of his own, Shakespeare decided that the core of Richard's being must remain enigmatic. Cibber softened that enigma not only by using lines from *3 Henry VI*, but also by adding soliloquies and revealing choric asides throughout the play.

For instance, the courtship of Lady Ann is prefaced by a thirty-line dialogue between Stanley and Tressel which fills in the historical background and addresses Richard's surprising suit to the "Widow to the late Prince *Edward*." (In Cibber's play, Richard had initiated his courtship sometime prior to this scene. See a passing reference to this initial suit at II.i.31–34.) Richard himself then enters to speak another three dozen lines preparing the audience for the audacious wooing which follows:

> But see, my Love appears: Look where she shines,
> Darting pale Lustre, like the Silver Moon
> Through her dark Veil of Rainy sorrow;
> . . .
> 'Tis true, my Form perhaps will little move her,
> But I've a Tongue shall wheadle with the Devil.
>
> (Cibber II.i.55–57; 60–61)

Like Shakespeare's Richard, this one later says *"I'll have her: But I will not keep her long"* (Cibber II.i.255). Unlike Shakespeare's, however, Cibber's Richard admits at the outset that he "cannot blame" Ann for initially rejecting his professions of love. Moreover, he at first appears to yearn for the love which foreswore him in his mother's womb: "am I then a man to be belov'd?/O Monstrous Thought! more vain my Ambition" (44–45). While the courtship scene turns out to have been as elaborate a charade as the one in Shakespeare, Cibber's has the added poignancy of Richard's explicit appreciation of Ann's beauty and his deep fear of rejection by her. Moreover, in Cibber, Richard's courtship includes a more apparent note of contrition for his crimes (and more baldly expressed) than anything in Shakespeare:

> I swear, bright Saint, I am not what I was:
> Those Eyes have turn'd my stubborn heart to Woman,
> Thy goodness makes me soft in Penitence,
> And my harsh thoughts are tun'd to Peace and Love.
>
> (Cibber II.i.228–31)

Actors using this text had excuses to portray Richard as a serious and penitent wooer—without all of the winking asides—and thus "explain" Ann's remarkable change of heart. Cibber takes further steps to discourage a scoffing response to the scene: he gives one of his characters lines that might well be uttered by unconvinced theater-goers. In an aside, Tressel says "I scarce can credit what I see. . . . /When future Chronicles shall speak of this/They will be thought Romance, not History" (II.i.201; 203–04). Tressel's astonishment helps to account for any astonishment that may be experienced in the audience. (This scene could have been played to suggest Richard has hoodwinked Tressel as well as Ann.)

In the wooing, Cibber's Richard performs as he does throughout the tragedy. He is at once lover and cynic, simultaneously self-hating and self-congratulating. Cibber's character plays up the pathos of a deep and soul-warping fear of rejection while acting as if normal human feelings have no effect upon him. To his credit, Cibber largely embellishes hints and suggestions from Shakespeare's portrait of Richard. He does not simply put forward a fully original Richard III. Among the results of this embellishment, however, is a more melodramatic victim of circumstances than the original Gloucester.

In the second scene of Act II, following the wooing of Ann, Cibber combines events between Shakespeare's I.iii (the first court scene) and II.ii (the death of King Edward and provisions for the coronation of the Prince). This 140-line episode allows him to condense six scenes from the original and to remove about 1,000 lines from Shakespeare's text. Because the absences of Clarence and Margaret account for most of the cuts, the result of this surgery is that the focus remains on Richard as he moves quickly from one successful plot to another. The first half of the tragedy thus presents Richard's career in terms of three major confrontations: the murder of Henry VI (i.iii), the wooing of Ann (II.i), and the "capture" of the Prince (III.i), all in fewer than half the lines in Shakespeare's text.

The third act contains two new soliloquies and the added scene between Richard and Lady Ann. At the end of III.i, where Richard and Buckingham set the trap for Hastings, the original Gloucester blandly comments that "afterwards/We may digest our complots in some form" (199–200). With this line, all exit. At the same stage of the plot, Cibber's character speaks nearly two dozen lines in which he comments upon his struggles with his conscience, and then expresses an almost Marlovian delight in his overreaching appetite for power: "Ev'n all Mankind to some lov'd Ills incline,/Great Men chuse Greater Sins—Ambition's mine" (III.i.177–78). It is typical of the two plays that Shakespeare's Richard frequently declines comment at the very moments when Cibber's Richard explores the depths of his thoughts and feelings. At this stage of the play, Shakespeare's Gloucester is more the chilling villain than his troubled successor in Cibber's play.

On the surface, the new scene with Lady Ann (Cibber III.ii) seems implausibly melodramatic, but Cibber of course had the idea from historical record (including many of the most melodramatic touches). For more than twenty lines Ann laments the agony of her life with her husband before Richard enters to describe his plans in an aside:

> The fair *Elizabeth* hath caught my Eye,
> My Heart's vacant; and she shall fill her place—
> They say that Women have but tender hearts,
> 'Tis a mistake, I doubt; I've found them tough:
> They'll bend, indeed: But he must strain that cracks 'em.
> All I can hope's to throw her into sickness:
> Then I may send her a Physicians help.
>
> (Cibber III.ii.27–33)

One of Richard's hopes is to drive his wife to a despairing illness so he can then arrange a "natural" death for her. When she begs him to kill her, he refuses, saying "The medling World will call it murder" and he "wou'd have 'em think me pitifull" (III.ii.47–48). Hence he challenges his wife: "wert thou not afraid of self-Destruction,/Thou hast a fair excuse for't" (49–50). Ann fails to comply, and later in the play Richard comments in an aside that a physician has indeed seen to her death (IV.ii.61).

In both plays, Richard wishes to secure his throne by his marriage to the young Elizabeth:

> *I must be married to my Brother's Daughter,*
> At whom I know the *Brittain Richmond* aims;
> *And by that knot looks proudly on the Crown.*
> (Cibber IV.ii.62–64)

But in Cibber's version there are hints that this ambitious Richard is intermittently prey to the softer stirrings of love. When Ann accuses him of having dissembled his earlier vows to her, he responds, "For when I told thee so, I lov'd:/Thou art the only Soul I never yet deceived" (III.ii.58–59). He tells Ann that his rejection of her stems not merely from "the dull'd edge of sated Appetite," but "from the eager Love I bear another" (53–54). Characteristically, Richard follows these revelations with an aside—"If this have no Effect, she is immortal" (62)—that suggests his professions of love are merely weapons to use against his wife. Yet as in the wooing scene of II.i, Cibber's Richard seems to be having it both ways. He teases the audience with glimpses of an inner emotional life which he then immediately denies. For most of the play, for instance, he rejects the claims of conscience while repeatedly returning to the theme. Conscience, despite his denials, preys upon him. In similar fashion, his pragmatically political approach to marriage masks brief moments in which he seems to yearn for love.

The new episode with Lady Ann is followed immediately by the charade for the citizens and the Lord Mayor. As in Shakespeare, Richard and Buckingham have tried and failed to rouse the people to Richard's standard, but now lure the Mayor to Richard's home. In the original tragedy, Richard plays his part, entering *"aloft, between two* Bishops" (III.vi.93 s.d.). Cibber's Richard enters alone to the stage, *"with a* Book" (Cibber III.ii.160 s.d.) to demonstrate his earnest Christian mediation. At the conclusion to this scene of playacting, Shakespeare's Richard pretends to continue his prayers, and says for benefit of the departing Mayor and Buckingham, "Come, let us to our holy work again. / Farewell my cousin, farewell gentle friends" (III.vii.245–46). With that, all exit. Cibber could not let such a dramatic moment go by without elaboration. His Richard remains onstage to speak another of the classic Cibberian soliloquies:

> Why now my golden dream is out—
> Ambition like an early Friend throws back
> My Curtains with an eager Hand, o'rejoy'd
> To Tell me what I dreamt is true—A Crown!
> (Cibber III.ii.270–73)

And in good Cibberian fashion, he ends the scene, struggling yet again with a conscience that refuses to lie dormant: "Conscience, lie still—More lives must yet be drain'd,/Crowns got with Blood must be with Blood maintain'd" (Cibber III.ii.281–82).

Shakespeare opens his fourth act with the visit of Queen Elizabeth, the Duchess of York, and Lady Anne to the Tower. (Shakespeare's character is "Anne." Cibber's is "Ann.") The royal ladies are prevented from visiting the imprisoned princes, and Stanley arrives to accompany Lady Anne to Richard's coronation. Cibber duplicates this action, but adds a sequence in which he allows the tearful women an entire scene with the children before Ann's summons. The reviser thus gains a series of near-operatic moments of high emotion:

PR. ED.: Wou'd I but knew at what my Uncle aims;

If 'twere my Crown, I'd freely give it him,

So he'd but let me 'joy my life in quiet.

. . .

> QUEEN: I cannot bear to see 'em thus.—
>
> (Cibber IV.i.17–19; 22)

Cibber, as Albert Kalson observes, found the Prince's plaintive lines in Holinshed and Stow (Kalson [1963] 261–62), and thus shares the credit or blame for this episode with anti-Ricardian historians.

Cibber's coronation scene parallels the original version, although it is more detailed. Shakespeare's Richard, for instance, merely asks Buckingham, "But shall we wear these honours for a day? . . . /Young Edward lives: think now what I would say" (IV.ii.5, 10). Cibber's Richard typically exploits this dramatic moment with vivid imagery. He does not mention the clock which was an important aspect of Shakespeare's speech: rather, he turns to spiders:

> I tell thee, Cuz, I've lately had two Spiders
> Crawling upon my startled hopes: Now tho'
> Thy friendly hand has brush'd 'em from me,
> Yet still they Crawl offensive to my Eyes,
> I wou'd have some Friend to tread upon 'em.
> *I wou'd be King, my Cousin—*
>
> (IV.ii.14–19)

Both Richards meet with feigned incomprehension, and both resort to identical plain speaking: "*I wish the Bastards dead*" (Cibber IV.ii.25; Shakespeare IV.ii.18). Cibber's Richard has previously given "Tirrel" certain "sums of Gold" as inducement to serve him, and now Richard sends for him to do the deed. Shakespeare's Richard had no previous dealings with the assassin. Cibber's despot thus typically reveals himself as several steps ahead in the game.

In both plays, IV.iii is devoted to the murder. In Shakespeare, Tyrrel makes a solo entrance to report "The tyrannous and bloody act is done" (IV.iii.1). In Cibber, Richard skulks in the precincts of the Tower as Tirrel, Dighton, and Forest carry out the bloody deed. Richard's soliloquy at the moment of the off-stage murder brings to mind Macbeth's midnight reflections as he moves toward the sleeping Duncan's room: "Is this a dagger which I see before me" (see *Macbeth,* II.i.33–64). Macbeth's imagination forces him to confront the awful implications of his bloody deeds. Cibber's Richard similarly reflects upon the imminent crime:

> Nature too,
>
> . . . .
>
> Tugs at my Heart-Strings with complaining Cries,
> To talk me from my Purpose—
> And then the thought of what Mens Tongues will say,

> Of what their Hearts must think; To have no Creature
> Love me Living, nor my Memory when Dead.
>
> . . . .
>
> Hark! the Murder's doing; Princes farewel,
> To me there's Musick in your Passing-Bell.
> (IV.iii.21; 23–24; 26–27; 37–38)

In both *Macbeth* and in Cibber's *Richard III,* the quiet night is punctuated with the sound of a bell which marks the point of no return. (In his first version of the play, Cibber included an on-stage murder of the princes. He removed it from early productions, probably after the death of Princess Anne's eleven-year-old son William in July, 1700. [See Sprague (1927) 29–32].)

Cibber's reading of history affected his handling of IV.iii. His Richard asks for a coffin "Full of holes" which would be thrown into the Thames: "once in, they'll find the way to the' bottom" (IV.iii.52). Shakespeare's Tyrrel merely reports "The chaplain of the Tower hath buried them, / But where, to say the truth, I do not know" (29–30). Kalson cites the historians cited by Cibber who mention burial by water (264). Oddly enough, Shakespeare's "unhistorical" details turn out to have been closer to the truth. A burial place in the Tower was discovered in the seventeenth century, and the remains were declared in 1933 to have been those of the princes (Ross 97–98).

Shakespeare's IV.iv (the grieving, wailing queens and Richard's suit to Elizabeth) is 538 lines long. Cibber, as usual, manages his version in less than half Shakespeare's length. Margaret, of course, never appears in Cibber's play, but Cibber also reduces the contrapuntal wailing he allows the remaining characters. Because of the Senecan choric laments, the entrance of Shakespeare's Richard is delayed by 137 lines. Cibber's comes on after only nineteen lines of such lamentation. Not wishing to risk fourth-act fatigue, Cibber and many later directors have turned one of the longest scenes in the play into one that plays briskly. Shakespeare's Richard takes 230 lines to assault Queen Elizabeth's resistance to him. Cibber's tries (and fails) in only seventy-five lines: in the revision Elizabeth says, "I may seemingly comply, and thus/By sending *Richmond* word of his Intent,/Shall gain some time to let my Child escape him" (Cibber IV.iv.114–16). Elizabeth's motives in Shakespeare's play are more ambiguous. She is sometimes played as if she capitulates to Richard, only to double-cross him later (See the discussion of the Alexander-Sher production).

In the original text, much of the dialogue between Richard and Elizabeth concerns the moral consequences of human actions. The Queen repeatedly asks Richard how he can seek the hand of a young woman whose brothers he has murdered. Richard persistently denies that past events have anything to do with future hopes:

> Look what is done cannot be now amended:
> Men shall deal unadvisedly sometimes,
> Which after-hours give leisure to repent.
> If I did take the kingdom from your sons,
> To make amends I'll give it to your daughter.
> (Shakespeare IV.iv.291–295)

While Cibber's Elizabeth reminds Richard of his previous crimes, the dialogue is much less given to Richard's denials of the force of history. The moral debate vanishes. Cibber's scene becomes a struggle between two persons, and less an allegory about the past, guilt, retribution, or moral consequences. Shakespeare's IV.iv is as long as it is because he used it to develop a moral theme. Cibber employs the same scene to heighten the psychological rather than the moral drama.

It is at the end of Cibber's Act IV that one of his most famous lines is heard. As messengers rush on and off stage, Richard finally learns from Catesby that *"The Duke of Buckingham is taken."* Cibber's Richard savagely responds, *"Off with his head, So much for Buckingham"* (IV.iv. 187; 188). This line was so popular with the audiences that it not only appeared in later productions of Shakespeare's text (including Olivier's film), but also made its way into the *Oxford Dictionary of Quotations*. It is at the end of IV.iv that Cibber's Richard is most unlike Shakespeare's. The revised Gloucester does not become unhinged when messengers bring him bad news: he does not forget nor contradict his orders, nor does he strike the bearer of good news. This new Richard faces his greatest crisis with *sang-froid*.

Cibber's final act is just over half the length of Shakespeare's: 286 as opposed to 458 lines. Gone are Buckingham's final words before his execution as well as two-thirds of both Richmond's and Richard's several orations to their armies. Richmond's final speech of the play ("We'll twine the Roses red and white together," Cibber V.ix.50) is cut by half. While Cibber's entire ghost scene is nearly the length of Shakespeare's, there are remarkable differences between the two. Perhaps the most remarkable of these differences is Richard's new Macbeth-like moment before his ghostly dream. In Shakespeare's play, Richard dismisses his companions—"Leave me, I say" (V.iii.78)—and simply goes to sleep. As Richard sleeps, Richmond and his associates gather at a tent across the stage and engage in nearly fifty lines of dialogue. The Elizabethan audience was apparently less troubled than Cibber's by this example of simultaneous staging. In Shakespeare, it is Richmond's prayer which serves as prologue to the appearance of the ghosts, and indeed, it is the prayer which seems to beckon the spirits to appear. Before he sleeps, Richmond kneels and begs God to

> Make us thy ministers of chastisement,
> That we may praise thee in the victory!

> To thee I do commend my watchful soul
> Ere I let fall the windows of mine eyes:
> Sleeping and waking, O, defend me still!
> (Shakespeare V.iii.113–17)

The prayer demonstrates that Richmond is indeed defended both in sleeping and in waking, for as he drifts into slumber, the first of eleven ghosts makes its entrance to speak both to the villain and to the minister of chastisement. As is common in Shakespeare, the ghosts are played as if real and present. Upon awakening, both generals recall the visits of the ghosts, and both understand their significance. Richard realizes vengeance has been called upon his head (although he quickly rallies to deny his insight) and Richmond understands that he has been urged on to victory (See V.iii.204–06; 230–33). In Shakespeare's play, of course, the audience observes the visits to both sleeping figures. Cibber's Richmond briefly mentions his dream about the ghosts (V.v.10–11), but the force of his dream is lessened because it is merely reported, and not presented on the stage.

Thus in Cibber, only Richard's tent stands onstage, and only he is addressed by the spirits. In this version, it is not a prayer that calls forth the ghosts, but another of Richard's despairing, Macbeth-like moments of fearful self-understanding. Using some lines from the Prologue to Act IV of *Henry V,* Cibber describes the "clink of hammers closing rivets up" (17) and other pre-battle preparations, as Richard nervously paces back and forth. The conscience-stricken tyrant hears a ghastly groan as he readies himself for sleep and recognizes it as

> The Eccho of some yawning Grave,
> That teems with an untimely Ghost.—'Tis gone!
> 'Twas but my Fancy, or perhaps the Wind
> Forcing his entrance thro' some hollow Cavern;
> No matter what—I feel my eyes grow heavy.
> (Cibber V.v.27–31)

This Richard suspects his fancy has caused him to hear the strange sound, thus suggesting to the audience that the following visit of the ghosts is similarly a bad dream stimulated by an unquiet mind. While Shakespeare's haunting went on for nearly sixty lines, Cibber's four ghosts manage their appearance in less than thirty. The ghosts of King Henry, Lady Ann, and the two Princes (the younger of whom has no lines) enter as a group to haunt the king and then disappear as suddenly as they had appeared. Shakespeare's near-dozen spirits waft by in procession from one sleeping figure to the other, making the original haunting a much more extensive (and time-consuming) ritual.

Richard's agonizing words upon awakening are among the most powerful of the many words spoken in Shakespeare's play. Finally, Richard admits what is happening beneath the surface of his mind. Half-awake, starting from his dream-vision, calling for a horse, Richard suddenly realizes the root of his fear: "O coward conscience, how dost thou afflict me!" (Shakespeare V.iii.180). In the next twenty-seven lines, Shakespeare's Richard vividly recognizes the terrible self-hatred and isolation that torment him:

> What do I fear? Myself? There's none else by.
> Richard loves Richard, that is, I [am] I.
> Is there a murtherer here? No. Yes, I am.
> Then fly. What, from myself? Great reason why—
> Lest I revenge. What, myself upon myself?
> Alack, I love myself. Wherefore? For any good
> That I myself have done unto myself?
> O no! Alas, I rather hate myself. . . .
>
> (V.iii.183–89)

The fractured syntax, the starts and stops, the assertions and denials, all represent a dramatic voice not previously heard in the play. Richard has shown brilliant mastery of language throughout the tragedy, but here for the first time, something distorted in the inner man emerges in his troubled, syncopated speech. It is an extraordinary moment in the play—almost electric in effect— all the more striking because the audience has not previously encountered such rhythms. In this drama of Senecan lamentation, stichomythia, and secure blank verse, here suddenly is a natural cry from deep in the human psyche.

Cibber apparently could not stomach the shocking change in Richard's diction and character. The revised Richard knows he has dreamed, and knows the root of the dream is a troubled conscience. Yet he levels his response to something more rational than Shakespeare's character would express:

> O Tyrant Conscience! how dost thou afflict me!
> When I look back, 'tis terrible Retreating:
> I cannot bear the thought, nor dare repent:
> I am but Man, and Fate, do thou dispose me,
>
> (Cibber V.v.65–68)

Four straightforward lines replace Shakespeare's two dozen. Cibber's Richard "cannot bear the thought" and therefore invites Fate to "dispose" him as it will. Shakespeare's character explores the thoughts that swirl in his head, coming to recognize how far apart he exists from others. He visualizes a courtroom in which witnesses to his crimes crowd to the bar shouting "Guilty! guilty!" The troubled king realizes no soul will pity him: "And, wherefore should they, since that I myself/Find in myself no pity to myself?" (Shakespeare V.iii.202–03). The soliloquy is the only moment in the two versions of the play in which Shakespeare's character devotes more lines to introspection than does Cibber's.

Both Richards confess that

> shadows to night
> *Have struck more terror to the Soul of* Richard
> *Than can the substance of ten Thousand Soldiers*
> *Arm'd all in Proof, and led by shallow* Richmond.
> (Cibber V.iii.75–78; Shakespeare V.iii.216–19)

Shakespeare's Richard rallies himself by telling Ratcliffe to accompany him as he plays "the ease-dropper,/To see if any mean to shrink from me" (V.iii.221–22). With that threat, he simply exits. Cibber's roused tyrant pronounces a more boisterous conclusion to his momentary fright:

> No, never be it said,
> That Fate it self could awe the Soul of *Richard.*
> Hence, Babbling dreams, you threaten here in vain:
> Conscience avant; *Richard's* himself again.
> Hark! the shrill Trumpet sounds, to Horse: Away!
> My Soul's in Arms, and eager for the Fray.
> (Cibber V.iii.82–87)

This Richard is not off to skulk under tents to overhear treasonous mutterings, but with a mighty couplet he is ready to take on his foe. The line "Conscience avant; *Richard's* himself again" has been roared by hundreds of Gloucesters over the years, and was adopted by Olivier in his highly edited film version of the play.

Cibber's alterations of this scene, as usual, make good sense. It has struck many actors as incredible that Shakespeare's Richard could awaken from a terrible vision, utter those soul-searing words, and then just as suddenly snap back into a primitive version of his original character. One almost expects him to rub his hands in glee as he vows to eavesdrop. Cibber's Richard thus engages in fewer self-doubts than the original, and presents a more convincing transition to his more normal self-assurance. He explains the thought processes that allow him to be eager for the fray. In a similar spirit, most of the important Shakespearean Richards of the nineteenth century— Phelps, Irving, Edwin Booth, Calvert, and Benson—cut Richard's awakening speech nearly to the length of Cibber's, and removed Richard's most tortured expressions of self-hatred and remorse (that is, lines 188–92 and 202–03). Audiences schooled by Freudian and other psychological characterizations in novels and plays have seemed better able to accept Shakespeare's writing of Richard's soliloquy than have earlier playgoers.

Both plays present the orations of the opposing generals, although Cibber's renditions are only a third the length of Shakespeare's. Both Richards scoff at the satiric doggerel found near the tents: "Jockey of Norfolk, be not so bold," but it is Cibber's Richard who utters the famous line "A weak invention of the enemy" (Cibber V.vii.17), one that has found its way even into succeeding performances of Shakespeare's text. Both plays delay the execution of young Stanley until after the battle. But there are significant differences in the two battle scenes. Shakespeare's Richard enters the battle invoking "the spleen of fiery dragons" (V.iii.351), while Cibber's character more elegantly calls upon the king of beasts: "St. *George* inspire me with the Rage of Lyons" (V. vii.39). This lion-hearted Richard is more heroic than one who calls upon a satanic monster. Continuing in the heroic vein, Cibber's Richard has much more to say upon the battlefield than does the original. Once the fray begins, Shakespeare's Richard has a scant half-dozen lines, including his famous cry for "A horse! a horse!" (V.iv.7). Cibber's Richard has five times more to say. In Shakespeare's play, the end comes wordlessly: the stage directions in the Folio simply note: "*Enter* King Richard *and* Richmond; *they fight. | Richard is slain. Then, retrait*" (V.v.i s.d). After shouting for his horse, Shakespeare's king lets his sword speak for him. He says nothing more for himself.

Cibber, on the other hand, gives his adversaries an exchange of two-dozen lines of challenges and counter-challenges. Indeed, Richard is allowed a stirring speech at his death in which he draws heavily upon two dramatic moments in the first and second parts of *Henry IV:*

> the vast Renown thou has acquired
> In Conquering *Richard,* does afflict him more
> Than even his Bodies parting with its Soul:
> 'Now let the World no longer be a Stage
> 'To feed contention in a lingering Act:
> 'But let one spirit of the First-born *Cain*
> 'Reign in all bosoms, that each heart being set
> 'On bloody Actions the rude Scene may end,
> 'And darkness be the Burier of the Dead.
> (Cibber V.ix.12–20)

The dying Hotspur had said, "I better brook the loss of brittle life/That those proud titles thou hast won of me" (*1 Henry IV,* V.iv.78–79). Cibber clearly had the gallant young warrior in mind when he fashioned Richard's battle scene. Moreover, Richard's final six lines are taken from Northumberland's lament at Hotspur's death: "And let this world no longer be a stage" (*2 Henry IV* I.i.155–60). In the Cibber revision, it is no longer a moment when the victors can say "The day is ours; the bloody dog is dead"(Shakespeare V.v.2). Richard is hardly presented as a bloody dog, but rather as a kind of fallen angel. Indeed, in the generous spirit of Prince Hal, the victorious Richmond pays homage to his heroic enemy:

> Had thy aspiring Soul but stir'd in Vertue
> With half the Spirit it has dar'd in Evil,
> How might thy Fame have grac'd our *English* Annals. . . .
> (Cibber V.ix.23–25)

Stanley immediately enters with the crown: "Tis doubly thine by Conquest and by Choice" (Cibber V.ix.35)—Richmond is virtually elected by acclamation—and the first Tudor can then call for the union of the white rose and the red.

Shakespeare's play ends with three prayerful words: "God say amen!" (V.v.41); Cibber's, in a more secular mood, with a hope for "fair *England's* Peace" (V.ix.62). The shift from a spiritual to a secular perspective colors Cibber's entire concluding speech. His Henry VII does not pray, "smile, heaven, upon this fair conjunction" (20), nor does he claim that the heirs of York and Lancaster "By God's fair ordinance conjoin together" (31). The revised play is grounded in the here and now. Richmond's political and military skills have brought him victory, and not his service as a minister of God's chastisement upon an evil king. Cibber's play thus comes to an end, the fallen angel lying dead, his heroic adversary secure and triumphant. As in Shakespeare's play, Richmond wins his battlefield prize and pronounces the final words of the tragedy.

The concluding scenes, like many other elements in Cibber's version, retain the crucial elements of the original. In the depiction of the rise and fall of Richard III, Cibber thus duplicates more than in silhouette what Shakespeare had written about his central character. A version of the famous soliloquy is there, the wooing of Ann remains, as do the charade for the Lord Mayor, the baiting of Buckingham, the wooing of Elizabeth, the ghostly dream, the furious battle—Richard's grand moments are vividly present. So much of the outline of Richard's adventures remains, in fact, that theatergoers accepted Cibber's as a legitimate substitute for Shakespeare's text. Contemporary reviews of Cibber's play, oddly enough, sound as if they had been written about Shakespeare's. We can still gain insights into Shakespeare's play by reading reviews of Garrick's, Kemble's, or Kean's performances of the revised tragedy. Cibber indeed captured something that lies at the core of Shakespeare's Gloucester.

He also caught more than is obvious about Shakespeare's Gloucester. Cibber's villain-hero is bolstered by implied comparisons to Richard II, Hotspur, and even Macbeth, and is given lines from Shakespearean contexts quite alien to *Richard III*. Even the additions to the play from chronicle history add dimensions to the character that are absent in Shakespeare's version of the play. Given that only half of Cibber's *Richard III* is from the original, it is remarkable that the sleight-of-hand exchange of one text for another went so smoothly. Not only did he bring off the switch smoothly, Cibber was lauded in his time and afterwards by actors for having done a better job, in many respects, than the original playwright, in producing a tragedy that played well in performance.

Another oddity of theater history is the tone of much criticism of Cibber's accomplishment. The players, by and large, respected his accomplishment. Reviewers of the famous productions describe a dramatic experience of Shakespearean proportions. And yet critics of the text (as opposed to critics of theatrical performance) have lambasted him frequently and often satirically. A good deal that is written about Cibber's revision itself is untrustworthy, particularly those aphoristic critical judgments that stick in one's memory. Cibber's reputation from his time to ours has been touched by Pope's remarkable verses about the King of the Dunces. Cibber's self-defense hardly helped his own cause. His unselfconscious, self-confessing tone and a rambling prose style made the *Apology* indeed seem, to many, the work of a dunce. Literate commentators of succeeding ages have been conditioned to trust the clever satirists and to dismiss a laureate who was surrounded by his poetic betters.

Cibber's accomplishment was to make a well-structured, coherent, and psychologically convincing play out of the sprawling, mysterious, and ambiguously archetypal original. He reached his goals successfully, and apparently reached the goals that Garrick, Kemble, Cooke, Kean, and a hundred others could claim as their own. The laureate playwright certainly had no intention of replacing Shakespeare, just as modern directors who cut and rearrange have no wish ultimately to replace the text that has come down to us from Shakespeare's time. Cibber's *Richard III* stands as an inspired product of a remarkable theatrical intelligence. We recognize now, as Phelps, Edwin Booth, and Irving did in their own time, that Shakespeare's *Richard III* goes beyond inspiration to the level of theatrical genius. Cibber's tragedy, simply put, only shadows the greatness of his model. Once we remove Pope's dunce's crown from Cibber's head, however, we can recognize his achievement as a major one.

Texts Cited

Cibber, Colley. *An Apology for the Life of Colley Cibber.* Ed. B. R. S. Fone. Ann Arbor MI: 1948.
Davies, Thomas. *Memoirs of the Life of David Garrick.* 2 vols. London: 1808.
Downes, John. *Roscius Anglicanus, or an Historical View of the Stage from 1660 to 1706.* Ed. Judith Milhous and Robert M. Hume. London: 1997.
Hill, Aaron, and William Popple. *The Prompter: A Theatrical Paper (1734–1736).* Ed. William W. Appleton and Kalman A Burnim. New York: 1966.
Kalson, Albert E. "The Chronicles in Cibber's *Richard III.*" *S.E.L.* 3 (1963): 253–67.
Odell, George C. D. *Shakespeare from Betterton to Irving.* 2 vols. New York: 1920.
Rabkin, Norman S. *Shakespeare and the Problem of Meaning.* Chicago: 1981.
Sprague, Arthur Colby. *Shakespeare's Histories: Plays for the Stage.* New York: 1964.
Stone, George Winchester. "Bloody, Cold, and Complex. Richard: David Garrick's Interpretation." *On Stage and Off: Eight Essays in English Literature.* Ed. John R. Elwood and Robert C McLean. Pullman: 1968.
Vickers, Brian. *Shakespeare: the Critical Heritage. Vol. 2: 1693–1733.* London: 1974; *Vol. 3: 1733–1752.* London: 1975; *Vol. 6: 1774–1801.* London: 1981.
Wilson, John Dover, ed. *Richard III.* Cambridge: 1954; rpr. with corrections, 1968.

Macbeth and Richard III

THOMAS WHATELY

Every Play of Shakespeare abounds with instances of his excellence in distin-guishing characters. It would be difficult to determine which is the most striking of all that he drew; but his merit will appear most conspicuously by comparing two opposite characters, who happen to be placed in similar cir-cumstances:—not that on such occasions he marks them more strongly than on others, but because the contrast makes the distinction more apparent; and of these none seem to agree so much in situation, and to differ so much in dis-position, as RICHARD THE THIRD AND MACBETH. Both are soldiers, both usurpers; both attain the throne by the same means, by treason and murther; and both lose it too in the same manner, in battle against the person claiming it as lawful heir. Perfidy, violence, and tyranny are common to both; and those only, their obvious qualities, would have been attributed indiscrimi-nately to both by an ordinary dramatic writer. But Shakespeare, in confor-mity to the truth of history as far as it led him, and by improving upon the fables which have been blended with it, has ascribed opposite principles and motives to the same designs and actions, and various effects to the operation of the same events upon different tempers. Richard and Macbeth, as repre-sented by him, agree in nothing but their fortunes. . . .

The first thought of acceding to the throne is suggested, and success in the attempt is promised, to Macbeth by the witches: he is therefore repre-sented as a man, whose natural temper would have deterred him from such a design, if he had not been immediately tempted, and strongly impelled to it. Richard, on the other hand, brought with him into the world the signs of ambition and cruelty: his disposition, therefore, is suited to those symptoms; and he is not discouraged from indulging it by the improbability of succeed-ing, or by any difficulties and dangers which obstruct his way.

Agreeably to these ideas, Macbeth appears to be a man not destitute of the feelings of humanity. His lady gives him that character:

From Thomas Whately *Remarks on Some of the Characters in Shakespeare,* ed. Joseph Whately, (Oxford: J. Parker, 1785).

> ————I fear thy nature;
> It is too full o' th' milk of human kindness,
> To catch the nearest way.————

Which apprehension was well founded; for his reluctance to commit the murther is owing in a great measure to reflexions which arise from sensibility:

> ————He's here in double trust:
> First, as I am his kinsman and his subject;
> Strong both against the deed; then, as his host,
> Who should against his murtherer shut the door,
> Not bear the knife myself.————

Immediately after he tells Lady Macbeth,

> We will proceed no further in this business;
> He hath honour'd me of late.

And thus giving way to his natural feelings of kindred, hospitality, and gratitude, he for a while lays aside his purpose.

A man of such a disposition will esteem, as they ought to be esteemed, all gentle and amiable qualities in another: and therefore Macbeth is affected by the mild virtues of Duncan; and reveres them in his sovereign when he stifles them in himself. That

> ————This Duncan
> Hath borne his faculties so meekly; hath been
> So clear in his great office,————

is one of his reasons against the murther: and when he is tortured with the thought of Banquo's issue succeeding him in the throne, he aggravates his misery by observing, that,

> For them the gracious Duncan have I murther'd:

which epithet of *gracious* would not have occurred to one who was not struck with the particular merit it expresses.

The frequent references to the prophecy in favour of Banquo's issue, is another symptom of the same disposition: for it is not always from fear, but sometimes from envy, that he alludes to it: and being himself very susceptible of those domestic affections, which raise a desire and love of posterity, he repines at the succession assured to the family of his rival, and which in his estimation seems more valuable than his own actual possession. He therefore reproaches the sisters for their partiality. . . .

Thus, in a variety of instances, does the tenderness in his character shew itself; and one who has these feelings, though he may have no principles, cannot easily be induced to commit a murther. The intervention of a supernatural cause accounts for his acting so contrary to his disposition. But that alone is not sufficient to prevail entirely over his nature: the instigations of his wife are also necessary to keep him to his purpose; and she, knowing his temper, not only stimulates his courage to the deed, but sensible that, besides a backwardness in daring, he had a degree of softness which wanted hardening, endeavours to remove all remains of humanity from his breast, by the horrid comparison she makes between him and herself:

> ———I have given suck, and know
> How tender 'tis to love the babe that milks me:
> I would, while it was smiling in my face,
> Have pluck'd my nipple from his boneless gums,
> And dash'd the brains out, had I but so sworn
> As you have done to this.———

The argument is, that the strongest and most natural affections are to be stifled upon so great an occasion: and such an argument is proper to persuade one who is liable to be swayed by them; but is no incentive either to his courage or his ambition.

Richard is in all these particulars the very reverse to Macbeth. He is totally destitute of every softer feeling:

> I that have neither pity, love, nor fear,

is the character he gives of himself, and which he preserves throughout; insensible to his habitudes with a brother, to his connexion with a wife, to the piety of the king, and the innocence of the babes, whom he murthers. The deformity of his body was supposed to indicate a similar depravity of mind; and Shakespeare makes great use both of that, and of the current stories of the times concerning the circumstances of his birth, to intimate that his actions proceeded not from the occasion, but from a savageness of nature. Henry therefore tells him,

> Thy mother felt more than a mother's pain,
> And yet brought forth less than a mother's hope;
> To wit, an indigested, deform'd lump,
> Not like the fruit of such a goodly tree.
> Teeth hadst thou in thy head when thou wast born,
> To signify thou cam'st to bite the world;
> And, if the rest be true which I have heard,
> Thou cam'st into the world with thy legs forward.

Which violent invective does not affect Richard as a reproach; it serves him only for a pretence to commit the murther he came resolved on; and his answer while he is killing Henry is,

> I'll hear no more; die, prophet, in thy speech!
> For this, among the rest, was I ordain'd.

Immediately afterwards he resumes the subject himself; and, priding himself that the signs given at his birth were verified in his conduct, he says,

> Indeed 'tis true that Henry told me of;
> For I have often heard my mother say,
> I came into the world with my legs forward.
> Had I not reason, think ye, to make haste,
> And seek their ruin that usurp'd our right?
> The midwife wonder'd; and the women cry'd,
> O Jesus bless us! he is born with teeth!
> And so I was; which plainly signified
> That I should snarl, and bite, and play the dog.
> Then, since the Heavens have shap'd my body so,
> Let Hell make crook'd my mind to answer it.

Several other passages to the same effect imply that he has a natural propensity to evil; crimes are his delight: but Macbeth is always in an agony when he thinks of them. He is sensible, before he proceeds, of

> ————the heat-oppressed brain.

He feels

> ————the present horror of the time
> Which now suits with it.————

And immediately after he has committed the murther, he is

> ————afraid to think what he has done.

He is pensive even while he is enjoying the effect of his crimes; but Richard is in spirits merely at the prospect of committing them; and what is effort in the one, is sport to the other. An extraordinary gaiety of heart shews itself upon those occasions, which to Macbeth seem most awful; and whether he forms or executes, contemplates the means, or looks back on the success, of the most wicked and desperate designs, they are at all times to him subjects of merriment. Upon parting from his brother, he bids him

> Go, tread the path that thou shalt ne'er return;
> Simple, plain Clarence! I do love thee so,
> That I will shortly send thy soul to Heaven,
> If Heaven will take the present at our hands.

His amusement, when he is meditating the murther of his nephews, is the application of some proverbs to their discourse and situation:

> So wise so young, they say, do ne'er live long.

And,

> Short summer lightly has a forward spring.

His ironical address to Tyrrel,

> Dar'st thou resolve to kill a friend of mine?

is agreeable to the rest of his deportment: and his pleasantry does not forsake him when he considers some of his worst deeds, after he has committed them; for the terms in which he mentions them are, that,

> The sons of Edward sleep in Abraham's bosom;
> And Ann my wife hath bid the world good night.

But he gives a still greater loose to his humour, when his deformity, and the omens attending his birth, are alluded to, either by himself or by others, as symptoms of the wickedness of his nature. . . .

But the characters of Richard and Macbeth are marked not only by opposite qualities; but even the same qualities in each differ so much in the cause, the kind, and the degree, that the distinction in them is as evident as in the others. Ambition is common to both; but in Macbeth it proceeds only from vanity, which is flattered and satisfied by the splendor of a throne: in Richard it is founded upon pride; his ruling passion is the lust of power:

> ——this earth affords no joy to him,
> But to command, to check, and to o'erbear.

And so great is that joy, that he enumerates among the delights of war,

> To fright the souls of fearful adversaries;

which is a pleasure brave men do not very sensibly feel; they rather value

——Battles
Nobly, hardly fought.——

But, in Richard, the sentiments natural to his high courage are lost in the greater satisfaction of trampling on mankind, and seeing even those whom he despises crouching beneath him: at the same time, to submit himself to any authority, is incompatible with his eager desire of ruling over all; nothing less than the first place can satiate his love of dominion: he declares that he shall

Count himself but bad, till he is best:

and,

While I live account this world but hell,
Until the mis-shap'd trunk that bears this head
Be round impaled with a glorious crown.

Which crown he hardly ever mentions, except in swelling terms of exultation; and which, even after he has obtained it, he calls

The high imperial type of this earth's glory.

But the crown is not Macbeth's pursuit through life: he had never thought of it till it was suggested to him by the witches; he receives their promise, and the subsequent earnest of the truth of it, with calmness. But his wife, whose thoughts are always more aspiring, hears the tidings with rapture, and greets him with the most extravagant congratulations; she complains of his moderation; the utmost merit she can allow him is, that he is

——not without ambition.

But it is cold and faint, for the subject of it is that of a weak mind; it is only pre-eminence of place, not dominion. He never carries his idea beyond the honour of the situation he aims at; and therefore he considers it as a situation which Lady Macbeth will partake of equally with him: and in his letter tells her,

This have I thought good to deliver thee, my dearest partner of greatness, that thou might'st not lose the dues of rejoicing, by being ignorant of what greatness is promis'd thee.

But it was his rank alone, not his power, in which she could share: and that indeed is all which he afterwards seems to think he had attained by his usurpation. He styles himself,

——high-plac'd Macbeth:

but in no other light does he ever contemplate his advancement with satisfaction; and when he finds that it is not attended with that adulation and respect which he had promised himself, and which would have soothed his vanity, he sinks under the disappointment, and complains that

> ————my way of life
> Is fallen into the sear, the yellow leaf;
> And that which should accompany old age,
> As honour, love, obedience, troops of friends,
> I must not look to have.————

These blessings, so desirable to him, are widely different from the pursuits of Richard. He wishes not to gain the affections, but to secure the submission of his subjects, and is happy to see men shrink under his controul. . . .

Nothing can be conceived more directly opposite to the agitations of Macbeth's mind, than the serenity of Richard in parallel circumstances. Upon the murther of the Prince of Wales, he immediately resolves on the assassination of Henry; and stays only to say to Clarence,

RICH.: Clarence, excuse me to the king my brother; I'll hence to London, on a serious matter:

Ere ye come there, be sure to hear some news.

CLA.: What? What?

RICH.: The Tower, man, the Tower! I'll root them out.

It is a thought of his own, which just then occurs to him: he determines upon it without hesitation; it requires no consideration, and admits of no delay: he is eager to put it in execution; but his eagerness proceeds from ardor, not from anxiety; and is not hurry, but dispatch. He does not wait to communicate to the king his brother; he only hints the thought, as he had conceived it, to Clarence; and supposes that the name alone of the Tower will sufficiently indicate his business there. When come thither, he proceeds directly without relenting; it is not to him, as to Macbeth, *a terrible feat*, but only *a serious matter:* and

> Sir, leave us to ourselves, we must confer,

is all the preparation he makes for it; and indeed with him it is little more than a conference with an enemy: his animosity and his insolence are the same, both before and after the assassination; and nothing retards, staggers, or alarms him. The humour which breaks from him, upon this and other occasions, has been taken notice of already, as a mark of his depravity; it is at the same time a proof of his calmness, and of the composure he preserves when he does not indulge himself in ridicule. It is with the most unfeeling steadiness that he tells the first tidings of the death of Clarence to Edward, when, on the Queen's intercession in his favour, he occasionally introduces it as a notorious fact, and tells her,

> Who knows not that the gentle duke is dead'
> You do him injury to scorn his corse.

He feels no remorse for the deed, nor fear of discovery; and therefore does not drop a word which can betray him, but artfully endeavours to impute it to others; and, without the least appearance of ostentation, makes the most natural and most pertinent reflections upon the fruits of rashness, and the vengeance of God against such offenders. . . .

Richard is able to put on a general character, directly the reverse of his disposition; and it is ready to him upon every occasion. But Macbeth cannot effectually conceal his sensations, when it is most necessary to conceal them; nor act a part which does not belong to him with any degree of consistency: and the same weakness of mind, which disqualifies him from maintaining such a force upon his nature, shews itself still further in that hesitation and dullness to dare, which he feels in himself, and allows in others. . . .

Thus, from the beginning of their history to their last moments, are the characters of Macbeth and Richard preserved entire and distinct: and though probably Shakespeare, when he was drawing the one, had no attention to the other; yet, as he conceived them to be widely different, expressed his conceptions exactly, and copied both from nature, they necessarily became contrasts to each other; and, by seeing them together, that contrast is more apparent, especially where the comparison is not between opposite qualities, but arises from the different degrees, or from a particular display, or total omission, of the same quality. This last must often happen, as the character of Macbeth is much more complicated than that of Richard; and therefore, when they are set in opposition, the judgement of the poet shews itself as much in what he has left out of the latter as in what he has inserted. The picture of Macbeth is also, for the same reason, much the more highly finished of the two; for it required a greater variety, and a greater delicacy of painting, to express and to blend with consistency all the several properties which are ascribed to him. That of Richard is marked by more careless strokes, but they are, notwithstanding, perfectly just.

Richard III as Climax to Henry VI

Augustus William Schlegel

The part of Richard the Third has become highly celebrated in England from its having been filled by excellent performers, and this has naturally had an influence on the admiration of the piece itself: for many readers of Shakspeare stand in want of good interpreters of the poet to understand him properly. This admiration is certainly, in every respect, well founded, though I cannot help thinking there is an injustice in considering the three parts of *Henry the Sixth* as of small value compared with *Richard the Third.* These four plays were undoubtedly composed in succession, as is proved by the style and the spirit in the manner of handling the subject; the last is definitely announced in the one which precedes it, and is also full of references to it: the same views run through the series; in a word, the whole make together only one single work. Even the deep characterization of Richard is by no means an exclusive advantage of the piece which bears his name: his character is very distinctly drawn in the two last parts of *Henry the Sixth;* nay even his first speeches lead us already to form the most unfavourable prognostications respecting him. He lowers obliquely like a dark thunder-cloud on the horizon, which gradually approaches nearer and nearer, and first pours out the elements of devastation with which it is charged when it hangs over the heads of mortals. Two of the most significant monologues of Richard, and which enable us to draw the most important conclusions respecting his constitution of mind, are to be found in *The Last Part of Henry the Sixth.* Respecting the value and the justice of actions those who are impelled to them by passions may be blind, but wickedness cannot mistake its own essence: Richard, as well as Iago, is a villain with full consciousness. That they should say this in so many words, is not perhaps in human nature: but the poet has the right in soliloquies to lend a voice to the most hidden thoughts, otherwise the form of the monologue would, generally speaking, be censurable. Richard's deformity is the expression of his internal malice, and perhaps in part the effect of it: for where is the ugliness that would not be softened by benevolence and openness? He however considers it as an iniquitous neglect of nature, which justifies him in tak-

From Augustus William Schlegel the Twelfth Lecture, in *A Course of Lectures on Dramatic Art and Literature,* trans. John Black (London: Baldwin, Craddock, and Joy, 1815).

ing his revenge on that human society from which it is the means of exclud-
ing him. Hence these sublime lines:

> And this word love, which graybeards call desire,
> Be resident in men like one another,
> And not in me. I am myself alone.

Wickedness is nothing but an egotism designedly unconscientious; however
it can never do altogether without the form of morality, as this is the law of all
thinking beings,—it must seek to found its depraved way of acting on something like principles. Although Richard is thoroughly acquainted with the
blackness of his mind and his hellish mission, he yet endeavours to justify this
to himself by a sophism: the happiness of being beloved is denied to him;
what then remains to him but the happiness of ruling? All that stands in the
way of this must be removed. This envy of the enjoyment of love is so much
the more natural in Richard, as his brother Edward, who besides preceded
him in the possession of the crown, distinguished for the nobleness and
beauty of his figure, was an almost irresistible conqueror of female hearts.
Notwithstanding his pretended remuneration Richard places his chief vanity
in being able to please and win over the women, if not by his figure at least
by his insinuating discourse. Shakspeare here shows us, with his accustomed
acuteness of observation, that human nature, even when it is altogether
decided in goodness or wickedness, is still subject to petty infirmities.
Richard's most favourate entertainment is to ridicule others, and he possesses
satirical wit in an eminent degree. He entertains at bottom a contempt for all
mankind, as he is confident of his ability to deceive them whether they may
be his instruments or adversaries. In hypocrisy he is particularly fond of using
religious forms, as if actuated by a desire of profaning in the service of hell the
religion of which he had inwardly abjured the blessings.

So much for the main features of Richard's character. The play named
after him embraces also the latter half of the reign of Edward IV, in the whole
a period of eight years. It exhibits all the machinations by which Richard
obtained the throne, and the deeds which he perpetrated to secure himself in
its possession, which lasted however only two years. Shakspeare intended that
terror rather than compassion should prevail throughout this tragedy: he has
rather gone out of the way of the pathetic scenes which he had at command,
than sought after them. Of all the sacrifices to Richard's lust of power,
Clarence alone is put to death on the stage: his dream excites a deep horror,
and proves the omnipotence of the poet's fancy: his conversation with the
murderers is powerfully agitating; but the earlier crimes of Clarence merited
death, although not from his brother. The most innocent and unspotted sacrifices are the two Princes: we see but little of them, and their murder is merely
related. Anne disappears without our learning any thing farther respecting
her: she has shown a weakness almost incredible in marrying the murderer of

her husband. The parts of Lord Rivers, and other friends of the Queen, are of too secondary a nature to excite a powerful sympathy; Hastings, from his triumph at the fall of his friend, forfeits all title to compassion; Buckingham is the satellite of the tyrant, who is afterwards consigned by him to the axe of the executioner. In the back-ground the widowed Queen Margaret appears, as the fury of the past who calls forth the curse on the future: every calamity, which her enemies draw down on each other is a cordial to her revengeful heart. Other female voices join, from time to time, in the lamentations and imprecations. But Richard is the soul or rather the dæmon, of the whole tragedy. He fulfils the promise which he formerly made of leading the murderous Macchiavel to school. Besides the uniform aversion with which he inspires us, he occupies us in the greatest variety of ways by his profound skill in dissimulation, his wit, his prudence, his presence of mind, his quick activity, and his valour. He fights at last against Richmond like a desperado, and dies the honourable death of the hero on the field of battle. Shakspeare could not change this historical issue, and yet it is by no means satisfactory to our moral feelings, as Lessing, when speaking of a German play on the same subject, has very judiciously remarked. How has Shakspeare solved this difficulty? By a wonderful invention he opens a prospect into the other world, and shows us Richard in his last moments already branded with the stamp of reprobation. We see Richard and Richmond in the night before the battle sleeping in their tents; the spirits of those murdered by the tyrant ascend in succession, and pour out their curses against him, and their blessings on his adversary. These apparitions are properly merely the dreams of the two generals rendered visible. It is no doubt contrary to sensible probability that their tents should only be separated by such a small space; but Shakspeare could reckon on poetical spectators, who were ready to take the breadth of the stage for the distance between two camps, if by such a favour they were to be recompensed by beauties of so sublime a nature as this series of spectres and the soliloquy of Richard on his awaking. The catastrophe of *Richard the Third* is, in respect of external events, very like that of *Macbeth:* we have only to compare the complete difference of the manner of treatment to be convinced that Shakspeare has observed, in the most accurate manner, poetical justice in the genuine sense of the word, namely, where it signifies the revelation of the invisible blessing or curse which hangs over human sentiments and actions.

The Character of Richard III

WILLIAM HAZLITT

Richard III may be considered as properly a stage-play: it belongs to the theatre, rather than to the closet. We shall therefore criticize it chiefly with a reference to the manner in which we have seen it performed. It is the character in which Garrick came out: it was the second character in which Mr. Kean appeared, and in which he acquired his fame. Shakespeare we have always with us: actors we have only for a few seasons; and therefore some account of them may be acceptable, if not to our contemporaries, to those who come after us, if "that rich and idle personage, Posterity," should deign to look into our writings.

It is possible to form a higher conception of the character of Richard than that given by Mr. Kean: but we cannot imagine any character represented with greater distinctness and precision, more perfectly *articulated* in every part. Perhaps indeed there is too much of what is technically called execution. When we first saw this celebrated actor in the part, we thought he sometimes failed from an exuberance of manner, and dissipated the impression of the general character by the variety of his resources. To be complete, his delineation of it should have more solidity, depth, sustained and impassioned feeling, with somewhat less brilliancy, with fewer glancing lights, pointed transitions, and pantomimic evolutions.

The Richard of Shakespeare is towering and lofty; equally impetuous and commanding; haughty, violent, and subtle; bold and treacherous; confident in his strength as well as in his cunning; raised high by his birth, and higher by his talents and his crimes; a royal usurper, a princely hypocrite, a tyrant and a murderer of the house of Plantagenet.

> But I was born so high:
> Our aery buildeth in the cedar's top,
> And dallies with the wind, and scorns the sun.

The idea conveyed in these lines (which are indeed omitted in the miserable medley acted for *Richard III*) is never lost sight of by Shakespeare, and should not be out of the actor's mind for a moment. The restless and sanguinary

From William Hazlitt *The Characters of Shakespeare's Plays* (London: Hunt, 1817).

Richard is not a man striving to be great, but to be greater than he is; conscious of his strength of will, his power of intellect, his daring courage, his elevated station; and making use of these advantages to commit unheard-of crimes, and to shield himself from remorse and infamy.

If Mr. Kean does not entirely succeed in concentrating all the lines of the character, as drawn by Shakespeare, he gives an animation, vigour, and relief to the part which we have not seen equalled. He is more refined than Cooke; more bold, varied, and original than Kemble in the same character. In some parts he is deficient in dignity, and particularly in the scenes of state business, he has by no means an air of artificial authority. There is at times an aspiring elevation, an enthusiastic rapture in his expectations of attaining the crown, and at others a gloating expression of sullen delight, as if he already clenched the bauble, and held it in his grasp. The courtship scene with Lady Anne is an admirable exhibition of smooth and smiling villainy. The progress of wily adulation, of encroaching humility, is finely marked by his action, voice and eye. He seems, like the first Tempter, to approach his prey, secure of the event, and as if success had smoothed his way before him. The late Mr. Cooke's manner of representing this scene was more vehement, hurried, and full of anxious uncertainty. This, though more natural in general, was less in character in this particular instance. Richard should woo less as a lover than as an actor—to show his mental superiority, and power of making others the playthings of his purposes. Mr. Kean's attitude in leaning against the side of the stage before he comes forward to address Lady Anne, is one of the most graceful and striking ever witnessed on the stage. It would do for Titian to paint. The frequent and rapid transition of his voice from the expression of the fiercest passion to the most familiar tones of conversation was that which gave a peculiar grace of novelty to his acting on his first appearance. This has been since imitated and caricatured by others, and he himself uses the artifice more sparingly than he did. His by-play is excellent. His manner of bidding his friends "Good night," after pausing with the point of his sword drawn slowly backward and forward on the ground, as if considering the plan of the battle next day, is a particularly happy and natural thought. He gives to the two last acts of the play the greatest animation and effect. He fills every part of the stage; and makes up for the deficiency of his person by what has been sometimes objected to as an excess of action. The concluding scene in which he is killed by Richmond is the most brilliant of the whole. He fights at last like one drunk with wounds; and the attitude in which he stands with his hands stretched out, after his sword is wrested from him, has a preternatural and terrific grandeur, as if his will could not be disarmed, and the very phantoms of his despair had power to kill.—Mr. Kean has since in a great measure effaced the impression of his Richard III by the superior efforts of his genius in Othello (his master-piece), in the murder-scene in Macbeth, in Richard II, in Sir Giles Overreach, and lastly in Oroonoko; but we still like to look back to his first performance of this part, both because it first assured his admirers of his future success, and because we bore our feeble but, at that time, not useless testimony to the merits of this very original actor, on which the town was considerably divided for no other reason than because they *were* original.

The manner in which Shakespeare's plays have been generally altered or rather mangled by modern mechanists, is a disgrace to the English stage. The patch-work *Richard III* which is acted under the sanction of his name, and which was manufactured by Cibber, is a striking example of this remark.

The play itself is undoubtedly a very powerful effusion of Shakespeare's genius. The ground-work of the character of Richard, that mixture of intellectual vigour with moral depravity, in which Shakespeare delighted to show his strength—gave full scope as well as temptation to the exercise of his imagination. The character of his hero is almost everywhere predominant, and marks its lurid track throughout. The original play is, however, too long for representation, and there are some few scenes which might be better spared than preserved, and by omitting which it would remain a complete whole. The only rule, indeed, for altering Shakespeare is to retrench certain passages which may be considered either as superfluous or obsolete, but not to add or transpose anything. The arrangement and development of the story, and the mutual contrast and combination of the *dramatis personae,* are in general as finely managed as the development of the characters or the expression of the passions.

This rule has not been adhered to in the present instance. Some of the most important and striking passages in the principal character have been omitted, to make room for idle and misplaced extracts from other plays; the only intention of which seems to have been to make the character of Richard as odious and disgusting as possible. It is apparently for no other purpose than to make Gloucester stab King Henry on the stage, that the fine abrupt introduction of the character in the opening of the play is lost in the tedious whining morality of the uxorious king (taken from another play);—we say *tedious,* because it interrupts the business of the scene, and loses its beauty and effect by having no intelligible connexion with the previous character of the mild, well-meaning monarch. The passages which the unfortunate Henry has to recite are beautiful and pathetic in themselves, but they have nothing to do with the world that Richard has to "bustle in." In the same spirit of vulgar caricature is the scene between Richard and Lady Anne (when his wife) interpolated without any authority, merely to gratify this favourite propensity to disgust and loathing. With the same perverse consistency, Richard, after his last fatal struggle, is raised up by some galvanic process, to utter the imprecation, without any motive but pure malignity, which Shakespeare has so properly put into the mouth of Northumberland on hearing of Percy's death. To make room for these worse than needless additions, many of the most striking passages in the real play have been omitted by the foppery and ignorance of the prompt-book critics. We do not mean to insist merely on passages which are fine as poetry and to the reader, such as Clarence's dream, &c., but on those which are important to the understanding of the character, and peculiarly adapted for stage-effect. We will give the following as instances among several others. The first is the scene where Richard enters abruptly to the queen and her friends to defend himself:

GLOUCESTER: They do me wrong, and I will not endure it.

Who are they that complain unto the king.

That I forsooth am stern, and love them not?

By holy Paul, they love his grace but lightly,

That fill his ears with such dissentious rumours:

Because I cannot flatter and look fair,

Smile in men's faces, smooth, deceive, and cog.

Duck with French nods, and apish courtesy,

I must be held a rancorous enemy.

Cannot a plain man live, and think no harm,

But thus his simple truth must be abus'd

With silken, sly, insinuating Jacks?

GRAY: To whom in all this presence speaks your grace?

GLOUCESTER: To thee, that hast nor honesty nor grace;

When have I injur'd thee, when done thee wrong?

Or thee? or thee? or any of your faction?

A plague upon you all!

Nothing can be more characteristic than the turbulent pretensions to meekness and simplicity in this address. Again, the versatility and adroitness of Richard is admirably described in the following ironical conversation with Brakenbury:

BRAKENBURY: I beseech your graces both to pardon me.

His majesty hath straitly given in charge,

That no man shall have private conference,

Of what degree soever, with your brother.

GLOUCESTER: E'en so, and please your worship,

Brakenbury,

You may partake of anything we say:

We speak no treason, man—we say the king

Is wise and virtuous, and his noble queen

Well strook in years, fair, and not jealous.

We say that Shore's wife hath a pretty foot,

A cherry lip,
A bonny eye, a passing pleasing tongue;
That the queen's kindred are made gentlefolks.
How say you, sir? Can you deny all this?
BRAKENBURY: With this, my lord, myself have nought to do.
GLOUCESTER: What, fellow, naught to do with mistress Shore?
I tell you, sir, he that doth naught with her,
Excepting one, were best to do it secretly alone.
BRAKENBURY: What one, my lord?
GLOUCESTER: Her husband, knave—would'st thou betray me?

The feigned reconciliation of Gloucester with the queen's kinsmen is also a masterpiece. One of the finest strokes in the play, and which serves to show as much as anything the deep, plausible manners of Richard, is the unsuspecting security of Hastings, at the very time when the former is plotting his death, and when that very appearance of cordiality and good-humour on which Hastings builds his confidence arises from Richard's consciousness of having betrayed him to his ruin. This, with the whole character of Hastings, is omitted.

Perhaps the two most beautiful passages in the original play are the farewell apostrophe of the queen to the Tower, where the children are shut up from her, and Tyrrel's description of their death. We will finish our quotations with them.

QUEEN: Stay, yet look back with me unto the Tower;
Pity, you ancient stones, those tender babes,
Whom envy hath immured within your walls;
Rough cradle for such little pretty ones.
Rude, rugged nurse, old sullen play-fellow,
For tender princes!

The other passage is the account of their death by Tyrrel:

Dighton and Forrest, whom I did suborn
To do this piece of ruthless butchery,
Albeit they were flesh'd villains, bloody dogs,—
Wept like to children in their death's sad story:
O thus! quoth Dighton, lay the gentle babes;
Thus, thus, quoth Forrest, girdling one another
Within their innocent alabaster arms;
Their lips were four red roses on a stalk,

> And in that summer beauty kissed each other;
> A book of prayers on their pillow lay,
> Which once, quoth Forrest, almost changed my mind:
> But oh the devil!—there the villain stopped;
> When Dighton thus told on—we smothered
> The most replenished sweet work of nature,
> That from the prime creation ere she framed.

These are some of those wonderful bursts of feeling, done to the life, to the very height of fancy and nature, which our Shakespeare alone could give. We do not insist on the repetition of these last passages as proper for the stage: we should indeed be loath to trust them in the mouth of almost any actor: but we should wish them to be retained in preference at least to the fantoccini exhibition of the young princes, Edward and York, bandying childish wit with their uncle.

Shakespeare's Richard III
and Milton's Satan

NATHAN DRAKE

The character of Richard the Third, which had been opened in so masterly a manner in the Concluding Part of *Henry the Sixth,* is, in this play, developed in all its horrible grandeur.

It is, in fact, the picture of a demoniacal incarnation, moulding the passions and foibles of mankind, with super-human precision, to its own iniquitous purposes. Of this isolated and peculiar state of being Richard himself seems sensible, when he declares—

> I have no brother, I am like no brother:
> And this word love, which grey-beards call divine,
> Be resident in men like one another,
> And not in me: I am myself alone.
> [*3 Henry VI,* V. vi. 80–3]

From a delineation like this Milton must have caught many of the most striking features of his Satanic portrait [in *Paradise Lost*]. The same union of unmitigated depravity, and consummate intellectual energy, characterises both, and renders what would otherwise be loathsome and disgusting, an object of sublimity and shuddering admiration.

Richard, stript as he is of all the softer feelings, and all the common charities, of humanity, possessed of "neither pity, love, nor fear" [*3 Henry VI,* V. vi. 68], and loaded with every dangerous and dreadful vice, would, were it not for his unconquerable powers of mind, be insufferably revolting. But, though insatiate in his ambition, envious, and hypocritical in his disposition, cruel, bloody, and remorseless in all his deeds, he displays such an extraordinary share of cool and determined courage, such alacrity and buoyancy of spirit, such constant self-possession, such an intuitive intimacy with the workings of the human heart, and such matchless skill in rendering them subservient to his views, as so far to subdue our detestation and abhorrence of

From Nathan Drake, "Observations on *King Richard III,*" in *Shakespeare and His Times* (London: T. Cadell, 1817).

his villany, that we, at length, contemplate this fiend in human shape with a mingled sensation of intense curiosity and grateful terror.

The task, however, which Shakspeare undertook was, in one instance, more arduous than that which Milton subsequently attempted; for, in addition to the hateful constitution of Richard's moral character, he had to contend also against the prejudices arising from personal deformity, from a figure

> ————curtail'd of it's fair proportion,
> Cheated of feature by dissembling nature,
> Deform'd, unfinish'd, sent before it's time
> Into this breathing world, scarce half made up;
> [I. i. 18–21]

and yet, in spite of these striking personal defects, which were considered, also, as indicative of the depravity and wickedness of his nature, the poet has contrived, through the medium of the high mental endowments just enumerated, not only to obviate disgust, but to excite extraordinary admiration.

One of the most prominent and detestable vices indeed, in Richard's character, his hypocrisy, connected, as it always is, in his person, with the most profound skill and dissimulation, has, owing to the various parts which it induces him to assume, most materially contributed to the popularity of this play, both on the stage and in the closet. He is one who can "frame his face to all occasions" [3 Henry VI, III. ii. 185], and accordingly appears, during the course of his career, under the contrasted forms of a subject and a monarch, a politician and a wit, a soldier and a suitor, a sinner and a saint. . . .

So overwhelming and exclusive is the character of Richard, that the comparative insignificance of all the other persons of the drama may be necessarily inferred; they are reflected to us, as it were, from his mirror, and become more or less important, and more or less developed, as he finds it necessary to act upon them; so that our estimate of their character is entirely founded on his relative conduct, through which we may very correctly appreciate their strength or weakness.

The only exception to this remark is in the person of Queen Margaret, who, apart from the agency of Richard, and dimly seen in the darkest recesses of the picture, pours forth, in union with the deep tone of this tragedy, the most dreadful curses and imprecations; with such a wild and prophetic fury, indeed, as to involve the whole scene in tenfold gloom and horror.

We have to add that the moral of this play is great and impressive. Richard, having excited a general sense of indignation, and a general desire of revenge, and, unaware of his danger from having lost, through familiarity with guilt, all idea of moral obligation, becomes at length the victim of his own enormous crimes; he falls not unvisited by the terrors of conscience, for, on the eve of danger and of death, the retribution of another world is placed before him; the spirits of those whom he had murdered reveal the awful sentence of his fate, and his bosom heaves with the infliction of eternal torture.

RICHARD III RECOGNIZED

◆

The following section reflects the outcome of a reevaluation of the history plays established by E. M. W. Tillyard, as applied to *Richard III.* The essays attempt to explicate and evaluate the text in terms of the critical, social, and theatrical values of the later twentieth century. Among these concerns are the psychological preoccupations encouraged by Freud, as seen in the work of Murray Krieger and Richard P. Wheeler, among others. Marjorie B. Garber investigates the major role of dreams in the play. Modern delight in the play's complexity and ambiguity is heralded by A. P. Rossiter's essay. Current preoccupations with gender are anticipated in Madonne M. Miner's study. Above all, as shown in Nicholas Brooke's application of linguistic nuances to performance, there is an increasing sense in modern critics of this text as a script inviting, indeed requiring, consideration of performance as a key determinant of composition and outcome. A validation of such theatrical considerations is seen in Henry Fenwick's account of the BBC televised version of the play and in Roy W. Battenhouse's attempt to place its audience affect in the context of classical dramatic theory.

These commentaries also stress close textual analysis resulting from the procedures of the new criticism. The detailed workings of the dynamics of individual scenes are explored, as accomplished by Emrys Jones, with a thoroughness not previously sustained, though implicit in Wolfgang H. Clemen's earlier explorations of traditional theatrical motifs and devices. All the commentators display a conviction of the importance of recognizing the full Shakespearean text rather than Colley Cibber's ingenious reworking and simplification. There seemed to me no point in including writers who consider the work to be merely as Cibber conceived it: a facile melodrama, basically an aesthetic failure, or at least deeply flawed in its original form. By contrast, M. M. Mahood seeks to validate the function of every role in an exceptionally large cast, including many usually cut as insignificant. All the cited texts assume this obligation to validate the original play in the face of persistent censures of *Richard III* as a laborious melodrama written to reinforce political dogma and an archaic value system of patriarchy and religious dogmatism. From its first performances, the script has achieved archetypal status as an artifact that each generation must rework to validate its own prejudices and preoccupations—as we have seen recently with the revisionism of Al Pacino and Ian McKellen. The following section reflects the most sustained and convincing effort to accomplish this charge of assimilation since the romantics, on behalf of the post–World War II generation.

Richard III and the First Tetralogy

E. M. W. Tillyard

When there is already so much evidence that Shakespeare wrote his tetralogy deliberately and academically and that he was deeply influenced by the Morality tradition with its medieval passion for equivalences, it is not pressing things to assert that Shakespeare fully intended the cross-references between the first and last plays of his series. However, the greatest bond uniting all four plays is the steady political theme: the theme of order and chaos, of proper political degree and civil war, of crime and punishment, of God's mercy finally tempering his justice, of the belief that such had been God's way with England.

I noticed that in each part of *Henry VI* there was some positive, usually very formal or stylised reference to the principle of order. In *1 Henry VI* there was the scene of Talbot doing homage to his king, in *2 Henry VI* the blameless conduct of Iden and his perfect contentment with his own station in life, in *3 Henry VI* Henry's pathetic longing for the precisely ordered life of a shepherd. In *Richard III* Shakespeare both continues this technique by inserting the choric scene of the three citizens, and at the end of the play comes out with his full declaration of the principle of order, thus giving final and unmistakable shape to what, though largely implicit, had been all along the animating principle of the tetralogy. His instrument, obviously and inevitably, is Richmond; and that this instrument should be largely passive, truly an instrument (hence likely to be overlooked or made little of by the modern reader) was also inevitable in the sort of drama Shakespeare was writing. In the tremendous evolution of God's plans the accidents of character must not be obtruded. Every sentence of Richmond's last speech, today regarded as a competent piece of formality, would have raised the Elizabethans to an ecstasy of feeling. Richmond gets everything right and refers to all the things they minded about. He is conventionally pious, his first words after the victory being, "God and your arms be prais'd, victorious friends"; just as Talbot after his capture of Rouen had said "Yet heavens have glory for this victory." Then he thinks of the immediate problems and asks about the dead. Hearing of them, he begins his last speech,

From E. M. W. Tillyard, *Shakespeare's History Plays* (London: Chatto and Windus, 1944). Reprinted with permission of Stephen Tillyard.

> Inter their bodies as becomes their birth,
> (V.iv.28)

and thereby implies: after thanks to God, the keeping of due degree on earth. And again he duplicates Talbot, who in the same scene, after thanking God, said

> let's not forget
> The noble Duke of Bedford late deceas'd,
> But see his exequies fulfill'd in Roan.
> (IHVI, III.ii.131–33)

Then, after degree, mercy:

> Proclaim a pardon to the soldiers fled
> That in submission will return to us.
> (V.iv.29–30)

And lastly an oath, taken with full religious solemnity and duly observed, and the healing of the wounds of civil war, with an insensible and indeed very subtle transfer of reference from the epoch of Bosworth to the very hour of the play's performance, from the supposed feelings of Richmond's supporters to what Shakespeare's own audience felt so ardently about the health of their country. The reference to father killing son and son killing father served at a single stroke both to recall the battle of Towton and to take the audience out of the Wars of the Roses to the wider context of civil wars in general; to Israel, France, and Germany; to the writers of chronicles and the Homilies; to what they had heard endlessly repeated on the subject by fireside or in tavern.

> And then, as we have ta'en the sacrament,
> We will unite the White Rose and the Red.
> Smile heaven upon this fair conjunction,
> That long have frown'd upon their enmity!
> What traitor hears me and says not amen?
> England hath long been mad and scarr'd herself:
> The brother blindly shed the brother's blood;
> The father rashly slaughter'd his own son;
> The son, compell'd, been butcher to the sire.
> All this divided York and Lancaster,
> Divided in their dire division,
> O now let Richmond and Elizabeth,
> The true succeeders of each royal house,
> By God's fair ordinance conjoin together;
> And let their heirs, God, if thy will be so,
> Enrich the time to come with smooth-fac'd peace,
> With smiling plenty and fair prosperous days.

> Abate the edge of traitors, gracious Lord,
> That would reduce these bloody days again,
> And make poor England weep in streams of blood.
> Let them not live to taste this land's increase
> That would with treason wound this fair land's peace.
> Now civil wars are stopp'd, peace lives again:
> That she may long live here God say amen.
>
> (V.ii.31–53)

An Elizabethan audience would take the dramatist's final amen with a transport of affirmation.

But Richmond's final speech not only voiced popular opinion, it showed Shakespeare fulfilling his old debt to Hall, when he invested the very practical and politic match between Richmond and Elizabeth with a mysterious and religious significance. True, Shakespeare quite omits the Tudors' ancient British ancestry; but his references to the marriage are in the very spirit of Hall's title, *The Union of the two noble and illustre Families of Lancaster and York* and his statement in his preface of the "godly matrimony" being "the final end of all dissensions titles and debates." Nor is this the only place in the play that sends us back to Hall and Tudor conceptions of history. There are some rather queer lines in III. 1, where Edward V, Richard, and Buckingham talk about oral and written tradition. They serve to bring out Edward's precociousness but they also take us into the centre of contemporary opinions on history. Edward, before the Tower, asks if Julius Caesar built it. Buckingham tells him that Julius Caesar began it; and Edward asks:

> Is it upon record, or else reported
> Successively from age to age, he built it?
>
> (III.i.71–72)

Buckingham answers it is "upon record," and Edward goes on:

> But say, my lord, it were not register'd,
> Methinks the truth should live from age to age,
> As 'twere retail'd to all posterity,
> Even to the general all-ending day.
>
> (III.i.75–78)

His words take us to the familiar medieval and renaissance context of fame: its capriciousness, its relation to all history and to all time. And he goes on to a more specifically historical commonplace:

> That Julius Caesar was a famous man.
> With what his valour did enrich his wit,
> His wit set down to make his valour live.

> Death makes no conquest of this conqueror,
> For now he lives in fame though not in life.
> (III.i.84–88)

It was a stock saying in discussions on history that Caesar provided both the material of history and its memorial. Shakespeare was telling his audience that they must put his tetralogy among other solemn documents of history, that he is striving to continue the high tradition of Polydore and Hall.

Above, I put the theme of *Richard III* partly in terms of God's intentions. As it is usual to put it in terms of Richard's character, I had better expand my thesis. But it is a delicate matter. People are so fond of Shakespeare that they are desperately anxious to have him of their own way of thinking. A reviewer in the *New Statesman* was greatly upset when I quoted a passage in *Measure for Measure* as evidence that Shakespeare was familiar with the doctrine of the Atonement: he at once assumed I meant that Shakespeare believed the doctrine personally. And if one were to say that in *Richard III* Shakespeare pictures England restored to order through God's grace, one gravely risks being lauded or execrated for attributing to Shakespeare personally the full doctrine of prevenient Grace according to Calvin. When therefore I say that *Richard III* is a very religious play, I want to be understood as speaking of the play and not of Shakespeare. For the purposes of the tetralogy and most obviously for this play Shakespeare accepted the prevalent belief that God had guided England into her haven of Tudor prosperity. And he had accepted it with his whole heart, as later he did not accept the supposed siding of God with the English against the French he so loudly proclaimed in *Henry V.* There is no atom of doubt in Richmond's prayer before he falls asleep in his tent at Bosworth. He is utterly God's minister, as he claims to be:

> O Thou, whose captain I account myself,
> Look on my forces with a gracious eye;
> Put in their hands thy bruising irons of wrath,
> That they may crush down with a heavy fall
> The usurping helmets of our adversaries,
> Make us thy ministers of chastisement,
> That we may praise thee in the victory.
> To thee I do commend my watchful soul,
> Ere I let fall the windows of mine eyes.
> Sleeping and waking, O, defend me still.
> (V.iv.108–17)

In the same spirit Shakespeare drops hints of a divine purpose in the mass of vengeance that forms the substance of the play, of a direction in the seemingly endless concatenation of crime and punishment. In *3 Henry VI*, York at Wakefield, Young Clifford at Towton, Warwick at Barnet, and Prince Edward at Tewkesbury die defiantly without remorse. In *Richard III* the great men die acknowledging their guilt and thinking of others. Clarence, before his murderers enter, says:

> O God, if my deep prayers cannot appease thee,
> But thou wilt be aveng'd on my misdeeds,
> Yet execute thy wrath in me alone:
> O spare my guiltless wife and my poor children.
> (I.iv.69–72)

Edward IV, near his death, repents his having signed a warrant for Clarence's death and while blaming others for not having restrained him blames himself the most:

> But for my brother not a man would speak,
> Nor I, ungracious, speak unto myself
> For him, poor soul. The proudest of you all
> Have been beholding to him in his life;
> Yet none of you would once plead for his life.
> O God, I fear thy justice will take hold
> On me and you and mine and yours for this.
> (II.i.126–32)

The Duchess of York, who once rejoiced when her family prospered, now in humility acknowledges the futility of ambitious strife.

> Accursed and unquiet wrangling days,
> How many of you have mine eyes beheld.
> My husband lost his life to get the crown,
> And often up and down my sons were toss'd
> For me to joy and weep their gain and loss.
> And, being seated and domestic broils
> Clean overblown, themselves, the conquerors,
> Make war upon themselves: blood against blood,
> Self against self. O, preposterous
> And frantic outrage, end thy damned spleen.
> (II.iv.55–64)

All this penitence cannot be fortuitous; and it is the prelude to forgiveness and regeneration. But the full religious temper of the play only comes out in the two great scenes in the last third of the play: the lamentations of the three queens after Richard has murdered the princes in the Tower, and the ghosts appearing to Richard and Richmond before Bosworth. These are both extreme and splendid examples of the formal style which should be considered the norm rather than the exception in the tetralogy. Both scenes are ritual and incantatory to a high degree, suggesting an ecclesiastical context; both are implicitly or explicitly pious; and both are archaic, suggesting the prevalent piety of the Middle Ages. The incantation takes the form not only of an obvious antiphony like Queen Margaret's balancing of her own woes with Queen Elizabeth's—

> I had an Edward, till a Richard kill'd him;
> I had a Harry, till a Richard kill'd him:
> Thou hadst an Edward, till a Richard kill'd him;
> Thou hadst a Richard, till a Richard kill'd him—
> (IV.iv.40–43)

but of a more complicated balance of rhythmic phrases and of varied repetitions, as in the Duchess of York's self-address:

> Blind sight, dead life, poor mortal living ghost,
> Woe's scene, world's shame, grave's due by life usurp'd,
> Brief abstract and record of tedious days,
> Rest thy unrest on England's lawful earth,
> Unlawfully made drunk with innocents' blood.
> (IV.iv.25–29)

The piety in this scene is implicit rather than explicit, and the two passages just quoted will illustrate it. Queen Margaret is thinking of Richard's crimes and the vengeance he will incur, yet by repeating a phrase in four successive lines she expresses unconsciously the new and fruitful unity that God is to construct out of Richard's impartial wickedness. The Duchess's mention of England's *lawful* earth is in itself an assertion of the principle of order and an implicit prayer for a juster age. The medievalism and its accompanying suggestion of piety comes out in Margaret's great speech to Elizabeth, itself an example of incantation and antiphony. She refers to her prophecies made earlier in the play and now fulfilled.

> I call'd thee then vain flourish of my fortune.
> I call'd thee then poor shadow, painted queen;
> The presentation of but what I was;
> The flattering index of a direful pageant;
> One heav'd a-high, to be hurl'd down below;
> A mother only mock'd with two sweet babes;
> A dream of what thou wert, a breath, a bubble,
> A sign of dignity, a garish flag,
> To be the aim of every dangerous shot;
> A queen in jest, only to fill the scene.
> Where is thy husband now? where be thy brothers?
> Where are thy children? wherein dost thou joy?
> Who sues to thee and cries "God save the queen"?
> Where be the bending peers that flatter'd thee?
> Where be the thronging troops that follow'd thee?—

Decline all this and see what now thou art:
For happy wife a most distressed widow;
For joyful mother one that wails the name;
For queen a very caitiff crown'd with care;
For one being sued to one that humbly sues:
For one that scorn'd at me now scorn'd of me;
For one being fear'd of all now fearing one;
For one commanding all obey'd of none.
Thus hath the course of justice wheel'd about
And left thee but a very prey to time;
Having no more but thought of what thou wert
To torture thee the more being what thou art.
(IV.iv.82–108)

The speech takes us back to the Middle Ages; to the laments of the fickleness of fortune, to the constant burden of *Ubi sunt,* and to the consequent contempt of the world. . . .

The scene of the ghosts of those Richard has murdered follows immediately on Richmond's solemn prayer. It is essentially of the Morality pattern. Respublica or England is the hero, invisible yet present, contended for by the forces of heaven represented by Richmond and of hell represented by Richard. Each ghost as it were gives his vote for heaven, Lancaster and York being at last unanimous. And God is above, surveying the event. The medieval strain is continued when Richard, awaking in terror, rants like Judas in the Miracle Plays about to hang himself. The scene, like Richmond's prayer and his last speech, is very moving. It may have issued from Shakespeare's official self, from Shakespeare identifying himself with an obvious and simple phase of public opinion. But the identification is entirely sincere, and the opinion strong and right, to be shared alike by the most sophisticated and the humblest. The scene becomes almost an act of common worship, ending with Buckingham's assertion:

God and good angels fight on Richmond's side;
And Richard falls in height of all his pride.
(V.iii.176–77)

And just because he participates so fully, because he holds nothing of himself back, Shakespeare can be at his best, can give to his language the maximum of personal differentiation of which he was at the time capable. This differentiation he achieves, not as in some of the other great places in the play by surprising conjunctions of words or new imagery but by subtle musical variations within a context of incantation. He seems indeed to have learnt and applied the lessons of Spenser. At the same time the substance of what each ghost says is entirely appropriate to the speaker and by referring back to past events in the tetralogy serves to reinforce the structure of the plot. There may be better scenes in Shakespeare, but of these none is like this one. Of its kind it is the best.

That the play's main end is to show the working out of God's will in English history does not detract from the importance of Richard in the process and from his dominance as a character. And it is through his dominance that he is able to be the instrument of God's ends. Whereas the sins of other men had merely bred more sins, Richard's are so vast that they are absorptive, not contagious. He is the great ulcer of the body politic into which all its impurity is drained and against which all the members of the body politic are united. It is no longer a case of limb fighting limb but of the war of the whole organism against an ill which has now ceased to be organic. The metaphor of poison is constantly applied to Richard, and that of beast, as if here were something to be excluded from the human norm. Queen Margaret unites the two metaphors when she calls him "that poisonous bunchback'd toad" and that "bottled spider," the spider being proverbially venomous.

In making Richard thus subservient to a greater scheme I do not deny that for many years now the main attraction of the play has actually been Richard's character in itself, like Satan's in *Paradise Lost.* Nor was this attraction lacking from the first. Indeed it antedates the play, going back to More's *History of Richard III,* which was inserted with trifling modifications into Hall's chronicle and repeated thence by Holinshed. Shakespeare in singling out Richard III and later Henry V for special treatment as characters is not therefore departing from tradition but following closely his own main teacher of the philosophy of history, Hall.

One would like to think of Shakespeare hailing More (through Hall) as a kindred spirit and using his charm as an inspiration. Actually, though Shakespeare accepts More's heightened picture of Richard as an arch-villain, he can very coolly reject the episodes of which More made much. He quite omits Edward's wonderful speech on his deathbed and the most moving scene of all, the Archbishop persuading Queen Elizabeth to give up her younger son out of sanctuary. It may be however that More's abundant sense of humour encouraged Shakespeare to add to Richard that touch of comedy that makes him so distinguished a villain. His aside after he has gone on his knees to ask his mother's blessing is very much in More's spirit:

> DUCH.: God bless thee, and put meekness in thy mind,
> Love, charity, obedience, and true duty.
> RICH.: Amen; and make me die a good old man.
> That is the butt-end of a mother's blessing:
> I marvel why her grace did leave it out.

> (II.ii.107–11)

A number of people have written well on the character of Richard: in one place or another all has been said that need be said. It remains now to think less in terms of alternatives and to include more than is usually done in Richard's character, even at the sacrifice of consistency. Lamb, for instance, who in his brief references raised most of the pertinent questions, wants to exclude the melodramatic side:

> Shakespeare has not made Richard so black a monster as is supposed. Wherever he is monstrous, it was to conform to vulgar opinion. But he is generally a Man.[1]

Actually Shakespeare was already at one with vulgar opinion and willingly makes him a monster. But only in some places; in others he keeps him human. Similarly we need not choose between Richard the psychological study in compensation for physical disability and Richard the embodiment of sheer demonic will, for he is both. It *is* true that, as Lamb notes, Richard in the allusions to his deformity

> mingles . . . a perpetual reference to his own powers and capacities, by which he is enabled to surmount these petty objections; and the joy of a defect *conquered*, or *turned* into an advantage, is one cause of these very allusions, and of the satisfaction, with which his mind recurs to them.

But Dowden also is right when he says of Richard that

> his dominant characteristic is not intellectual; it is rather a daemonic energy of will. . . . He is of the diabolical class. . . . He is single-hearted in his devotion to evil. . . . He has a fierce joy, and he is an intense believer,—in the creed of hell. And therefore he is strong. He inverts the moral order of things, and tries to live in this inverted system. He does not succeed; he dashes himself to pieces against the laws of the world which he has outraged.[2]

It might be retorted that the above distinction is superfluous, because an extreme manifestation of demonic will can only arise from the additional drive set in motion by an unusual need to compensate for a defect. But the point is that Shakespeare does actually make the distinction and that Richard, within the limits of the play, is psychologically both possible and impossible. He ranges from credibly motivated villain to a symbol, psychologically absurd however useful dramatically, of the diabolic.

This shift, however, is not irregular. In the first two scenes, containing his opening soliloquy, his dealings with Clarence, his interruption of the funeral of Henry VI with his courtship of Ann Nevil, he is predominantly the psychological study. Shakespeare here builds up his private character. And he is credible; with his humour, his irony, and his artistry in crime acting as differentiating agents, creating a sense of the individual. After this he carries his established private character into the public arena, where he is more than a match for anyone except Queen Margaret. Of her alone he is afraid; and her curse establishes, along with the psychologically probable picture just created, the competing and ultimately victorious picture of the monstrosity, the country's scapegoat, the vast impostume of the commonwealth. She makes him both a cosmic symbol, the "troubler of the poor world's peace," and subhuman, a "rooting hog," "the slave of nature and the son of hell." She calls on him the curse of insomnia, which later we find to have been fulfilled. Clearly this does not apply to the exulting ironic Richard: *he* must always have slept with infant tranquillity. Thus Margaret's curse is prospective, and though he continues to pile up the materials for the construction of his monstrosity, it is the credible Richard, glorying in his will and his success in compensating his disabilities, who persists till the end of the third act and the attainment of the throne. Thenceforward, apart from his outburst of energy in courting Queen Elizabeth for her daughter's hand, he melts from credible character into a combination of sheer melodrama villain and symbol of diabolism. His irony forsakes him; he is unguarded not secretive in making his plans; he is no longer cool but confused in his energy, giving and retracting orders; he *really* does not sleep; and, when on the eve of Bosworth he calls for a bowl of wine because he has not "that alacrity of spirit nor cheer of mind that I was wont to have," he is the genuine ancestor of the villain in a nineteenth century melodrama calling for whiskey when things look black. Then, with the ghosts and his awakening into his Judas-like monologue, psychological probability and melodramatic villainy alike melt into the symbol of sheer denial and diabolism. Nor does his momentary resurrection at Bosworth with his memorable shout for a horse destroy that abiding impression. That a character should shift from credible human being to symbol would not have troubled a generation nurtured on Spenser. Richard in this respect resembles one of Spenser's masterpieces, Malbecco, who from a realistic old cuckold is actually transformed into an allegorical figure called Jealousy.

Finally we must not forget that Richard is the vehicle of an orthodox doctrine about kingship. It was a terrible thing to fight the ruling monarch, and Richard had been crowned. However, he was so clearly both a usurper and a murderer that he had qualified as a tyrant; and against an authentic tyrant it was lawful to rebel. Richmond, addressing his army before Bosworth, makes the point absolutely clear:

> Richard except, those whom we fight against
> Had rather have us win than him they follow.
> For what is he they follow? truly, gentlemen,
> A bloody tyrant and a homicide;
> One rais'd in blood and one in blood establish'd;

> One that made means to come by what he hath
> And slaughter'd those that were the means to help him; . . .
> One that hath ever been God's enemy.
> Then if you fight against God's enemy,
> God will in justice ward you as his soldiers;
> If you do sweat to put a tyrant down,
> You sleep in peace, the tyrant being slain.
>
> (V. iii. 243–49, 252–56)

And Derby, handing Henry the crown after the battle, calls it "this long-usurped royalty."

I have indicated in outline the course of the play: the emerging of unity from and through discord, the simultaneous change in Richard from accomplished villain to the despairing embodiment of evil. Shakespeare gives it coherence through the dominant and now scarcely human figure of Queen Margaret: the one character who appears in every play. Being thus a connecting thread, it is fitting that she give structural coherence to the crowning drama. As Richard's downfall goes back to her curse, so do the fates of most of the characters who perish in the play go back to her curses or prophecies in the same scene, 1. 3. Nor are her curses mere explosions of personal spite; they agree with the tit-for-tat scheme of crime and punishment that has so far prevailed in the tetralogy. She begins by recalling York's curse on her at Wakefield for the cruelty of her party to Rutland and the penalty she has paid; and then enumerates the precisely balanced scheme of retribution appointed for the house of York:

> If not by war, by surfeit die your king,
> As ours by murder, to make him a king.
> Edward thy son, which now is Prince of Wales,
> For Edward my son, which was Prince of Wales,
> Die in his youth by like untimely violence.
> Thyself a queen, for me that was a queen,
> Outlive thy glory like my wretched self.
>
> (I.iii.197–203)

Curses on minor characters follow, but Richard, as befits, has a speech to himself. His peculiar curse is the gnawing of conscience, sleeplessness, and the mistake of taking friends for enemies and enemies for friends. I have spoken of the sleeplessness above, how it could not apply to the Richard of the first three acts. Similarly it is not till Bosworth that the curse of thinking his enemies friends comes true. We are meant to think of it when Richmond says in lines quoted above that "those whom we fight against had rather have us win than him they follow." The man with the best brain in the play ends by being the most pitifully deceived.

Notes

1. *Lamb* in his Letter to Lloyd 26 July 1801 and *G. F. Cooke* in *"Richard III"* (1802).

2. Edward Dowden, in *Shakspere: A Critical Study of His Mind and Art* (9th Edition, London: K. Paul, 1889), pp. 182, 189.

"Angel with Horns": The Unity of *Richard III*

A. P. Rossiter

Let's write "good angel" on the devil's horn

—Measure for Measure, II. iv. 16

In the Second Part of *Henry IV* (III. i.) the King and Warwick are talking away the midnight, or the King's insomnia; and the King remembers how Richard spoke like a prophet of the future treachery of the Percies. Warwick replies that those who look for rotations in history can indeed appear to be prophets:

> There is a history in all men's lives,
> Figuring the nature of the times deceas'd;
> The which observ'd, a man may prophesy,
> With a near aim, of the main chance of things
> As yet not come to life, who in their seeds
> And weak beginnings lie intreasured.
> Such things become the hatch and brood of time.

Richard, he explains, had observed "the necessary form" of the events he had seen happen; and from that he could "create a perfect guess" of some that were to ensue as "the hatch and brood of time."

Men have always looked for such a predictability in history: it gives the illusion of a comfortably ordered world. They have also often read—and written—historical records to show that the course of events has been guided by a simple process of divine justice, dispensing rewards and punishments here on earth and seeing to it that the wicked do *not* thrive like the green bay-tree (as the Psalmist thought), and that virtue is not "triumphant only in theatrical performances" (as the humane Mikado put it: being a Gilbertian Japanese, not an Elizabethan Christian). The story-matter of the Henry VI plays and of *Richard III* accepted both of these comforting and comfortable principles.

When I say "story-matter" I mean what the Chronicles gave the author (or authors) of these four plays, and I wish to remain uncommitted as to whether their *plots* (and especially that of *Richard III*) work entirely within those reassuring limitations.

Reprinted by permission of Addison Wesley Longman Ltd.

I am averse to source-study, as material for lectures. Yet sad experience of human nature (and perhaps of historians) leads me to remind you how the Richard III myth (*"story"*) came to reach Shakespeare. In the play, you remember, the Bishop of Ely, Morton, plots with Buckingham and runs away to join Richmond (Henry Tudor). He duly became one of Henry's ministers; and Thomas More grew up in his household—and later wrote the life of Richard III. It would only be human if Morton recounted all the worst that was ever said of the master he had betrayed: it is not surprising that Edward Halle should accept More's account, in writing his vast book on the "noble and illustre families of Lancastre and York"; and still more human that Raphael Holinshed (whom no one could call a historian) should copy extensively from Halle—and so leave room for all those since Horace Walpole who have had doubts about the historical character of this terrible monarch and the events of his times.

To think that we are seeing anything like sober history in this play is derisible naïvety. What we are offered is a formally patterned sequence presenting two things: on the one hand, a rigid Tudor *schema* of retributive justice (a sort of analogy to Newton's Third Law in the field of moral dynamics: "Action and reaction are equal and apposite"); and, on the other, a huge triumphant stage-personality, an early old masterpiece of the art of rhetorical stage-writing, a monstrous being incredible in any sober, historical scheme of things—Richard himself.

I will talk about the first, first. The basic pattern of retributive justice (or God's vengeance) is well enough illustrated in Holinshed, in the passage telling how Prince Edward (Henry VI's son and Margaret's) was murdered at the Battle of Tewkesbury. The Prince was handed over to Edward IV on the proclamation of a promise that he would not be harmed; he was brought before the King, asked why he "durst so presumptuously enter into his realm" and replied courageously "To recover my father's kingdom and heritage" (and more to that purpose)—but let Holinshed say the rest:

> At which words king Edward said nothing, but with his hand thrust him from him, or (as some saie) stroke him with his gantlet; whom incontinentlie, George duke of Clarence, Richard duke of Glocester, Thomas Greie marquesse Dorcet, and William lord Hastings, that stood by, suddenlie murthered; for the which cruell act, the more part of the dooers in their latter daies dranke of the like cup, by the righteous justice and due punishment of God.

There you have the notional pattern, in little, of the whole framework of *Richard III:* Clarence—"false, fleeting, perjur'd Clarence" (who took the sacrament to remain true to Henry VI of Lancaster and deserted him); Gray—one of the group of Queen Elizabeth Woodeville's relations, who fall to Richard and Buckingham next after Clarence; Hastings, who says he will see "this crown of mine hewn from its shoulders/Before I see the crown so foul misplaced" (on Richard's head)—and *does* (if a man can be said to see his own decapitation). Holinshed really understates the matter in writing "the more part of the dooers . . . dranke of the like cup"; for of those he names, everyone did. On the one hand, that is what *Richard III* is about: what it is composed of. A heavy-handed justice commends the ingredients of a poisoned [cup].

This notional pattern of historic events rigidly determined by a mechanical necessity is partly paralleled by, partly modified by, the formal patterns of the episodes (or scenes) and the language. By "formal patterns" I mean the unmistakably iterated goings-on in scenes so exactly parallel that if the first *is* passable on a modern stage as quasi-realistic costume-play stuff, the second (repeating it always *more* unrealistically) cannot be. The two wooing-scenes (Richard with Anne and Elizabeth) are the simplest case; but in the lamentation-scenes—where a collection of bereft females comes together and goes through a dismal catalogue of *Who was Who and Who has lost Whom* (like a gathering of historical Mrs. Gummidges, each "thinking of the old 'un" with shattering simultaneity)—there, even editors have found the proceedings absurd; and readers difficult. When Queen Margaret, for example, says:

> I had an Edward, till a Richard kill'd him;
> I had a husband, till a Richard kill'd him:
> Thou hadst an Edward, till a Richard kill'd him;
> Thou hadst a Richard, till a Richard kill'd him.
> (IV. iv. 40–43)

a reader may *just* keep up (and realize that the last two are the Princes in the Tower, so that Queen Elizabeth is being addressed); but when the Duchess of York takes up with

> I had a Richard too, and thou didst kill him;
> I had a Rutland too, thou holp'st to kill him,

it is likely that you are lost, unless your recollection of a *Henry VI* and the ends of Richard, Duke of York and his young son (Edmund) is unusually clear.

It is not only the iteration of scene that is stylized: the stiffly formal manipulation of echoing phrase and sequence of words within the scenes is even more unrealistic. A closely related parallelism exists in the repeated occurrence of a sort of "single line traffic" in sentences: the classicist's *stichomythia*. One speaker takes from the other exactly the same ration of syllables, and rejoins as if under contract to repeat the form of the given sentence as exactly as possible, using the maximum number of the same words or their logical opposites, or (failing that) words closely associated with them. I describe the game pedantically, because it *is* an exact and scientific game with language, and one of the graces and beauties of the play Shakespeare wrote. If we cannot accept the "patterned speech" of *Richard III*, its quality must remain unknown to us. "Early work" is an evasive, criticism-dodging term. Early it may be; but the play is a triumphant contrivance in a manner which cannot properly be compared with that of any other tragedy—nor of any history, except *3 Henry VI* (where the manner takes shape, and particularly in III. ii.) and *King John* (which is not half so well built or integrated as this).

I have emphasized the stylization of verbal patterning (with its neatly over-exact adjustments of stroke to stroke, as in royal tennis), because the sequence of most of the important events offers very much the same pattern. I might remark, in passing, that these verbal devices were offering to the Elizabethans an accomplished English equivalent to the neat dexterities they admired in Seneca (a point made by T. S. Eliot years ago; though he did not examine how the dramatic ironies of the action run in parallel with these counter-stroke reversals of verbal meaning, and form a kind of harmony). But we miss something more than Shakespeare's rhetorical game of tennis if merely irritated by, e.g.:

ANNE:	I would I knew thy heart.
RICHARD:	'Tis figured in my tongue.
ANNE:	I fear me, both are false.
RICHARD:	Then never man was true.

Those reversals of intention (*heart-tongue; false-true*) are on precisely the pattern of the repeated reversals of human expectation, the reversals of events, the anticipated reversals (foreseen only by the audience), which make "dramatic irony." The patterned speech of the dialogue—the wit that demonstrates that a sentence is but a cheveril glove, quickly turned the other way—is fundamentally one with the ironic patterns of the plot. "Dramatic irony" here is verbal *peripeteia*.

You will see that simply exemplified if you read Buckingham's speech at the beginning of Act II, where he calls a curse on himself if ever he goes back on his reconciliation with the Queen (and is quite specific about it); then turn straight to his last lines in V. i., when he is on the way to execution: "That high All-seer, which I dallied with." He has got exactly what he asked for. He did not mean the words he used, but they have been reversed into actuality, in exactly the same way as verbal terms are reversed in the tennis-court game of rhetoric.

The same irony plays all over *Richard III*. It lurks like a shadow behind the naïvely self-confident Hastings; it hovers a moment over Buckingham when Margaret warns him against "younder dog" (Richard), and, on Richard's asking what she said, he replies, "Nothing that I respect, my gracious lord" (I. iii. 296)—and this at a time when Buckingham is under no threat whatsoever.

Its cumulative effect is to present the personages as existing in a state of total and terrible uncertainty. This is enhanced if we know the details of what comes into the play from *3 Henry VI,* but is there even if we know only a few bare essentials of what has gone before. We need to know who Margaret is; how Lancaster has been utterly defeated, and King Henry and his son murdered; how Clarence betrayed his King and returned to the Yorkists; and how Richard, his younger brother, has already marked him as his immediate obstruction on his intended way to the crown. We need to know too that the Duchess of York is mother to that unrewarding trio, Edward IV, Clarence, Gloucester; that Edward IV has married an aspiring commoner, Elizabeth Grey (*née* Woodeville); and that she has jacked up her relations into nobility. Beyond those half-dozen facts we do not need back-reference to *3 Henry VI* for any but the finer points—so far as the essential ironies of the plot go.

Far more important than these details is the simple overriding principle derived from the Tudor historians: that England rests under a chronic curse— the curse of faction, civil dissension and fundamental anarchy, resulting from the deposition and murder of the Lord's Anointed (Richard II) and the usurpation of the House of Lancaster. The savageries of the Wars of the Roses follow logically (almost theologically) from that; and Elizabeth's "All-seeing heaven, what a world is this!" says but half. It is a world of absolute and hereditary moral ill, in which *everyone* (till the appearance of Richmond-Tudor in Act V) is tainted with the treacheries, the blood and the barbarities of civil strife, and internally blasted with the curse of a moral anarchy which leaves but three human *genera:* the strong in evil, the feebly wicked and the help-lessly guilt-tainted (such as the Princes, Anne—all those despairing, lament-ing women, whose choric wailings are a penitentional psalm of guilt and sor-row: England's guilt, the individual's sorrow). The "poor painted Queen's" "What a world" needs supplementing with the words of the pessimistically clear-sighted Third Citizen:

> All may be well; but, if God sort it so,
> 'Tis more than we deserve or I expect.
> (II. iii. 36)

I have in effect described the meaning of the framework of the play: pre-sented it as "moral history," to be interpreted in abstract terms. But the play itself is also a symphonic structure which I can only describe in terms of music: a rhetorical symphony of five movements, with first and second sub-jects and some Wagnerian *Leitmotifs.* The play-making framework is Senecan revenge, the characterization largely Marlovian; but the orchestration is not only original, but unique. It can be sketched like this.

The first movement employs five "subjects": Richard himself, his own overture; the wooing-theme (to be repeated in the fourth movement); Richard among his enemies (repeating the duplicity with which he has fooled

Clarence); Margaret's curse; and the long dying fall of Clarence. It occupies the whole of Act I.

The second movement includes Act II. and scenes i.–iv. of Act III. It begins with the King's feeble peace-making—in which Buckingham invites his curse—and its other subjects are: a lamentation after the King's death (repeated in the fourth movement); the fall of the curse on Rivers, Grey and Vaughan (when the curse is remembered), and on Hastings (the curse briefly recalled again). The future subject of Richard's moves against the Princes is introduced between-whiles.

The third movement cuts across the Act-divisions and runs from III. v. to IV. iii. Its main subject is the Gloucester-Buckingham plot for the crown, with the magnificently sardonic fooling of the London *bourgeoisie* with a crisis-scare, a brace of bishops, and the headline-story that here is a highly respectable unlibidinous monarch for decent England. On its success, Anne is called to be Queen, and thus to meet the curse she herself called on Richard's wife before he wooed her in that humour and won her (the first movement is here caught up). Buckingham now makes himself one of Richard's future victims by showing reluctance for the plot against the Princes, and Richard throws him off with a snub. The Princes are dealt with (the account of Forrest and Deighton echoing that of the murderers of Clarence, one of whom had a temporary conscience); and Richard concludes with a brisk summary and prospectus:

> The sons of Edward sleep in Abraham's bosom,
> And Anne my wife hath bid this world good night;

and so, since Richmond plans to marry "young Elizabeth, my brother's daughter," "To her go I, a jolly thriving wooer." (Richard's last jocularity). The movement ends with the first murmurs of Richmond. Previously there has been slipped in the trivial-sounding prophecy about "Rugemount," besides Henry VI's prophecy (IV. ii. 99 f.). The flight of the Bishop of Ely (Morton) really troubles Richard.

The fourth movement brings down the curse on Buckingham (V.i. is obviously misplaced, so the movement runs from IV. iv. to V.i. inclusive). Mainly it repeats themes heard before: with a long lamentation-scene (the Blake-like weeping Queens); a repetition of Margaret's curse with the curse of Richard's mother added; the second wooing-scene; the subject of Nemesis repeated by Buckingham. In it the sound of Richmond's advance has become clearer; and Richard's self-command and certainty begin to waver.

The fifth movement is all at Bosworth: the fall of the curse on Richard himself. There is the dream-prologue of the procession of contrapuntal Ghosts (including all those so qualified from the four previous movements) and, like all ghosts, they are reminiscent and repetitive. The play ends with the epilogue to the Wars of the Roses—spoken by Queen Elizabeth's grandfather—calling a blessing on the English future, and inverting the opening lines of Richard's prologue:

> Now is the winter of our discontent
> Made glorious summer . . .

The deliberateness of this highly controlled workmanship needs but little comment. I shall take up a single musical phrase: one that intertwines its plangent undertones throughout the whole symphony, a true *Leitmotif.*

At first sight, Clarence's dream (I. iv. 9 f.) appears to contribute little to the play, nothing to the plot; and it may seem a rhetorical indulgence, even if we accept Mr. Eliot's judgement that it shows "a real approximation in English to the magnificence of Senecan Latin at its best. . . . The best of Seneca has here been absorbed into English."[1] But first recollect the setting. Clarence has been sent to the Tower, by the machinations of the Queen's party (so he thinks), and he is confident that his brother Richard will stand good friend to him. He believes Richard's worried "We are not safe, Clarence; we are not safe"; cannot possibly see the ironical joke Richard is cracking with himself; has no idea that he has been first on Richard's list since that moment in *3 Henry VI* (V. vi. 84) when his brother muttered, "Clarence, beware; thou keep'st me from the light."[2] (A line that follows a passage predetermining the gulling of both Clarence and Anne to follow:

> I have no brother, I am like no brother;
> And this word "love," which greybeards call divine,
> Be resident in men like one another,
> And not in me! I am myself alone).

Clarence had not been there to hear that: knows nothing of the typically sharp reversal of Richard's solemnly hypocritical fooling now with:

> Go tread the path that thou shalt ne'er return.
> Simple, plain Clarence, I do love thee so
> That I will shortly send thy soul to heaven,
> If heaven will take the present at our hands.
> (I.i.117–20)

Clarence has his nightmare in the Tower: a vision prophetic of doom, and thick with curdled guilt. He dreams that Richard blunderingly knocks him overboard from a vessel; he drowns; goes to hell; and his guilt-sick mind spews up its own evil:

> KEEPER: Awak'd you not in this sore agony?
> CLARENCE: No, no, my dream was lengthen'd after life.
>   O, then began the tempest to my soul!

> I pass'd, methought, the melancholy flood
> With that sour ferryman which poets write of,
> Unto the kingdom of perpetual night.
> The first that there did greet my stranger soul
> Was my great father-in-law, renowned Warwick,
> Who spake aloud "What scourge for perjury
> Can this dark monarchy afford false Clarence?"
> And so he vanish'd. Then came wand'ring by
> A shadow like an angel, with bright hair
> Dabbled in blood, and he shriek'd out aloud
> "Clarence is come—false, fleeting, perjur'd Clarence,
> That stabb'd me in the field by Tewkesbury.
> Seize on him, Furies, take him unto torment!"
>
> (I. iv. 42–57)

It is as fine a passage in that style as English can offer: calculated to leave its solemn music in even half-attentive ears. In the second movement of the play (II. ii. 43 f.), Queen Elizabeth announces the King's death:

> If you will live, lament; if die, be brief,
> That our swift-winged souls may catch the King's,
> Or like obedient subjects follow him
> To his new kingdom of ne'er-changing night.

It is scarcely a proper-wifely expectation of the fate of her husband's spirit: but the echo of "Unto the kingdom of perpetual night" is the effect intended, not Elizabeth's notions. The actors who put together the Q. text of 1597 showed that they appreciated, if clumsily, the author's intention. They made it "To his new kingdom of perpetuall rest": catching the echo rightly, while missing the point.

The same "dark monarchy" awaits all these people: they are the living damned. That is the translation of this echo-technique of *Leitmotifs;* and why I call the play's anatomy "musical." Nor is that all: the phrase returns again. But before I come to that, remark how Hastings philosophizes on his fall at the end of the second movement:

> O momentary grace of mortal men,
> Which we more hunt for than the grace of God!
> Who builds his hope in air of your good looks
> Lives like a drunken sailor on a mast,
> Ready with every nod to tumble down
> Into the fatal bowels of the deep.
>
> (III. iv. 98–103)

We have heard that surging rhythm before. And with it the feeling of being aloft, in air, unbalanced: the rhythm of Clarence dreaming:

> As we pac'd along
> Upon the giddy footing of the hatches,
> Methought that Gloucester stumbled, and in falling
> Struck me, that thought to stay him, overboard
> Into the tumbling billows of the main.
>
> (I. iv. 16–20)

Pattern repeats pattern with remarkable exactitude. "Into the fatal bowels of the deep" is where the giddy Hastings also goes. "O Lord, methought what pain it was to drown" might be extended to all these desperate swimmers in the tide of pomp and history. The elaboration of the dream is no mere exercise in fine phrase on Latin models: it offers a symbol of choking suspense above black depths (the ocean, and perpetual night) which epitomizes the "momentary grace" of all these "mortal men" and women. And the sea as figure of "the destructive element" appears again in Elizabeth's lines in the second wooing-scene:

> But that still use of grief makes wild grief tame,
> My tongue should to thy ears not name my boys
> Till that my nails were anchor'd in thine eyes;
> And I, in such a desp'rate bay of death,
> Like a poor bark, of sails and tackling reft,
> Rush all to pieces on thy rocky bosom.
>
> (IV. iv. 229–34)

"Bay" of death suggests also an animal at bay; just plausibly relevant, since Richard (the boar) would be at bay when she *could* scratch his eyes out. But the repetition of the rather too emphatic anchors and the eyes from Clarence's dream is much more striking.

You will find a further echo of the "night-motif" in the last movement. Richard suspects Stanley (confusingly also called Derby), and reasonably so: for he was husband to the Countess of Richmond, Henry Tudor's mother, the famous Lady Margaret Beaufort; and therefore keeps his son, George Stanley, as hostage. Before Bosworth, he sends a brisk message to warn the father of the black depths beneath the son; and again Shakespeare sounds his doom-music from the Clarence sequence:

> bid him bring his power
> Before sunrising, lest his son George fall
> Into the blind cave of eternal night.
>
> (V. iii. 60–2)

Need I remark that Clarence was "George" too, and lightly called that by Richard when he was afraid that King Edward might die before he signed his brother's death-warrant?

> He cannot live, I hope, and must not die
> Till George be packed with post-horse up to heaven.
> (I. ii. 145)

I could further exemplify the play's tight-woven artistry by taking up that very remarkable prose-speech on "conscience" by Clarence's Second Murderer (I. iv. 133 f.), and following the word into Richard's troubled mind in Act V. before Margaret's curse attains its last fulfilment. But to reduce attention to Richard himself in his own play, beyond what I am already committed to by my insistence on taking the play as a *whole* (as a dramatic pattern, not an exposition of "character"), would be to do it—and Shakespeare—an injustice.

Richard Plantagenet is alone with Macbeth as the Shakespearian version of the thoroughly bad man in the role of monarch and hero; he is unique in combining with that role that of the diabolic humorist. It is this quality which makes it an inadequate account to say that the play is "moral history," or that the protagonists are the personality of Richard and the curse of Margaret (or what it stood for in orthodox Tudor thinking about retributive justice in history)—for all that these opposed "forces" *are* central throughout. The first movement establishes both, and emphatically. First, Richard, stumping down the stage on his unequal legs, forcing his hitched-up left shoulder and his withered arm on us, till we realize that *this* is what the "winter of our discontent" in *3 Henry VI* has produced, *this* the proper "hatch and brood of time"; and then, Richard established, his cruel and sardonic effectiveness demonstrated on Clarence and Anne, there arises against his brazen Carl Orff-like music the one voice he quails before (if but slightly): the sub-dominant notes of Margaret and her prophecy of doom, to which the ghosts will walk in the visionary night before Bosworth. It is a conflict between a spirit and a ghost: between Richard, the spirit of ruthless will, of daemonic pride, energy and self-sufficiency, of devilish gusto and *Schadenfreude* (he *enjoys* wickedness even when it is of no practical advantage to his ambitions or to securing himself by murder: it may be only wickedness in *words,* but the spirit revealed is no less evilly exultant for that); and the ghost, as I call her—for what else is Margaret Reignier's daughter picked up on a battlefield by Suffolk and married to that most etiolated of Shakespeare's husbands, Henry VI, but the living ghost of Lancaster, the walking dead, memorializing the long, cruel, treacherous, bloody conflict of the years of civil strife and pitiless butchery?

You can, of course, see more there if you will. Make her the last stage or age of woman-in-politics: she who has been beautiful, fiercely passionate, queenly, dominating, master of armies, *generalissima:* now old, defeated, empty of everything but fierce bitterness, the illimitable bitterness and rancour of political zeal. What did Yeats write of *his* equivalent symbol?[3] It is in *A Prayer for my Daughter.* For her he prays:

> An intellectual hatred is the worst,
> So let her think opinions are accursed.
> Have I not seen the loveliest woman born
> Out of the mouth of Plenty's horn,
> Because of her opinionated mind
> Barter that horn and every good
> By quiet natures understood
> For an old bellows full of angry wind?

Margaret is that, if you like; but, not to go beyond Shakespeare, I cannot but think that when the old Duchess of York sits down upon the ground for the second lamentation-scene (to tell "sad stories of the death of kings"), the *author's* mind ran more upon Margaret as he wrote:

> Dead life, blind sight, poor mortal living ghost, . . .
> Brief abstract and record of tedious days,
> Rest thy unrest on England's lawful earth,
> Unlawfully made drunk with innocent blood.
> (IV. iv. 26, 28–30)

Here Shakespeare devises a new variation on the Senecan visitant from another world howling for revenge, by making the spectre nominal flesh and blood; the tune of the Dance of Death to which all dance to damnation is played by Margaret; and one aspect of the play is our watching the rats go into the Weser, compelled by that fatal tune.

But Richard himself is not simply the last and most important (and worst) of the victims—if those justly destroyed can be called "victims." That is just where the label "moral history" is inadequate. For Richard has grown a new dimension since his abrupt and remarkable development in *3 Henry VI:* he has become a wit, a mocking comedian, a "vice of kings"—but with a clear inheritance from the old Vice of the Moralities: part symbol of evil, part comic devil, and chiefly, on the stage, the generator of roars of laughter at wickednesses (whether of deed or word) which the audience would immediately condemn in real life. On the one hand, his literary relations with the Senecan "Tyrant" (author of "In regna mea Mors impetratur," etc.) are clear enough; as they are with the Elizabethan myth of "the murderous Machiavel" ("feared am I more than loved/Let me be feared," etc.): enough has been written on them. But only the medieval heritage—from the comic devils with their *Schadenfreude,* and the Vice as comic inverter of order and decency—can fully explain the new Richard of this apparent sequel to the *Henry VI* series.

I have said that the Christian pattern imposed on history gives the simple plot of a cast accursed, where all are evil beings, all deserve punishment. Look, then, with a believing Tudor eye, and ought you not to *approve* Richard's doings? *Per se*, they are the judgment of God on the wicked; and he

> *Ein Teil von jener Kraft*
> *Die stets das Böse will, und stets das Gute schafft.*[4]

But that is not all. Richard's sense of humour, his function as clown, his comic irreverences and sarcastic or sardonic appropriations of things to (at any rate) *his* occasions: all those act as underminers of our assumed naïve and proper Tudor principles; and we are on his side much rather because he makes us (as the Second Murderer put it) "take the devil in [our] mind," than for any "historical-philosophical-Christian-retributional" sort of motive. In this respect a good third of the play is a kind of grisly *comedy;* in which we meet the fools to be taken in on Richard's terms, see them with his mind, and rejoice with him in their stultification (in which execution is the ultimate and unanswerable practical joke, the absolutely final laugh this side of the Day of Judgment). Here, Richard is a middle-term between Barabas, the Jew of Malta (*c.* 1590) and Volpone (1606). He inhabits a world where everyone deserves everything he can do to them; and in his murderous practical joking he is *inclusively* the comic exposer of the mental shortcomings (the intellectual and moral deformities) of this world of beings depraved and besotted. If we forget to pity them awhile (and he does his best to help us), then his impish spirit urges us towards a positive reversal of "Christian charity" until the play's fourth movement (which is when the Elizabethan spectator began to back out, I take it)—or even beyond that point.

An aspect of Richard's appeal, which has, I fancy, passed relatively unexamined,[5] is one that we can be confident that William Shakespeare felt and reflected on. I mean the appeal of the actor: the talented being who can assume every mood and passion at will, at all events to the extent of making others believe in it. Beyond question, all our great actors have regarded the part as a fine opportunity. The extent to which the histrionic art (as Shakespeare thought and felt about it) contributed to the making of this great stage-figure is to me more interesting.

The specific interest here is the *power* that would be in the hands of an actor consummate enough to make (quite literally) "all the world a stage" and to work on humanity by the perfect simulation of every feeling: the appropriate delivery of every word and phrase that will serve his immediate purpose; together with the complete dissimulation of everything that might betray him (whether it be his intentions, or such obstructive feelings as compunction, pity or uncertainty of mind). This appears at once when Gloucester first takes shape as the man self-made to be King, in the long soliloquy in *3 Henry VI* (III. ii. 124 f.). The closing lines are specifically on histrionic genius:

> Why, I can smile, and murder whiles I smile,
> And cry "Content!" to that which grieves my heart,
> And wet my cheeks with artificial tears,
> And frame my face to all occasions.
>
> (ibid. 182–5)

And then, after a little bragging prospectus on his intended deadliness, he ends:

> I can add colours to the chameleon,
> Change shapes with Protheus for advantages,
> And set the murderous Machiavel to school.
> Can I do this, and cannot get a crown?
> Tut, were it farther off, I'll pluck it down.
>
> (ibid. 191–5)

M. R. Ridley notes here that "Machiavelli . . . seems to have been to the Elizabethans a type of one who advocated murder as a method of cold-blooded policy."[6] It is true that that marks off one point of difference between the "Senecan" tyrant-villainy (which is primarily for revenge) and the "Machiavellian" (which is for power, or self-aggrandizement: "We that are great, our own self-good still moves us"): though I do not think that the distinction can be maintained, if you read Seneca. But surely Ridley's note misses the point, in its context? What the "Machiavel" allusion represents is, I believe, Shakespeare's recognition that the programme set before the Prince in *Il Principe* is one that demands exactly those histrionic qualities I have just described: a lifelong, unremitting vigilance in relentless simulation and impenetrable deception. There, precisely, lies the super-humanity of the Superman. The will-to-power is shorn of its effective power without it. He is an *artist* in evil.

Now Richard in his own play shows this power—these powers—to perfection. Except to the audience, he is invisible; but the audience he keeps reminded not only of his real intentions, but equally of his actor's artistries. The bluff plain Englishman, shocked at ambitious go-getters and grievingly misunderstood, is perfectly "done" before the Queen's relations:

> Because I cannot flatter and look fair,
> Smile in men's faces, smooth, deceive, and cog,
> Duck with French nods and apish courtesy,
> I must be held a rancorous enemy.
> Cannot a plain man live and think no harm
> But thus his simple truth must be abus'd
> With silken, sly, insinuating Jacks?
>
> (I. iii. 47–53)

A little later, it is: "I am too childish-foolish for this world," (ibid., 142); and even: "I thank my God for my humility." (II. i. 72).

Then, left to himself and the audience, after egging on all their quarrels:

> But then I sigh and, with a piece of Scripture,
> Tell them that God bids us do good for evil.
> And thus I clothe my naked villainy
> With odd old ends stol'n forth of holy writ,
> And seem a saint when most I play the devil.
>
> (I. iii. 334–8)

The stage-direction, *"Enter two Murderers,"* caps this nicely. It is not simply that Richard is a hypocrite and (like other stage-villains) tells us so. The actor's technique of "asides" is the essence of his chuckling private jokes—made to "myself alone." (You might say that Shakespeare is giving not merely "the acting of drama," but also "the drama of consummate *acting*.")

The same reminders, nudging the audience's attention, appear in his swift-switched actual asides: e.g., his thoroughly unholy reception of his mother's blessing, spoken as he gets up off his dutiful knees:

> Amen! And make me die a good old man!
> That is the butt end of a mother's blessing;
> I marvel that her Grace did leave it out.
>
> (II. ii. 109–11)

Or, again, we have Richard's insinuating equivocations in talking to the prattling little Princes; in one of which he acknowledges his theatrical-historical legacy from the Moralities: "Thus, like the formal vice, Iniquity,/I moralize two meanings in one word." (III. i. 82–3). Over and above this there is that striking passage (III. v. 1–11) where he and Buckingham are working up a crisis (appearing ill-dressed in old rusty armour, as if they had armed in desperate haste), when Richard specifically inquires whether Buckingham can "do the stage-tragedian":

> RICHARD: Come, cousin, canst thou quake and change thy colour,
> Murder thy breath in middle of a word,
> And then again begin, and stop again,
> As if thou wert distraught and mad with terror?
> BUCKINGHAM: Tut, I can counterfeit the deep tragedian;
> Speak and look back, and pry on every side,
> Tremble and start at wagging of a straw,
> Intending deep suspicion. Ghastly looks
> Are at my service, like enforced smiles;
> And both are ready in their offices
> At any time to grace my stratagems.

It is all sardonically jocular; but nothing shows more clearly the artist's delight in his craft: call it illusion or deception, it makes no odds. It is this dexterity that his other rapid reversals of tone keep us aware of; whether he is half-amazedly rejoicing in his conquest of Anne, or poking unfilial fun at his mother (a performance more shocking to Elizabethans than to our more child-foolish days).

Yet again, there is that admirable moment when the Londoners are being fooled into believing that he must be persuaded to be king; when Buckingham pretends to lose patience, with "Zounds, I'll entreat no more." And Richard, bracketed aloft with two Bishops, is distressed: "O, do not swear, my lord of Buckingham." (III. vii. 220). (It is like the moment in *Eric or Little by Little* (ch. 8) when Eric refers to the usher as a "surly devil"; and the virtuous Russell exclaims: "O Eric, that is the first time that I have heard you swear.") It is this unholy jocularity, the readiness of sarcastic, sardonic, profane and sometimes blasphemous wit, the demonic gusto of it all, which not only wins the audience over to accepting the Devil as hero, but also points us towards the central paradox of the play. And, through that, to a full critical awareness of its unity: with a few remarks on which I shall conclude.

To begin with Richard. On the face of it, he is the demon-Prince, the cacodemon born of hell, the misshapen toad, etc. (all things ugly and ill). But through his prowess as actor and his embodiment of the comic Vice and impish-to-fiendish humour, he offers the false as more attractive than the true (the actor's function), and the ugly and evil as admirable and amusing (the clown's game of value-reversals). You can say, "We don't take him seriously." I reply, "That is exactly what gets most of his acquaintances into Hell: just what the devil-clown relies on." But he is not only this demon incarnate, he is in effect God's agent in a predetermined plan of divine retribution: the "scourge of God." Now by Tudor-Christian historical principles, this plan is *right*. Thus, in a real sense, Richard is a King who "can do no wrong"; for in the pattern of the justice of divine retribution on the wicked, he functions as an avenging angel. Hence my paradoxical title, "Angel with Horns."

The paradox is sharpened by what I have mainly passed by: the repulsiveness, humanely speaking, of the "justice." God's will it may be, but it sickens us: it is as pitiless as the Devil's (who is called in to execute it). The contrast with Marlowe's painless, dehumanized slaughterings in *Tamburlaine* is patent.

This overall system of *paradox* is the play's unity. It is revealed as a constant displaying of inversions, or reversals of meaning: whether we consider the verbal patterns (the *peripeteias* or reversals of act and intention or expectation); the antithesis of false and true in the histrionic character; or the constant inversions of irony. Those verbal capsizings I began by talking about, with their deliberate reversals to the opposite meaning in equivocal terms, are the exact correlatives of both the nature of man (or man in power: Richard) and of the nature of events (history); and of language too, in which all is conveyed.

But, start where you will, you come back to history; or to the pattern made out of the conflict of two "historical myths." The orthodox Tudor myth made history God-controlled, divinely prescribed and dispensed, to move things towards a God-ordained perfection: Tudor England. Such was the *frame* that Shakespeare took. But the total effect of Shakespeare's "plot" has quite a different effect from Halle: a very different meaning. Dr. Duthie may write, "But there is no doubt that Shakespeare saw history in the same light as Halle saw it."[7] I say there *is* doubt. Dover Wilson has nothing to offer but what he summarizes from Moulton, but his last sentence points my doubting way: "it appears, to me at least, unlikely that Shakespeare's 'main end' in *Richard III* was 'to show the working out of God's will in English history.' "[8] (The quotation he is discussing is from Tillyard's *Shakespeare's History Plays.*)[9] He can go no further because his own limitations on *Henry IV* inhibit his ever observing that the comic Richard has no more place in Halle's scheme than Falstaff has.

The other myth is that of Richard the Devil-King: the Crookback *monstrum deforme, ingens* whom Shakespeare *found* as a ready-made Senecan tyrant and converted into a quite different inverter of moral order: a ruthless, demonic comedian with a most un-Senecan sense of humour and the seductive appeal of an irresistible gusto, besides his volcanic Renaissance energies. They are themselves demoralizing: *Tapfer sein ist gut*[10] is the antithesis of a Christian sentiment.

The outcome of this conflict of myths was Shakespeare's display of constant inversions of meaning; in all of which, two systems of meaning impinge and go over to their opposites, like the two "ways" of the cheveril glove. This applies equally to words and word-patterns; to the actor-nature; to dramatic ironies; and to events, as the hatch and brood of time, contrasted with opposite expectations.

As a result of the paradoxical ironic structure built from these inversions of meaning—built above all by Richard's demonic appeal—the naïve, optimistic, "Christian" principle of history, consoling and comfortable, modulates into its opposite. The "Christian" system of retribution is undermined, counter-balanced, by historic irony. (Do I need to insist that the coupling of "Christian" and "retribution" itself is a paradox? That the God of vengeance is *not* a Christian God; that his opposite is a God of mercy who has no representation in this play. If I do, I had better add that the so-called "Christian" frame is indistinguishable from a pagan one of Nemesis in which the "High all-seer" is a Fate with a cruel sense of humour.)

But do not suppose I am saying that the play is a "debunking of Tudor myth," or that Shakespeare is disproving it. He is not "proving" anything: not even that "Blind belief is sure to err/And scan his works in vain" (though I think that is *shown,* nevertheless). Contemporary "order"-thought spoke as if naïve faith saw true: God was above God's Englishmen and ruled with justice—which meant summary vengeance. This historic myth offered absolutes, certainties. Shakespeare in the Histories always leaves us with relatives, ambiguities, irony, a process thoroughly dialectical. Had he entirely accepted the Tudor myth, the frame and pattern of order, his way would have led, I suppose, towards writing *moral history* (which is what Dr. Tillyard and Dr. Dover Wilson and Professor Duthie have made *out* of him). Instead, his way led him towards writing *comic history.* The former would never have taken him to tragedy: the latter (paradoxically) did. Look the right way through the cruel-comic side of Richard and you glimpse Iago. Look back at him through his energy presented as evil, and you see Macbeth. And if you look at the irony of men's struggles in the nets of historic circumstance, the ironies of their pride and self-assurance, you will see Coriolanus; and you are past the great tragic phase and back in history again.

Notes

1.   T. S., *Selected Essays* (New York: Harcourt Brace, 1932), p. 90; reprinted from Introduction to *Seneca His Tenne Tragedies,* 1927.

2.   This contradicts, R. G. Moulton, *Shakespeare as a Dramatic Artist* (Oxford: Clarendon Press, 1885), p. 92, who says Richard is *not* "ambitious" (as Macbeth is): "never found dwelling upon the prize in view." This presumes a complete disconnection between *3 Henry VI* and *Richard III.* No such assumption is acceptable nowadays—nor was it sensible even then.

3.   W. B. Yeats, *The Collected Poems,* 2d ed. (New York: Macmillan, 1950), p. 187.

4.   "A part of that Power which always wills evil and yet always brings about good." (Goethe's *Faust Part I.* iii. 159–60)

5.   J. Middleton Murry, *Shakespeare,* (London: Cape, 1936), pp. 125–6, quotes the theatrical metaphors and remarks briefly on the conception of Richard as an actor.

6.   *New Temple* edn., William Shakespeare, *King Richard III,* ed. M. R. Ridley (London: J. M. Dent, 1935), p. 140.

7.   G. I. Duthie, *Shakespeare,* (London: Hutchinson, 1951), p. 118.

8.   *Richard III* ed., J. D. Wilson, (Cambridge: Cambridge University Press, 1954), p. xiv.

9.   E. M. W. Tillyard, *Shakespeare's History Plays* (London: Chatto and Windus, 1944), p. 208.

10.   "To be bold is good."

The Dark Generations of *Richard III*

MURRAY KRIEGER

Let me begin by remarking that I had half-jestingly thought of calling this essay "Richard III as Scourge and Purge." Not a highly serious way to begin a study of a work of the highest seriousness; but it should immediately indicate that I intend to break radically with the conventional treatments of the play as a Marlovian tragedy, even with those that allow the master Shakespeare a few extensions of the formula in his manipulation of it. For if we call Richard a scourge, then we are assuming that his victims somewhat deserve what he inflicts upon them; that they have been cruelly active themselves even if at the hands of Richard they are now rendered passive. And if we call him a purge, then we are assuming that he is in the service of the gods of a righteous future who must start afresh; that a guilt-ridden past, with all its weighty burdens, must be cast off by one of its own. If we think of Richard in these ways, then it is clear that the play is not uniquely his, nor the power and the evil uniquely his, as the Marlovian formula would have it.[1]

Even looking only at Richard's motivations, however, we find more than is in the world of Marlovian psychology. One need hardly invoke the insights of Freud to see that the lust which impels him is not solely directed toward power. Admittedly, one can point to his opening soliloquy where—in a Marlovian manner which denies the possibility of self-deception and the psychological complexity that goes with it—he announces his villain's role and his prideful assumption of it. Indeed one can strike this note earlier, as early as his perhaps finer soliloquy in *III Henry VI* (III.ii.124–195). Richard, then, does confront his villainy with a consciousness as candid as the actions which ensue from his villainy are consistent. But there is another and a less conscious motive being continually revealed in these speeches. He invariably couples the assertion of political power with the sexual assertion of manliness. And he admits that he embraces the former only because he is, as monster, denied the embrace of sexual love.

Early in the soliloquy from *III Henry VI* Richard despairs of ever attaining the crown as he lists those who would precede him in the line of succes-

From Murray Krieger, *Criticism* 1 (1959): 32–48.

sion. Well, then, he must turn to another source of masculine satisfaction: "I'll make my heaven in a lady's lap." But the dialectic proceeds:

> O miserable thought! and more unlikely
> Than to accomplish twenty golden crowns.
> Why, love forswore me in my mother's womb:
> And, for I should not deal in her soft laws,
> She did corrupt frail nature with some bribe, . . .
> (III.ii.151–155)

There is no alternative, then. However impossible to attain, it must be power after all: "I'll make my heaven to dream upon the crown." In the opening soliloquy of *Richard III* he notes that the advent of peace demands that the warrior be transformed into the lover. Significantly, it is by a sexual image that he describes the warrior, so that the role as lover may follow naturally from the battle's end. The image tells us something also of Richard's deeper motives in the public life as well as in the private life.

> Grim-visag'd war hath smooth'd his wrinkled front;
> And now, instead of mounting barbed steeds
> To fright the souls of fearful adversaries,
> He capers nimbly in a lady's chamber
> To the lascivious pleasing of a lute.
> (I.i.9–13)

It is clear from Richard's language that he dotes, perhaps perversely, on the sensual abandon in the battle of love—on the "sportive tricks" one plays with "a wanton ambling nymph." And again he decides there is nothing left for him but "to prove a villain" since he "cannot prove a lover."

His villainy seems to him to be chargeable to the heavens since it is but a moral reflection of his deformity.

> The midwife wonder'd, and the women cried
> "O! Jesus bless us. He is born with teeth!"
> And so I was; which plainly signified
> That I should snarl and bite and play the dog.
> Then, since the heavens have shap'd my body so,
> Let hell make crook'd my mind to answer it.
> I have no brother, I am like no brother;
> And this word "love," which greybeards call divine,
> Be resident in men like one another,
> And not in me: I am myself alone.
> (*III Henry VI,* V.vi.74–83)

But if he is not a man among men, neither, of course, is he a beast. He may "play the dog," but he does so as a monstrous perversion of man. As he answers Anne, who insists that even the fiercest beast knows pity, "But I know none, and therefore am no beast" (*Richard III*, I.ii.72). A unique monster, then, excluded from the order of men as from the order of beasts, he sees himself indeed as representing a gap in nature, a lump of chaos thrust into the midst of the natural order. And so he will do the business of chaos in the political and moral order. This dedication to chaos, physical and political, stirs him from his early soliloquy,

> [Love] did corrupt frail nature with some bribe,
> To shrink mine arm up like a wither'd shrub;
> To make an envious mountain on my back,
> Where sits deformity to mock my body;
> To shape my legs of an unequal size;
> To disproportion me in every part,
> Like a chaos, or an unlick'd bear-whelp
> That carries no impression like the dam.
> (*III Henry VI*, III.ii.155–162)

to the speech before his final battle:

> March on, join bravely, let us to 't pell-mell;
> If not to heaven, then hand in hand to hell.
> (*Richard III*, V.iii.312–313)

And since force is the arm of chaos even as right is the sometimes feeble arm of order, so must he dedicate himself to force as well. It should be clear, however, that, far from being his essential motivation force, like the power to which it leads, is a very derivative one. Shakespeare's probing instruments are too delicate to stop, with Marlowe short of cutting away a little lower layer.

But there is even more psychological complexity than this to Richard. His will to political power is not merely a substitute for his frustrated will to sexual power, but, as his "mounting" warrior may have intimated, is a perversion of it so that sexual elements become curiously intermingled with political ones. His incapacities as a lover continue to torment him, but he welcomes and even relishes the torment. He parades his deformity before women even as he parades it before himself. And he takes an "underground" delight in both displays. His dialogue with Anne is a brilliant manifestation of this strange exhibitionism. Surely we cannot account for Richard's behavior in this scene solely on the grounds of his lust for power. Granted that Richard feels this marriage to be a political necessity (as he tells us I.i.157–159), that by their union the houses of York and Lancaster can be joined; nevertheless he hardly undertakes his wooing in a way that will ensure success. On the contrary he seems to enjoy this occasion since it presents every conceivable obstacle. It is the most inauspicious moment for him to woo her. Further, he makes it perfectly clear (I.i.160–162) that other foul deeds remain to be done before the marriage can serve its purpose; in other words, that there is no rush about wooing Anne, that he can await a more favorable opportunity.

Let us note the circumstances of the present occasion: Anne is the mourner in the funeral procession of her father-in-law, Henry VI, murdered by Richard, as Anne knows. And it is still but very little more time since the death of her husband whom Richard co-murdered (*III Henry VI,* V.v). Of course, Richard's physical handicaps, in such marked contrast to Anne's murdered Edward—"fram'd in the prodigality of nature," as Richard disdainfully acknowledges—will always damage his chances; but they surely should prompt him to seek out a better time, if success is his primary objective. But both before and after the scene Richard indicates his special pleasure in wooing her at such a disadvantage. And he begins in the worst way possible, by forcibly interrupting the funeral procession, by allowing the conversation to enter those channels which must render him most hateful to Anne, by leading her to engage with him in a repartee that is on his side callously witty. His bantering appears calculated to inspire in her a loathing that must issue in her humiliating outcry, "thou lump of foul deformity." His love of self-torture having accomplished this much, he pursues her, still as her lover lest her revulsion abate. He speaks of the fitness of Henry VI for heaven and she, of Richard's for hell. Richard insists there is one other place for which he is fit:

ANNE:	Some dungeon.
RICH:	Your bedchamber.
ANNE:	Ill rest betide the chamber where thou liest!
RICH:	So will it, madam, till I lie with you.

(I.ii.111–113)

At this point fair Richard has turned Petrarchan lover. He blames Anne's beauty for his murderous actions, and when she threatens to destroy that beauty, like the sonneteer he answers,

> These eyes could not endure that beauty's wreck;
> You should not blemish it, if I stood by:
> As all the world is cheered by the sun,
> So I by that; it is my day, my life.
> (I.ii.127–130)

When she wishes that her eyes were basilisks to strike him dead, he again has the appropriate retort, even using the appropriate conceit:

> I would they were, that I might die at once;
> For now they kill me with a living death.
> (I.ii.152–153)

Having won her, Richard matches his contempt for her with his pride in himself.

> Was ever woman in this humour woo'd?
> Was ever woman in this humour won?
> I'll have her; but I will not keep her long.
> What! I, that kill'd her husband and his father,
> To take her in her heart's extremest hate;
> With curses in her mouth, tears in her eyes,
> The bleeding witness of her hatred by;
> Having God, her conscience, and these bars against me,
> And I no friends to back my suit withal,
> But the plain devil and dissembling looks,
> And yet to win her, all the world to nothing!
>
> (I.ii.128–138)

And his perverse self-mockery returns. If in spite of all these obstacles he has won the right to succeed his handsome predecessor, then, he ironically reasons, he must suppose himself to have underestimated his sexual attractiveness all along. He shall have to get mirrors and tailors to care for his fine figure and make a proper lover. In the opening soliloquy of the play he remarked that in this time of peace he, as a warrior who could not be a lover, had

> . . . no delight to pass away the time,
> Unless to see my shadow in the sun
> And descant on mine own deformity.
>
> (I.i.25–27)

Now he closes the soliloquy which follows his success with Anne by reverting to this idea, this time with the bitterness only renewed by his amatory conquest:

> Shine out, fair sun, till I have bought a glass,
> That I may see my shadow as I pass.
>
> (I.ii.263–264)

Toward the end of the play there is the similar scene with Queen Elizabeth when he woos her for her daughter's hand. Again he chooses the worst possible time since, his murder of her children having only recently occurred, she has come with his mother to join in cursing him. Again he seems to succeed and again his success produces in him only contempt for her. Does it not appear possible, then, not merely that Richard pursues power as single-mindedly as he would a mistress, but also that he pursues power so that he may coerce a mistress—one who will have to play the game of treating him as lover and who, though it only aggravates her revulsion, will painfully sport with him as with one "fram'd in the prodigality of nature?" And in self-laceration Richard will enjoy it both ways: because his villainous intelligence has forced his mistress to receive him as lover and because his monstrous ugliness increases her horror and his pain in his unnatural role. Surely this is hardly a hero-villain of a single dimension.

I should like now to return briefly to the scene between Richard and Anne in order to ask an obvious question, one answer to which I find most illuminating. How is it, in view of Richard's handicaps of person and occasion and in view of his tactics, that Anne accepts him? We may ask a similar question about Elizabeth in the other scene I referred to—if we assume that she was sincere in her acceptance of him, an assumption that her later acceptance of Richmond makes doubtful for some readers. And we may ask similar questions about many other characters, some of them mostly openly at odds with Richard, who at times seem not to see through his transparent dissembling. Rivers, for example, whom Richard is shortly to dispose of, commends a sentiment of Richard's as "virtuous" and "Christian-like"; and Hastings, just before he learns that Richard has condemned him to death, says of Richard after observing his apparent good humor,

> I think there's never a man in Christendom
> Can lesser hide his love or hate than he;
> For by his face straight shall you know his heart.
> (III.iv.53–55)

The usual answer to these questions seems unacceptable. If we take these characters at their face value, then Shakespeare is asking us to believe the unbelievable: that otherwise intelligent and sometimes brilliant characters (his women, for example, prove their brilliance in their repartee with Richard) are somehow fooled by an open hypocrite who has continually proved a villain even before the events of the play begin. Even if there were no other instance of this but the scene with Anne, does it not seem preposterous that Shakespeare would try to foist it upon his audience? Nor can the insistence upon Shakespeare's youth and inexperience in this early play and upon the improbabilities encouraged by Elizabethan dramatic convention explain away so irresponsible an attitude toward dramatic propriety.

The alternative explanation is obvious. These characters know from first to last that Richard is a villain, so that they are never fooled by him. What they do they do in full knowledge of the truth. If they appear to be convinced by any poses he assumes, it is because they themselves are playing the hypocrite's role. Much of the difficulty in interpreting the play arises from an inability to recognize the villainy that pervades the entire stage. Perhaps once again it is because we have been too quick to see the play as if it were written by Marlowe, with a hero-villain gigantically alone in an inexorable surge which drowns all the innocents in his path. I shall eventually suggest that in *Richard III* there are no innocents; that rather than intruding himself as an alien force into the world of the play, Richard is a purified and thus extreme symbol, a distillation, of that world; that the evil stems not from Richard but from a history he shares with the others even if it finds its essential representative in him. Even the young princes, still children and thus still unsinning, must share with their forebears the burden of guilt.

The answer which common-sense dictates—that the characters are not taken in by Richard but, consciously or unconsciously, must be engaging in deception themselves—finds support at several points in the play. It finds support, for example, in those minor and yet telling scenes in which Shakespeare lets us see what political facts are so obvious that even the common man is aware of them. Thus in a discussion of the affairs of the commonwealth by a group of citizens, one of them simply states, "O! full of danger is the Duke of Gloucester" (II.iii.27). Even more precisely to the point, we find a scrivener commenting on the published report of Hastings' indictment issued after his execution in order to justify it:

> Here's a good world the while! Who is so gross
> That cannot see this palpable device?
> Yet who so bold, but says he sees it not?
> Bad is the world; and will come to nought,
> When such ill dealing must be seen in thought.
>
> (III.vi.10–14)

We are evidently being informed here of the deception, however enforced, which pervades the court. Surely we must acknowledge that what the scrivener and even the "gross" cannot help but see, the high characters of the play must see. Hastings himself, conscious that his pretended trust in Richard, quoted in part above, did not save his head, says in comment and in warning to the still remaining fawners as he is led off to execution, "They smile at me who shortly shall be dead" (III.iv.109). He is recalling, no doubt, his own recent satisfaction in hearing of the execution of Rivers, Grey, and Vaughan, when he, still seemingly beguiled by Richard, could confidently mock (even as we know he himself has already been marked for execution):

> But I shall laugh at this a twelve-month hence,
> That they which brought me in my master's hate,
> I live to look upon their tragedy.
>
> (III.ii.57–59)

Finally, it is quite likely that the confessed villainy and hypocrisy of Richard's first victim in the play, "false, fleeting, perjur'd Clarence," set the precedent for our moral evaluation of those who follow.

Richard, then, is a fox among foxes. He is wittier than the others and more successful. But his victories can be attributed not so much to the fact that he is more villainous than the rest, as to the fact that he is more consistently and self-admittedly villainous. Whatever reason Anne may give herself or him, she can accept him as successor to her sweet and lovely gentleman, his victim, for but one reason—her self-interest. A widow of the ousted House of Lancaster, she must sense that the ruthless Richard's star is rising. Thus she is serious in her toying acknowledgment to Richard, ". . . you teach me how to flatter you" (I.ii.224). Disdaining the bitter role of her mother-in-law, Queen Margaret, she must instead take Richard, swallowing her curses and pretending to have been successfully wooed—which is of course precisely the game that Richard expects her to play and that his perverseness, as we have seen, demands that she play. It is one of the satisfactions he seeks in power. We must either believe this or believe not only in her apparent conviction that "the murderous Machiavel" has turned Petrarchan lover but also in her apparent desire for him, deformity and all.

Elizabeth is later equally politic in her reception of Richard's addresses to her daughter. One may argue that she is merely putting him off for the moment since she has intended her daughter for Richmond, as we learn in the next scene. But there is no evidence in her scene with Richard that she need fear him, nor does she fear him; for she is as outspoken as she pleases. Why, then, pretend to accept him? Why, having come to curse, does she remain to welcome his addresses? Is it not more likely that, with Richard still in power and Richmond's venture surely questionable at best, she will play it safe and mother a queen regardless of the victor? So she pretends to be won by Richard's oath (IV.iv.397–417) and by his promised moral conversion.

And so it is with the others of his victims who play at being deceived by him. But like Anne and Elizabeth, these others have moral pretensions as well. We see these pretensions on display frequently: for example, in the solicitous mannerisms of the court (I.iii and II.i) and in the self-righteousness of the lamenting women (IV.iv.). It may be that there is this difference between Richard's seeming hypocrisy and theirs. Richard's is only seeming; theirs is real. When Richard insists that he "cannot flatter and look fair," that as "a plain man" he wants only to "live and think no harm"; when he chides himself for being "too childish-foolish for this world," he knows he is in no danger of being believed. He is laughing at his pose and at their reception of it (often explicitly in an aside), knowing that as deceivers themselves they must play the game with a straight face. His wit enables him to delight in the farce as he forces them to appear to accept the most outrageous of his moralizing utterances. In short, while the others are pretending at being decent, Richard is rather pretending at being a hypocrite. No thorough-going and utterly unscrupulous villain need actually be one.

Richard would seem to be a self-conscious and consistent version of the other characters. They cannot bear to witness in Richard the logical consequence of their own tendencies—which is perhaps another reason that they often rush to accept his pretended pretensions. Nor can they endure to live with this purified reflection of their self-destructive instincts—which may metaphorically justify the fact that so many of them fall prey to him. Each falls prey to his own worst self. Anne is perhaps a perfect symbol here. Early in the action, as we learn more explicitly later, she is led by her personal and political ills to curse Richard and his future wife. It is of course herself she has damned: the torment she suffers while alive, and the unnatural death which it is implied she suffers, are inflicted by Richard only insofar as he is her agent carrying out her curse.

There are yet other indications of the unrelieved ugliness of the world of *Richard III*. Some of those who defend the Marlovian character of the play cite its humorlessness as evidence. No low-comedy vaudeville routines seem to be found here. But this is only a superficial view. For example, the scene between the two murderers as they confront each other and then Clarence (I.iv) has all the earmarks of such a routine. We may miss the similarities because of the morbidity of the occasion: it is, after all, cold-blooded fratricide that is being committed. This stark reality may nag at us and mar our enjoyment of the quips leading to the brilliantly cynical discourse on conscience which may well rival Falstaff's on honor in *I Henry IV*. But this is precisely Shakespeare's point, I take it. While much of the scene takes the form of so-called comic relief, it is a bitter perversion of this device. The scene indicates what has become of humor in the world Shakespeare creates here: it is a humor bitterly transformed to callous irony, a humor too chill to sustain even a suggestion of human warmth.

In the witty dialogue between the murderers all moral values are inverted. Conscience, "a dangerous thing," finally becomes "the devil," so that to obey it and spare Clarence is now a diabolical act. To resist it and murder Clarence is to be "a tall man that respects thy reputation." The lively and biting duels of wit between Richard and Anne and between Richard and Elizabeth are of course other examples of these fearful analogues to comic routines. They may even suggest to us, in an unguarded moment, the brilliance of Benedick and Beatrice in *Much Ado*. Even the terrifying moment of Queen Margaret's systematic and all-inclusive curse is not immune to Richard's ready and deadly wit (I.iii.233–240). He toys with her at the height of her ritualistic fervor until, deflated, she weakly pleads with him, "O, let me make a period to my curse!" And even here his bantering does not stop.

There is bitter humor too in those moments when Richard turns his wit on himself in his public poses, although, of course, always in an aside or a soliloquy. When, responsible for it himself, he speaks forgivingly of those who have caused the imprisonment of his brother Clarence, Rivers congratulates him:

> A virtuous and a Christian-like conclusion,
> To pray for them that have done scath to us.
> (I.iii.316–317)

Richard says aloud, "So do I ever." To himself he adds, "Being well-advis'd; For had I curs'd now, I had curs'd myself." Always there is this final bitter twist. We can argue about whether all this ought to go by the name of humor or comedy, but the term is not important. It is important, however, to note that these passages are analogous to what in many other plays seems more properly comic and, therefore, that this brutal wit is as close to the comic as Shakespeare can come in the infernal world he is creating. It is true to this world and, in its differences from his wit elsewhere, it tells us much about the moral darkness through which his characters wander to their deaths—symbolically self-inflicted through Richard, one of their own.

There is yet a rather evident argument for the general viciousness of the characters; but it is an argument which is conclusive. It asserts its force as early as Act I, Scene iii, when Queen Margaret appears and interrupts the self-righteous and yet haggling claims and counterclaims of the members of the royal court. And since to some extent she is Chorus as well as Nemesis, we must give credence to her characterization of them:

> Hear me, you wrangling pirates, that fall out
> In sharing that which you have pill'd from me!
> Which of you trembles not that looks on me?
> If not, that, I am queen, you bow like subjects,
> Yet that, by you depos'd, you quake like rebels?
> (I.iii.158–161)

There is another reason why we should be especially moved by her words. She is, after all, the widow of the last king of the now deposed Lancastrian line, the line dear to the hearts of the Elizabethans who associated the Tudors intimately with it; and she is addressing the far less favored Yorkists. They are, then, usurpers all, and all fall under her curse. Strangely, although it is Richard whom she most detests and most heatedly condemns, it is he who becomes the instrument of her vengeance. True, she cannot rest content until he is also fallen (IV.iv.71–78). But before this final prayer for his death Margaret has recounted the murderous services which Richard, the Yorkist to end Yorkists, has performed for her; she has, in effect, thanked God for him.

> O upright, just, and true-disposing God,
> How do I thank thee, that this carnal cur
> Preys on the issue of his mother's body,
> And makes her pew-fellow with others' moan.
> (IV.iv.55–58)

So Richard does serve, in part, as an arm of Lancastrian justice.

But our problem is not so simple or so simply factional. For neither Margaret nor the Lancastrian cause is, after all, much less vicious than the Yorkist. We hear in the play about the previous curse laid on Margaret by Richard's father, the nobler Richard, Duke of York. It is the success of this curse which leads her to match it with her own. When we turn back to *III Henry VI* (I.iv), the circumstances which lead to York's curse frighten us with what they reveal of Margaret's unrestrained cruelty in her days of power. She is a termagant in the earlier play. Hers is a ruthlessness to match the later Richard's: she merits the curses she brings down upon herself as Richard merits his. We can, then, look to the Lancastrian—the injured party, the summoner of vengeance, in *Richard III*—for moral righteousness no more than we can look to the Yorkists for it. If Margaret's curses settle our judgment of the Yorkists, immediate history as revealed in *III Henry VI* makes up our minds similarly about their predecessors.

History indeed holds the answer to all questions about the moral atmosphere of the play—or rather Shakespeare's dramatic version of history in the *Henry VI* plays which precede *Richard III* and in the plays from *Richard II* through *Henry V* to which he turned shortly after *Richard III*. It seems reasonable to assume that Shakespeare, after *Richard III*, followed history back to Richard II in order to trace the origin and the course of the troubles that culminate in the War of the Roses and that—from the viewpoint of the confident Elizabethans—are removed with the death of the remover, Richard III, and with the advent of the Tudors. Shakespeare appears to have viewed English political history from the fall of Richard II until the rise of Henry VII as a single drama; and it is rewarding for us briefly to do so even though Shakespeare produced the first four sections after he had completed the final four. It is the usurpation-theme which dominates the plays. The unruly, destructive forces unleashed by Bolingbroke roar uncontrolled through the land. What the eminently practical and calculating Bolingbroke meant to be a slight and limited blood-letting for the health of the state becomes a blood-bath which drowns generation after generation. Finally Richard III, the blood-bath personified in its purest form, cleanses the land of the last of the guilt-ridden generations, so that with his own bloody end England may begin anew with Henry Tudor, symbol of the conciliation of the past and its feuds. We see, then, why the world of this play must be so unqualifiedly ugly. It is worth noting too that England's salvation, Richmond, must come from outside, from France, like a breath of fresh air, since this world of England is so entirely foul.

As there is this spatial gap between bloody England and the forces of a new day, so in the beginning there was the temporal gap of a generation between the last of those who had a sound view of kingship and those, like Richard II and Bolingbroke, who courted national ill-health. In *Richard II*, only Gaunt and York, the last of the older generation, of the "seven vials" "of Edward's sacred blood," have a full and traditional sense both of the obligations owing to kingship and of the obligations owed by kingship. Richard II, with a decadent version of absolutism, is selfishly aware only of the former of these obligations. Bolingbroke, a modern who has broken with the absolutist principle, has no principle of governmental order to which to appeal except force and expedience; and these are hardly principles conducive to lasting order. Thus he usurps. And, unable to replace the dogma of divine right with another that would equally symbolize the maintenance of the state as an orderly and continuing establishment, he cannot re-order the chaos he has loosed.[2] Nor can those who follow, and blood begets blood.

It may hardly be original to state that Shakespeare relates analogically the traditional views of reason and emotion in the individual to those of order and chaos in the state. But it may be more original to use this analogy in order to establish the extent to which Richard III symbolizes his political and moral milieu. We need say little about the chaos which for Shakespeare must join with usurpation as ruler, upon the deposition of a rightful king—symbol of reason in the state—except to point to Ulysses' famous speech about cosmic, political, and psychological order in *Troilus and Cressida* (I.iii.75–137). Toward the end of this speech is the intimation that when reason is perverted through enslavement to emotion, an overthrow of the proper hierarchy has occurred—a usurpation of mental authority and an introduction of chaos in the individual personality. It is the extremity mentioned in *Venus and Adonis* (792), "When reason is the bawd to lust's abuse." But to return to the words of Ulysses concerned with the loss of order:

> Force should be right; or rather, right and wrong,
> Between whose endless jar justice resides,
> Should lose their names, and so should justice too.
> Then every thing includes itself in power,
> Power into will, will into appetite;
> And appetite, an universal wolf,
> So doubly seconded with will and power,
> Must make perforce an universal prey,
> And last eat up himself.
>
> (*Troilus and Cressida,* I.iii.116–124)

But are these lines not a fine description of Richard as I delineated him earlier? Richard is surely the darling of almost a century of English history which has seized upon him and created in him a reflection of itself: he is an incarnation of the spirit of usurpation and thus of chaos. And we saw at the outset that he is, almost literally, a lump of chaos, physical and political, whose very existence defies the natural order. If chaos in the state reflects politically the perversion of the proper government of emotion, then we should expect this perversion in Richard. And we saw earlier too that in Richard the two most forceful emotions, the will to sexual power and the will to political power, are seriously perverted. Finally in Richard we have a brilliance of intellect, but criminally distorted in order to serve his perverse desires—again just what is required of usurpation incarnate.

But if history realizes itself in Richard as its representative, it also uses him—the embodied perfection of its horrors—to purge the world of itself, to end its reign. In a way English history is thus converted to eschatology with

Richmond and the Tudors representing a Second Coming which gives birth to the golden world. I have already noted that Richmond returns from another country to be England's salvation. Only under his aegis, according to Elizabeth, can Dorset be safe "from the reach of hell" (IV.i.43). Richmond, who looms throughout the play as a source of help from afar, in effect plays the Saviour, even as the saintly if ineffectual Henry VI has served, like John the Baptist, to prophesy his dominion.

The spirit of usurpation and of chaos has been abroad in varying degrees among all of Shakespeare's characters after the deposition of Richard II. Thus Richard III, as we have seen, is their symbol too—a fearful projection of that worst self which they never dare confront. And for them to confront it reflected in Richard—as many of them have to—is usually fatal, since they are overcome by the unrelieved darkness of its aspect.

There is one final way in which the deadly weight of history enters the play: it asserts itself as ritual. The force of the dark generations past is felt especially, through their curses. And the curse is a formalized affair, as we have seen from Margaret's insistence on giving it a proper ending. It must be formalized into ritual if, as a form of magic, it is to be efficacious. It invariably is efficacious. Margaret's extended curse contributes a structural framework to the play. In it she dispenses the fates of almost all the characters. The subsequent action is constructed largely in order to see her curse realized as, one after another, its objects succumb. Shakespeare induces us to keep count of them as her victims by the use of various devices: for example, by inserting brief pre-execution scenes in which the power of the curse is explicitly attested, and even once by having her reappear to calculate her bloody gains. And, in the realm of ritual and magic, the victims are hers rather than Richard's; for Richard is also her victim, one who is sufficiently destructive before turning self-destructive. I have already noted that Anne's earlier curse, of which we do not learn fully until considerably later, works only too well. Although it comes finally to be aimed at herself as well as at Richard, the curse once spoken cannot be unsaid nor its effects neutralized. Even the Duchess of York, the widow who matches in generation the Lancastrian widow (even as Elizabeth matches Anne), must add her curse to the others her son must bear. And the night before Bosworth the ghosts of Richard's victims deliver, again in proper form, the final curse, the same curse that Faustus had delivered upon himself: "Despair and die!" They also bless Richmond and, since they represent York as well as Lancaster, they put the seal of reconciliation on the House of Tudor. For example, the ghosts of the Yorkist princes say to the sleeping Richmond,

> Live, and beget a happy race of kings!
> Edward's unhappy sons do bid thee flourish.
> (V.iii.157–158)

But Margaret's is not the first curse in the play. We have seen that it is inspired by what has seemed to be the efficacy of York's earlier curse in *III Henry VI*. If his curse has bereft her of power and family, then why should she not answer it with one aimed at those who have been the executioners of his curse? With Margaret's curse reaching for its precedent back into the history that precedes the action of the play, it seems as if we could trace curse upon curse back through the bloody generations to Richard II. And when we turn to *Richard II* (written, of course, not long after *Richard III*), we find at the very start of civil strife speeches by Richard (III.iii.85–100) and by Carlisle (IV.i.136–149) which are half prophecy of the bloodshed ahead and half curse calling for it.

There is another form of ritual in the play—the lamentation of the women and children. It is a competitive telling over of their woes, which, since they are of royal blood, are the woes of history. It takes the form of a stylized, chant-like rivalry of grief among those left by the dark generations to linger on the stage. A simple passage will reveal how rigidly formalized it can be:

Q. ELIZ.:   Give me no help in lamentation;
           I am not barren to bring forth complaints:
           All springs reduce their currents to mine eyes
           That I, being govern'd by the watery moon,
           May send forth plenteous tears to drown the world!
           Ah! for my husband, for my dear lord Edward.

CHIL.:   Ah! for our father, for our dear lord Clarence.

DUCH.:   Alas! for both, both mine, Edward and Clarence.

Q. ELIZ.:   What stay had I but Edward? and he's gone.

CHIL.:   What stay had we but Clarence? and he's gone.

DUCH.:   What stays had I but they? and they are gone.

Q. ELIZ.:   Was never widow had so dear a loss.

CHIL.:   Were never orphans had so dear a loss.

DUCH.:   Was never mother had so dear a loss.
           Alas! I am the mother of these griefs:
           Their woes are parcell'd, mine is general.
           She for an Edward weeps, and so do I;
           I for a Clarence weep, so doth not she;
           These babes for Clarence weep, and so do I;
           I for an Edward weep, so do not they:
           Alas! you three on me, threefold distress'd,

> Pour all your tears, I am your sorrow's nurse,
> And I will pamper it with lamentation.

> (II.ii.66–88)

There is no need to comment at length about the echoes and refrains in the passage, its symmetry, the effective closing of its first and last lines with the word "lamentation." Similar comparisons of sorrows occur among Margaret, the Duchess of York, and Elizabeth (IV.iv), and (though less clearly in the ritual pattern) between Elizabeth and Anne (IV.i). The very impersonality of the lamentation suggests its historic rather than individual authenticity. The characters are taking a recognized role, playing once for their generation a part that has been played many times, borrowing from history words and tears that have rarely gone unused.

In the ritual of lamentation and in the ritualistic curses which successive generations form in answer to one another, we are eventually carried back far beyond Richard II in history and tradition—back to those other dramas of lust and blood and Nemesis, to those extended cycles about family and domain with which Western tragedy began. Perhaps it is with Greek tragedy, rather than with Marlowe or even Seneca, the *Richard III* has its most essential and most intimate connections.

Notes

1. It ought perhaps to be added that, from my unorthodox point of view, Sir Laurence Olivier's film version of the play falls into most of the usual traps of interpretation.

2. For evidence of a similarly corrupt moral atmosphere in the plays about reigns earlier than Richard III's see LEONARD UNGER, "Deception and Self-Deception in Shakespeare's *Henry IV*," in *The Man in the Name* (Minneapolis: University of Minnesota Press, 1956), pp. 3–17.

Linguistic Contrasts in *Richard III*

Nicholas Brooke

1

The theatrical success of the role of Richard himself has tended to obscure the fact that his play presents any important critical problems. It was a very early play, the earliest of those which have consistently held the stage; and if it seemed dull in parts, or inconsistent, or in any way puzzling, that was easily accounted for by Shakespeare's immaturity. The fact that it is a work of outstanding technical virtuosity, in words and stagecraft, has not always been given the stress it needs; still less that the elaborate patterns worked out in it give it an exceptionally firm sense of structural unity.[1] It was treated in the eighteenth century as a tragedy, and compared (unfavourably, of course) with *Macbeth;* in the nineteenth century it was hardly allowed the tragic dignity, but rather regarded as melodrama, a prototype for *The Red Barn,* and fit matter for Lewis Carroll's parody. But the play thus criticized was scarcely the one that Shakespeare wrote: Colley Cibber's version was first acted at Drury Lane in July 1700, and though the proportion of Shakespeare's words gradually increased, Cibber's arrangement of material dominated stage versions until very recently indeed.[2] It concentrated exclusively on Richard himself; omitted scenes in which he did not appear, minimized Margaret's role (which was often cut entirely), and drastically pruned the formalized patterning of language which is so conspicuous a feature of the play, on the grounds that it was undramatic. This selective procedure is still often followed, most notably in Sir Laurence Olivier's film. And although the critics usually did read Shakespeare's text, their attention was for two centuries as selective as the actors'.

Recent critical history, and even more recent theatrical history, have however offered us a totally different view of the play, stressing the elements which Cibber excised: the tendency to ritual, the formalized staging and language, are held to be devices for binding together and rounding off the epically conceived sequence of moral-history plays about the Wars of the Roses. This attitude is not altogether irreconcilable with Cibber's activities, for it likewise assumes that the play is not viable as an independent unit, but is only intelligible when played in series with its predecessors. The dominant

From Nicholas Brooke, *Shakespeare's Early Tragedies* (London: Methuen, 1968). Reprinted with permission of the publisher.

role of Richard can be assimilated if he is seen as the instrument of divine ret-ribution on a guilty society; but the notion that his career has any significance as tragedy is nowadays rarely expressed. The usual attitude seems to be that the play results from a rather uncomfortable fusion of two distinct purposes: a formal conclusion to the series on the one hand, and a lively melodrama about Richard himself on the other.

I am not concerned to deny that the formal aspects of the play develop from 2 and 3 *Henry VI,* nor that it is intended to conclude an impressive sequence. But it does not seem to me to be dependent on that sequence for its own quality, and it does seem to me to have its own most interesting unity. I want to argue here that the play, once deprived of its moral-history, was deprived of any adequate opposition to Richard; so that his stature, which Cibber might seem to have enhanced, was in fact diminished, and the decline from tragedy to melodrama became inevitable. On the other hand, concen-tration on the moral-history has tended to divert attention from the central-ity of Richard's disturbing vitality in the play, and so has tended also to pro-duce an unintelligent and boring play. My assertion is, therefore, that the two aspects of the play require each other, and that the contrast between them is not a technical accident which Shakespeare should have been concerned to minimize, but an important structural device, elaborated to its maximum effect in the use of contrasting linguistic and dramatic modes, with a conse-quence which can properly be called tragic.

II

Such a contrast is by no means new in this play. As the series of histories moves towards its conclusion, we become aware of a mounting weight of rit-ual on the stage; an echoing series of scenes in patterned form and patterned speech lead on from 2 and 3 *Henry VI* into the highly formalized structure and writing of *Richard III* itself. This mounting tide of ritual is punctuated by actions of violence—battles, murders, executions; a sequence which itself becomes by repetition a pattern, a kind of anti-ritual of chaotic violence, which is inclined towards grotesque comedy in Richard's famous comment on Hastings:

> Chop off his head—something we will determine.
> (III.i. 193)

Simultaneously, as the actions of men accumulate in destruction, the lamentations of women mount in chorus from the solo voice of Margaret in Act I to the assembly of weeping dowagers in Act IV:

> I had an Edward, till a Richard kill'd him;
> I had a husband, till a Richard kill'd him:
> Thou hadst an Edward, till a Richard kill'd him;
> Thou hadst a Richard, till a Richard kill'd him.
>
> (IV. iv. 40–3)

And so on—as we may easily feel—for far too long. Too long because, among other reasons, we cannot for the life of us remember who these Edwards were, though we remember well enough who the Richard is that concludes every line. The theory runs that seeing *Richard III* in series with the other histories would give this jingle new significance, for we should then know all the references. This I do not believe; not simply because in practice (e.g. at Stratford in 1964) it hardly works out that way, but because it seems to me that the form of language itself precludes such precise intelligence. Even if we have studied the cast lists and the genealogical table and carried our knowledge fresh to the performance of this scene, as Margaret speaks we shall forget the detailed identifications: the names roll on in ritualized accumulation until their whole weight is laid on the single focus, Richard:

> From forth the kennel of thy womb hath crept
> A hell-hound that doth hunt us all to death.
>
> (47–8)

The ritual repetition piles up the roll of the accusing dead in *un*-particularized accumulation to convert Richard from his natural state of man into that of a sub-human figure of evil. In this process the identical names fit easily; it is the more singular titles that are awkward to assimilate. We forget the Harrys and the Edwards; but Rivers, Vaughan, and Grey stick out. Shakespeare absorbs them adroitly into the anonymous pattern by an exceptional use of rhyme:

> And the beholders of this frantic play,
> Th' adulterate Hastings, Rivers, Vaughan, Grey . . .
>
> (68–9)

The jingling rhyme distracts attention from the names and makes even them part of the sing-song litany, the generalized accumulation of death. The intensity of the ritual incantation was first developed from more ordinary blank verse through couplets in Margaret's asides.

This technical device clinches the function of language I have been dwelling on: it is to generalize and to de-humanize the sense of events; not to recapitulate our knowledge of detail, but to transcend the detail in creation of a larger pattern in which individuals lose their independence and identity. Just as the litany of the church overwhelms us with the *number* of evils from which the good Lord should deliver us, rather than calls our attention to their separate identities. One aspect of the rhetoric of the play finds its climax here, not in imitation of Seneca, but in echo of liturgical forms, such as the ancient "Ubi sunt" theme to which Margaret proceeds:

> Where is thy husband now? Where be thy brothers?
> Where be thy two sons? Wherein dost thou joy?
>
> (92–3)

And so on.

I have somewhat laboured this rather obvious point, because awareness of it seems to me necessary to what I want to say about the play. It is this aggregation of events into a generalized momentum which seems to me to represent the fundamental sense of "history" in the play; and it is this development which links it most closely to *Henry VI*. None of Shakespeare's histories, not even *1 Henry VI*, is a mere chronicle; but *Richard III* is the most remote of them all from mere chronicling. The events are there, but in unfamiliar proportions, so that (for instance) the murder of Clarence is more conspicuous than that of the boy princes. Interpretation is always more prominent than event: Richard's coronation is not shown, so that the stress remains on the blasphemous parody of election by which he reaches the throne. History, the legacy from the earlier plays, becomes an order of chaos, a ritual of destruction that grows in power until it destroys the destroyer, Richard himself. Strictly speaking it is not Margaret and her pupils who destroy Richard, it is Richmond; and Richmond is something which they decidedly are not, an unequivocally "good"character. But it is quite impossible to see him as Richard's "mighty opposite" in the dramatic conflict of the play: the force that builds up against Richard till his fall becomes inevitable is not Richmond, but the ritual of history, the swelling chorus of a more-than-human force. Richmond is a *tertium quid,* the inheritor of the new land when the conflicting forces have destroyed each other.

History, therefore, becomes imaginatively felt as an impersonal force rolling on beyond the lives of individual men, who are thereby belittled and cannot achieve the stature of a tragic figure. It is against this weight that Richard's personality is pitted, with impressive wit and force. The conflict in the play becomes therefore almost a matter of conflicting genres, for the historical and the tragic as shown here represent radically contrasting ideas of value—history has no place for tragedy, and in the end we must balance one against the other.

III

The first need is to explore the technical means by which Richard is thus isolated from the ritual sense of the play, in order to define the significance of this isolation. For it is not, I think, simply a matter of his being a different character; nor is our response to him a simple matter. One way of accounting for our fascination with so repulsive a figure is indeed simple enough: it is psychologically fairly obvious that while we can delight in the machinations of a clever dog who cocks a snook at all rectitude, authority, and religion, we can simultaneously be complacently satisfied when he is properly punished in the end. This is a simple and familiar ambivalence; but how Shakespeare establishes this double delight, and what he constructs out of it, call for more precise attention to the play, and particularly to the different kinds of utterance found there.

I have pointed to the generalizing ritual patterns of words in IV. iv; that is the furthest the play goes in formality of speech. In contrast, I quoted also Richard's "Chop off his head," a shockingly *informal* treatment of an (obviously) serious matter. Opposite as those two utterances are, it is Margaret's which is closer to the play's norm, which is more insistently rhetorical than that of any other; ejaculations of the flexibility of private speech are almost confined to Richard himself. Even with him they are not common, but by virtue of their repeated surprise come to seem characteristic of his personality. Accepting his mother's blessing in II. ii, he continues aside:

> And make me die a good old man!
> That is the butt end of a mother's blessing;
> I marvel that her Grace did leave it out.
> (II. ii. 109–11)

It is not a gentlemanly tone, but it adds a dimension to the scene, not only by its caustic wit, but also by momentarily introducing a mundane level far from the rhetorical pitch at which the scene has been proceeding. The effect is the same in III. v when Richard recalls his mother as he plans to rumour her adultery:

> Yet touch this sparingly, as 'twere far off;
> Because, my lord, you know my mother lives.
> (III. v. 93–4)

The sentiment is hardly touching, because it is so inevitably ironic: but the possibility of sentiment is glanced at, more sharply than in all the wailing of the queens.

This punctuation of rhetorical formality with sudden penetrations of the mundanely human adds, by itself, a whole critical dimension to the play; and it is something peculiarly associated with Richard himself. He makes the contrast felt in the end of I. i:

> Which done, God take King Edward to his mercy,
> And leave the world for me to bustle in!
> (I. i. 151–2)

God's mercy versus the world, formal language versus "bustle"; and, one may now add, the formal structure of the play versus Richard. That awareness is sustained in I. ii, the *tour de force* of the wooing of Anne, which I shall discuss later. The scene is surprisingly convincing; but it is also a performance. And it must be a very good performance, or it does not work. The words are virtuoso, so must the acting be. The tendency of all Richards that I have seen is to do what Lamb condemned in Cooke's performance: to make the underlying villainy obvious all the time.[3] That is what Olivier did, and the scene lost all power. But the full descriptive notes which survive on Kean's performance make it clear that he did not do this.[4] He made the scene brilliantly persuasive, the charm real, and he triumphed. So that when he was alone on the stage after Anne's departure, and blew the gaff on his performance, the audience felt a sense of shock. A shock, of course, not of total surprise, but of recognition, of what had been always known yet almost forgotten.

Almost forgotten, but never quite: the scene was always rhetorical in an obtrusive if brilliant way. A spectacle of persuasion, not quite persuasion itself, however brilliantly based on psychological observation. This is what is made clear in Richard's soliloquy:

> Was ever woman in this humour woo'd?
> Was ever woman in this humour won?
> (I. ii. 227–8)

These lines are a parody of the rhetorical performance he has just given, and the point is enforced by the characteristically abrupt switch to direct speech which follows:

> I'll have her; but I will not keep her long.
> (229)

The abrupt change of utterance makes a sharp critical comment on the whole mode of the scene; in a way, on the whole play. The rhetorical mode in which *Richard III* is so ostentatiously written, and the formal structure which matches it, are not the result of Shakespeare uncritically doing his best in a given theatrical fashion (Senecan or otherwise): the rhetorical mode is known and placed, both for its splendour and its falsity, within the play. The distance which I have noted in general terms between Richard's interjections and the general tone of the play, can here be seen as directly critical exposure. A distinction is felt which is finally made explicit in Margaret's advice on how to curse:

> Think that thy babes were sweeter than they were,
> And he that slew them fouler than he is.
> Bett'ring thy loss makes the bad-causer worse;
> Revolving this will teach thee how to curse.
> (IV. iv. 120–3)

The relationship between rhetoric and reality could not be more plainly stated; that the words are put in Margaret's mouth confirms her as the only antagonist comparable to Richard himself. Elsewhere the agent of this critical exposure is, almost always, Richard alone; and this fact as much as any other sets him apart from the other actors and, what is more, sets him in a favourable light to other people's disadvantage. It is not a question of whether he is better or worse than other people, but simply that he is more real.

This sense of him makes everyone else mere actors in a play. It is one aspect of the rhetorical mode that it confines the actors within its limitations, from which only Richard and Margaret stand apart. In a sense this is ironical, because Richard himself is the supreme actor. From the actor's point of view, this is not one role, but many: the ardent wooer, the honest blunt puritan at the court of King Edward, the witty uncle with his nephew York, the devout scholar with his clerical tutors, and so on—it is a long list. It is this protean quality which makes him so theatrically brilliant, provided that the actor, like Kean, gives every role its full value, and does not, like Cooke, attempt the super-subtlety of reducing them all to one.

This condition in Richard's part has a further consequence. In *his* performance, the difference between "being" and "acting" is very clear; and it is when he is with others on the stage that he is acting, as (each in their single roles) so are they. Thus, as I said, it is with him alone that a dimension of reality is felt. It follows that his relation to the audience—to us—is essentially different from anyone else's and this is established in his very first speech, in the unusual manner of opening a play with the solo appearance of the leading actor.

Unusual, that is to say, for Shakespeare. Marlowe had opened *The Jew of Malta* and *Dr Faustus* with soliloquies from the heroes; but each of their speeches follows a prologue, so that they are already within the play. Richard's speech is itself a prologue as well as a soliloquy from the hero, though to some extent it shifts from the one into the other; from:

> Now is the winter of our discontent
> Made glorious summer by this sun of York;
> (I. i. 1–2)

into:

> But I—that am not shap'd for sportive tricks . . .
> (14)

This is not, however, soliloquy in the sense of the speaker talking to himself: it is an address to the audience, not so much taking them into his confidence as describing himself. This mode of initial self-description is, of course, taken over here from the old tradition of the morality play. But it is a mistake, I think, to suppose that Shakespeare uses it simply because this is an early play following familiar conventions. He did not do it in any other play, and it is very rare among his contemporaries; nor does he follow it in this play with similar speeches for any other character. In other words, this should be seen as a deliberately bold technique used for specific purposes in establishing the distinctive character of *this* play.

The first effect to note is that it supplies, very economically, a traditional role for Richard from the moralities, that of the Vice: a sardonic humorist, by origin a kind of clown, who attracted to himself the attributes of anti-Christ bent on the mocking destruction of accepted virtues: a singularly welcome figure whenever virtue becomes tedious or oppressive; but one in whom the audience's delight is always coupled with condemnation. This, of course, is Richard's role, as he claims in III. i:

> Thus, like the formal vice, Iniquity,
> I moralize two meanings in one word.
> (III. i. 82–3)

The Vice was commonly the star of a morality play, what the audience most wanted to see. He had, like other kinds of clown, a special relationship with the audience, a kind of sly ironic confidence insinuated between them and the other players; and this is also Richard's. Like most ironists, he secures the audience "on his side," and yet involves us even further when (again like most ironists) he betrays our trust, and turns out to be way beyond us, leaving us embarrassed as Baudelaire did: "Vous! hypocrite lecteur: mon semblable! mon frère!" Our condemnation of his evil is involved in recognition of our brotherhood with it.

This relationship between Richard and the audience is given a special emphasis because, as I said, he alone is given the morality address, he alone has any direct contact with the audience at all. It follows that, in the technical construction of the play, Richard is set apart from the other actors, not just in character, nor just in mode of speech, but also in theatrical mode. Everyone else is distanced from the audience, is in a sense taking part in a play within a play of which Richard is the presenter. We are forced to know them as actors acting just as, when Richard joins them, he is (more obviously) an actor acting; and the consequence of this alienation (the Brechtian term is appropriate) is a carefully imposed limitation on the sympathy or approval that other figures can have. The audience can never become closely involved with Anne or Elizabeth, Hastings or Buckingham. It is this critical detachment which is enforced in the unusually sustained rhetorical language of the play. The result is that the whole play is set in a perspective which I have compared to that of a play within a play: we have, continually revived by Richard's rare but very telling asides, a double view of what is happening: we view the patterns of formal development for themselves, and we know them for an artefact, a coldly formal order *imposed* on the warmer but less orderly matter of human life. If this alienation were less marked, we could more easily detach ourselves from Richard in sympathy for his victims.

Notes

1. This has been fully argued by A. P. Rossiter in *Angel with Horns* (London: Longmans, Green, 1961).

2. See Clifford Leech: "Shakespeare, Cibber, and The Tudor Myth" in *Shakespearian Essays,* ed. A. Thaler and N. Sanders, *Tennessee Studies in Literature,* 1964.

3. See *Lamb's Criticism,* ed. E. M. W. Tillyard (Cambridge: Cambridge University Press, 1923), pp. 52–3.

4. See *Oxberry's 1822 Edition of King Richard III, with the Descriptive Notes Recording Edmund Kean's Performance Made by James H. Hackett,* ed. A. S. Donner (London: Society for Theatre Research, 1959).

Richard III and Aristotelian Catharsis

ROY W. BATTENHOUSE

The Elizabethan apologists for tragedy, in those samples of their literary criticism which have come down to us, to some degree lack a sense of the full dimensions of tragedy's art. They incline to see in tragedy a moral exemplum. This emphasis stems in part from the influence of Horace and Seneca on Renaissance interpretations of Aristotle; and in part it is sometimes reinforced by a strain of puritanism among Elizabethan critics. Too often, therefore, poetry is defended chiefly for its moral utilitarianism. Thus, for Sidney, tragedy is "high and excellent" because it makes kings fear to be tyrants; and Puttenham praises it for showing "the just punishment of God in revenge of a vicious and evill life." In Nashe's view, tragedies are "sower pills of reprehension, wrapt up in sweete words"; for they never encourage any man to rebellion without also showing the wretched end of usurpers and "how just God is evermore in punishing of murther." Thomas Newton's apology for translating Seneca's tragedies was that the whole issue of every one of them beats down sin. And Thomas Heywood explained in his *Apology for Actors:* "If we present a Tragedy, we include the fatall and abortive ends of such as commit notorious murders, which is aggravated and acted with all the Art that may be, to terrifie men from the like abhorred practises."[1] By all these critics, tragedy is more or less reduced to the lesson that crime does not pay. In their eagerness to answer Plato's objection to poetry, that it stirs up unhealthy emotions, they commonly argue that it serves, rather, to warn against vice by exhibiting its depravity and punishment, so as to terrify the spectator into avoiding crimes. In drama we can see the effect of this emphasis, for instance, in the *Tragedy of Cleopatra* by Samuel Daniel. Daniel openly moralizes on Cleopatra's fall, and does much less justice than Shakespeare to the natural grace and fascination of her arts. The spectator is allowed too Olympian a stance; he is not lured into a quasi-identification with Cleopatra's emotional life.

For many Elizabethans the tragedies of Seneca, built about a contrast between passionate villains and men of reason, were influential as literary

Roy W. Battenhouse: *"Richard III and Aristotelian Catharsis,"* reprinted from Roy W. Battenhouse, *Shakespearean Tragedy: Its Art and Its Christian Premises.* Reprinted with the permission of Mrs. Marian Battenhouse.

models. According to Stoic philosophy, all virtue is comprehended in rational self-control, while all vice is attributed to passion devoid of reason. A man of upright character will negate evil by becoming impervious to passion; but when character is deteriorated by passion it becomes rampantly mad. In Seneca's dramas, therefore, moral character is either black or white, and there is no mixed state of the human soul. His tragic heroes, typically, are murderous criminals crazed with blood and power.[2] The punishment they suffer is chiefly psychological, a loss of contentment of mind, which the onset of rage automatically entails. In much of Elizabethan drama these Senecan features are more or less reflected.

But does this pattern for tragedy resemble Shakespeare's? If we look at Shakespearean villains such as Iago or Richard III, we discover not hysterical revengers but singularly cold and adroit schemers. These men take pride in their reason's control of passion. Iago and Richard are fascinating to us because of their wit and their skill in playacting. In going about murder, they do not act for blood lust, but in proof of their cleverness and self-importance. When ultimately they suffer a downfall, this takes the form of an external loss of power through some final inadequacy in their vision or tactics, while internally their punishment is mainly that of a self-imprisonment within their own loveless existence.

In what sense does a spectator feel pity and fear while watching the drama of Richard III? Perhaps in this case we may feel pity chiefly for his victims, and a fear because we imagine ourselves in their predicament. If so, what purgation of our emotions takes place as we watch? Could it be that the quality of our emotion changes—that if we begin with pity for their plight, we find this pity qualified by an awareness of mistakes of theirs which are abetting it, so that ultimately our pity is for the ruin to which their blindness is making them liable? Our pity is in that way educated, refined from its initial sentimentality.

But is it only by these victims that our pity and fear are exercised? Do we feel toward Richard, the protagonist, merely a disapprobation and then a moral satisfaction when finally he is destroyed? I doubt this is the case. For surely Richard's despair in Act V draws our pity. Here we see him tormented by a conscience he had previously ignored. It is an aspect of the self he has not considered in his doctrine that "Richard loves Richard: that is, I am I." His self-love is revealed as self-hate. "There is no creature loves me," he cries, "And if I die, no soul shall pity me." Here his statement is only half-correct, for we of the audience who have been given this insight into his misery of soul pity him even now. He has committed his crimes in ignorance, we realize, of who he really is. Moreover, Shakespeare allows us a further ground for our pity. Richard in his despair is still ignoring a potential aspect of his conscience—the one voiced in the cry with which he began his soliloquy—"Have mercy, Jesu!" He neglects to give further consideration to mercy as a cure for guilt. This leaves us pitying the incompleteness of his penitence. For now when he tries to be courageous, he can do so only by banishing conscience and wasting what remains of his life in an empty show of outward bravado. There is a dramatic irony in his swearing "By the Apostle Paul" that he has been terrified by "shadows," since we know that in the Apostle's case a conversion came by probing the shadows of conscience—coming to terms with them rather than dismissing them. Some readers may not catch this irony. But for those who do, it furnishes an additional reason for pitying Richard and for fearing his disaster as one we might suffer.

All told, Shakespeare's drama is inviting a more enlightened pity and fear than Aristotle had envisaged, yet the goal of purifying these emotions through exercising them in viewing a tragedy is the same. Aristotle, it is true, in describing the best kind of plot for a tragedy, advised against one in which the downfall of an utter villain is exhibited. Yet, as Butcher has remarked, we need not infer a banning of the villain from all tragedies, since Aristotle elsewhere refers twice to the Menelaus of Euripides' *Orestes* as a character "gratuitously bad";[3] this Menelaus was perhaps tolerable in a tragedy of lesser kind emphasizing spectacle. Aristotle's objection was that a downright villain inspires neither pity nor fear. For "pity is aroused by unmerited misfortune, fear by the misfortune of a man like ourselves." This statement must be understood, however, in the context of Aristotle's whole philosophy. By "unmerited" misfortunes, he means miseries disproportionate to a man's faults; and he considers this the case whenever a man of typically healthy nature has acted from ignorance, not intending to do evil. Since the evil comes about accidentally to such a man's purpose, and not through deliberate choice, the misfortune is unmerited. (Christian thought is more complex on this point: earthly misfortunes may be visited on a man of good intentions to try him, rather than simply to reward the merit of his intentions; and also they may punish secret faults of which he is unaware.) On the other hand, Aristotle thinks of a villain as one whose purposes are no longer properly human but rather those of a bestial depravity. Such a man is not "like us" and therefore cannot arouse our fear. In Shakespeare's outlook we can discern a modification of these premises. Richard's crimes are shown to be motivated not by animalistic depravity, but by a desire for revenge against nature for giving him a crooked back. They are intended by Richard as a means to the good of self-esteem. He pursues this good in ignorance of his true self, not realizing that his warped body ought not to be identified with his basic nature, since he has in fact a hidden or repressed soul capable of conscience. Thus Richard acts without intending the misfortune of self-hate and despair, yet faultily adopts a means to his intended good which lands him in this misfortune.

We may say that insofar as Richard has acted from ignorance, there is an element of involuntariness in his crimes. And is he not "like us"? Not like, perhaps, the run of the mill fellows among us whom we consider healthy; nevertheless, he is an instance of a spiritual blindness potential in everyman.

This implication, more penetrating than Aristotle's view of villainy, depends on Shakespeare's inheritance of Christian philosophical principles. These enlarge the contextual circumstances of action and our reasons for pity and fear. They deepen, without abandoning, Aristotle's argument.[4]

St. Augustine, in his *Confessions* II. v. 11, takes up the matter of the so-called "gratuitously evil" man. That is what Sallust had called Catiline. But Augustine remarks that not even Catiline loved his own villainies; he loved rather something else, for whose sake he did them. "Would any commit murder upon no cause, delighted simply in murdering? Who would believe it?" Augustine asks. A criminal acts always for the sake of some beguiling good. A villain's monstrousness is merely an extraordinary case within the range of potential error to which human beings are liable. Shakespeare, with this background of understanding, could use a villain-hero in tragedy simply by treating Richard as not merely a villain. Though we hear Richard announce himself as a villain at the play's very beginning, that is not the whole truth about him. We are made aware that "villain" is the role Richard would make-believe as his nature, superimposing it on the human nature he would mock; and later we see the consequences of his having equated himself with his melodramatic self—with that shadow-self on which he preens himself at the end of II. i, asking for a mirror in which to admire it. These Shakespearean insights into the psychology of villainy give *Richard III* a subtlety lacking in a play such as Jonson's *Catiline.*

In the light of our discussion, we can amend somewhat a comment by Butcher. Rightly, he defends *Richard III* as a tragedy rather than a melodrama, but on grounds that are rather romantic:

> Wickedness on a grand scale, resolute and intellectual, may raise the criminal above the commonplace and invest him with a sort of dignity. There is something terrible and sublime in mere will-power working its evil way, dominating its surroundings with a superhuman energy. The wreck of such power excites in us a certain tragic sympathy; not indeed the genuine pity which is inspired by unmerited suffering, but a sense of loss and regret over the waste or misuse of gifts so splendid. (*Aristotle's Theory,* p. 313)

I can agree that we feel at the end a regret over Richard's misuse of his energies. But do we then still regard those energies as having been "superhuman" and sublime? When Richard declares before his last battle,

> Conscience is but a word that cowards use,
> Devised at first to keep the strong in awe.
> Our strong arms be our conscience, swords our law

he is being as resolute as ever in his kind of dignity; yet surely we perceive by now the intellectual bankruptcy of such a dignity. Only in Richard's own foolish estimate is he superhuman. His oration to his army cannot make appeal, as Richmond's does, to "God and our good cause"; it must resort instead to a picturing of his adversary as a "milksop" attended by vagabonds and rats. Richard's oration is obviously tawdry. And then when he exits invoking the spleen of dragons, but reappears crying "My kingdom for a horse!" any sense we might have had of something terrible and sublime is quite undone by our sense of the pitiableness of such absurdity. We remember perhaps, and apply to Richard, the play's earlier image of "a drunken sailor on a mast" (III. iv, 101). Rather then than Butcher's sympathy for "the wreck of such power," I think we feel a pity for Richard's misestimate of his capacities, and for his having (like Hastings) built "his hopes in air."

Also we come away fearing that such a disaster might have been ours too, had we been placed in Richard's circumstances. If we were deformed of body amid a society deformed by license, perjury, and opportunism—a society in which the King is living scandalously with Mistress Shore and the Archbishop is a trimmer easily cajoled into betraying "blessed sanctuary "—might not we, like Richard, take a morbid delight in outdoing this society on its own terms, by using Machiavellian arts to achieve a wooer's mastery over widow Anne and in all situations a mockery of traditional holiness? Is there not something almost sublime in the pleasure of becoming lyric about "my own deformity," studying "my shadow in the sun," and then demonstrating the power of one's actor-self to astound, plague, and dominate the less skilful hypocrisy of one's neighbors? Yet Shakespeare's drama, while tempting us by this dream of dignity, has in the course of its action shown us the dream's ultimate blindspot. Richard cannot beguile Queen Elizabeth in Act IV with the techniques he used on Anne in Act I. "Relenting fool, and shallow, changing woman!" he has boasted after she has given him in fact only an equivocal answer; and thus it is he who is fooled, and his wit proved shallow. His realism, which depends on supposing that immediate vantage and an illusion of security can be counted on to sway anyone but himself, is but a realism manqué, and he is self-deceived by a mistaken premise. Moreover, we have seen his intellect lapse into a misjudgment of Buckingham and a giving of confused commands when he finds his power evaded and then challenged by unanticipated events. And on the eve of the showdown at Bosworth field we have heard him confess:

> I have not the alacrity of spirit,
> Nor cheer of mind, that I was wont to have.

An attrition of his energies has overtaken him, comparable to that of Macbeth's in Shakespeare's later play, and its sequel is self-doubt, remorse, and despair, and then death in the service of a futile and vain activism.

How, then, does such a story purge our pity and fear? By arousing at the outset, I would say, our interest in the *seemingly* superhuman intelligence of Richard. We are encouraged, that is, to take a romantic view of evil. Out of a pity for Richard's deformity or because we find awesome his bold resourceful-ness, we can become half-enchanted by this criminal. We then can perhaps let ourselves make-believe, as he does, that an unscrupulous wit is justifiable in a corrupt society, and that its skilful use may provide a sublime adventure. If we respond in this way we are releasing, for its exercise, the impure state of our own pity—i.e., of a pity in us which has become corroded more or less by our penchant for self-pity, pitiless toward society. The pleasure we take, with Richard, in making sport of the weaknesses of neighbors is, essentially, a deformed form of pity—the dried up version of it which the play magnifies in a Richard who pities only his bodily ugliness and fears nothing but the ignominy of losing out in the competition for worldly eminence. Such a per-son is fearless of outcries such as Anne's.

> Either Heaven with lightning strike the murderer dead,
> Or earth, gape open wide and eat him quick.

For in this hero the emotion of fear has been deformed too, by a corrosive cynicism which has evaporated all credence in the reality of the supernatural. Hence Richard can make mock of "old odd ends" stolen out of Scripture (not realizing that his own end will turn out to be the "old odd" one Scripture tells of). But who of us can say we never have similar predilections? If and insofar as our own emotions of pity and fear have in them impurities like Richard's, we can be enlisted in a quasi-identification with him. Then the subsequent events of the drama work on our emotions, much as does a furnace fire when applied to a meltingpot containing rusty metal or crude ore. As the play pro-ceeds, the accumulating crises stimulate in us insights which break down our initial form of pity and fear, eliminating the dross and allowing these emo-tions to recollocate. A purgation of this kind, it seems to me, is effected whenever a played tragedy is properly structured and its auditors are properly responsive.

Notes

1. A review of these samplings of Elizabethan theory, and of others like them, can be found in Lily B. Campbell, *Shakespeare's Tragic Heroes* (New York, 1959 reprint), pp. 25–38; in Virgil Whitaker, *The Mirror Up To Nature* (San Marino, 1965), pp. 56–81; and in my *Marlowe's Tamburlaine* (Vanderbilt University Press, 1941), pp. 114–20.

2. See Norman Pratt, "The Stoic Base of Senecan Drama," *TAPA*, LXXIX (1948), 1–11.

3. S. H. Butcher, *Aristotle's Theory of Poetry and Fine Art,* fourth edition (New York, 1951), p. 316.

4. Note how Aquinas, in *S.T.* II–II, 1–3, sets Aristotle's understanding of pity in the context of the virtue of mercy.

History, Character and Conscience in *Richard III*

RICHARD P. WHEELER

Criticism of Shakespeare's second tetralogy of English history plays has moved away from the attempt to correlate precisely the history dramatized in these plays with that presented by official Tudor apologists. C. L. Barber's essay on the *Henry IV* plays,[1] for instance, finds in them a much more profound understanding of historical rhythms and of human involvement in the dynamics of power than E. M. W. Tillyard could establish by interpreting Shakespeare through concepts expressed in the chronicles and other sixteenth century poetry.[2] Alvin B. Kernan, in his recent essay on the Henriad, demonstrates the sophisticated artistry through which Shakespeare comprehends the essential conflict of power and self as it is presented to modern western civilization.[3] The first tetralogy and *King John* perhaps fail to achieve this sophistication, but in these plays Shakespeare begins to win for himself a difficult and sobering emancipation from official historical attitudes. I will examine this struggle as it shapes the drama of *Richard III*.

A wide range of historical attitudes have been assigned to *Richard III*. The extremes are represented by Jan Kott's stunning, free-wheeling essay on "The Kings" and Tillyard's scholarly, background-oriented study of *Shakespeare's History Plays*. From Shakespeare's histories, writes Kott, "there gradually emerges the image of history itself. The image of the Grand Mechanism."[4] Shakespeare presents a history stripped of all illusion and mythology, indeed, of all meaning, a cruel, amoral, impersonal history of manipulators and victims. Inevitably the manipulators, the kings and the king-makers, become the victims of history's "recurring and unchanging circles" (p. 8). Gloucester understands and expresses the essence of this history, though he, too, becomes its "victim, caught in the wheel" (p. 51). Richmond's victory at Bosworth Field begins a new variation of the old pattern of kingship. Henry VII becomes the new face and voice of history, smoother, higher sounding, but equally implicated in the power process. Tillyard, on the other hand, sees Shakespeare faithfully dramatizing the Tudor myth of a divinely ordained

By permission of the editors of *Comparative Drama* and Medieval Institute Publications.

unification of the houses of York and Lancaster. For Tillyard, *Richard III* is a profoundly religious play: "The play's main end is to show the working out of God's will in English history. . . ."[5] Victorious Richmond represents the sacred force of right providentially triumphing over the forces of evil.

What is remarkable is not that these polar approaches to *Richard III* have been made, but that the play can so readily accommodate both. Historical outlooks close to each are essential to this play. *Richard III* dramatizes a struggle, never quite resolved, between conflicting ways of interpreting historical experience. In this play Shakespeare is finding his way toward an understanding that ultimately undermines a simple adherence to Tudor historic myth, but is not yet in full awareness and control of its disturbing implications.

Caught between contradictory conceptions of history, Shakespeare is profoundly drawn toward both. The two point toward views which, according to Mircea Eliade,[6] distinguish the modern historical sense from that of earlier cultures. The Tudor historic myth—a strange adaptation of reactionary trends in Reformation and Counter-reformation political thought to the need for an official apologetic which could celebrate and stabilize Tudor succession—develops a traditional view of history which denies that life is tied to an irreversible procession of time which cannot be redeemed. Throughout the various levels of sophistication developed within this view of history, there runs the central idea of redeeming time-bound, worldly experience by immersing it in transcendent systems of meaning. Redemptive destiny makes the suffering of life bearable. By giving historical cycles a profound regenerative meaning, it invests the moment of suffering with a quality of meaningful, historical necessity:

> . . . whether history was governed by the movements of the heavenly bodies or purely and simply by the cosmic process, which necessarily demanded a disintegration inevitably linked to an original integration, whether, again, it was subject to the will of God, a will that the prophets had been able to glimpse, the result was the same: none of the catastrophes manifested in history was arbitrary. (*Cosmos and History*, p. 133)

This way of understanding the present through a redemptive destiny makes history sacred. In contrast, "modern non-religious man" has come to regard himself

> solely as the subject and agent of history, and he refuses all appeal to transcendence. In other words, he accepts no model for humanity outside the human condition as it can be seen in the various historical situations. Man *makes himself*, and he only makes himself completely in proportion as he desacralizes himself and the world. The sacred is the prime obstacle to his freedom. He will become himself only when he is totally demysticized. He will not be truly free until he has killed the last god. (*The Sacred and the Profane*, p. 203)

To the extent that profane man can "create" history without submission to archetypal prescriptives, he has a freedom and individuality that mythic, sacred history denies. On the other hand, profane history has no means of justifying the terrors of history because it can neither escape nor regenerate time. Paterns continue to repeat themselves, but devoid of their redemptive content.

> But *repetition emptied of its religious content necessarily leads to a pessimistic vision of existence.* When it is no longer a vehicle for reintegrating a primordial situation, and hence for recovering the mysterious presence of the gods, that is, *when it is desacralized,* cyclic time becomes terrifying; it is seen as a circle forever turning on itself, repeating itself to infinity. (Ibid., p. 107)

Profane man must come to terms with a history in which "time presents itself as a precarious and evanescent duration, leading irremediably to death" (Ibid, p. 113).

In *Richard III* a disturbing awareness of the possibility of a profane view of history suggesting the lines sketched by Eliade is eating into Shakespeare's faith in regenerative, historic myth. Eliade's distinction between sacred and profane history thus provides a useful interpretive frame for approaching the conflict in this play between Shakespeare's allegiance to an old order of thought and the doubts and discoveries which trouble that allegiance. But the relationship between the tensions of the play and the dichotomies of the modern writer's theoretical speculations is also to be understood as a mythology in common. This shared myth identifies the persistence in our time of the problem that worries Shakespeare's play. Eliade's writings are saturated with a profound nostalgia for the lost order, which he is able to preserve through his own Christian position. His vision of profane history—which he sees as necessarily a process in which the price of freedom for a few strong individuals is paid with the terror, futility, and constraint of the many—is shaped by this commitment to a sacred order which alone can infuse human life with meaning and comfort. Just so, Shakespeare needs at this stage to approach history through the assurance of the Tudor myth, solidly grounded in a Christianity that invests all historical events with the quality of meaningful necessity. With this need he confronts the England of the 1590's, and the result, projected into the past, is the delightful but nightmarish monster of individual will, Richard III, whose terrible presence is a source of fascination so long as it can be shrouded with the very ordered meaning of history which he threatens.

Richmond's victory is shaped by the Tydor myth of divine union; the blood-soaked land is regenerated and the violence is redeemed with peace and joy. This triumph culminates a thematic structure that can be clearly traced throughout the play. *Richard III* explicitly provides a single, well-defined interpretive frame for its events. Irving Ribner sums it up as a stern morality which combines a Senecan notion of Nemesis with a Christian faith in providence, for the evil path of Richard is a cleansing operation which roots evil out of society and restores the world at last to the God-oriented goodness embodied in the new rule of Henry VII.[7]

Once it is understood that Richard is the scourge of God, his actions, however evil, serve a divinely ordained end. He becomes the paradoxical "Angel With Horns" brilliantly analyzed by A. P. Rossiter.[8] But trends toward a profane view of history which emerge from the action of the play threaten the controlling power of the mythic structure. Whereas Richmond *fulfills* the destiny of one kind of history, Richard appears to *make* the other kind. Richard embodies the creative individuality that profane history grants its agents, just as he comes to embody the doom that such history demands.

The play is carefully constructed so that two levels of reality interact through the mediating agency of Margaret's curse. Richard's cruel manipulation of profane existence fulfills Margaret's prophetic curse, which in turn fulfills the divine plan, purging England of evil and clearing the way for Tudor ascension through Richmond. The play asks us to endorse such a view, but it also invites us to question it. The very structure that uses Richard as the scourge of God destined to aid providence is also constructed so as to put a severe and disruptive strain on its providential message. This threat is created by strong pressures toward a profane view which are never allowed thematically to break out of the sacred view which encloses them, but which show through the sacred veneer. The thematic structure surrounds but cannot completely control the violent energy of the inner, emotive structure. What follows is an attempt to locate those trends in the play that disrupt its stated meaning.

The desacralizing quality of the play cannot easily be accounted for in the thematic development toward an optimistic resolution. The roles of Margaret and Richmond are too carefully controlled to allow that. Steeped in vengeful anguish, Margaret delivers and presides over a prophetic curse which comes to be realized in the action of the play. First go Rivers, Vaughan and Grey: "Now Margaret's curse is fall'n upon our heads" (III.3.16)[9]; then Hastings: "O Margaret, Margaret, now thy heavy curse/Is lighted on poor Hastings' wretched head!" (III.4.91–93); then Buckingham: "Thus Margaret's curse falls heavy on my neck" (V.1.25). Richard himself is served his end according to Margaret's explicit predictions—betrayed by friends, his soul victim to "the worm of conscience," sleepless except for "some tormenting dream." Richmond's name is brought into the play as a potential counter to Richard just after Richard has become king. As Richmond draws nearer to England, his power steadily growing, Richard becomes increasingly troubled, his self control visibly shaken. A sense of fatefulness attaches itself to the approaching victory of Richmond that is experienced as destiny.

But even within the roles played by Margaret and Richmond there are tendencies which either disrupt the complete assimilation of history to a mythical pattern, or fail to make that assimilation completely convincing. The very fact that Margaret's prophetic power is manifested in a curse obscures the clarity of the sacred perspective. There is a difference between Richard's thematic function as scourge of God—one who can only serve divine ends regardless of the depths of his evil—and Margaret's as conscious agent of God's will—one who would have her curse "pierce the clouds and enter heaven." She tarnishes the purity of the sacred, for she serves God only as she serves her own gluttonous revenge: "I am hungry for revenge,/And now I cloy me with beholding it" (IV.4.61–62). Margaret finds the same cruel delight in her bloodthirsty success that Richard does. Margaret's purpose conforms to a divine end, but her presence suggests what Eliade describes as the "magico-religious paraphernalia" of "hybrid forms of black magic and sheer travesty of religion," steps in "the process of the desacralization of human existence" (*The Sacred and the Profane,* p. 206).

When Richmond arrives with his army (V.2), he encourages his troops "To reap the harvest of perpetual peace/By this one bloody trial of sharp war." He plans his battle for the next day, and prays that his forces may be able to serve God as "ministers of chastisement." Asleep, he dreams the "fairest-boding" half of a dream he shares with Richard. Richmond inspires his soldiers with the prospect of glory and peace through "God and Saint George! Richmond and victory!" Finally he defeats and kills Richard in the Battle of Bosworth Field, accepts the crown, and promises Tudor union, worthy heirs, and peace. This is a work of historical redemption done with God's sanction and in his presence. Richmond's speeches and the action of the final scenes bring the play to a thematic conclusion wholly consistent with the Tudor historic myth. The play demands a peaceful world to succeed a world of misery. The structuring of this theme insists that Richmond first be kept to the background, then austerely brought into the center of the action. But such a strategy, though adequate thematically, is simply not able to balance the tremendous emotional investment in its counter-theme. In the early parts of the play, Shakespeare pushes unrelieved terror and misery toward the status of general human conditions. The play presents a world, as Queen Elizabeth tells Richard, "full of thy foul wrongs." The cumulative effect of this expansive emphasis on cruelty, deceit and misery creates a lingering impression that becomes independent of the simple cause (Richard) and effect (evil in the world) system that is thematically, but not emotionally, absorbed by the optimistic structure of the play.

Richmond's promise is fulfilled hope and perpetual peace. But Richmond must take over a rhetoric that has already been colored by the sardonic humor of Richard and the prolonged laments of his victims. Richmond's person simply does not carry enough force to jolt his key terms free from associations that have accrued to them in the course of the previous four acts. Through Richard's victims, the prospect of peace becomes fused with false hope and deception, as in the sickening irony of King Edward's wish to leave behind him a united kingdom.

> And more at peace my soul shall part to heaven,
> Since I have made my friends at peace on earth,

followed by,

> There wanteth now our brother Gloucester here
> To make the blessed period of the peace.
>   (II.1.3–4; 43–44)

Richard makes peace a tool of his savage wit, and uses the promise of peace in his various deceits. He would be reconciled to King Edward's "friendly peace," and entreats "true peace" of Queen Elizabeth. With Edward dead, Richard hopes that "the king made peace with all of us;/ And the compact is firm and true in me." Hastings is executed for the "peace of England." Wooing Elizabeth for her daughter, Richard argues, "Infer fair England's peace from this alliance." But only the peace of death is salvable in the world Richard rules, and this is turned to when access even to false hope is impossible, as it becomes for the Duchess of York: "I to my grave, where peace and rest lie with me."

Richmond's purpose, of course, is to change all this. He brings "perpetual peace," "sleep in peace," and "smooth-faced peace" that "lives again." But because the preceding parts of the play identify the quest for peace so strongly with false hope, despair, blasphemy, and deceit, the language of peace carries into the last act affective associations that Richmond's promises are not entirely able to dispel. Behind the optimistic conclusion presided over by Richmond is an affective content already created by the earlier parts of the play, and which attaches itself to the language of the last act even though it contradicts the redemptive theme. This affective power is generated by the force of Richard's actions earlier, and to Richard we must turn in order to clarify the implications of this force.

The keys to Shakespeare's presentation of history in this play lie primarily in the relationship between Richard and the thematic apparatus used to subdue him. Richard's outstanding features are, of course, his extraordinary wit, his exceptional abundance of energy which this wit channels and releases, his total lack of scruples in the pursuit of power, his skill as an actor, and his penetrating insight into the psychology of persons with whom he deals. As master of face to face encounter, Richard is without peer. His virtuosity is demonstrated from the first, in his meeting with Clarence, where Richard displays his knack for playing on the weakened position of others to win their total confidence. But Clarence is a pushover, the real triumphs are to come. A more subtle development within this scene (I.1) is the side exchange with

Brackenbury, who feels the bind between the royal order to let no one speak with Clarence and Richard's witty confiding as he violates this order. The quiet, almost inconspicuous terror conveyed in Brackenbury's response to Richard's intimidating congeniality establishes a quality that grows in magnitude and intensity throughout the play.

Richard's technique builds on his knowledge of the human tendency to substitute wish for reality when the facts of reality are intolerable. Richard can create both the oppressive reality and the outlet of illusory escape through false hope. By the end of the first devastating courtship scene, the easiest alternative for Anne is to hope for a redeeming sincerity in Richard's appeal for her hand in marriage, though she should better know the futility of this hope than anyone. Faced with the gruesomely real prospect of stabbing Richard's bared breast (killing him by word or deed in her mind are equal alternatives by this point, so thoroughly has Richard constructed a false reality through words), Anne slides into a realm of false hope in which Richard's remarkable love rhetoric becomes credible, however distant it is from the true situation. Instead of acting she pauses, "I would I knew thy heart," and the moment is Richard's. So is Anne Richard's, but the moment is what counts, not the woman: "I'll have her; but I will not keep her long."

This power to manipulate the wishes of others works both to create and shatter illusions. When Richard, ranting of injustice and violations of the social hierarchy, bursts in on the queen and her group (I.3), Elizabeth knows well what is on his mind:

> Come, come, we know your meaning, brother Gloucester;
> You envy my advancement and my friends!
> God grant we never may have need of you!

But during the long intrusion of Margaret's curse, Richard is able to deflect their animosity for him toward her, and bind the group to him with a kind of fellow feeling against the widow of Henry VI. His master stroke of feigned forgiveness when Margaret leaves is praised by Rivers as a "virtuous and Christian-like conclusion." Richard reverses this process of building from insecurities a false sense of good faith in his next encounter with the court regulars (II.1). He first enters into the spirit of dying King Edward's wish to reconcile the affairs of family and state before his death. Then still in his pious mode, Richard shatters this wishful optimism with the news of Clarence's death—as if by the king's too slowly rescinded order.

Richard retains his power to dominate intimate personal encounter through the last chance he has to exercise it—the courtship of Queen Elizabeth for her daughter (IV.4). Once again he triumphs over incredibly formidable conditions in getting this woman to relent. Queen Elizabeth is no more able than Anne had been to withstand Richard's psychic assault; she does not fend him off with a false promise, but is driven to consent to his request. The difference between the two courtship scenes is the changed nature of the play's political situation, which does not allow Richard to sustain the triumph of the moment in the time that follows it. Richard brings Elizabeth to relent, but he now faces a problem in power that extends far beyond the limited time and space of intimate personal encounter. Offstage, Elizabeth realizes what has happened to her, just as Anne did, but Elizabeth simply slips away to the camp of Richmond, a possibility that did not exist in the power arrangement that Anne faced.

Richard is the most famous of Elizabethan Machiavels, but the Machiavelli who wrote *The Prince* would have little patience with his tactics. Rule by fear is, of course, a principle Machiavelli endorses, but this rule is effective only when carefully controlled:

> A prince, however, should make himself feared in such a manner that, if he has not won the affection of his people, he shall not incur their hatred.[10]

Machiavelli repeatedly asserts that a prince must "avoid everything that would make him odious and despised. And in proportion as he avoids that will he have performed his part well, and need fear no danger" (Ibid., p. 79). Richard, on the contrary, does everything possible to make himself "odious and despised." His very triumphs create the conditions that result in his downfall.

Nobody protests the execution of Hastings. The contrivance which traps Hastings into falsely but fatally condemning himself (III.4) is one of Richard's most impressive exhibitions of imaginative coercion. But although no one protests, neither is anyone fooled by this trumped up charge of treason, as the Scrivener indicates:

> Here's a good world the while! Who is so gross
> That cannot see this palpable device?
> Yet who so bold but says he sees it not?
> Bad is the world; and all will come to naught,
> When such ill dealing must be seen in thought.
> (III.6.10–14)

The political reaction against Richard that follows from the proliferation of such attitudes as the Scrivener's need not be considered the response of a divinely guided universe to Richard's wickedness. Machiavelli would have foreseen it. That the successful exercise of political power derives from a broad base is not a divine nor a mythic nor even a moral law. "Never," writes José Ortega y Gassett,

> has anyone ruled on this earth by basing his rule essentially on any other thing than public opinion. . . . The fact that public opinion is the basic force which produces the phenomenon of rule in human societies is as old, and as lasting, as mankind.[11]

Richard the master of palace politics does everything possible to prevent himself from attaining this broad base in popular support, which in his England was manifested in the strength of the nobility.

Richard's strategy in winning the crown (III.7) exhibits the discrepancy between his brilliance as an actor and his failure as a politician of real strength. The crowd, long silent, that finally concedes a reluctant "amen" to Richard's acceptance of the title of "England's worthy king," is simply joining, for the expedience of the moment, the play that Richard and Buckingham have staged using the rusty armor, the priests, and the lord mayor as props. It is an impressive display of acting virtuosity, but an artifice is created, not a solid political reality, which is no more able to sustain itself in the broad world of political power than any such artifice not solidly grounded. Judged only by conditions of a political reality that the play establishes, Richard's power is so disintegrated by the last act that virtually anyone able to attract to himself the eager support of the frustrated and fearful English nobility could have unseated him. Richard, politically, ironically is the "bottled spider" that Margaret calls him, able to poison whomever ventures into his web, but not able to extend this web as a means of embracing the power of the kingdom. The force of Richmond as Agent of God is diminished by there being no need for a resort to a higher system of causality, of what Paul Goodman[12] calls a "miracle" to relieve England of the "impasse" of Richard's tyranny. There is no impasse. Richard's political and military might have been so drained that there is little doubt about the outcome. This, of course, does not deny the play's prerogative to interpret the events of history in terms of the sacred or mythic, as it does. But *Richard III* establishes a rigorous inner integrity within an essentially profane system of political causality which makes the Tudor-Christian myth seem more the ornament of history than its essence.

The arc of Richard's development through a series of triumphs to final defeat best can be understood through his highly self-conscious role as an actor who imposes the conditions of stage onto the real world. Richard's vice role reflects far more than Shakespeare's indebtedness to an old theatrical tradition. Anne Righter comments that Richard—who "through the power of illusion . . . blinds honest men and accomplishes their overthrow"—"seems to be regarded by Shakespeare more as an example of the power wielded by the actor than as a figure of treachery and evil."[13] But Shakespeare also shows, through Richard, the limits of the actor, both in controlling power and in controlling the whole person that lies behind the actor's mask.

Machiavelli, of course, insists that a ruler be an actor, a dissembler who appears to act in the interest of the good while actually contriving to maintain and extend his power by any means necessary. Richard's ascent to power is grounded in his acting artistry, in his ability to fabricate reality, to create a world of illusion that others accept as real. He turns his world into a stage, history into a play which he creates. But similarly, his failure is an artistic one. Shakespeare's Richard violates the basic laws of mimesis; he distorts the world so out of shape in his play-acting that the artificiality of it becomes only too clear. By the time he has become king, he simply is no longer fooling anyone. Instead of adapting himself to a part dictated by the precarious political conditions he encounters, Richard attempts to re-shape these conditions in terms of the part he craves to play. No artist is more powerful than his materials, and Richard's attempt to be so leads to his destruction at their hands. Richard's theatricality, through which he manifests his strength, is also his essential political weakness, because he believes the momentary illusion of reality that he creates by acting can be extended through time over the real sources of political power.

Just as Richard's relations to the external world are focused through his role as actor, so are his relations to himself. The vice role allows him to avoid facing the complicating demands of his inner self, and is essential to the defensive structure of his character. As Hazlitt saw, Richard uses his talents and his drive for power "to shield himself from remorse. . . ."[14] Richard feels, as do most men, a need for power, a need for love, and a bondage to conscience. Rather than attempt a working compromise of these inner demands, Richard strives for an identity built solely around an unmitigated drive for power. He substitutes sadistic violence for the need for love; he transforms shame for his own deformity into disgust for others. The guilt that such an inversion arouses is consciously warded off through a total commitment to sadistic aggression, although this maneuver divides Richard against himself. He is fierce and cunning in the manipulation of others, but as his queen tells us, at night he has "timorous dreams."

Richard has constructed a role that projects onto the outer world the violence of his inner conflicts. As the objective power structure he has created begins to crumble, there is a corresponding weakening of Richard's capacity to keep repressed needs at a distance. Eventually, Richard is forced to see himself from the vantage point he has outrageously flaunted before. Helpless before his accumulated guilt in the dramatized dream in which his victims return to accuse him, Richard finds himself alone, afraid, and unloved:

> My conscience hath a thousand several tongues,
> And every tongue brings in a several tale,
> And every tale condemns me for a villain.
> Perjury, perjury, in the highest degree,
> Murder, stern murder, in the direst degree,
> All several sins, all used in each degree,
> Throng to the bar, crying all, "Guilty, guilty!"
> I shall despair. There is no creature loves me;
> And if I die, no soul will pity me.
>
> (V.3.194–202)

The culturally defined conflict to which Richard finally succumbs—that of a Christian political morality opposed to the individual rage for power—corresponds psychologically to an unresolved ambivalence belonging to the earliest stages of infancy. Richard is driven by inner needs which present themselves to him in the contradictory extremes of the infantile imagination: the need for a feeling of omnipotence, around which he builds his aggressive drive for power; and the need for love of a sort which could be achieved only by total, selfless submission. So long as he has before him the promise of an ever growing sense of externally realized power, Richard can relegate his self-disgust and the fear of being unloved to the domain of witty detachment, as in the famous opening soliloquy. Richard, "not shaped for sportive tricks/ Nor made to court an amorous looking glass," delights in his "own deformity," and decides to "prove a villain" since he "cannot prove a lover." The need for power and the consciously repudiated need to be seen as the worthy object of the love of others both appear, however, in his major triumphs. The aggressive drive for power furnishes the propelling force, but the need to be loved emerges—to be mocked—in the disguise. He bares his breast to Lady Anne, offering her the option to destroy him or to love him. He presents himself as victim and martyr—"too childish-foolish for this world"—to the court of dying Edward. He plays "the maid's part" before his London audience, reluctantly accepting the burden of a crown forced upon him. Even in persuading Queen Elizabeth to woo her daughter for him, Richard attempts to picture a situation in which he and the queen and her daughter are all helpless before the conditions of the time, duty bound to effect the marriage:

> In her consists my happiness and thine;
> Without her, follows to myself and thee,
> Herself, the land, and many a Christian soul,
> Death, desolation, ruin and decay.
> It cannot be avoided but by this;
> It will not be avoided but by this.
>
> (IV.4.407–11)

Richard's guise to "seem a saint, when most I play the devil" (I.3.337) is not only a clever expedient, but reflects his conflicting drives to be both, one of which is necessarily repressed in order that the other may be asserted. An exchange between Richard and the Duchess of York provides an essential key to these contradictory needs. Richard turns to her after the death of Edward:

> Madam, my mother, I do cry you mercy;
> I did not see your grace. Humbly on my knee
> I crave your blessing.
>
> DUCHESS OF YORK: God bless thee, and put meekness in thy breast,
> Love, charity, obedience, and true duty!

RICHARD: Amen! [aside] and make me die a good old man!
            That is the butt-end of a mother's blessing;
            I marvel that her grace did leave it out.

(II.2.104–11)

His mother's blessing, for Richard, amounts to a curse. Christian obedience and the possibility of receiving love are fused in Richard's mind with passive, effeminate submissiveness to others and to the force of conscience. The demands of love and duty can lead only to frustration of his drive for power. And power, for Richard, means the narcissistic triumph of unbounded self-esteem through the sadistic reduction of others to helpless, inferior, repugnant objects. He strives for self love through a destructive repudiation of the need to be loved. The real pleasure in this power—which betrays its origins in early infantile ambivalences—comes through inflicting suffering on women. Men must be destroyed in order for Richard to gain his power; the sequence of killing started in *3 Henry VI* is extended by the deaths of Clarence, of Rivers, Vaughan and Grey, of Hastings, of the two princes, of Buckingham. But the real pleasure of sadistic aggression begins for Richard in the cruel courtship of Anne, and the real suffering of the play comes to be focused in the voices of widowed mothers. Richard does not kill men so much as he kills sons and husbands.

As the play progresses, and all of Richard's visible enemies are destroyed, the dramatic situation is polarized into a verbal battle between Richard—the terrible son his mother's "womb let loose to chase us to our graves"—and a chorus of bereaved mothers—old Queen Margaret, Queen Elizabeth, and the Duchess of York. It is appropriate that just after Richard's own mother leaves him with her "most grievous curse," Richard persuades Elizabeth to court her daughter for him, for it is as to a mother that he turns to Edward's widowed queen.

If I did take the kingdom from your sons,
To make amends I'll give it to your daughter;
If I have killed the issue of your womb,
To quicken your increase I will beget
More issue of your blood upon your daughter.
(IV.4.294–98)

He goes on to promise her first "grandam's name," then the chance to be "mother of a king." As he moves toward increased intimacy, he calls her "my mother," then "dear mother." He celebrates his success by calling her "happy mother."

As before with Anne, the triumph gives Richard a chance to confirm his disgust with female weakness: "Relenting fool, and shallow, changing woman!" But this time the effort shatters Richard's self-composure. Confronted almost immediately with news of Richmond's increasing power,

Richard is irritable, shaken, and confused. His conquest of Elizabeth, like that of Anne, has expressed his defensive hatred of women, as it has parodied his deep but denied need to purify himself through the love of a woman, ideally of a mother. But the disintegration of the power situation, which has previously allowed the separation of defense and need, has created a corresponding interior disintegration. The inner defensive balance—which sacrificed the need to be loved for the narcissistic feeling of omnipotence achieved through sadistic aggression—is completely tied to the external situation. The victory over Elizabeth parodies and mocks but does not fulfill a deeply repressed need; without the compensatory assurance of power, Richard feels the absence of what he has pretended to gain.

As the political artifice crumbles, the actor's mask is pulled away, and the weakness of Richard, his human susceptibility to conflicting needs, comes to the surface. Before lying down on the eve of the battle, Richard is baffled by the disappearance of his vigor and self-assurance: "I have not that alacrity of spirit/Nor cheer of mind that I was wont to have." During the night, he confronts his guilt, and shudders before it. The inner torment is fiercer now than any danger he can face in the field:

> By the apostle Paul, shadows to-night
> Have struck more terror to the soul of Richard
> Than can the substance of ten thousand soldiers
> Armed in proof and led by shallow Richmond.

His speech before the troops the next day is an attempt to reassert a power that is no longer his. Richard bolsters his courage with a magnificent half-truth in which he defines the nature of conscience as he would still like to regard it:

> Conscience is but a word that cowards use,
> Devised at first to keep the strong in awe:
> Our strong arms be our conscience, swords our law!
> (V.3.310–12)

He dies in the same vein, true in the action of battle to a private obsession with power that has lost its sway in the public realm and its unchallenged supremacy in his personal struggle for an omnipotent self: "Slave, I have set my life upon a cast,/And I will stand the hazard of the die."

Richard, who becomes an actor-king with near demonic powers by repudiating a part of his own humanity, eventually becomes a slave to the role he has created for himself. His realization that he must marry the daughter of Elizabeth brings with it an ironic step toward self-recognition:

> I must be married to my brother's daughter,
> Or else my kingdom stands on brittle glass;

> Murder her brothers, and then marry her—
> Uncertain way of gain! But I am in
> So far in blood that sin will pluck on sin.
> Tear-falling pity dwells not in this eye.
>
> (IV.2.59–64)

Though Richard tries to turn this oblique step toward self-understanding into an assertion of his pitiless cruelty, the irony lies in his partial awareness of the political and psychological determinants that have made him their pawn. The role Richard has created has become a part in a play no longer shaped solely by his egoistic drive for power, but by forces not within his control. These forces—within him, within the play, and within Shakespeare—are moral and religious in form, but do not reflect precisely the historical morality of Tudor chroniclers.

The return of the suppressed forces of conscience in a moment of personal vulnerability is a major organizing principle in the play. When Clarence's dream on the eve of his execution releases a surer knowledge of his relationship to Richard than he has conscious access to, his fear is accompanied by waves of guilt and retribution. As the two murderers prepare themselves for killing Clarence, the second murderer shudders to find that "some certain dregs of conscience are yet within me" (I.4.120–21). The murderers openly regard conscience as the enemy to manly assertion: "'Tis a blushing, shame-faced spirit that mutinies in a man's bosom; . . . and every man that means to live well endeavors to trust to himself and live without it." Of the two murderers, only one will accept his reward once the killing is accomplished; the other would wash his hands "of this most grievous murder!" What is interesting, however, about the extraordinary scene in which Clarence's killing is carried out, is the means by which the assassins prepare themselves for it. In order to escape the obstructions of a conscience they regard as effeminate and inhibiting, they turn to an outrageous delight in the cruelty of their plan:

1 Murderer: Take him on the costard with the hilts of thy sword, and then throw him into the malmsy butt in the next room.

2 Murderer: O excellent device! and make a sop of him.

The murderous identity they achieve through sadistic activity that simply seems to fly in the face of internal restraint presents in small the story of Richard himself.

A clear pattern emerges, developed in large by Richard and elaborated by lesser figures, Clarence, the assassins, and Buckingham: a violent release of cruel energy—which serves an egoistic need for power, which is expressed through sadistic aggression, and which must overcome the inner restraints of conscience by projecting its self-tormenting force onto the outside world—is finally unable to elude the grasp of conscience, and succumbs to it. This pattern accounts for the action of Richard as a character, and also for his relationship to the moral theme of the play. This latter relationship expresses in an external, cultural context the same drama that goes on inside the character of Richard. The night before the battle, Richard's dream of omnipotence is destroyed; during the battle the political objectification of that dream is dealt its final blow. With the rhetoric of Richmond's victory, Shakespeare clears his own conscience by destroying the egoistic monster through which he has eluded it.

The relationship of Richard to the moral theme is presented by Shakespeare as the message bequeathed by past history, but it actually expresses better the historical conditions under which the play was written. *Richard III* dramatizes, ultimately, neither the past as it had been interpreted by Tudor historians (Tillyard), nor the confrontation with history we face today (Kott), but the historical pressures experienced by Shakespeare and his contemporaries anxious about the approaching death of the last, aging Tudor. This is an experience which created in the Elizabethan theater fascination with Richard, tolerance for Margaret, and the need for Richmond. The massive cultural pressures presented by the power struggle of church and state, by the economic forces which dissolved feudalism and threatened the stability of class distinctions, by the emergence of an intellectual freedom and awareness which overthrew the shackling dominance of medieval thought, these and other powerful social disruptions brought confusion, anxiety and opportunity into the key relationships which bind an individual to his society. Zevedei Barbu speculates suggestively on the experience of inhabiting this world in which traditional answers are shaken by the prospects of an emerging but as yet unclarified social reality greatly changed from the one that created them:

> On the psychological level, the situation was characterized by an outburst of primary mental energy—instincts and wishes—which escaped the moulding and repressing influence of traditional values and patterns of behaviour. People passed through a period of reorientation of their mental structure, and particularly their conscience. It would perhaps be appropriate in this case to speak about a period of interlude in the human conscience in the sense that the conscience articulated by the old world of values was weak while the new was not yet formed. Thus, the period was one of mental freedom verging on inner anarchy.[15]

Barbu's remarks seem to describe aptly a condition out of which Shakespeare's *Richard III* might arise, since Richard builds his success around the explosive force of crude instinctual demands masked by a role that parodies traditional values. Richard's rampant egoism would appear to channel into shared, theatrical fantasy the released energies of a people who not only were "becoming more and more prepared to admit that their minds were often activated by primitive egoistic impulses, but also that this should be so."[16]

Apt as Barbu's comments may seem, a contradiction nevertheless emerges. Richard's egoism is not condoned but condemned by the play. Richard must privately face the terrors of his conscience and publicly succumb to the restorative power of Richmond. The contradiction points to a mis-emphasis in Barbu's analysis of the historical experience. Barbu posits a weakening and a reshaping of the individual conscience, but Freud has stressed the persistence in the individual of values formed in the past even when altered social and economic conditions draw men toward activities which contradict them.

> Mankind never lives entirely in the present. The past, the tradition of the race and of the people, lives on in the ideologies of the super-ego; and so long as it operates through the super-ego it plays a powerful part in human life, independently of economic conditions.[17]

The release of energy given dramatic expression in Richard is a release that incurs the wrath of a conscience still powerful in the inner life even if violated in the pursuit of egoistic opportunity. Richard as a character offered to Elizabethan audiences the chance to indulge through the vicarious medium of theater egoistic drives striving for liberation; *Richard III* the play allowed them a rapport with the persisting demands of an old morality. Indeed, the relationship is even more thoroughly pervaded by the power of conscience than this, because the special delight in cruelty that characterizes the play derives from the cruelty of super-ego forces projected into relationships with others. That the attempt of the play to contain Richard within an optimistic historical frame is only partially successful points to the very precariousness of the historical situation as it was faced by the individual of Elizabethan England. In attempting to resolve Richard's cruelty into an optimistic re-integration of past values, Shakespeare projects into dramatic form the division of moral, religious self against egoistic self central to the crisis of the individual during his lifetime. This division within the individual corresponds to the opposing trends toward sacred and profane history with which we started, for it is Shakespeare's age that faced the exhilarating and terrifying origins of that conflict in historical awareness that is still in progress.

The collapse of a unifying perspective within the play yields a volatile mixture of insight, fantasy and cliché ignited by the collision of doubt with faith in the historical order, release with restraint in the personal order. Richard as a character expresses Shakespeare's fascination with the possibility of a creative, self-assertive individuality, unleashes his intoxicating delight with the escape from traditional, moral restrictions through the power of imagination as it serves egoistic demands. But as a figure exercising his egoistic freedom in the world of other men, Richard presents to Shakespeare the possibilities for terror and destruction which can accompany that freedom. The grotesque proportions of Richard's evil reflect Shakespeare's radical distrust of the individual not controlled by a divine moral plan. Shakespeare's "villainizing" of the idea of individuality in the person of Richard expresses his disbelief that there can be any real power to sustain order located in agencies (social, economic, political, institutional, etc.) which mediate between the divine scheme of things and the demands of individual men. With the inner disintegration of Richard, Shakespeare sees deeply into the psychological persistence of internal restraints in those who will to escape them. In presenting Richard's political triumph and defeat, Shakespeare discovers in dramatic action the rigid causality of Machiavellian politics. But the sacralization of history through Richmond's triumph is an attempt to nullify these discoveries, to hold in check the fascinating and terrifying Richard by assimilating him to a view of history Shakespeare can no longer quite believe and not yet afford to abandon.

Notes

1. "Rule and Misrule in *Henry IV*," *Shakespeare's Festive Comedy* (Princeton, N.J.: Princeton University Press, 1959), pp. 192–221.

2. *Shakespeare's History Plays* (New York: Collier Books ed., 1962).

3. "The Henriad: Shakespeare's Major History Plays," *Modern Shakespearean Criticism*, ed. Alvin B. Kernan (New York: Harcourt, Brace & World, 1970), pp. 245–75.

4. *Shakespeare Our Contemporary*, trans. Boleslaw Taborski (Garden City, N.Y.: Anchor Books, 1966), p. 10.

5. *Shakespeare's History Plays*, p. 238. A. L. French has recently argued that *Richard III* "by no means conforms to the Tudor morality-play pattern proposed by Tillyard and others. . . ." and that "the play enlists feelings wide of any conceivable Tudor mark." "The World of *Richard III*," *Shakespeare Studies*, IV (1968), 31–32. But French fails to appreciate the anxieties aroused by diminishing the control over historical experience offered by the official Tudor view.

6. The discussion of Eliade's ideas derives primarily from *Cosmos and History: The Myth of the Eternal Return* (New York: Harper Torchbook, 1959) and from *The Sacred and the Profane: The Nature of Religion* (Harper Torchbook, 1961), both translated by Willard R. Trask.

7. *The English History Play in the Age of Shakespeare*, revised ed. (London: Methuen, 1965), p. 118.

8. *Angels With Horns*, ed. Graham Storey (New York: Theatre Arts Books, 1961), pp. 1–22.

9. Quotations from *Richard III* are from the Pelican Shakespeare text, ed. G. Blakemore Evans, in *William Shakespeare: The Complete Works*, gen. ed. Alfred Harbage (Baltimore, Maryland: Penguin Books, 1969).

10. *The Prince*, trans. Christian E. Detmold, ed. Lester G. Crocker (New York: Washington Square Press, 1963), p. 73.

11. *The Revolt of the Masses*, authorized trans. (New York: W. W. Norton, 1932), pp. 126–27.

12. *The Structure of Literature* (Chicago: Phoenix Books ed., 1962), p. 55.

13. *Shakespeare and the Idea of the Play* (Harmondsworth, England: Penguin Shakespeare Library ed., 1967), pp. 87, 88.

14. *Characters of Shakespear's plays,* quoted in F. E. Halliday, *Shakespeare and His Critics,* revised ed. (London: Gerald Duckworth and Co., 1958), p. 138.

15. *Problems of Historical Psychology* (New York: Grove Press, 1960), p. 154.

16. Ibid., p. 155.

17. "The Dissection of the Psychical Personality," *The Complete Introductory Lectures on Psychoanalysis,* trans. and ed. James Strachey (New York: W. W. Norton, 1966), p. 531.

Dream and Plot in *Richard III*

Marjorie B. Garber

The great popularity of the dream as a dramatic device among the Elizabethans is surely due at least in part to its versatility as a mode of presentation. Both structurally and psychologically the prophetic dream was useful to
the playwright; it foreshadowed events of plot, providing the audience with
needed information, and at the same time it imparted to the world of the play
a vivid atmosphere of mystery and foreboding. Thus the Senecan ghost
stalked the boards to applause for decades, while the cryptic dumb show,
itself a survival of earlier forms, remained as a ghostly harbinger of events to
come.

Even in his earliest plays, Shakespeare began to extend and develop
these prophetic glimpses, so that they became ways of presenting the process
of the mind at work in memory, emotion, and imagination. What was essentially a predictive device of plot thus became, at the same time, a significant
aspect of meaning. Dream episodes, in short, began to work within the plays
as metaphors for the larger action, functioning at once as a form of presentation and as a concept presented. This is clearly the case with the dramatic
action of *Richard III*. From Queen Margaret's curse to Clarence's monitory
dream and the haunting nightmare of Bosworth Field, omen and apparition
define and delimit the play's world.

The consciousness of dreaming which is to dominate the play throughout makes its first striking appearance in Richard's opening soliloquy:

> Plots have I laid, inductions dangerous,
> By drunken prophecies, libels and dreams,
> To set my brother Clarence and the king
> In deadly hate the one against the other.
> (1.1.32–35)

Dreams here appear in what will become a familiar context for the early
plays, clearly analogous to "plots," "prophecies," and "libels" as elements of
the malign irrational. Richard has deftly contrived to manipulate circum-

From Marjorie B. Garber, *Dream in Shakespeare: From Metaphor to Metamorphosis* (New Haven, Conn.:
Yale University Press, 1974). Reprinted with permission of the publisher.

stance by preying upon the vulnerability of the superstitious king. Encountering his brother Clarence on his way to the Tower, he is told what he already knows: the king, says Clarence,

> harkens after prophecies and dreams,
> And from the crossbow plucks the letter G,
> And says a wizard told him that by G
> His issue disinherited should be;
> And, for my name of George begins with G,
> It follows in his thought that I am he.
>
> (1.1.54–59)

The poetry here halts and stammers, a mirror of the simplicity and confusion which make Clarence such an easy target. He considers himself a reasonable man, and, confronted by unreason, he is both impotent and outraged. Yet such an absolute rejection of the irrational is a fatal misjudgment in the world of *Richard III,* and Clarence's skepticism becomes a means to his destruction, just as later his determined denial of the truth of his own dream will lead directly to his death.

Here, in the first scene of the play, a sharp contrast is already apparent between the poles of dream and reason. Significantly, Richard, the Machiavel, defines himself as a realist, in contrast to the foolish Clarence and the lascivious Edward; he intends to control his fate and the fate of others through an exercise of reason. Yet the very first evidence of his supposed control, the false prophecy of "G," is truer than he knows: not George but Gloucester will disinherit Edward's sons. Clarence's passive skepticism about the irrational is but an image of Richard's more active scorn, and Richard's vulnerability to the powers of the imagination at Bosworth is prefigured by Clarence's prophetic dream of death.

The basic pattern of dream as prophecy is exemplified in simplest form by the dream of Lord Stanley as it is reported to Hastings in act 3:

> He dreamt the boar had rased off his helm.
> . . . .
> Therefore he sends to know your lordship's pleasure,
> If you will presently take horse with him
> And with all speed post with him to the north
> To shun the danger that his soul divines.
>
> (3.2.11, 15–18)

But Hastings, like Clarence, reacts with instinctive disbelief:

> Tell him his fears are shallow, without instance;
> And for his dreams, I wonder he's so simple
> To trust the mock'ry of unquiet slumbers.
>
> (3.2.25–27)

In the dream and its reception we have the fundamental design of early Shakespearean dream: the monitory dream which is true, but not believed. Stanley dreams that Richard—the boar—will cut off their heads, and Hastings rejects this suggestion absolutely. He reasons, further, that to react to it will have the undesirable effect of making the prophecy come true, since if it is known that they distrust him, Richard will give them reasons for distrust.

> To fly the boar before the boar pursues
> Were to incense the boar to follow us
> And make pursuit where he did mean no chase.
>
> (3.2.28–30)

This is a politic and sophisticated conclusion; it is also a false one, and it places Hastings in the revealing category of those who scoff at omens. He is in fact a prisoner of his own reason. "A marvelous case it is," remarks Holinshed, with customary exactitude, "to hear either the warning that he should have voided or the tokens that he could not void." It is only hours later, when he hears himself condemned, that he at last grasps the enormity of his mistake.

> For I, too fond, might have prevented this.
> Stanley did dream the boar did rase our helms,
> And I did scorn it and disdain to fly.
> Three times today my footcloth horse did stumble,
> And started when he looked upon the Tower,
> As loath to bear me to the slaughterhouse.
>
> (3.4.80–85)

This belated account of an earlier omen, equally disregarded, establishes even more clearly Hasting's distrust of the entire realm of the irrational. It is only in the developing context of supernatural warnings that he, too late, can interpret the sign correctly.

For his part, Richard follows the same course with Hastings as he did with Clarence and Edward: he pretends to have discovered "devilish plots / Of damnèd witchcraft" (3.4.59–60), ostensible reasons for his own deformity, and condemns Hastings to death for his cautious skepticism. Once again, he employs witchcraft as a device, something to be used rather than believed in. Apparently, then, he and Hastings occupy positions at opposite ends of the rationalist scale: Hastings the victim, warned by true omens he chooses to ignore; Richard the victor, creating false signs and prophecies through which he controls the superstitious and the skeptical alike. Yet they are more alike than they seem at first. When Richard himself becomes the dreamer, the recipient of omens and supernatural warnings, his rationalist posture is susceptible to the same immediate collapse; the terrifying world of dream overwhelms him, as it has overwhelmed Clarence and Hastings, at the critical moment of his ill-starred defense on Bosworth Field.

The double dream at Bosworth is an apparition dream, related to the risen spirits in *2 Henry VI* and *Macbeth* as well as to the ghosts of *Hamlet* and *Julius Caesar*. Richard and Richmond, encamped at opposite ends of the field, are each in turn visited by a series of ghosts representing Richard's victims: Edward Prince of Wales, Henry VI, Clarence, Rivers, Gray and Vaughan, Hastings, the two young princes, Anne, and Buckingham. As each spirit pauses he speaks to Richard like a voice of conscience within the soul: "Dream on thy cousins smothered in the Tower" (5.3.152); "Dream on, dream on, of bloody deeds and death" (l. 172). And then, in a formal counterpoint, each turns to Richmond and wishes him well. The whole scene is symmetrically arranged, the contrast of sleeping and waking, despair and hopefulness, emphasized by the rigidity of the form. For Richard, "guiltily awake" (l. 147), this is the fulfillment of the last term of Margaret's curse:

> The worm of conscience still begnaw thy soul!
> Thy friends suspect for traitors while thou liv'st,
> And take deep traitors for thy dearest friends!
> No sleep close up that deadly eye of thine,
> Unless it be while some tormenting dream
> Affrights thee with a hell of ugly devils!
>
> (1.3.221–26)

Richard's sleeplessness, like Macbeth's, is the mark of a troubled condition of soul, the outward sign of an inward sin. Margaret in her self-chosen role as "prophetess" (1.3.300) has called it down upon him, adding yet another to the series of omens which culminate in dream.

The terror which this dream evokes in Richard's mind is explicitly shown in his frightened soliloquy ("Is there a murderer here? No. Yes, I am" [5.3.185]), and even more in his subsequent conversation with Ratcliff. "O Ratcliff," he exclaims, "I have dreamed a fearful dream!" This is a very different man from the bloodless Machiavellian who plants the seeds of Clarence's execution in his brother's brain. His cry is now the Shakespearean equivalent of Faustus's last speech:

KING RICHARD: O Ratcliff; I fear, I fear!

RATCLIFF: Nay, good my lord, be not afraid of shadows.

KING RICHARD: By the apostle Paul, shadows tonight
Have struck more terror to the soul of Richard
Than can the substance of ten thousand soldiers.

(5.3.215–19)

In his fear he hits the point precisely: the "shadows," because they arise from the symbol-making unconscious, are more threatening than the substance.

The Richard who can say "Richard loves Richard: that is, I am I" (5.3.184) must create his own omens if they are to strike him with terror. Consciousness is the one enemy he can neither trick nor silence. From the controller of dreams he has become the controlled, the victim of his own horrible imaginings.

The Bosworth dream, like the predictive dream of Stanley, serves a structural purpose as well as a psychological one. The apparitions of murdered friends and kinsmen recall to the onlooker all the atrocities that have gone before, the perfidies of 3 Henry VI as well as the events of the present play. The device is dramatically useful because of the complexity of the historical events involved; many in the audience will probably not remember whose corpse is being mourned at the play's beginning, nor what relation the Lady Anne bears to the Lancastrian monarchy. Points of history are thus clarified at the same time that a psychologically convincing "replay" takes place in Richard's mind. The direct inverse of the prophetic dream, this recapitulation simultaneously furthers the ends of psychological observation, historical summation, and structural unity, so that the sequence of dreams and omens which are the formal controlling agents of Richard III are all embodied in the last revelation at Bosworth.

As useful a device as this final dream proves to be, it carries with it several inherent drawbacks. The apparatus of the serial ghosts is cumbersome and formal, analogous to (and probably derived from) the older pageantry of Deadly Sins and Heavenly Virtues. Holinshed, again a useful touchstone, describes the assemblage merely as "divers images like terrible devils" and rejects any supernatural interpretation: "But I think this was no dream but a punction and prick of his sinful conscience." His eagerness to moralize causes him to miss a more significant point: the very equivalence of *dream* with "the punction and prick of conscience" goes deep into the structural and psychological roots of the play. But Holinshed's devils are simply punishment figures of a generalized and abstract sort; by replacing them with the pageant of Richard's victims seeking retributive justice, Shakespeare transforms the entire significance of the last dream. He will use such a formal array only once more, in the series of apparitions which address Macbeth on the heath. There, again, the ghostly figures will become part of the king's private and terrible mythology of symbols, at the same time that they recall the ominous, monitory procession of deadly sins common to Tudor drama.

But the interior world of dream in Richard III was to undergo yet another alteration and expansion, quitting the specific formalism of the Bosworth dream for a freer and richer exploration of the subconscious. Just as Richard's apparent control of "prophecies, libels, and dreams" was abruptly replaced by subjugation to internal terrors, so, in Clarence's dream, imagination and the creative unconscious begin to replace the mechanism of witchcraft and omen as the proper architects of dream. Clarence's prophetic dream falls into three structurally distinct parts, each of which is important to the

pattern of dream use in the play. The first part (1.4.9–20) recounts his supposed sea journey with Gloucester, their reminiscences of the wars, and
Gloucester's accidental fall:

> As we paced along
> Upon the giddy footing of the hatches,
> Methought that Gloucester stumbled, and in falling
> Struck me (that thought to stay him) overboard
> Into the tumbling billows of the main.
>
> (1.4.16–20)

There is both psychological and symbolic truth in this passage. What Freud
called the "dream-work," the process by which the latent dream thoughts are
transformed into the manifest dream content, has rendered Clarence's latent
suspicion of Richard, a suspicion he finds emotionally unbearable, into more
reassuring terms. The subconscious thought "Gloucester wants to murder
me," rejected by the conscious, here appears in the disguised form "Gloucester will kill me by accident, though he doesn't want to." Outwardly, of
course, this prediction falls into the category of monitory dreams, the "tumbling billows of the main" anticipating the butt of malmsey in which
Clarence is to be ingloriously drowned. We may, if we choose, regard it solely
as another ignored or misunderstood omen, a class for which there is precedent in Shakespeare's works and in those of his contemporaries. But the passage, like the play, offers more than one possibility. While it fits into the pattern of unheeded warnings, it also begins to become an intrinsic part of the
mind of the speaker, communicating to us something even he himself does
not know.

Gloucester "stumbles" metaphorically in seeking the crown. This information is conveyed more directly in his own words; his soliloquies are psychological revelations, his disappointments and ambitions shown in psychological terms. He is a wholly new kind of character in Shakespeare, and we are
able to follow the workings of his mind in a wholly new way. When he thinks
aloud at the close of *3 Henry VI*, "Clarence, beware. Thou keep'st me from the
light" (5.6.84), he gives to us the same warning which is given in Clarence's
dream. And though we enter Clarence's consciousness only once, in the
dream itself, it is clear that some part of him suspects what we know to be a
certainty: Richard's design on his life. To read the accident passage as merely
another foreshadowing is to ignore the remarkably acute psychology with
which the poet approaches the unique occasion of the dream. Through the
dream device he permits us to enter Clarence's consciousness for a moment,
in the same way we have entered Richard's. This is why the dream appears so
different in style and imagery from anything else in the play. The latent suspicion Clarence harbors is authentically presented in masked form by his subconscious mind. And what is most interesting is that the process of masking
here takes the form of *metaphor.*

The mention of the "tumbling billows" meantime precipitates the dream into its second phase, the lyrical description of a world undersea. The chief characteristic of this vision—for that is what it really appears to be—is a striking contrast of mortality and eternity, the obscenely decaying body and the insensate but highly valued jewels which endure unchanged.

> A thousand men that fishes gnawed upon;
> Wedges of gold, great anchors, heaps of pearl,
> Inestimable stones, unvalued jewels,
> All scatt'red in the bottom of the sea.
>
> (1.4.25–28)

The ambiguity in "unvalued" is key to the whole. To Clarence in the extremity of his fear the jewels, though priceless, are without value as compared to human life. "Some lay in dead men's skulls," he continues,

> and in the holes
> Where eyes did once inhabit there were crept,
> As 'twere in scorn of eyes, reflecting gems
> That wooed the slimy bottom of the deep
> And mocked the dead bones that lay scatt'red by.
>
> (1.4.29–33)

What is chiefly remarkable about this image is its sheer physicality, the fascinated horror of a man contemplating his own imminent death. When the same image next appears in Shakespeare, it will have been curiously purified of passion:

> Those are pearls that were his eyes:
> Nothing of him that doth fade,
> But doth suffer a sea change
> Into something rich and strange.
>
> (*Tempest,* 1.2.401–4)

In Ariel's song mortality has become immortality, the eyes not replaced by pearls but transformed into them. The difference between this view and Clarence's suggests the direction in which vision and dream will develop in the plays. In *Richard III,* however, the undersea passage is nightmare to the dreamer, though its language is touched with a strange and haunting lyricism.

The passage which succeeds it, by contrast, is vividly dramatic, working through dialogue rather than through images. Two spirits appear to Clarence and confront him with his crimes, much as Richard's victims do on Bosworth Field. The tradition here evoked is that of the underworld visit of classical epic, the dead man greeted by the shades of those he knew on earth.

> I passed, methought, the melancholy flood,
> With that sour ferryman which poets write of,
> Unto the kingdom of perpetual night.
>
> (1.4.45–47)

Here is yet another sea journey, parallel to the channel crossing of the dream's first section. This generally unnoticed parallel is significant, for it again utilizes authentic dream logic to clarify the total meaning of the dream. In the first sea journey, as we have seen, Clarence overtly ascribes the cause of his fall to accident, though he betrays a latent distrust of his brother Richard. Here, in the second journey, he pictures his destination as hell, and supplies vivid reasons—in the forms of Warwick and Edward, prince of Wales—why he deserves damnation. The displaced figure of the stumbling Richard is strongly related to Clarence's assessment of his own guilt: he has perjured himself (i.e., dissembled about his allegiance) and slain the heir to the throne. But Richard, too, is a perjurer and will become a murderer; he has had Clarence falsely imprisoned and has then pretended ignorance and concern over the event; he will later have him killed because he stands in the line of succession. Clarence thus displaces his unacceptable distrust of Richard, by transferring his just suspicions to analogous episodes in his own life. Simultaneously he punishes himself for having these suspicions by turning them against himself. The ghosts of Warwick and Edward thus possess a multiple significance for the dream's meaning, establishing even further the psychological accuracy of its form.

The more direct significance of these figures is of course historical recapitulation, as it will be in Bosworth dream. The magnificent tongue twister of a line,

> "What scourge for perjury
> Can this dark monarchy afford false Clarence?"
>
> (1.4.50–51)

is meant to recall the elaborate chain of events by which, in *3 Henry VI,* Clarence first pledges his support to Warwick and then deserts him. On that occasion Warwick rebukes him as a "passing traitor, perjured and unjust" (5.1.106), and the charge is repeated by the prince of Wales: "Thou perjur'd George," he taunts (5.5.34), and when Clarence joins with his brothers to stab the prince to death, he does so in a spirit of resentment as well as anger, retorting, "there's for twitting me with perjury" (l. 40). The accusations made by the ghosts in his dream are thus authentic reminders of Clarence's history. The prince's ghost resembles the accusatory apparitions of Bosworth, but is much more closely assimilated into the consciousness of the dreamer:

> A shadow like an angel, with bright hair
> Dabbled in blood, and he shricked out aloud,

"Clarence is come, false, fleeting, perjured Clarence,
Seize on him, Furies, take him unto torment!"
(1.4.53–57)

This is no ceremonial intoning, but rather a visionary visitation. The prince is not identified by name, but is only presented in fragmented detail, as if hastily glimpsed—"a shadow like an angel," "bright hair," "blood." We are inside the mind of Clarence, and we see the ghost through his eyes. In keeping with the play's general design, the ghosts of Clarence's mental landscape appear only secondhand, as related through his dream. It is Richard's consciousness with which we are continually in contact, and only Richard's ghosts make actual appearances on stage.

Yet there is something extremely important about the relationship of Clarence's vision of Warwick and Edward to the actual ghosts of act 5. Clarence's dream internalizes the ghosts, portrays them directly as elements of imagination. Gone is the cumbersome apparatus of the Bosworth dream, and gone likewise is the aura of artificiality created by the mechanical pattern of omen and fulfillment. Dream here is an agency of liberation, a means of freeing prophecy from device and relating it to psychological intuition. Imagery bears a bigger part, and association is legitimately employed to make images into symbols. The materials of Clarence's dream are still embryonic, and its technique stands in marked contrast to that of the rest of *Richard III*. But it is the first real anticipation of a new use of dream, to be refined and expanded in the later plays.

Richard III and Queen Elizabeth

EMRYS JONES

Richard's wooing of Elizabeth for her daughter's hand is usually taken as a repeat performance, but feebler and more long-drawn-out, of his wooing of Anne. And, though there are one or two dissentients, it is usually understood that Elizabeth finally consents to Richard's proposal.[1] In Hall's historical account the Queen does in fact allow herself to be flattered into receiving overtures from Richard, and moves out of sanctuary with her daughters into his power, though it is not clear whether she knows of his designs on her daughter; but later, when "young Elizabeth" hears of them, she is affronted— Richard was her uncle, and marriage would have been within the forbidden degrees. Although the scene has its faults—it probably is too long—it is a mistake to see Richard repeating his triumph over another intellectually feeble woman. Shakespeare had a quite different end in view.

The dialogue is more elusive in tone than it may first appear. There is from the start a studied ambiguity—and the ambiguity is Shakespeare's, not Richard's. Richard opens the subject as follows:

> You have a daughter call'd Elizabeth,
> Virtuous and fair, royal and gracious.

One notices a peculiar neutrality of tone; it has the ring of a formal utterance. It might have been spoken by anyone, good or bad. We could certainly not infer from it that a "villain" was the speaker. We could, on the contrary, imagine it spoken by someone as virtuous in the play's world as Richmond. Richard is speaking with, for him, a strange objectivity; his speeches are usually coloured with personality and rich in histrionic or parodic tone-effects, but this one is different. The Queen responds with alarm, fearing that since Elizabeth is her daughter she too, like the Princes, must die. Richard replies in the same graciously formal tone: "Wrong not her birth, she is a royal princess." But Elizabeth still mistakes his purpose and bitterly reminds him of her murdered sons. And he makes yet another effort to switch the subject to his present good intentions:

> K. RICH.: . . . I intend more good to you and yours
>
> Than ever you or yours by me were harm'd!
>
> Q. ELIZ.: What good is cover'd with the face of heaven,
>
> To be discover'd, that can do me good?
>
> K. RICH.: Th' advancement of your children, gentle lady.
>
> Q. ELIZ.: Up to some scaffold, there to lose their heads?
>
> K. RICH.: Unto the dignity and height of Fortune,
>
> The high imperial type of this earth's glory.
>
> Q. ELIZ.: Flatter my sorrow with report of it;
>
> Tell me what state, what dignity, what honour,
>
> Canst thou demise to any child of mine?

The bearing of this is not obvious at once. But one notices that the terms in which the dialogue is couched are such as to induce us to contemplate the future—the real future—of the Queen's daughter, "young Elizabeth," upon whom Richard now has his eye fixed. And this too is the effect of the slightly unctuous, almost "official," neutrality of tone with which he opened ("You have a daughter call'd Elizabeth . . ."). We remember in fact that "young Elizabeth" was to become the first Tudor queen, wife of Henry VII and mother of Henry VIII. Officially speaking, she was exactly what Richard here calls her: "Virtuous and fair, royal and gracious." And so on throughout the dialogue: when Richard promises to advance Elizabeth's children "Unto the dignity and height of Fortune" we can't help knowing that that is what—inadvertently—he actually did. And that this—the historical irony of this extraordinary situation—is what Shakespeare had in mind is proved by his use of the unusual word "demise" in the rhetorical position of climax in the speech of Elizabeth's last quoted. This is a legal word, used only here by Shakespeare. Its general meaning is "convey," "transmit," but a further, more specialized meaning also seems present, although the earliest example cited by the *O.E.D.* belongs to 1670: "To convey or transfer (a title or dignity); *esp.* said of the transmission of sovereignty, as by the abdication or death of the sovereign." Shakespeare must intend his audience to pick up, once again, the allusion to Bosworth, the fact that Richard was soon to "demise" his "state," "dignity," and "honour" to his successor. A little later the dialogue receives similar added point through the ambiguity of reference: but first, Elizabeth prepares for it by deliberately mistaking Richard's meaning. When he says "from my soul I love thy daughter," she quibblingly takes "from" to mean "at variance with," "away from" his soul. Richard corrects her, but in doing so introduces the notion of "confounding" meaning, so making Shakespeare's purpose more explicit, and more conscious, for the audience.

K. RICH.:   Be not so hasty to confound my meaning.
               I mean that with my soul I love thy daughter
               And do intend to make her Queen of England.
Q. ELIZ.:   Well, then, who dost thou mean shall be her king?
K. RICH.:   Even he that makes her queen. Who else should be?
Q. ELIZ.:   What, thou?
K. RICH.:   Even so. How think you of it?

Here Shakespeare has made his point more clearly. Elizabeth might actually be in the author's secret, privately enjoying the equivocation, so relaxed and colloquial her words sound: "Well, then, who dost thou mean shall be her king?" Her next remark ("What, thou?") recalls a moment in an earlier scene, when she hears for the first time that Richard has seized the royal power: Brakenbury has just refused to admit her to the Tower to visit her sons:

BRAK.:   The King hath strictly charg'd the contrary.
Q. ELIZ.:   The King! Who's that?
BRAK.:   I mean the Lord Protector.
Q. ELIZ.:   The Lord protect him from that kingly title!

The two situations, as far as Elizabeth is concerned, have a kind of antithetical symmetry: in the first she was unaware that her son had been deposed; in the second she is (necessarily, of course) unaware that her daughter is to be made queen.

Historical irony of this kind informs the whole of this second "out of time" wooing scene. The topics of conversation turn pointedly on what is going to happen in the immediate future—we are constantly made to apply our historical knowledge of the outcome to the present situation. In Richard's long speech (for example) of would-be overwhelmingly forceful persuasion (291–336), he dwells on the pleasure Elizabeth will enjoy as the mother of another queen:

> The King, that calls your beauteous daughter wife,
> Familiarly shall call thy Dorset brother;
> Again shall you be mother to a king . . .

—but the effect is once more to remind us that the situation envisaged, though certainly to be brought about, will see a different "King" on the throne. Entirely in keeping with this conception is Richard's final choice of something by which to swear: "The time to come" (IV. iv. 387). That is what the whole scene is about.

Taken in this light, the apparent wavering of Elizabeth is seen to be deliberately plotted by Shakespeare. Richard never makes any headway in his long attempt on her: all he does on his own behalf is utter a solemn curse upon himself shortly before the end of the scene, which at this point in the play we take "straight"—this is no histrionically amusing blasphemy but is premonitory, like so much else in this dialogue, of the ultimate despair expressed in the ghost scene of V.iii. Elizabeth, on the other hand, never loses her intensely bitter sense of maternal loss. In this Shakespeare firmly departs from the chroniclers, who say (as Hall does) that she "putting in oblivion the murther of her innocente children . . . blynded by avaricious affeccion and seduced by flatterynge wordes, first delivered into kyng Richards handes her v. daughters as Lambes once agayne committed to the custody of the ravenous wolfe. . . ."[2] Shakespeare has nothing about delivering her daughters into Richard's hands. Hall goes on to comment sharply on the culpable frailty of Elizabeth ("Surely the inconstancie of this woman were muche to be marveled at . . ."), but this is not Shakespeare's position. He gives this contemptuous expression of surprise to Richard ("Relenting fool, and shallow, changing woman!"), but made more use of it earlier, after the subjugation of Anne, where it was more deserved. (For just as he transferred the chroniclers' conception of Richard's dream to Clarence's, so he transfers their contempt for Elizabeth to Anne.) Elizabeth's final words in this scene, like so much else in it, are ambiguous: they temporarily placate Richard, but convey a different meaning to the audience:

> Shall I be tempted of the devil thus? . . .
> Shall I forget myself to be myself? . . .
> Yet thou didst kill my children. . . .
> Shall I go win my daughter to thy will? . . .
> I go. Write to me very shortly,
> And you shall understand from me her mind.

What we hear at the beginning of the next scene is that "The Queen hath heartily consented / He should espouse Elizabeth her daughter"—where "He" refers to Richmond. We certainly have an impression of Elizabeth's weakness—she is no Margaret. And the questions just quoted make her instability apparent to the end. But even here, in their midst, comes the flat statement "Yet thou didst kill my children." There is no "putting in oblivion"; that, as she said earlier, is a string she will harp on till death.

This wooing scene, like everything else in this second movement, is orientated towards Bosworth.

Notes

1. E. A. J. Honigmann, ed., *Richard III* (Harmondsworth: Penguin, 1968), pp. 27–8, believes that Elizabeth does not consent; Wolfgang Clemen (*A commentary on Shakespeare's "Richard III,"* London, Methuen, 1968, pp. 190–4) is more orthodox in thinking she does; while Dover Wilson (William Shakespeare, *Richard III,* ed. John Dover Wilson, Cambridge: Cambridge University Press, 1961, p. 234) takes up a more complicated position: Shakespeare, he thinks, leads the audience to believe that she yields to Richard but "undeceives them almost immediately after, i.e. in 4.5."

2. *Narrative and Dramatic Sources,* ed. G. Bullough (New York: Columbia, 1960), iii. 287.

Bit Parts in *Richard III*

M. M. MAHOOD

"My lord, stand back, and let the coffin pass." The words and their accompanying action are a high point in most productions of *Richard the Third*. Richard, who has peremptorily halted the funeral procession of Henry the Sixth, finds a halberd pointed at his breast. This combination of axe and spear is a formidable weapon, and when the play is over we may recall the visual prolepsis of the incident: the axe portending Richard's ruthless dismissal of his opponents as they are escorted to the block by halberdiers, the spear foreboding the manner in which the Boar is finally hunted down by those who have escaped his tyranny.

Telling as the line is, it is not clear who should say it. The heading "Gent[leman]" suggests the speaker is one of the pair whom the mourning Lady Anne addresses as Tressel and Berkeley, and this attribution would give verbal substance to one of these walking shadows, whose names so mysteriously persist in programmes and even in the character lists of modern editions. The words are, however, more courageous, more a protest made on our behalf if they come from one of the halberdiers; the generalised term, "the coffin," then expresses the common man's sense of outrage (one thinks of recent Irish incidents) at the indecency of stopping a funeral. Directors certainly prefer the line to provoke the eyeball-to-eyeball confrontation between Richard and the halberdier:

> Unmannered dog, stand'st thou when I command.
> Advance thy halberd higher than my breast,
> Or by Saint Paul I'll strike thee to my foot,
> And spurn upon thee, beggar, for thy boldness.
> (1.2.39–42)

Edmund Kean struck the halberd up with his sword, Laurence Olivier (in his film version) knocked the man down and put his foot on him, and Anthony Sher went one better by felling two halberdiers with his crutches.[1]

Violence such as this, however, is more characteristic of the disintegrating Richard of the Messengers episode, late in the fourth act. What the encounter with the halberdier brings out is Richard's power to dominate by mean of a dark charisma, a power best conveyed through the slow return of the halberd to an upright position and through the deferential hesitancy of the words which, on Anne's departure, complete this small part: "Towards Chertsey, noble lord?" (225). The effect is helped, as Shakespeare may have guessed it would be, by the small-part actor being genuinely awestruck in the presence of a star performer.[2]

The point made is that Richard allows nothing to stand in his way. Every man, woman and child in his path must be made to serve his ends or be eliminated; the halberdier is only one of many minor figures, in this play of fifty-two speaking parts, whom he cows, silences, and renders ineffectual. Though this astonishing ascendancy is a triumph of the dramatist's art, it creates a major dramaturgical problem. Drama is by definition an interplay of forces, but here the juggernaut hero scatters or crushes all in his advance to the throne. There is a risk of Richard the playwright inhibiting Shakespeare's inventiveness with his lesser characters, of the dramatist being upstaged by his own marvellous creation. How Shakespeare faces and attempts to overcome this difficulty is the theme of this chapter, and I hope to show that, despite Richard's dominance, only a very small number of the minor figures deserve to be called shadows. Like Truth at the opening of another Elizabethan play about Richard the Third, Shakespeare finds ways to give substance to the rest:

> TRUTH: . . . Poetry, what makes thou upon a stage?
> POETRY: Shadows.
> TRUTH: Then will I add bodies to the shadows . . . [3]

A gang of four, comprising King Richard, Francis Lord Lovel, Sir William Catesby and Sir Richard Ratcliffe, was an essential part of the Elizabethan folk-memory of Richard the Third's reign.

> The Cat, the Rat, and Lovel our Dog,
> Do rule all England under the Hog

ran the rhyme which cost William Collingbourne his life. Collingbourne is allocated a cautionary monologue in *The Mirror for Magistrates,* between those of Buckingham and of Richard himself, and its arresting beginning makes it unlikely that Shakespeare skipped the story:

> Beware, take heed, take heed, beware, beware,
> You poets you, that purpose to rehearse
> By any art what tyrants' doings are . . . [4]

In fact the Cat, the Rat and the Dog all figure in *Richard the Third,* even though the exigencies of doubling made it impossible for Shakespeare to keep them together as a gang. Lovel's part is tiny but consistent. One line echoes Ratcliffe's eagerness to see Hastings beheaded, and the other two—

> Here is the head of that ignoble traitor,
> The dangerous and unsuspected Hastings
> (3.5.22–3)

—are a bit of zestful role-playing, in the manner of Catesby, in order to impress the Mayor. Lovel is thus a shadow to Richard's other two shadows, and his absence from the Quarto indicates that he may have been dropped at an early point in the play's stage history.[5] But whether or not he appears in a modern production, his title should serve as a reminder that these accomplices in Richard's crimes, though they are not great nobles like Buckingham, should not be played as waged "minders," they *did* rule all England under the Boar, Ratcliffe being particularly powerful as Richard's agent in the North, and Catesby, who was connected with him by marriage, being a member of Richard's Council, and Lord Chamberlain after Hastings' death.

High birth and high office do not of course exclude barbarous behaviour. Ratcliffe in particular carries an aura of physical brutality which comes straight from More's description of him as "short and rude in speech, rough and boistrous of behaviour, bold in mischief, as far from pity as from all fear of God."[6] He is something more than a bodyguard: an extension of Richard's body, a replacement for his withered right arm. The horror of Hastings' beheading and of the executions at Pomfret is heightened by the callousness ("He longs to see your head") with which he oversees them. After the play was written, the actors, or Shakespeare himself, noticed that Ratcliffe could not have been present at both events, so in the Quarto Catesby replaces him at the Tower. But if Shakespeare's first version was logistically wrong, it was dramatically right. Nor does the Quarto compensate for the change when it saves a part by letting Ratcliffe preside over a later execution, that of Buckingham, in place of the Sheriff. Ratcliffe could never have uttered the Sheriff's mild words.

If Ratcliffe by his violence of speech is the shadow of Richard's brutality, Catesby, "well learned in the laws of this land,"[7] is an extension of Richard's intellect, the shadow of his inventiveness and dissimulation. He is cockahoop at being sent by Richard and Buckingham (3.1.186–9) to discover Hastings' reaction to the notion of Richard as king. It proves to be outrage: "God knows I will not do it, to the death!" (3.2.55). That Catesby's sardonic "God keep your lordship in that gracious mind!" is followed by a moment of rapt private triumph while Hastings' thoughts are dwelling with satisfaction on his enemies' fate at Pomfret, is made clear by the way the dialogue is resumed at line 60—

> I tell thee, Catesby.
> CATESBY: What, my lord?[8]

Now, with the blend of assumed piety and gleeful private irony that we meet time and again in Richard, the Cat begins to play with his victim:

> 'Tis a vile thing to die, my gracious lord,
> When men are unprepared, and look not for it,
> (62–3)

and he emphasises his role-playing by throwing a further aside straight at the audience, exactly in the manner of the reverend Vice, Richard himself:

> The princes both make high account of you
> [*aside*] For they account his head upon the bridge.
> (69–70)

Shakespeare has perforce simplified Catesby's relationship with Hastings. More, who felt the need to supply, at least in his Latin text, motives for Catesby's behaviour, tells us that he coveted Hastings' state offices, and an awareness of this may be of help to the actor. But Shakespeare transfers this sort of self-interest to a very minor character in the same scene, the Pursuivant with whom Hastings hubristically rejoices on his way to the Tower, and whose words drip with oily expectation of his share in Hastings' improved fortunes. Catesby does not need motives. He exists as the zealous imitator of Richard's dissimulations, most in his element in the two scenes in which Richard outwits the Citizens in their reluctance to see him crowned. At the Tower he finds great opportunities to mime his pretended concern for Richard's safety, and at Baynard's Castle he bustles back and forth between the parties, adding to Buckingham's efforts a proper satisfaction at the legality of the proceeding: "Oh, make them joyful, grant their lawful suit!" (3.7.203).

Still as Richard's shadow, Catesby reflects the changes that come over the tyrant in the second part of the play. He watches with alarm the effect on Richard of Buckingham's reluctance to be involved in the murder of the two Princes. It is a no longer gleeful Richard who wants Catesby to rumour abroad that the Queen is near to death, and Catesby's hesitation ("Look how thou dream'st!"—4.2.56) shows that for him this is one order that will not be executed with zest. Later in the same act, in the confusions of the Messengers scene, both principal and supporting actor fluff their parts as the pressures increase. In the final battle a distraught Catesby, shouting for his master to be rescued, is flung aside by him as a "Slave" (5.4.9). But there is nothing moving in this fidelity or in its rejection. Walking shadows cannot outlive the body that cast them, and Shakespeare does not bother to inform us that Ratcliffe dies at Bosworth or that Catesby will be executed after it. Despite his several appearances, Catesby has in the end no more substance than have his cronies Ratcliffe and Lovel. The Cat, the Rat and the Dog are executioners in that older sense in which the word is still used by Holinshed: they execute Richard's designs, and apart from this have no other life or function.

The up-to-date meaning of "executioner" was "assassin," and Richard uses it thus in 1.3 for the two men he employs to kill Clarence. In the murder scene which follows there is a marked difference in the language used by the Murderers to each other and that they use to Clarence after he wakes, and some critics believe the cross-talk of the pair to be an addition, perhaps made when Shakespeare realised that the parts would be played by the company's comedians. But ordinary people have never had much difficulty in shifting their speech register according to those they are addressing. The Murderers, having talked with Richard in blank verse, drop naturally enough into prose for a dialogue which, by its important bearings on the succeeding verse exchanges with Clarence, is integral to the scene as Shakespeare wrote it.

In the prose, both in turn express remorse at what they have to do. It is pretty clear from the sudden reversal of roles and rapid shifts of feeling in lines 145–51 that the First Murderer is "taking off" the Second's misgivings. What has not always been as clear to critics as it is to many actors is that those misgivings, which began with "The urging of the word 'judgment' hath bred a kind of remorse in me" (107), can also be a piece of play-acting. The stage business of counting twenty to give the pang time to pass, and the account, stylised in the manner of the comic monologues of Launce and Lancelot, of the ways conscience attacks a man, form part of an act the audience would readily have recognised: by 1591, the Remorseful Murderer was sufficiently well established on the Elizabethan stage to be the object of parody.[9] Even if we are not quite sure whether the Second Murderer is just pretending or if he is pretending to pretend, the recognisable element of theatrical burlesque serves a number of functions. It provides a few minutes of relaxation for the audience after the anguish of Clarence's dream, to which the prose dialogue is linked by the theme of conscience. It is also anticipatory, in the manner of *Henry the Fourth, Part One* 4.3: prior parody draws off irrelevant responses from the powerful scene that follows. A third, and for our purpose the most important, function of the prose dialogue is that its deliberate staginess emphasises that the two Murderers want nothing better than to be creatures made in Richard's likeness. Each flings himself into his metadrama, as eager as his master to "play the devil" and "prove a villain." Their sudden entry is in the recognisable Gloucester manner (the actors, to judge by the Quarto, saw the importance of this and polished up the effect), and they do not forget that Richard has called them likeable lads such as would have no qualms of remorse—"Your eyes drop millstones when fools' eyes fall tears" (1.3.352). Helping themselves, perhaps, to the wine on hand, they enter with relish into their appointed roles of conscience-free villains, loudly parodying the scruples felt by old-fashioned stage murderers.

This back-slapping cheerfulness wakes their victim, and they launch into a different genre of metadrama. In verse and in the lofty tones of revenge tragedy, they portray themselves as the instruments of divine retribution against one who helped at Tewkesbury to slay Prince Edward of Lancaster. Histrionic as it all is, Clarence knows they are not going to "murder in jest" and undercuts their posturings with the cold self-awareness that this knowledge brings:

> CLARENCE: Take not the quarrel from his powerful arm.
> He needs no indirect or lawless course
> To cut off those that have offended him.
> FIRST MURDERER: Who made thee, then, a bloody minister,
> When gallant-springing brave Plantagenet,
> That princely novice, was struck dead by thee?
> CLARENCE: My brother's love, the devil, and my rage.
>
> (1.4.217–23)

The First Murderer's retort to this—

> Thy brother's love, our duty, and thy faults
> Provoke us hither now to slaughter thee

—represents another aspect of the stage murderer's behaviour: the revelation to the victim of the crime's real instigator. Both join in this gratuitous cruelty, and to Clarence's insistence that Richard "would labour my delivery" (246) the First Murderer replies in the very voice Richard used when speaking of Clarence in the play's first scene,

> Why, so he doth, when he delivers you
> From this earth's thralldom to the joys of Heaven.

But the thought calls forth from the Second Murderer a line—"Make peace with God, for you must die, my lord"—which hardly belongs to the brutal parts "lessoned" (240) them by Richard. Perhaps there is just enough regret and uncertainty in his voice for Clarence to seize upon in a plea beginning "Have you that holy feeling in your souls?" which in turn elicits the faltering, bewildered "What shall we do?" (256). The First Murderer is in no such doubt: "Relent? no: 'tis cowardly and womanish."[10] This harsh rebuttal drives Clarence to direct all his pleading to the man who has faltered. This is his undoing, for it gives the First Murderer the chance to strike from behind. All that remains for the Second Murderer is bitter regret that his warning cry— "Look behind you, my lord!"(268)—came too late to save Clarence.

As with all good theatrical surprises, we find on looking back at the script that the Second Murderer's turnabout was far from being unprepared.

He is the one who wants to kill Clarence in his sleep and thus avoid the confrontation that the ruthless First Murderer so eagerly undertakes.[11] When Clarence wakes, it is significantly the Second Murderer who is out of his part and cannot stammer his intention until prompted by his victim. Most important of all, he has been the first to play with the notion of remorse, and in the richly Falstaffian speech on conscience we can, with hindsight, see an attempt to exorcise feelings which in the end, since God is not mocked, he will be unable to suppress.

Of course, it is Clarence's scene. Our dominant emotion must be horror at the murder, and in this the Murderers are merely Richard's instruments. But that the Second Murderer is something besides prepares us for later matters, and in particular for the revulsion experienced by two other assassins whom we never see and by the man who suborns them and whom we do see, Tyrrel. This revulsion is so central to the dramatic effect of the play's last two acts, which are built upon the chronicles' insistence that Richard's downfall was retribution for his murder of the Princes in the Tower, that inevitably the question arises: why, when Shakespeare had so powerfully portrayed the death of Clarence, did he choose not to stage the children's deaths? Reluctance to repeat himself can hardly be the reason, since duplication—Margaret's two appearances, the two formal keenings, the two outrageous wooings, Richard's two playlets at the Tower and Baynard's Castle—is a structural feature of the play. It has been suggested that, in order to avoid the charge of plagiarism, Shakespeare took care not to use episodes already exploited in *The True Tragedy*.[12] A cruder but more plausible explanation is that he originally intended the play, which has a remarkably leisurely and inventive first act, to be in instalments, like his own *Henry the Sixth,* and like a University play he might have known, Legge's *Richardus Tertius.* A belated decision to portray the whole reign in one play would have forced him to be highly selective of later incidents. But dramatic artistry is explanation enough. Concealed violence, the fate of *los disparados,* can be even more horrifying to those who become aware of it than is overt brutality, and our revulsion at the unseen murder is deepened by the effect it has on those who carry out Richard's wish to have "the bastards dead" (4.2.18).

Tyrrel's alacrity in undertaking the murder, coming as it does in the wake of Buckingham's distress at the proposal, immediately places him in the company of those who closely imitate Richard's own ruthlessness—so much so that the actors reconstructing the quarto text mixed his lines with others belonging to Catesby.[13] And because we thus think of Tyrrel as a recruit to the totally unscrupulous group round Richard, his soliloquy on his return overwhelms us. Not until *Macbeth* will Shakespeare again show a character so traumatised by his own action. Tyrrel discovers an evil deed is not "done, when 'tis done" when he encounters the anguish of Dighton and Forrest who, "fleshed villains" as they were, are now "gone [i.e. overwhelmed] with conscience and remorse." How deeply Tyrrel is himself touched by these feelings is evident from his realisation that he has been instrumental in

> The most arch deed of pitious massacre
> That ever yet this land was guilty of.
> (4.3.2–3)

But the shock wave stops at Tyrrel, whose report to Richard is charged—especially if we recall that one meaning of "sovereign" is "life-giving"—with a desperate and futile irony:

> All health, my sovereign lord!
>
> RICHARD: Kind Tyrrell, am I happy in thy news?
>
> TYRREL: If to have done the thing you gave in charge
> Beget your happiness, be happy then,
> For it is done.
>
> (23–7)

Deaf to Tyrrel's tone, Richard looks forward to hearing all the details after supper:

> Meantime, but think how I may do thee good,
> And be inheritor of thy desire.
> (32–4)

Tyrrel has, however, other thoughts and a different inheritance. The burden of both is expressed in an exit (silent, without leavetaking, in the Quarto) as different as the actor can make it from the eagerness with which, only sixty lines earlier, he sped to do Richard's bidding. Of the play's five paid assassins, four are appalled by their task, and this revulsion gives them a human substantiality denied the flush of court cards that Richard holds in his hand.

Not only Richard's henchmen are carried away by his zest for villainy. The audience too rides in his triumph, its power fantasies fed by the ease with which he crushes his victims. Nor do all of these earn a full measure of sympathy. Our admiration at the ingenuity of the bottled spider overrides most of the pity we might otherwise feel for poor foolish Anne or the trustful and complacent Hastings, and Buckingham forfeits our concern when he has second thoughts about Richard's plan to murder the Princes. Even Clarence in his time has been a ready accessory after Richard's crimes. Yet to counter Richard's dramatic supremacy, there must be victims who deserve and get our total compassion. Shakespeare provides them in the small roles of Queen Elizabeth's kindred—most notably in her brother Rivers and her two younger sons.

There is a second brother, but his role is slight. Shakespeare follows the writer of *The True Tragedy* in making Sir Richard Grey the Queen's brother rather than a son by her earlier marriage; the effect of the Princes' deaths would be undermined if Elizabeth were to lose a son at Pomfret.[14] The playwright's awareness that he is taking a liberty with history may be the reason Grey is a shadowy figure until the moment he gladdens the audience's hearts with the parting shot

> God bless the prince from all the pack of you!
> A knot you are of damned bloodsuckers.
>
> (3.3.5–6)

He shares his fate with an even more sketchy figure, Sir Thomas Vaughan, who speaks one truculent line on his way to the scaffold and helps to swell the muster of ghosts before the Battle of Bosworth.[15] This looks like a beginner's part.

This scaffold defiance is Shakespeare's only concession to the notion, aired not only by Buckingham, an unreliable witness (2.2.150), but also by the Third Citizen (2.3.28), that the Queen's family are "proud." Pride is no part of the character of Lord Rivers as Shakespeare develops it, giving him a prominence which is in keeping with that afforded him in *The Mirror for Magistrates,* where his Tragedy is the first of those added to the 1563 volume. Richard's allusion to him in the opening scene as

> that good man of worship
> Anthony Woodvile, her brother there
>
> (66–7)

is meant to disparage, by denying Rivers his two noble titles and using a phrase suggestive of citizen worth.[16] But since an audience in the early 1590s contained a sizeable proportion of citizens and would-be citizens, the term prepared them to view Rivers according to his description in the Chronicles, "a wise, hardy, and honourable personage, as valiant of hands as politic of counsel."[17] And this is the impression Rivers makes in 1.3 and 2.1, where his responses to Richard's open and covert provocations are moderate and conciliatory:

> My lord of Gloucester, in those busy days
> Which here you urge to prove us enemies,
> We followed then our lord, our sovereign king.
> So should we you, if you should be our king.
>
> (1.3.144–7)

This simple fealty which prompts him after Edward's death to look forward to the crowning of Edward's son is an obstacle Richard must remove, and

Rivers' other citizen-like virtues make him an easy victim. There is no reason to assume that he is speaking sarcastically when he calls Richard's invocation of God's pardon on those responsible for Clarence's imprisonment "A virtuous and a Christian-like conclusion" (1.3.315). Such earnest piety implies that his own vows of reconciliation are genuine. It also prepares us for his failure to recognise the duplicity with which, in 2.1, Richard and Buckingham tender theirs. An equally citizen-like sense of the properties causes him to insist that the crazed Queen Margaret ought to be kept away from the court; and there is, too, a genuine and "worthy" concern for law and order in the readiness with which he falls in with Buckingham's suggestion (2.2.120) that the young King be escorted to London without any display of armed power.[18]

Rivers' dramatic strength lies in the audience's ready identification with a figure who claims that he dies "For truth, for duty, and for loyalty" (3.3.4). All the more surprising therefore that his brother Grey, after speaking of their "guiltless blood," should recall Margaret's curse upon them "for standing by when Richard stabbed her son" (17). The Chronicles in no way substantiate this charge, and even the *Mirror for Magistrates* (whose authors were if anything more obsessed with retribution than was Edward Hall) visits no worse sin of commission upon Rivers than an avaricious marriage. Only at the very end of his monologue does Rivers' ghost make a further admission: he failed to call the uncrowned Richard to account for his murders of Henry the Sixth and Clarence. It is significant that Shakespeare should also attribute a sin of omission, however unjustifiably, to Rivers, for it serves to align him, victim though he is, with other characters still to be considered who bear out the truism that "All that is necessary for the triumph of evil is that good men should do nothing." Rivers' last words are those of a good man. But he is also an appeaser, who failed his prince in being all too ready to lay aside his halberd at Richard's command.

The death of Edward of Lancaster, to which he does not make Rivers a party, calls forth Hall's eloquence on the subject of retribution, but his strongest words on this subject are reserved for the death of the Princes in the Tower. He expands More's narrative into several pages, all expressive of the horror that the murder aroused both among the common people and among the friends and remaining kindred of Queen Elizabeth: "to slay and destroy innocent babes and young infants the whole world abhorreth, and the blood from the earth crieth for vengeance to almighty God."[19] Shakespeare builds likewise upon the universal revulsion awakened not only by child-murder but by any and every offence against children.

The play creates an awareness of more young victims than Shakespeare could bring onto the stage. Atrocities of the civil war are recalled: the deaths of "pretty Rutland" and young Edward of Lancaster. In the last act, Richard is still out-Heroding Herod when he gives the order for the young hostage George Stanley to be beheaded. Although Shakespeare, as the result of his having conjured up a throng of ghosts, is unable to follow the author of *The*

True Tragedy in reuniting George with his father onstage, we shall see that he serves as a powerful offstage presence. Another youthful near-victim is Princess Elizabeth of York, whose importance as Henry the Seventh's future queen has led directors to introduce her as a mute and sometimes even to transfer to her lines taken from other characters. Shakespeare had to be content with making us feel how much she is at risk. The Elizabethans may have accepted the idea of a young girl being used as a pawn in a political marriage, but they were deeply shocked, as *Hamlet* shows, by the notion of marriage within the prohibited degrees. What Richard contemplates in his second proposal is, Queen Elizabeth's reaction makes plain, nothing less than incest, and the Princess herself, according to Hall, "detested and abhorred this unlawful, and in manner unnatural, copulation."[20]

In Richard's realm, then, children are corrupted as well as butchered. Finding Buckingham unresponsive to his wish to see the Princes dead, Richard determines he will seek the help of

> iron-witted fools
> And unrespective boys; none are for me
> That look into me with considerate eyes,
> (4.2.28–30)

and accordingly summons the Page, who can, he hopes, tell him of an ambitious malcontent. Directors either let themselves be guided by "unrespective" into presenting the Page as an innocent playing with cup and ball on the steps of the throne while Richard and Tyrrel plot the murders over his head, or they recoil from the notion of a child in such a scene and follow Cibber in replacing the Page with Catesby. But More, a dispassionate observer of court life, saw the Page as a young Machiavel who observed that Tyrrel was kept under by Catesby and Ratcliffe, and decided "of very special friendship . . . to do him good, that all the enemies that he had (except the devil) could never have done him so much hurt and shame."[21] The author of *The True Tragedy* exploits this hint of diabolism by developing the Page into a kind of Vice, a part that Shakespeare preferred to keep for Richard; but it is clear from

> Knows't thou not any whom corrupting gold
> Will tempt unto a close exploit of death?
> (33–4)

that the Page has himself long since been corrupted by Richard and his circle.

If the audience half recognises in the Page the boy actor who previously played Clarence's son,[22] the effect of innocence destroyed is reinforced, for Clarence's two children have also fallen prey to Richard's malign influence. Shakespeare has been taken to task for not making sufficiently clear that these last Plantagenets are possible claimants to the throne. But so much would have been self-evident to the Elizabethans as the reason for Richard, later in the play, plotting a "mean" match for the girl and telling us that "The boy is foolish and I fear not him" (4.2.55). Not that Clarence's son shows himself in any way foolish in 2.2, the scene where both children appear shortly after their father's death. Though they seldom figure in modern productions, Shakespeare needs them to swell the numbers of child victims; and victims they are even at this stage for, as the talk with their grandmother shows, Richard has begun to corrupt them also. They round on the bereaved Queen with the cruelty of the very young who have been well instructed in hatred:

> BOY: Ah, Aunt, you wept not for our father's death;
>   How can we aid you with our kindred tears?
> GIRL: Our fatherless distress was left unmoaned;
>   Your widow-dolour likewise be unwept.
>
> (62–5)

Speech-patterning and diction are deliberately artificial, not only as a tuning-up for the choric role of the children in the highly formalised lament that follows, but also to make us feel how these "incapable and shallow innocents" (18) have been drilled into participation in adult vendettas.

A much more naturalistic presentation of a child occurs at the end of the same act, when during the wait for the young King's arrival the eleven-year-old Duke of York is scolded for being a little pitcher with big ears. What he has overheard has been talk of Richard's monstrosity, and to exemplify it there now comes the shattering news that the Queen's brothers have been arrested and taken to Pomfret. In the Quarto the place of the news-bearing Messenger is taken by Dorset, the Queen's elder son from her first marriage. Though this well illustrates the practice of giving messenger lines to any available minor character, the change is awkwardly made, with hardly any adaptation of the dialogue. It does, however, serve to satisfy the audience about Dorset's fate, by letting him be seen to go into sanctuary with the Queen.[23] In this way Dorset, really a middle-aged roué at the time, becomes a "sanctuary child" and so joins the number of Richard's youthful potential victims.

Eventually Dorset escapes. Not so York and his brother, who awaken the audience's compassion by reminding them of both the vulnerability of childhood and the limited weaponry it can wield against adult deceit. Vulnerability is made visible in the young King's entry, loomed over by Richard and Buckingham:

> RICHARD: The weary way hath made you melancholy.
> PRINCE: No, uncle; but our crosses on the way
>   Have made it tedious, wearisome, and heavy.
>   I want more uncles here to welcome me.
>
> (3.1.3–6)

After the arrest of his mother's brothers who had been escorting him on his journey to the capital, Edward knows he is alone among enemies, and defends himself by a bold appropriation of adult irony: "God keep me from false friends, but they were none" (16). This is no less mature than is the use of "crosses" to imply more than mishaps or troubles; the young King intuitively realises that this entry to London, though made ceremonious by the appearance of the Mayor, may be his *via crucis*. At the same time, he is still child enough to turn abruptly away from such pageantry to crave the presence of his mother and brother, and even to lend his voice to the plan to abduct the Duke of York.

Crosscurrents in this standing water between boy and man mingle again in the ensuing conversation between the young King and his self-appointed guardians. Though drastically cut in today's productions, the dialogue is of the minimum length necessary to indicate the time it might take to extricate the Duke of York from sanctuary—a prolonged episode in More's narrative. The universal belief of Shakespeare and his contemporaries that Richard, despite the absence of any written evidence, was guilty of the children's deaths in the Tower, doubles the irony with which Edward reflects on the tradition that the fortress was built by Julius Caesar:

> PRINCE: Is it upon record, or else reported
>
>   Successively from age to age, he built it?
>
> BUCKINGHAM: Upon record, my gracious lord.
>
> PRINCE: But say, my lord, it were not registered:
>
>   Methinks the truth should live from age to age,
>
>   As 'twere retailed to all posterity
>
>   Even to the general ending-day.
>
>   (72–8)

Richard's response to this shows that he knows the Prince to be thinking of his kinsmen's danger at Pomfret; we, of course, are put in mind of the children's danger in the Tower. Yet here again, as Edward tries to sustain an adult conversation by repeating lines he has learnt by rote—"Death makes no conquest of this conqueror"—there surfaces the child's dream over his schoolbook: "I'll win our ancient right in France again" (92). The sharp pathos of the moment is doubled by York's entry, marking as it does the successful completion of Richard's manoeuvres to get both children into his power.

The younger brother knows as well as the elder that Richard is their mortal enemy. But whereas Edward defends himself with a grown-up irony,[24] York, making use of one of the most effective strategies of childhood, reverts to behaviour that is younger than his years. The banter between him and his uncle, in which the boy's "flouts" culminate in the image of the hunchback

Richard carrying an ape on his shoulders, has frequently been turned into a wild romp in which York, playing the spoilt brat, leaps onto Richard's back and the goaded Boar whirls round and round in frustrated rage.[25] But to arouse our modern sensibility towards deformity is to misdirect the scene's pathos. As Richard's subsequent dialogue with Buckingham makes plain, he can afford to concede a dagger and tolerate a verbal prick or two, now that he is master of the situation. The real poignancy lies in York's flouting of the uncle who we know has him totally at his mercy, and in the bitter resignation of his brother's final exchange with the Protector:

> PRINCE: I fear no uncles dead.
>
> RICHARD: Nor none that live, I hope.
>
> PRINCE: And if they live, I hope I need not fear.
>   But come, my lord: and with a heavy heart,
>   Thinking on them, go I unto the Tower.
>
> (146–50)

Between Richard's accomplices and his ultimate opponents stand a number of lesser characters whose responses to the tyrant's misdeeds cover the whole gamut from Vicar-of-Bray opportunism to sullen resignation. Somewhere in the middle of the scale is Sir Richard Brakenbury, Lieutenant of the Tower. Immediately recognisable by his insignia, his appearance in the first scene reinforces the contrast on which Richard's opening monologue is constructed, between the court rejoicings, audible as offstage music and laughter, and the court machinations which have resulted in Clarence being sent under armed guard to the Tower. In trying to prevent talk between the royal dukes, Brakenbury does his best to appear the impersonal servant of the crown. Richard's reaction is to address him in a demoting sequence of terms—"your worship," "man," "sir" (often ironical, compare "sirrah"), "fellow," and then, jocularly but tellingly, "knave" (88–102). Flustered and uncertain how to respond, Brakenbury lets himself be trapped (as amused glances between the guards can confirm) into declaring that he has "naught to do" with Jane Shore. Richard's mockery is more than repartee: it exposes for us a man who will always make duty the excuse for keeping out of trouble. After this first encounter, the audience is not surprised to find that the King's signature is all that is needed to cause Brakenbury to surrender his keys to Clarence's murderers, nor that he fastidiously avoids contact by placing them on the table for the men to pick up:

> I will not reason what is meant hereby,
> Because I will be guiltless from the meaning.
> There lies the Duke asleep, and there the keys.
> (1.4.93–5)

The gesture is the more Pilate-like if Brakenbury has not already figured as the "kind keeper" to whom Clarence recounts his dream, but has entered only when Clarence is asleep, to muse, in a low-keyed and detached way, on the cares of princes.[26]

In the chronicles, Brakenbury stoutly resists the suggestion that he should himself give order for the murder of the little princes, and *The True Tragedy* has him recall this when he consigns his keys to Tyrrel "with tears."[27] Shakespeare's Brakenbury is incapable of such feelings. What clinches the character for the spectator is a slip of the tongue which the dramatist opportunely found in the Chronicles, though in a different context:

> LIEUTENANT: I may not suffer you to visit them.
> The King hath strictly charged the contrary.
> QUEEN: The King? who's that?
> LIEUTENANT: I mean, the Lord Protector.
>
> (4.1.16–18)

Nothing could make clearer that, for Shakespeare, Brakenbury's seeming duteousness is a cover to his acceptance that might is right. There is no justification, in modern productions, for Brakenbury being brought on at Bosworth as an adherent of Richmond. The historical Brakenbury died fighting for Richard, and Shakespeare's Brakenbury would surely have done the same.

The Church might reasonably be expected to be less compliant towards Richard's misdeeds than is a state official such as Brakenbury. At the beginning of the reign of terror, the Archbishop of York, who is also the Chancellor, shows a fighting spirit when he approves of the Queen's plan to take sanctuary and offers to bring her the Great Seal. But in the next scene the Archbishop of Canterbury, Cardinal Bourchier, is easily prevailed upon "for once" to infringe the rights of sanctuary (3.1.57): a once too often. Moreover it is by no means clear that the two prelates are not one and the same in Shakespeare's mind, as they appear to have been to More, who was perhaps misled into identifying the defiant York with the pusillanimous Cardinal by the fact that between the episodes York had meekly yielded up the Great Seal.[28] The two clerics are also one in the acting version represented by the Quarto.

Up, then, to the Council scene the relationship of the spiritual to the temporal powers appears to be one caricatured by Hastings' encounter with the sycophantic Priest on his way to the meeting. And this relationship is felt to continue if, at a critical moment in the Council, the Bishop of Ely bustles off, all becks and smiles, to meet Richard's request for strawberries. But his compliance can be merely courteous, and when, leaving the condemned Hastings to his fate, Richard orders "The rest that love me, rise, and follow me" (79), Ely may indicate a moment of vital choice by staying where he is, and joining the final exeunt in order to ensure that Hastings is allowed shriving time. Richard's subsequent alarm at the news of Ely's defection shows how pivotal has been this small part in the Council scene. Nor is its effect undermined by Richard's appearance at Baynard's Castle "between two bishops"; if the term is not a misnomer for the two popular preachers Penker and Shaw, and two episcopal figures do in fact flank the villain, the faces beneath the mitres may with great theatrical advantage be those of Ratcliffe and Lovel. The representative priest in the later part of the play is Sir Christopher Urswick, who throws in his lot with the Free English by helping to negotiate Richmond's marriage to Elizabeth.[29] As happens in other tyrannies, clerical discretion is at last overcome by valour, however belatedly.

In the Chronicles, one of Richard's most opportunist and ambitious supporters is Shaw's brother, the Mayor of London, who undertakes to win round the citizens: "upon trust of his own advancement, where he was of a proud heart highly desirous."[30] At least it can be said of the stage Mayor that he is motivated more by fear than the hope of gain. A problem that has to be solved in any production is at what point in 3.1, after his formal greeting to the young King, he and his train should leave the stage. There is much to be said for having the Mayor remain on stage throughout the rest of the scene, as a witness of Richard's triumph in getting both young princes into his power. Though he is not given any more lines, he can make the audience aware of his growing realisation that it will be prudent to support the all-powerful Protector. When subsequently he is sent for to the Tower, which Richard and Buckingham pretend to be defending against a rebellion, Hastings' head provides new and frightening evidence of *force majeure*. Richard's lament over the head, momentarily broken off as the Quarto indicates— "Look ye, my Lord Mayor"—by his thrusting it under the Mayor's nose, is designed, through its stress upon Hastings' affair with Jane Shore, to work upon citizen sensibilities.[31] But even the Mayor knows adultery is not treason, and his response to Buckingham's insistence that Hastings had intended to murder them both at the Council table sounds genuinely bewildered: "Had he done so?" The hesitation arouses nearly as much simulated passion in Richard as did Hastings' fatal "If," and in abject fright the Mayor not only concedes that Hastings deserved his death, but agrees to bring the City round to this view:

> And do not doubt, right noble princes both,
> But I'll acquaint our duteous citizens
> With all your just proceedings in this case.
> (3.5.64–6)

So he takes himself off, as fast as terror and the wish to appease Richard can propel him, to talk round the citizens of London. But he does not succeed.

London citizens appear in the play for the first time shortly after the death of Edward the Fourth, where their talk covers the passage of time between the departure of Richard and Buckingham, and their return to the capital with the young King. But 2.3 is much more than a bridge. A pointer to the way Shakespeare wanted it played lies in the Second Citizen's apparent inconsistency. The three speakers can be roughly characterised as a sanguine First Citizen and a pessimistic Second, who are joined by a reflective, analytically minded Third. But in lines 12–15 the Second Citizen suddenly reassures the Third that all is going to be well after all. Moreover, whereas he began the scene by saying to the First Citizen that he is going nowhere in particular, he ends it by telling the Third that they are both on their way to the Justices. The unconformity cannot be the result of misallocated or unblotted lines, because the Quarto, though it shuffles some lines between the First and Second Citizen, keeps the seeming anomalies in the Second Citizen's part.

It helps at this point to recall a comparable scene in *The True Tragedy* in which the destitute Jane Shore begs from a citizen and a servingman whom she has befriended in the past but who dare not give her anything because Richard's minions are enforcing the decree that no one is to relieve her—"hedges have eyes and highways have ears."[32] Shakespeare's citizens too know that anyone could be in Richard's pay. So when two of them are joined by a third who says "Woe to the land that's governed by a child" (11), the Second Citizen, who has been predicting "a giddy world" to his companion, suspects an *agent provocateur,* and hastily switches to the First Citizen's view that everything is going to be well under Edward the Fifth. The Third Citizen, who appears to be old—Alexander Leggett suggests that his nostalgia for, of all times, the minority of Henry the Sixth is a deliberate piece of irony on Shakespeare's part[33]—now goes out of his way to make clear to the others that his fear over the present king's minority does not mean he is supporting any other claimant to the throne: "Oh, full of danger is the Duke of Gloucester" (27). At this the Second Citizen is able to lower his defences, not only joining the Third in his foreboding that

> All may be well; but if God sort it so,
> 'Tis more than we deserve, or I expect
> (36–7)

but readily accepting his company "to the Justices," whereas before he was unwilling to give away this destination even to the First Citizen. Margaret Webster, in a mid-century production, well caught this atmosphere and dealt neatly with the inconsistency when she had members of the secret police enter in time to overhear the last two lines of the scene, which the Citizens quickly improvised for their benefit.[34] Other directors have reinforced the significance of two citizens' wariness in the presence of a third, by incorporating into the scene lines from the Scrivener's speech (usually dropped as a separate scene) which refer to the manner in which Hastings has been framed:

> Who is so gross,
> That cannot see this palpable device?
> Yet who so bold, but says he sees it not?
> Bad is the world, and all will come to nought,
> When such ill dealing must be seen in thought.
>
> (3.6.10–14)

But the Scrivener is not expendable. We have already seen that his monologue has the time-filling function of an interval between the two playlets staged by Richard—the first at the Tower, at the end of which he sends Buckingham to address the citizens at the Guildhall, and the second at Baynard's Castle, which has as prologue Buckingham's report of his failure after three efforts to get the citizens to proclaim Richard as King: "The citizens are mum, say not a word"(3.7.3). Placed thus, the Scrivener, appalled to discover his implication in Richard's abuse of justice, speaks for all those citizens who have realised, in the interim covered by his monologue, that they are expected to assent to a virtual usurpation. Before long, some of these citizens (including, presumably, the three of 2.3) arrive with the Mayor. In some productions the Londoners, swept along on the tide of Buckingham's eloquence, have chanted their agreement with his words. But Jan Kott surely responded more faithfully to the scene, in which Buckingham's account of the citizens' silence at the Guildhall has the effect of making their continued silence palpable beneath the torrent of words with which he and Richard now assail them, when he wrote: "Both the nobles and the townspeople are silent. They will only say "amen.""[35] Nor is it necessary that, at line 241, they should say even this. "All," as a speech heading, usually means "Somebody,"[36] and in the Quarto the speech heading is simply "Mayor." Nowhere in the text is there the great shout of "King Richard, King Richard!" recorded by More. Shakespeare's citizens as a body remain mum, except for the odd member of Buckingham's claque from whom the bystanders may be seen to draw away in distaste. And their exeunt can well be in line with More's description of their earlier departure after listening to Buckingham's oration at the Guildhall: sad for the most part, and some among them "fain . . . to turn their face to the wall, while the dolour of their hearts brast out of their eyes."[37] Of the departure from Baynard's Castle, More records that the citizens went away well aware that the acclamation had been stage-managed by Richard and Buckingham. His marvellously telling conclusion to the episode, as it is incorporated into Hall's Chronicle, makes plain that in his eyes Richard never gained the consent of the people, but only at most their cowed acquiescence in a carefully contrived charade:

And in a stage play, the people know right well that he that playeth the sultan is percase a souter [i.e. cobbler]; yet if one of acquaintance, perchance of little nurture, should call him by his name while he standeth in his majesty, one of his tormentors might fortune break his head for marring of the play. "And so," they said, "these matters be kings' games, as it were stage plays, and for the most part played upon scaffolds, in which poor men be but lookers-on; and they that wise be, will meddle no further, for they that step up with them when they cannot play their parts, they disorder the play and do themselves no good."[38]

It is a sombre conclusion to the story of Richard's accession. We have watched office-bearers in Court, Church and City succumb, albeit with varying degrees of readiness, to Richard's manipulations. Ordinary people can only resort to silence.

More's cobbler playing a "sultan" was in all probability acting Pharaoh in a guild play of the Exodus. Since this was a single episode in a cosmic drama stretching from the Creation to the Judgment, the deviser of the piece would have had no Aristotelian problem of how and when to finish. Shakespeare on the other hand has to satisfy his audience morally and aesthetically by bringing his tyrant to a bad end. This is a particularly difficult task for several reasons. One is that the playwright is almost out of time: by the point in 4.4 at which news of the impending invasion begins to arrive, the play is already over 3,000 lines long. Another reason is that Richard's overthrow is achieved by the founder of the Tudor dynasty, and Shakespeare may have judged it unwise to depict Henry the Seventh as anything other than a *deus ex machina*. Thus lack of time and excess of prudence may have prevented him from developing Richmond into the interestingly melancholy and self-doubting character revealed in the Chronicles.

A third reason why Shakespeare had problems with his ending was intrinsic to the play as he had so far written it. By his incessant role-playing Richard, as Ralph Berry has said, has "insulated himself against a central reality, the existence of a moral order,"[39] and this order is what we should feel to triumph in the play's conclusion. But the play-acting Richard, by a paradox of mimesis which Shakespeare would explore in later plays, is, as critics have repeatedly argued, much more "real" than those round him. How to bring in "real life" to put a stop to Richard's metadrama is thus in some ways the biggest of Shakespeare's problems. He tries a variety of solutions. One is to show Richard facing the truth about himself when alone before the battle; but this soliloquy is generally felt to be one of the least successful in Shakespeare. Another is to contrast Richmond's dignified address to his troops with Richard's rabble-rousing speech to his; but as an incitement to violence, Richard's performance wins all along the line. A third possible solution is to convince the audience of the earnestness and strength of the opposition to Richard's tyranny, and this is our concern here.

Under a reign of terror, the opposition has to take refuge in silence, exile and cunning. Richard's first intimation of failure comes in the reluctance of the London citizens to acclaim him as king; their silence exposes the unreality of first Buckingham's performance and then of his own in a way that words, simply because so much of the eloquence of other characters consists in highly artificial language, notably fail to do. The Chronicles state that the common people were brought to such desperation that they were ready in large numbers to join Richard's enemies when the time came, and even the forces which gathered round Richard to hear his oration on the eve of battle were disaffected: "So was his people to him unsure and unfaithful at his end, as he was to his nephews untrue and unnatural in his beginning."[40] But silent desperation is not easily staged, and it is one of the disappointments of *Richard the Third* that the Citizens do not figure in Richard's fall. Nor do the few allusions to those of the nobility who went into exile give us much sense of the strength of the opposition mustering in Brittany where, Hall tells us, defectors joined Richmond daily. Ely does not reappear; Dorset, though he is brought in among Richmond's followers, has nothing to say. We cannot be expected to involve ourselves in the hopes of Oxford, Blunt, Brandon and Herbert, none of whom we have ever seen before. Realising this, Shakespeare with some skill makes their tiny roles in 5.2 (Blunt alone has a line or two in a later scene) a choric statement[41] about Richard's friendlessness which does a little to make up for the absence of any dramatic focus upon popular resistance.

There remains cunning. Whether Queen Elizabeth, Richard's most able and most motivated enemy, deceives him with false hopes that she will consent to a marriage with her daughter is for the individual director and individual actress to decide. The news in 4.5 that she has "heartily consented" to Princess Elizabeth's marriage with Richmond does suggest that she has deliberately outwitted Richard, and the manner of her exit after their verbal tussle in the previous scene can imply as much to the audience, thus undercutting Richard's jubilation at his apparent success. This double-dealing, if such it is, has its counterpart at the end of the play in the behaviour of the "wily fox" Stanley, who pretends to the very last moment that he is on Richard's side. It is relevant to our concern with minimal and unseen characters that the cunning of both the Queen and Stanley is employed for the sake of a child's future. Neither the young Elizabeth nor young Stanley ever appears, but our awareness of them at the time of the battle, the one as virtually a prize for the victor and the other as a hostage doomed to die if Richard wins, lends urgency to Richmond's exhortation,

> If you do free your children from the sword,
> Your children's children quits it in your age.
> (5.3.261–2)

That Shakespeare wants to present Richmond's allies as fighting for their children's lives against a child-murderer is clear from the change he makes in the message delivered just before Stanley and his forces change sides. According to the Chronicles, Richard had sent word to Stanley that unless he brought up his troops "he would strike off his son's head before he dined" and received the reply "that if the king did so, he had more sons alive."[42] In the play Stanley's message is simply reported as "he doth deny to come" (343). If, as has been suggested, Shakespeare gave Stanley prominence at the battle because his patron at the time was Stanley's direct descendant Lord Strange,[43] he would have been loath to depict Stanley as ready to sacrifice the son who would be the first to bear the Strange title. But even without this extraneous motive for the change, Shakespeare could not show one of Richard's opponents as ready to throw away a child's life. Rather, by having Stanley confide in Richmond his fears for "tender George" (5.3.95), the dramatist suggests that the ambiguities of Stanley's behaviour (which in the Chronicles are discouraging for Richmond) were the means by which he deferred his defection till the actual onset of the fighting, and so preserved his son alive.

Though silence, exile and cunning lay the basis for Richard's overthrow, none of them furnishes the right material for a theatrical climax. Shakespeare needed stronger stuff if he was, in the last act, to build a powerful counter-stress to Richard's earlier triumphs. Still at this time a learner in stagecraft, he found the dramatic force and mass that he needed in two devices of the contemporary theatre, one from the popular and the other from the classical tradition. The excitement traditionally aroused by single combats in boxing-bouts, tourneys, folk drama, and popular theatrical romances is kindled afresh by the fight in which Richmond, a new St George, kills Richard, who has perversely called upon the national saint to infuse him with "the spleen of fiery dragons" (5.3.350). And the momentousness of the battle which culminates in this symbolic duel is built up by a re-engagement of a throng of the play's minimal characters in the role made popular by Senecan drama of the 1590s, that of the revengeful ghost.

One or two ghosts had sufficed for earlier dramatists. Shakespeare's eleven in all probability outnumber the forces required to fight the stage battle.[44] This is as it should be, because in a sense Richard's victims are the real counterweight to his triumph, and, though the director who showed them striking down Richard at the end of his fight with Richmond perhaps over-stressed the point,[45] we recognise in these shades that haunt the battlefield the moral realities needed to nullify Richard's illusions of grandeur: realities from which, were it not for the Ghosts' blessing upon their enterprise, Richmond and his army would otherwise appear oddly detached. To speak of the Ghosts as conveyors of reality may seem wrong-headed, especially since in the theatre their substantiality was for two centuries diminished by gauze curtains and subdued lighting. But for the Elizabethans the figure of Prince Edward of Lancaster, who so unexpectedly stepped forth (or sprang from the trap?), was the reality behind Clarence's dream of "a shadow like an angel, with bright hair / Dabbled in blood" (1.4.53), and Henry the Sixth who followed him was a powerful reanimation of the corpse they had seen unceremoniously trundled towards Whitefriars.

One substantial ghost succeeds another with overwhelming cumulative effect, their patterned utterances giving a voice to those who hitherto have not dared to speak what they know, and making sure at last that the truth (at least as the Tudors conceived it) "should live from age to age Even to the general ending-day." If for sixteenth-century audiences the Ghosts were the most thrilling and memorable part of *Richard the Third* the reason was not just the theatrical sensation they caused. Their accusations build up into a challenge that compensates us emotionally for the triumph of wrong in the earlier acts and lends to those who defeat Richard a credence far in excess of what their belated and somewhat perfunctory appearance can inspire in itself. The moral realities which were defied by Richard's minions, which slipped through the fingers of men such as Bourchier, or which suddenly overwhelmed a man such as the Second Murderer, in the end embody themselves in this far-from-disembodied throng. Their solemnly choric curses and blessings ensure that it is ultimately the tyrant and his attendant tormentors who are relegated to the shadows.

Notes

1. Julie Hankey, ed., William Shakespeare: *Richard III* (London: Junction Books), Plays in Performance edition, 1981, p. 98. Both Terry Hands (1980) and Bill Alexander (1984) cut the line in question.

2. And not helped by the cast spoonerising the line for him—"let the parson cough," etc.

3. *The True Tragedy of Richard III*, ed. W. W. Greg (Oxford: Oxford University Press, 1929), 8–10.

4. *The Mirror for Magistrates*, ed. L. B. Campbell. (Cambridge: Cambridge University Press, 1938) p. 347. The play's sources are discussed, with generous extracts, by Geoffrey Bullough in *Narrative and Dramatic Sources of Shakespeare* (New York: Columbia University Press, 1960), 3. The English and Latin versions of More's *The History of King Richard the Third* have been informatively edited by Richard S. Sylvester (*Complete Works*, 2, New Haven: Yale University Press, 1963).

5. The textual history of *Richard the Third* is very difficult to reconstruct. I have accepted Antony Hammond's view (Arden edition, London: Methuen, 1981) that the Folio is based on a collation of Shakespeare's foul papers (i.e. the play as completed to his satisfaction) with the Third (1602) and Fifth (1612) Quartos. The original (1597) Quarto represents a very good memorial reconstruction which perhaps incorporates Shakespeare's own revisions. Its reduced cast could reflect changes made for a touring production by Pembroke's Men in 1592, or when the play entered the repertory of the Lord Chamberlain's Men in 1594, or for a touring production by the Chamberlain's Men in 1597. Kristian Smidt has published an invaluable parallel-text edition, (New York: Humanities, 1969), and set out his theories about the text in *Injurious Imposters and Richard III*, (New York: Humanities, 1964), and *Memorial Transmission and Quarto copy in "Richard III"* (New York: Humanities Press 1970).

6. *Hall's Chronicle,* ed. J. Johnson, (London H. Ellis 1809), p. 364.

7. *Ibid.,* p. 359.

8. Only the Quarto has this exchange, which suggests the conversation has been broken off and then resumed.

9. See W. H. Clemen, *A Commentary on Shakespeare's "Richard III"* (London: Methuen, English translation 1968), p. 89. Extant plays with remorseful assassins include *The True Tragedy, King Leir,* and Shakespeare's own *Henry the Sixth, Part Two.*

10. This interpretation is based on the Folio text us it stands, rather than the rearrangement of lines 257 to 267 suggested by Harold Jenkins and incorporated into Antony Hammond's Arden edition (London: Methuen, 1981).

11. This is, I believe, Shakespeare's intention as revealed in the Folio, but it may have proved over-subtle, and in the Quarto the Second Murderer is the one who wants to "reason."

12. By J. Dover Wilson, New Shakespeare edition. William Shakespeare, *Richard III,* ed. John Dover Wilson (Cambridge: Cambridge University Press, 1954), p. xxxi.

13. "Shall we hear from thee, Tyrrel, ere we sleep?"—"You shall, my lord" is a typical memorial reiteration of 3.1.188–9.

14. On Grey, who is never addressed by name (presumably to avoid confusion with the Queen's first husband), see J. Dover Wilson, "Shakespeare's *Richard III* and *The True Tragedy of Richard the Third,* 1594," *SQ* 3 (1952), 299–306, p. 302.

15. He is called a relative of Queen Elizabeth only in More's Latin text.

16. I think it just possible that in the Folio, when Richard (2.1.67 following) addresses Rivers, Woodvile and Scales as three individuals, he is mocking Rivers' titles. But if there was a jest, it was again too subtle and the Quarto drops the line. The more usual explanation of Shakespeare's use of the three names is that he did not realise, when he first wrote the play, that they all belonged to Rivers, but that the error was corrected, either by the dramatist or by his fellow-actors, before the Quarto text was assembled.

17. *Hall's Chronicle,* p. 347.

18. The allocation of 137–9 to Rivers, like that of 1.3.315 quoted above, has been questioned, but it verbally echoes a speech by Rivers in *The True Tragedy.*

19. *Hall's Chronicle,* p. 379.

20. *Ibid.,* p. 407.

21. *Ibid.,* p. 377.

22. Compare pp. 13–14 above. Unless Margaret and the Duchess were played by grown men, I do not see how the play could have been performed with fewer than six boy actors. A boy could double as a woman and a child, but it is very unlikely that the same boy would play two child parts, as suggested by T. J. King in *Casting Shakespeare's Plays: London Actors and Their Roles 1590–1642* (Cambridge: Cambridge University Press, 1992). King also overlooks the Page entirely. Clarence's children appear rarely on the modern stage. Terry Hands made use of them, but did not give them any lines. Bill Alexander had them in the previews but then cut them as the performance needed to be shortened.

23. Hall, describing the risings which in the play are the subject of the various Messenger speeches in 4.4. says Dorset "came out of sanctuary" (p. 393).

24. But compare, R. S. White, *Innocent Victims: Poetic Injustice in Shakespearean Tragedy,* (Newcastle-upon-Tyne: Tyneside Free Press, 1986), p. 48.

25. This "business" appears to have started with Laurence Olivier.

26. The Quarto conflates the two roles.

27. *True Tragedy,* line 1204.

28. *Hall's Chronicle,* p. 350.

29. On the clergy, see E. A. J. Honigmann's Penguin edition (Harmondsworth: Penguin, 1968), pp. 32–3.

30. *Hall's Chronicle,* pp. 364–5.

31. In Cibber's version, the Mayor was a buffoon (much enjoyed by George II) and this tradition has persisted in productions of Shakespeare's original. But though the part has opportunities for comedy, it is not farcical: the Mayor's cooperation is important to Richard.

32. *True Tragedy,* lines 1103–4.

33. *"Henry VIII* and the ideal England." *SS* 38 (1985), 131–44, p. 134.

34. A. C. Sprague, "Shakespeare on the New York stage, 1953–4," *SQ* 5 (1954), 311–15, p. 312.

35. Jan Kott, *Shakespeare our Contempary,* (New York: Doubleday, 1964), p. 29.

36. See M. M. Mahood, *Bit Parts in Shakespeare's Plays,* p. 8.

37. *Hall's Chronicle,* p. 372.

38. *Ibid.,* p. 374.

39. Ralph Berry, *The Shakespearean Metaphor,* (London: Macmillan, 1978), p. 12.

40. *Hall's Chronicle,* p. 416.

41. In the quarto they are made even more choric by the generic speech headings "Lo[rd]."

42. *Hall's Chronicle,* p. 420.

43. See E. A. J. Honigmann, *Shakespeare: The Lost Years* (Manchester: Manchester University Press, 1985), pp. 63–4 and Andrew Gurr, *"Richard III* and the democratic process," *Essays in Criticism* 24 (1974), 39–47.

44. They still do, as Antony Sher's diary of the 1984 production shows: "we've run out of actors to man both armies. . . . At the moment Richard's army is made up entirely of 4 generals. . . Everyone is either in Richmond's army, preparing to be ghosts, female, or too posh to ask." And later: "My troops now number seven. We might win Bosworth at this rate" (*Year of the King* [London: Chatto and Windus, 1985], pp. 194 and 203).

45. Terry Hands in 1980 (promptbook).

The BBC Production of *Richard III*

HENRY FENWICK

The first scene of *Richard III* is a famous one; Richard's opening speech is a Shakespearian set piece, much quoted, much remembered. But in Jane Howell's production that set-piece quality fades into the background; the opening takes on again what must have been its primary function when the play was first staged—a piece of exposition, linking the play back to the three parts of *Henry VI*. As script editor David Snodin points out, "Since we're playing the play as the latest in a succession of four, 'Now is the winter of our discontent' becomes a story-so-far speech, with Richard saying, 'I am going to be a villain and this is what I'm going to do.' If one were doing the play as a single entity the temptation would be for an actor to put everything of his character into that speech, whereas we can do it very rapidly—and the verse benefits from that."

The links of the four plays are central to Howell's presentation of them. If *Richard III* is done without the build-up of the three parts of *Henry VI* and its chronicle of the bloody civil war that spawned him, it is impossible, she said during rehearsal, to appreciate Richard except as some sort of diabolical megalomaniac. "I've only ever seen *Richard* once," she says, "a production I didn't like, where he was certainly played as a megalomaniac." Doing the play in sequence, however, "you've seen why he is created, you know how such a man can be created: he was brought up in war, he saw and knew nothing else from his father but the struggle for the crown, and if you're brought up to fight, if you've got a great deal of energy, and physical handicaps, what do you do? You take to intrigue and plotting."

"Also," she adds thoughtfully, "I can see that if you didn't do the other three plays you'd have to cut an awful lot of *Richard* because it would make nonsense to the audience." "What usually happens," adds Snodin, "is that it's done as an entity to itself and a lot of the references to the earlier plays are taken out and it becomes a play about a megalomaniac rather than a play about the Wars of the Roses. For example, we have kept Margaret's long speeches because they obviously refer back to what's been going on. Usually she is cut out as a bit of a bore and as redundant to the story of Richard III, but she's *not* redundant to the idea of Richard becoming a sort of avenging devil, carrying out all the curses that have been made in the previous plays. She has a function as a sort of Cassandra."

"When we started in the studio," says Julia Foster, who has played Queen Margaret in all four plays, "and we started on Scene 3 [in which Margaret breaks in on the quarrelling court], one suddenly realised when one came into that 'Hear me, you wrangling pirates' speech that I actually brought the whole of everybody's past and the past of all the plays in with me and confronted Richard with it. One of the things that interested me most was that there is obviously from Margaret a slight admiration for Richard—he is successful at what he does. And her coming in and pointing out the crimes of the other characters balances out the evil as well: Richard is a baddy but these goodies are not as good as they appear to be."

There is, in Miss Foster's performance, a disturbing, slightly shocking quality that reminded me of the women who wander round the city streets with all their belongings in battered shopping bags, cursing to themselves. "That's what I thought about," she says when I tell her this. "So many people, when they talk about *Richard III*, talk about Mad Margaret, so it was superimposed on my mind that she was mad. But when I started reading it I began to think, 'She's not mad; she's *exceedingly sane.*' Everything she says is so precise and so accurate and right to the point. All those deaths and all those terrible things have driven her somewhere else, but not to madness . . . to a sort of muttering . . . and I started thinking about those ladies with all those bags: if you went up to them and said, 'Are you all right?' they'd probably hit you rather than say 'Help me'—that kind of aggressive eccentricity. You knew, as she stood there, that what she had with her was everything she had—no home, no pillow, no bed; everything was in the skirts or in the bag or underneath the hat. I imagined that the handkerchief with Rutland's blood on it was tucked in one sleeve, and Suffolk's skull under the skirt; that she was a complete identity on her own and wherever she went she took this whole world with her."

In many ways Queen Margaret is an appalling woman, bloody and ruthless, but, says Foster, "rightly or wrongly I always found a good reason for what she did—she did things out of passion and fire and out of ambition, not out of cold-bloodedness or calculation. She just had to do what she did! When she says finally, 'These English woes shall make me smile in France,' she vanishes from the play. She's been miserable for fifty years and now she makes sure that they are all miserable and leaves. I think she probably dies.

"It is obvious from the writing that the part is very stylised. It is not set on a realistic level, so if you approached it on the naturalistic level it became almost an impossibility. Why did they let her stay? Why did they let her speak? Why didn't Richard just knock her to the ground? I was very worried before we started, and then I thought, 'Well, Jane maybe in some way will stylise it, make it look as though I've appeared from heaven or . . . I don't know what I expected . . . but no, of course not, why did I even think of such a thing? Everything has to be approached from underneath, from the naturalistic level completely, and I realised that one just had to tackle it. It was very difficult if one thought about it. When I sat down and broke the scene down and did a little bit and thought about it, it was just a disaster. I couldn't find any level that was right and neither could Ron [Cook—playing Richard], but somehow when one took a dive at it, as an emotional heap of revenge and vulnerability, and just went 'Shaaa!' [she makes an awesome, charging sound] it just went wonderfully! Then it worked."

She, like many of Howell's actors, had had very little Shakespearian experience before this sequence of plays, but in *Richard III* she had some awesomely rhetorical, singing speeches, elaborate curses, which she handles with insouciance. It took her some time to come to terms with the verse, she confesses now. "I thought there was a way of playing Shakespeare disregarding the verse. I don't mean that completely: I mean that, by trying to make it more understandable to a young child like my daughter, I think maybe to start with I went slightly against the verse—or attempted to until Jane rapped one's knuckles very hard and explained that Shakespeare is like music. Unless you play the notes you can't play the music and unless you play the metre you can't play the play. Now after eight months Shakespeare is pouring out of one's pores and you practically speak like it at home."

David Snodin had spent a great deal of time throughout the rehearsal period of the earlier plays working with the actors on the verse, emphasising the importance of the Shakespearian line, which, he felt, was particularly important because of the comparative simplicity of the verse structure in the early plays. *Richard III* was a different matter; suddenly Shakespeare has taken on a new voice. There are remarkable scenes of formal poetry and equally remarkable scenes of flexible complex verse, "In *Richard,*" Snodin points out, "the verse is suddenly much more complicated. The danger is that it can become very versy and very rhythmic and in fact the language is very different from what's gone before. People are not saying what they mean." But fortunately for him, he says, by this stage in the work the actors had become so acclimatised to the Shakespearian line that "my only job was to tell them to forget the verse."

"No one in *Richard* any longer believes what they say or means what they say," emphasises Howell. "It is trick upon trick and layer upon layer, which is a very long journey from Talbot in the first play, who always said what he meant and said it very simply." The misuses and abuses of language echo the descent of the play into what she describes as "an appalling web of complex intrigue. In *Richard* we are involved in a very small world, and the set has been closed in, narrowed in. You feel the open air is no longer there until Richmond comes. Richmond brings back space and some sort of freedom, and the possibility of a horizon. The doors are now very dominant: they project forward from the towers so the set is almost a circle of doors. You never know who's coming out of which door. I think *Richard's* a bit like Watergate or any of our scandals over here—it's the atmosphere of those places where, when anyone opens a door, everyone looks—you don't know who's coming in from where, when, next."

"There are doors now everywhere," agrees Oliver Bayldon, designer of the set that has been a constant throughout the sequence of plays, changing moods from play to play. "Originally Jane had this feeling that there were corridors—everything took place along corridors, like a totalitarian state: there's a bit of paper and someone's signed it and stamped it, someone knocks on your door and the car's waiting and you're gone." This Kafkaesque aim was transmuted into the door-lined setting they now have. "There are fifteen or sixteen doors on the set and more behind those. The set has been all boarded up, it's like a derelict building site with rows of doors as fencing. The play-park of *Henry VI Part I* is now Belfast." Other details add to the sense of oppressiveness. The netting that hung around the set for the earlier plays has been looped up: "it looks sort of louring, like dark clouds up there."

The colours of the set, too, have changed. "*Richard* has a bit more colour again," says Bayldon. "Not a lot. It became more oppressive, almost into dark brown, which fitted that oppressive feel, and at the same time there's a curious mixture of comedy in the play, so we picked up colours. There's an orangey splash on the doors, for example. There's a curious scene where Richard and Buckingham frighten the Lord Mayor by putting on old armour and Jane felt it was farce. She wanted some sort of costume trunk for the armour, but we couldn't use a real costume skip because it didn't look right on the set. Everything had to be slightly bigger and cruder than reality or it just didn't fit, so we had this box made of split wood to look like a costume skip, and we wanted to hark back to the first play so we resurrected the old pink plumes and painted leather armour."

Another touch of colour came in the banners. "Richard has these very shiny black and white banners, with a fiercely aggressive-looking boar; then when Richmond come in his banners are green and white. We've never seen green before, we've kept green out of it, and they're bigger banners than we've ever had before, so when the green and white banners come on they come as a slight shock. I put a slightly dirty green on the set here and there just to prepare. The play does a sort of circle with Richmond and the Tudors coming on as the goodies, so, thinking of that full circle, I had thought of coming back to the blues and reds of *Part I*. But it didn't seem quite right, blue seemed too sharp; green and brown felt more appropriate."

"It's interesting to see how it's all developed from *Part I*," says John Peacock, the costume designer. "The armour in *Richard* is nearly all metal, very different from *Part I* where it was all painted. The scene where they dress up in armour from *Part I* looks very strange, it doesn't look real in the context of

Richard III." The overall attitude to clothes for *Richard III* was much more modern, more practical than it had been for the outset of the series. "Jane wanted the effect of three-piece suits, and since there's no such thing as three-piece suits in that period we used shirts and underjackets and jackets and tights with codpieces, and they've worn them in any way they wanted to— shirts with jackets, shirts with waistcoats or underjackets, people like Rivers and Grey are executed in their shirts and 'trousers.' All the buttons work, all the linings are finished, so Jane could dress and undress everybody in any way she wanted to. It feels and is practical. I based the costume designs on the right period, so though there are anachronisms—they didn't use buttons— basically it's the right shape with the right trimmings. I think because it's more practical it's becoming more sinister. You're not quite sure what's being covered up. In *Richard* there's a feeling that there are pockets everywhere and people can take things out to do nasty things with them."

"I'm going for greater contrast in this play than I did in the previous plays of the series," says lighting designer Sam Barclay. "The dark greys become black, the light greys become dark grey. I knew the costumes were going to be very dark and the scenes were generally conspiratorial, and when you start having lots of dark areas you start getting strange technical things happening, like looking at an ants' nest. Changing the gamma reduces the technical imperfections, you don't end up with strange blurrings. I'm also taking out colour for certain key scenes like the morning scenes— dawn, after all, is pretty colourless.

"Shakespeare makes Richard very conscious of light. In Shakespeare's time they couldn't switch on a switch and he's very conscious of what time of day it is, he's always on about the sun and the moon because light was a very basic thing in life. In *Part 3,* Richard is one of the sons of York and there's a play on the word sons: the three of them imagine they see three suns in the sky, one of which is in the ascendant, and the sun becomes a symbol. When you start reading *Richard III* the first scene talks about 'the sun of York' and Richard looks at his shadow in the sun, this distorted shadow, so our opening scene is, very specifically, Richard entering, leaving the party we left at the end of *Part 3,* and you see his shadow before you see him. He walks across the set and the shadow is a very dominant thing in the picture. Shadows are a very strong theme. In Scene 2 he says, 'Shine out, fair sun, till I have bought a glass, That I may see my shadow as I pass,' and since Richard is this shadowy character one puts stronger lighting on him." This made sometimes for problems in balancing the picture. "When Richard woos Ann over the bier one had to make her look good yet make him look strong and cruel. As one sits watching one thinks, 'That's too strong for her,' and one balances them. One has to go for the right thing for each moment and for each character. When we come to the battle where he meets his defeat the sun doesn't shine on him, it will be overcast; but when you see Richmond the sun *will* shine on his army.

"I've been to Bosworth field, I've got friends with a farm there, and it's just slightly undulating, a rather flattish landscape; there's no way we could go for realism. So I picked out the starkness of the set, and of course the use of smoke in the studio also helps to remove the sharpness of the set. Your imagination is allowed to roam a bit."

As a culmination for the battle of Bosworth, Howell has introduced a set piece of Queen Margaret sitting, laughing, the corpse of Richard in her arms, atop a pile of bodies—the whole company bloodied and finally bowed, in an image that encapsulates the butchery and horror of the long civil wars. This was something of a *pièce de résistance* for the make-up department. At first Howell had thought it would be impossible to have the corpse of Richard anything but fully clothed—the problems of his wounds, plus his withered arm, plus his hump, seemed insuperable and she assumed that the image she wanted of a reverse Pietà would have to be approximated—there would be no way of having the body stripped to the waist. But make-up artist Cecile Hay-Arthur argued otherwise, and her enthusiasm for the job and her confidence in the results won the director over. Made of foam latex, the all-important hump was created after they took casts of Ron Cook. They then experimented with various approaches, making fifteen humps in all. Then Cook came in for an experimental make-up session and they were persuaded that it would in fact work. As for the arm, Cook had already played three plays with a glove on, his hand twisted out of shape, so a definite visual image of what it should be like was already established. "We cast his hand as he held it in the glove, then we built up a deformed hand using a cast of this real hand in that position, building it with wax, then casting the wax and making a plastic hand." They also liaised extremely carefully with fight director Malcolm Ranson over the wounds that Richard sustains in the battle before he finally dies. Diagrams were made of every wound so that in the final make-up session each thrust could be shown accurately on his naked torso, in case any *aficionados* of such things were in the audience ready to catch out failures in continuity. "It's been quite fun," says Hay-Arthur contentedly.

One of the continuing problems for the make-up department was that of ageing. Many of the actors develop their characters through two or three parts—though only Julia Foster goes through all four-parts, ageing from young French princess to old crone. But actual historical age was no proper guide to the characters—Shakespeare's fidelity to historical fact was never 100%. There was no consistency in the way certain characters aged. And new characters, such as Annette Crosbie's dowager Duchess of York, appear in *Richard III* who would in theory have been older than Queen Margaret. Ageing was therefore decided to be a matter of minor details—no rubber wrinkles, no strict adherence to the details of physical decay. Another problem was that of the doubling of actors in different parts, which becomes especially prevalent in this, the last of the sequence. Faces seen before in major roles make reappearances in minor ones here, while certain faces that have been seen time and time again in an assortment of parts also continue to pop up. This appearance and reappearance of the same actors in different guises proved a problem in logistics, so again the decision was made to keep it simple. No great attempt was made to disguise each actor as he came on in a new role; changes were kept minimal: tinting hair, curling hair, straightening hair. (Most of the actors had grown their own hair long, so wiggery was not much needed.) "We tried to do things very, very simply," says Hay-Arthur.

In any case, too heavy a disguise for each actor would have run contrary to the point of the doubling. Jane's decision to use the same company throughout and have them double parts the way it was done in the theatre was first and foremost a pragmatic one, but nevertheless she felt there was a strong artistic reason too. "*Richard III* should be like a nightmare," she had said when in the early stages of preparation. "Faces will keep coming back. For example, the Duke of York from *Part 3* becomes one of the murderers in *Richard III*. The faces have a ricochet for the audience." In the event she was pleased with the effect she had planned. "*Richard* is a play haunted by the other three plays and also by the presence of the same actors. There's an extraordinary scene where Hastings is taken to the Tower. The pursuivant he meets is played by the actor who played Clarence, the priest he meets is played by Henry VI. Warwick becomes Tyrrel. And there are many other things in the doubling which I think are quite potent.

"I find it more frightening than any of the other plays because you don't see . . . you see nobody killed, just people going away, being taken away—so much like today: they're just removed. There's a knock on the door and people are almost willing to go. There's no way out of it. They're not dragged off, they walk off. *They* walk off. It's a very different fear, the fear in *Richard*. It's the fear of *unseen* violence." This is a marked contrast to the escalating, very visible violence of the three parts of *Henry VI*. "When you get to *Richard III*," adds Malcolm Ranson, the fight director, "the only person you actually see dying is Richard himself. Clarence is killed but you just see him stabbed rather ineffectually by the murderer, which is why he has to be dragged off and drowned, which you don't see. But the only person you see die is Richard, and that's done by having Richard fight the whole of the second company. It's quite a long death. Jane felt that by the time one had reached that point in the play and everybody had seen the character of Richard and his fighting ability in the earlier parts, you realise that he's a man who *can* fight, and who would instil fear into the opposing side. And he *is* still their king—until Richmond is crowned they are rebels and there is also that fear, which I hope we've brought out."

The fight, one man against so many, he had carefully prepared for. There had been a change in weaponry throughout the four parts: in *Part 1* "romantic swords and shields or single sword"; *Part 2* had a few more maces and Cade's rebels used an assortment of brutal though everyday implements for killing—pitchforks, sickles; in *Part 3* a lot of maces and axes were used, as well as bows and arrows, and halberds and spears were introduced "and shields started being used as an offensive weapon." The spears that the soldiers use against this feared figure of Richard, keeping him at a distance, had therefore been carefully placed in advance so that they were not totally new. The ball and chain which was the only possible weapon for Richard to use if he were to fend off large numbers of attackers was also introduced earlier. "I introduced a ball and chain in *Part 2* for Richard. He didn't fight with it, but you did see him with it, so that pre-empted the big fight at the end of *Richard III*. You can keep quite a few people away from you with a ball and chain: you don't go near somebody with one of those things swinging round their heads. The idea of that was to get the feeling still of fear of the soldiery for Richard. Even when he's wounded there's a feeling of "Do we go in and finish him off or is the man still alive?" No one actually wants to get in contact with this evil man, this possessed devil. It's quite grotesque and we've taken it to the point where it's just *difficult* to kill this man."

For any actor the part of Richard has to be a little intimidating. "Someone once described it as like one of those games you get at Christmas," says Ron Cook, who faced the challenge. "You have twenty little ball-bearings and you try to get them all in the holes. There are so many things to cram in, once you get one in another rolls out—you can't think of all the things at the same time. Sometimes you look at a scene and you can't see why it's there. Then you cut it in rehearsal and it doesn't work. You have to trust Shakespeare— I'm not saying he can't do anything wrong, but trusting him, trusting the words, trusting the shape of the play, very often will do it for you.

"One of the themes throughout the plays, and especially in *Richard III*, is conscience. What Richard decides in *Part 3* is that he will have no conscience, no morals whatsoever. Once he has killed Henry VI he finds there is no divine retribution, nothing happens, nothing strikes him dead. Up to that point he has been trained . . . he is a social animal and he's known nothing but war, he was brought up to fight and, especially because he's so good at it, at the end of *Part 3* it's boring for him, there's nothing for him to do but make mischief. Killing Henry in cold blood and finding nothing happens, he's become totally free, he has no conscience, guilt, pity, he has neither pity, love nor fear, and that's what makes him such an extraordinary figure."

Cook had begun to do historical background research for the part but, he says, "the historical figure of Richard is totally irrelevant—I stopped immediately." He found more relevance in the story of Faust, the man who bartered his soul for his desires. "And Richard is the antichrist as well—someone once told me there's only one story. Shakespeare makes Richard so funny, so irreligious, yet it's a very moral play. It's extraordinary that someone so morally bad comes across as such an attractive, charismatic figure. You love to watch his machinations going on, then in the middle of the play you begin to hate him but you are already implicated."

The precedent of Olivier's film performance has stamped the part indelibly in modern minds—a tough act to follow. "Faced with having to do

Richard with Olivier's shadow cast across the whole thing," says Cook, "you just have to forget that and enjoy the discovery of it, what is there, for yourself. Olivier did a very cut version—as I remember, he cut Margaret and added bits of *Part 3* and bits of Colley Cibber's version. And in a way, because we've done this in sequence with the other three plays, I think it makes it a different play. Olivier went for a very evil, charismatic figure, whereas for us it's to do with the whole picture of the Wars. Obviously Olivier's is a magnificent performance but it's a different Richard." *Richard III,* as part of the sequence of four plays, Cook sees rather as a picture of the breakdown of the country, England disintegrating from the unity of *Henry V,* "starting with the barons at each other, the breakdown of the political scene with factions against each other, resulting in a man out for his own, set against his own brother, finally divided even in his own soul."

"The play," Howell emphasises, "is about all the people, and not just about him. Playing the play as the final part of four in a sequence puts it in perspective. The big discovery for the actors was that because we've done the other three plays they always have pictures in their heads of the past, and that's terribly important if you're going to find out what *Richard III*'s about. It's not a play about a single man. It's a play about a society."

"Neither Mother, Wife, nor England's Queen": The Roles of Women in *Richard III*

Madonne M. Miner

> Richard sufficiently dominates the play so that analyses of his personality virtually exhaust the play's possibilities.
>
> *—Psychoanalysis and Shakespeare*

Although Norman Holland[1] speaks here primarily with reference to psychoanalytic interpretations of Shakespeare's *Richard III,* his comment actually serves as indication of the initial assumption behind almost all critical readings of the play; literary critics generally indulge in an a priori and unacknowledged Forsterian division of characters into round (Richard) and flat (everyone else), focus upon the former, and then weave their own particular analytic threads according to patterns perceived in the character of Richard.[2] Such threads comprise the traditional web of literary criticism—and deservedly so—but, because of the initial division of character and limitation of focus, certain questions raised by *Richard III* tend to fall outside the critical web. Why does one figure appear to assume a roundness of dimension while others, suffering from advanced anorexia, appear to atrophy? What is the nature of the interaction *among* "atrophied" figures as well as *between* such figures and the other, more "substantial" figure? This essay, organized into three sections, considers such questions with respect to one group of formerly ignored "flat characters": the women of *Richard III.* Section I studies the interaction between Richard and women, an interaction characterized by his determination to cast women in unattractive roles: as scapegoat for men, currency of exchange between men, and cipher without men. Section II suggests that interaction occurs among the women of the play, and Section III further substantiates the integrity of female figures with an analysis of the way in which metaphors of birth and pregnancy are used and abused throughout the play.

From Carolyn Ruth Swift Lenz, Gayle Greene, and Carol Thomas Neeley, eds., *The Woman's Part: Feminist Criticism of Shakespeare* (Urbana: University of Illinois Press, 1980). Reprinted with permission of the publisher.

I

Richard III opens with a soliloquy, in which Richard, Duke of Gloucester, distinguishes time past, time present, and what he perceives to be time future:

> Grim-visaged War hath smoothed his wrinkled front,
> And now, instead of mounting barbèd steeds
> To fright the souls of fearful adversaries,
> He capers nimbly in a lady's chamber
> To the lascivious pleasing of a lute.
> . . . .
> Why, I, in this weak piping time of peace,
> Have no delight to pass away the time.
> . . . .
> And therefore, since I cannot prove a lover
> To entertain these fair well-spoken days,
> I am determinèd to prove a villain.
> (I.i.9–13, 24–25, 28–30)[3]

Out of step with his time, Richard determines to force it into closer conformity with his own nature. Implicitly, the quality of the present which Richard finds so onerous is its femininity; present days belong to "wanton ambling nymphs," not to marching warriors, not to hunchbacked younger brothers.[4] The opposition between war and peace is expressed as opposition between male and female; "male" is associated with "bruisèd arms," "stern alarums," and "barbèd steeds," and "female" with "merry meetings," "delightful measures," and "sportive tricks."[5] It makes no difference whether we agree or disagree with Richard's sexual collocations; what is of importance is Richard's exclusive identification with one side of the antithesis and his determination to obliterate those who represent the opposite—those who, according to the imagery of Richard's soliloquy, are women.

In addition to introducing the poles of opposition in *Richard III*, Gloucester's opening soliloquy also introduces a tactic that Richard employs throughout: an allocation of guilt along sexual lines so that women are invariably at fault. Within the soliloquy it is apparent that women are to blame for effacing the countenance of "Grim-visaged War" and, immediately following the soliloquy, Richard explains to brother Clarence that women are to blame for other things as well. Even though Richard has just told us that he has spun "inductions dangerous" so as to set Clarence and Edward "in deadly hate the one against the other," when Clarence enters, under guard, Richard maintains that women are at the root of his woes:

> Why, this it is when men are ruled by women.
> 'Tis not the king that sends you to the Tower.

> My Lady Grey his wife, Clarence, 'tis she
> That tempers him to this extremity.
>
> (I.i.62–65)

Richard's allegation not only deflects suspicion from himself and onto Elizabeth, but also tends to unite the two brothers against an intruder (the sister-in-law, the "Other"). While challenging bonds of marriage, Richard appears to be reaffirming bonds of consanguinity. Clarence catches the impulse of Richard's comment and carries it yet further, naming Mistress Shore as another female force undermining the throne; if one woman is not to blame, another may be found. Clarence cites Shore's intervention in favor of Hastings and Richard agrees: "Humbly complaining to her deity/Got my Lord Chamberlain his liberty" (I.i.76–77). Obviously, according to Richard, when prostitutes capture the ear of kings, when wives wield more power than brothers, the time is out of joint.[6]

In the subsequent exchange with Anne, who follows the corpse of her father-in-law Henry to Chertsey, as in that with Clarence, Richard directs culpability from himself and onto the female figure.[7] He greets the recently widowed woman as "sweet saint" (I.ii.49), and bolsters this greeting with a string of compliments, to which she responds with curses. When Anne charges him with the slaughter of her father-in-law, Henry VI, and her husband, Edward, Richard initially scrambles for a surrogate (blaming Edward IV and Margaret) but then hits upon a far more effective line, accusing Anne as the primary "causer" of the deaths:

> Your beauty was the cause of that effect;
> Your beauty, that did haunt me in my sleep
> To undertake the death of all the world,
> So I might live one hour in your sweet bosom.
>
> (I.ii.121–24)

Thus, Anne is responsible; her beauty serves as incentive for murder. Richard, of course, lies; he kills Edward and Henry so as to come closer to the throne, and he woos Anne for the same reason. By the end of the scene, however, this hunchbacked Machiavellian is able to acknowledge his role in the murders of Edward and Henry, to offer Anne his sword to use against him, and to smile in the knowledge of his victory as she refuses to take vengeance.

> Nay, do not pause, for I did kill King Henry,
> But 'twas thy beauty that provokèd me.
> Nay, now dispatch; 'twas I that stabbed young Edward.
> But 'twas thy heavenly face that set me on.
> Take up the sword again, or take up me.
>
> (I.ii.179–83)

By focusing on her beauty, Richard insists that Anne fit the very flat definition of "womankind" he articulated in his opening soliloquy—a definition
that divides the world into male and female provinces, denying the latter any
possibility of communion with emblems (such as swords) of the former.
Focusing upon Anne's guilt, Richard deflects responsibility from himself, and
constructs a bond of alliance between Anne and himself, against the House of
Lancaster, rendering her powerless.

While the exchange between Richard and Anne may be the most dramatic example of Richard's aptitude with respect to sexual dynamics and the
allocation of guilt, it is by no means a final example. Another variation occurs
in Act III, scene iv, when Richard determines to weed out the ranks of those
in opposition to his coronation. Because Hastings is involved with Mistress
Shore, all Richard need do is accuse Shore, implicate Hastings (guilt by association) and be rid of him. Thus, in the midst of an assembly meeting,
Richard draws forth his withered arm and announces: "And this is Edward's
wife, that monstrous witch, Consorted with that harlot strumpet Shore,/That
by their witchcraft thus have markèd me" (III.iv.69–71). Hastings's reply, "If
they have done this deed, my noble lord" (72), is twisted by an enraged
Richard into unimpeachable evidence of guilt: "If! Thou protector of this
damnèd strumpet. Talk'st thou to me of ifs? Thou art a traitor. Off with his
head!" (73–75). In spite of the incredible and illogical nature of Richard's
accusation (his arm has always been withered; the association of Elizabeth
and Mistress Shore as conspirators is extremely unlikely), it holds: Hastings
loses his head on the basis of his involvement with a woman. Although the
dynamics in the three examples cited above vary considerably, in each
instance Richard blames women in order to benefit himself and, in so doing,
he creates or destroys associational bonds between men.

If, in the scenes above, Richard is able to manipulate women and blame
so as to cut or spin associational threads, his tailoring skills appear yet more
impressive when he sets himself to matchmaking—an activity which appears
to encourage the reduction of female status from "person" to "thing
exchanged." As Lévi-Strauss observes in *Structural Anthropology,* marriage
functions as the lowest common denominator of society; based as it has been
on the exchange of a woman between two men, marriage brings together two
formerly independent groups of men into a kinship system.[8] Richard takes
advantage of these associational possibilities, but, interestingly enough, the
impulse behind his marital connections most often appears to be one of
destruction rather than creation; society is wrenched apart rather than drawn
together. We see Richard play the role of suitor twice, with Lady Anne and
with Queen Elizabeth (whom he approaches to request the hand of her
daughter Elizabeth). To be sure, in formulating his marital plans, Richard
approaches women—an eligible widow and a widowed mother—but in both
cases, Richard actually focuses on men behind the women. Before meeting
Anne en route to Chertsey, he reveals his designs on her:

> For then I'll marry Warwick's youngest daughter.
> What though I killed her husband and her father?
> The readiest way to make the wench amends
> Is to become her husband and her father.
>
> (I.i.153–56)

"To make the wench amends"? Such, of course, is not the actual motivation behind Richard's system of substitution; he realizes that in order to substantiate his claims to the position previously held by Henry VI, it is politic to align himself with Henry's daughter-in-law. Further, maneuvering himself into Anne's bedchamber, Richard moves closer to replacing Edward, former occupant thereof, and former heir to the throne. Thus, after killing Anne's "husband and father," Richard can assume their sexual and political roles.[9] Finally, Richard's speech clarifies the function of women in the marital game: whether the game be one of exchange or one of substitution, the female serves as a piece to be moved *by others,* and a piece having value only *in relation* to others.

Political values, however, like those of the stock market, fluctuate wildly, and by Act IV, Richard (now king) recognizes that Anne has outlived her usefulness to him. After instructing Catesby to rumor it abroad that Anne is "very grievous sick," Richard ruminates alone: "I must be married to my brother's daughter,/Or else my kingdom stands on brittle glass./Murder her brothers and then marry her!" (iv.ii.58–60). As in his earlier choice of bride, Richard here pursues a woman from whom he has taken all male relatives; although not fully responsible for the death of Elizabeth's father, Richard conspires to lessen the natural term of Edward's life, and he employs more direct measures with respect to Clarence (Elizabeth's uncle) and the two princes (Elizabeth's brothers). However, not all possible rivals have been obliterated: Richmond also seeks the hand of Edward's daughter, and Richard's awareness of a living male rival sharpens his desire to legitimize his claim:

> Now, for I know the Britain Richmond aims
> At young Elizabeth, my brother's daughter,
> And by that knot looks proudly on the crown,
> To her go I, a jolly thriving wooer.
>
> (iv.iii.40–43)

Elizabeth, of course, has been a loose end; with the young princes dead ("cut off") she remains the only legitimate possibility of access to the throne. By tying his own knots, Richard plans to exclude Richmond from making any claims to the kingdom. In sum, Richard woos both Anne and Elizabeth because of the position they occupy with respect to men. However, in proposing marriage (which might lead to a bonding of male to male through female), Richard does not seek a union *with* other men but rather *replaces* them by assuming their roles with respect to women.

In considerations of the way Richard employs women as scapegoats and currency, younger female figures have received most attention. However, when we consider how Richard uses women as ciphers, three older women—Queen Elizabeth, Margaret, and the Duchess of York—step, reluctantly, into the foreground. All of these women suffer, on one level, a loss of definition at the hand of Richard. Caught in a society that conceives of women strictly in relational terms (that is, as wives to husbands, mothers to children, queens to kings), the women are subject to loss of title, position, and identity, as Richard destroys those by whom women are defined: husbands, children, kings.[10] Early in the play, Queen Elizabeth perceives the precarious nature of *her* position as her husband, King Edward, grows weaker and weaker. "The loss of such a lord includes all harms" (I.iii.8), she tells her son Grey. Elizabeth's words find verification not only in later scenes, but also, here, before Edward's death, in the figure of Margaret, England's former queen. Margaret, hiding in the wings, listens as Richard taunts Elizabeth and accuses her of promoting her favorites. When Elizabeth replies, "Small joy have I in being England's Queen" (109), Margaret can barely restrain herself; she says in an aside: "As little joy enjoys the queen thereof;/For I am she, and altogether joyless" (154–55). Margaret's aside pinpoints the confusion that results when women must depend upon men for identity and when Richard persists in removing these men. Is a woman to be considered "queen" after her "king" has been killed? Does one's title apply only as long as one's husband is alive? And, after her husband's death, what does the "queen" become? Margaret serves, of course, as model for the women of *Richard III;* she enters in Act I and shows Elizabeth and the Duchess of York what they have to expect from the future; like her, they are destined to years of sterile widowhood. But the women of York do not yet perceive Margaret's function; with Richard, they mock her and force her from the stage. Before leaving, however, Margaret further clarifies her relationship to Elizabeth by underlining the similarity of their woes:

> Thyself a queen, for me that was a queen,
> Outlive thy glory like my wretched self!
> Long mayst thou live to wail thy children's death;
> . . . .
> Long die thy happy days before thy death,
> And, after many length'ned hours of grief,
> Die neither mother, wife, nor England's Queen!
> (I.iii.201–3, 206–8)

Alive—but neither mother, wife, nor England's queen: the description may apply to Margaret, Elizabeth, and the Duchess. Only a very short time elapses between the day of Margaret's curse and the day Elizabeth suffers the death of her lord. Addressing the Duchess, the twice-widowed woman cries: "Edward, my lord, thy son, our king, is dead!/Why grow the branches when the root is gone?/Why wither not the leaves that want their sap?" (II.ii.40–42). Elizabeth's questions forecast her upcoming tragedy.

Not only does Richard subvert the role of queen, he also undermines roles of mother and wife. For example, while the death of Edward robs Elizabeth of a husband, it robs the Duchess of York of a son. Having lost son Clarence earlier, the Duchess's "stock" suffers a depletion of two-thirds. She turns to Elizabeth, commenting that years ago she lost a worthy husband,

> And lived with looking on his images;
> But now two mirrors of his princely semblance
> Are cracked in pieces by malignant death,
> And I for comfort have but one false glass
> That grieves me when I see my shame in him.
> Thou art a widow, yet thou art a mother
> And hast the comfort of thy children left.
> (II.ii.50–56)

Stressing Elizabeth's yet-current claim to motherhood, the Duchess appears to abjure her own; it is as if she no longer wants to assume the title of mother if Richard is the son who grants her this right; accepting "motherhood" means accepting responsibility for "all these griefs," for the losses sustained by Elizabeth and by Clarence's children.

It is not enough for one mother to abandon her claim to the title of mother; Richard pursues a course of action that eventually forces Elizabeth to relinquish her claim also (note that as the play proceeds, Elizabeth comes to bear a closer resemblance to Margaret). The process leading to Elizabeth's forfeiture of her title is more complicated than that of the Duchess and is accomplished in a series of steps: Buckingham and Richard override maternal authority and, parenthetically, the right of sanctuary, by "plucking" the Duke of York from the sheltering arms of his mother; Brakenbury, under order from Richard, denies Elizabeth entrance to the Tower, thereby denying her right to see her children; Richard casts doubt on the legitimacy of Edward's marriage to Elizabeth, and hence, on the legitimacy of her children; Richard preys upon Elizabeth to grant him her daughter in marriage while Elizabeth knows that to do so would be to sentence her daughter to a living death.

As this process is set in motion, the "Protector" refuses to grant Elizabeth her status as mother; as it comes to a close, Elizabeth freely abjures her motherhood in an attempt to protect her remaining child. Up until the murder of her sons, Elizabeth insists, often futilely, upon her maternal rights. When, for example, Brakenbury refuses to admit her to the Tower, she protests violently upon the grounds of familial relation: "Hath he set bounds between their love and me? I am their mother; who shall bar me from them?" (IV.i.20–21). Almost as if she were determined actively to dispute Richard's allegations that her children are illegitimate, Elizabeth reiterates, time and time again, the status of her relationship and that of her children to Edward. After the deaths of young Edward and Richard, however, Elizabeth is forced to perform an about-face. Because of Richard's manipulations, a "mother's name is ominous to children"; hence, she must deny her title of mother in order to express her genuine identity as a mother concerned for her children's welfare. She dispatches her son Dorset to France—"O Dorset, speak not to me, get thee gone!" (IV.i.38)—and expresses her willingness to deny the legitimacy of young Elizabeth's birth to save her from marriage to Richard.

> And must she die for this? O, let her live,
> And I'll corrupt her manners, stain her beauty,
> Slander myself as false to Edward's bed,
> Throw over her the veil of infamy;
> So she may live unscarred of bleeding slaughter,
> I will confess she was not Edward's daughter.
> (IV.iv.206–11)

It is the love of a mother for her daughter which prompts Elizabeth's offer; she willingly renounces her titles both of wife and legitimate mother.

In the examples cited above, Richard's general course of action is such to encourage women to abandon traditional titles, to de-identify themselves. Richard more specifically encourages this cipherization by confounding the integrity of titular markers: that is, by juggling titles without regard for the human beings behind these titles (although Richard does not restrict himself to female markers, females suffer more grievously from these verbal acrobatics than do males, who may draw upon a wider range of options with respect to identifying roles). Richard's changing choice of title for his sister-in-law Elizabeth most clearly exemplifies his policy of confoundment. Richard's first reference to Elizabeth occurs in a conversation with Clarence, in which Richard promises that he will employ any means to procure his brother's freedom: "And whatsoe'er you will employ me in,/Were it to call King Edward's widow sister,/I will perform it to enfranchise you" (I.i.108–10). Several things are happening here. First, as the wife of Edward, Richard's brother, Elizabeth *is* Richard's sister (sister-in-law); she need not solicit the title from Richard, although Richard certainly implies that it is his prerogative to grant or withhold the title at will. Second, the title Richard actually bestows on Elizabeth is "King Edward's widow," an equivocation of marvelous subtlety; Elizabeth *is* the widow of Grey but Richard's phrasing makes it possible to read this description as a prediction: Elizabeth will wear weeds again. And finally, when Richard and Elizabeth meet in the following scene, it is Elizabeth who twice addresses Richard as "Brother Gloucester"; Richard refuses to call her anything, because, at this time, he has nothing to gain by doing so. Later, in Act II, following the convenient demise of Edward IV, Richard, as if to ensure a smooth transference of power, attempts to placate Elizabeth: he calls her "sister." In Act IV, however, after Richard has approached Elizabeth for the hand of young Elizabeth, he calls her "mother": "Therefore, dear mother—I must call you so—/Be the attorney of my love to her" (IV.iv.412–13). The exchange between Richard and Elizabeth also supplies a rather startling example of Richard's indifference to the human beings who actually give substance to the titles he juggles with such apparent ease. Richard insists that he will provide substitutes for the children Elizabeth has lost at his hand:

> To quicken your increase I will beget
> Mine issue of your blood upon your daughter.
> A grandam's name is little less in love
> Than is the doting title of a mother.
> (IV.iv.297–300)

Focusing exclusively upon a "grandam's *name*" and the "*title* of a mother," Richard attempts to obscure the very real difference between these two positions; he attempts to confound all meaning attached to female position markers—a policy in keeping with his determination to confound women altogether.

II

Given Richard's perception of woman as enemy, as "Other," we should not be surprised that the action of the play depends upon a systematic denial of the human identity of women. Richard's apparently successful attempts to obscure Elizabeth's titular "sense of self" and Elizabeth's rejection of both her own identity and that of her daughter exemplify, on one level, the progression of women in *Richard III:* from mother to nonmother, wife to widow, queen to crone. However, this "progression" does not take into account a less obvious and more positive progression of women from a condition of bickering rivalry to a condition of sympathetic camaraderie. In the midst of loss, the women turn to each other. Thus, an interesting, but generally ignored, countermotion of interaction *among* women is introduced; having been reduced to the condition of nothing, Margaret, Elizabeth, and the Duchess evidence a new humanity, a humanity apparent nowhere else in the play. We need only explore the progression in the four scenes in *Richard III* in which women confront each other (I.iii; II.ii; IV.i; IV.iv) to see this countermotion. Act I, scene iii, opens with Elizabeth and Richard at each other's throat; with the entrance of Margaret, however, Richard is able to direct all hostility toward her. Even Elizabeth joins with crook-backed Gloucester in condemning the widow of Lancaster; angry words fly across the stage. When Elizabeth applauds

Richard for turning Margaret's curse back on herself, Margaret chides the "poor-painted queen":

> Why strew'st thou sugar on that bottled spider
> Whose deadly web ensnareth thee about?
> Fool, fool, thou whet'st a knife to kill thyself.
> The day will come that thou shalt wish for me
> To help thee curse this poisonous bunch-backed toad.
>
> (I.iii.241–45)

Margaret's prediction proves true, but the women must suffer first.

If the preceding scene depicts the hostility between women of different Houses, Act II, scene ii, depicts hostility between women of the same House. Instead of coming together in sympathy upon learning of the deaths of Clarence and Edward, the women of York and the children of Clarence engage in a chorus of moans, each claiming the greater loss. An appalling absence of empathy characterizes this meeting. A few lines may serve to indicate the mood of the entire scene:

> DUCH.: O, what cause have I,
>
> Thine being but a moi'ty of my moan,
>
> To overgo thy woes and drown thy cries!
>
> BOY: Ah, aunt, you wept not for our father's death.
>
> How can we aid you with our kindred tears?
>
> DAUGHTER: Our fatherless distress was left unmoaned;
>
> Your widow-dolor likewise be unwept!
>
> ELIZABETH: Give me no help in lamentation;
>
> I am not barren to bring forth complaints.
>
> (II.ii.59–67)

Obviously, the tendency here is away from commiseration and toward a selfish indulgence. It is not until Act IV, scene i, that a reversal of this tendency begins to make itself felt, the result of the women's sympathy as their position continues to erode. Elizabeth, the Duchess of York, Anne, and Clarence's daughter meet en route to the Tower to greet the young princes. When Elizabeth is denied visitation privileges, the Duchess and Anne support her maternal rights. Even when Stanley announces that Anne is to be crowned queen, the bond of sympathy between Anne and Elizabeth is not destroyed. Given her history of suffering, Elizabeth can respond now with feeling to Anne as Margaret could not when she was replaced by Elizabeth. When the new queen expresses her wish that the "inclusive verge of golden metal" were "red-hot steel to sear me to the brains," Elizabeth attempts to console her:

"Go, go, poor soul! I envy not thy glory. / To feed my humor wish thyself no harm" (IV.i.63–64). The Duchess of York adds her blessing also: "Go thou to Richard, and good angels tend thee!" (92). How different from the feeling of Act II, scene ii! Even though this union of sympathy may not generate any practical power (Richard continues to confound the women) it does prompt a revision in our responses to them: they attain a tragic dignity.

The most moving example of women-aiding-women, however, occurs in Act IV, scene iv, where the women of York join Margaret of Lancaster in cursing Richard. This union is achieved only gradually. Old Queen Margaret enters alone and withdraws to eavesdrop on Elizabeth and the Duchess of York, who sit down together to lament the death of the princes and lament their uselessness: "Ah that thou wouldst as soon afford a grave / As thou canst yield a melancholy seat" (IV.iv.31–32). When Margaret comes forward and joins the two women on the ground, she first claims that her griefs "frown on the upper hand" and it seems the scene will be a reiteration of the earlier contest.

> If sorrow can admit society,
> Tell o'er your woes again by viewing mine.
> I had an Edward, till a Richard killed him;
> I had a husband, till a Richard killed him.
> Thou hadst an Edward, till a Richard killed him;
> Thou hadst a Richard, till a Richard killed him.
> (IV.iv.38–43)

The Duchess, catching the rhythm of Margaret's refrain, interrupts in order to wail a few lines of her own. Margaret, however, regains voice, reminding the Duchess that it is her womb that has bred the cause of all their sorrows: "From forth the kennel of thy womb hath crept / A hellhound that doth hunt us all to death" (IV.iv.47–48). These words signal a reversal in the dynamics of the scene; no longer willing to recognize the legal ties to men which prohibit a communion between women of different parties, these women join together in sorrow, in suffering; it is easy enough to imagine the three of them, seated on the earth, hand in hand. The Duchess abandons her competition with Margaret for the title of most grief-stricken, and turns, in commiseration, to her: "O Harry's wife, triumph not in my woes! / God witness with me I have wept for thine" (59–60). Elizabeth, too, moves toward Margaret, admitting that the prophesied time has come for her to request Margaret's help in cursing the "foul bunch-backed toad" (81) Richard. Thus, the exchange among the women leads to the decision to arm themselves (to assume a male prerogative) with words; Margaret provides lessons in cursing and the Duchess suggests that they smother Richard in "the breath of bitter words" (133); no more wasted or feeble words—instead, the women now use words as weapons. Accordingly, when Richard enters a short while after Margaret's departure, Elizabeth and the Duchess verbally accost and accuse him. Unaccustomed to such noise, an indignant Richard commands: "Either be patient and entreat me fair, / Or with the clamorous report of war / Thus will I drown your exclamations" (152–54). Richard's response to these insistent female voices is worthy of note as it reiterates the alliance of Richard with war and against women, and as it serves as summary statement of Richard's policy with respect to women—they must be silenced. The Duchess, however, finds voice, and her final words to Richard take the form of a curse; she turns against her own House, prays for the adverse party, and damns her son Richard to a death of shame. Her ability to do so with such strength is surely a result of the communion of sympathy shared by the three women. If, in previous scenes, a meeting of women merely leads to angry words and altercation, the meeting of Act IV, scene iv, leads to the formation of bonds among the women against a single foe.[11] When the progression of female characters is charted on this level, it becomes apparent that they do not deserve the a priori dismissal they too frequently receive. Although attenuated by Richard, women take on an emotional solidity, a roundness of true humanity.

Notes

1. Norman Holland, *Psychoanalysis and Shakespeare* (New York: McGraw-Hill, 1966), p. 261.

2. Just to cite a few of the major examples: see Wolfgang H. Clemen, A *Commentary on Shakespeare's "Richard III."* trans. Jean Bonheim (London: Methuen and Co., 1968), and E. M. W. Tillyard, *Shakespeare's History Plays* (New York: Macmillan, 1946); as representative of historical-political interpretations, see John Palmer, *Political Characters of Shakespeare* (London: Macmillan, 1961) or M. M. Reese, *The Cease of Majesty* (New York: St. Martin's Press, 1961); for psychoanalytic interpretations, see essays in M. D. Faber, *The Design Within* (New York: Science House, 1970), or Holland, *Psychoanalysis and Shakespeare;* as representative of "type criticism" see Bernard Spivack, *Shakespeare and the Allegory of Evil* (New York: Columbia University Press, 1958). All of these works offer something to the history of criticism of *Richard III*, but all, initially, take their cue from the star performer-cum-director, Richard. The exception to this generalization is Leslie Fiedler. In *The Stranger in Shakespeare* (New York: Stein and Day, 1972), he shows his sensitivity to the "problem of woman" in Shakespeare; "Obviously, the beginning for Shakespeare is the problem of woman, or more exactly perhaps, his problem with women. Certainly, in his first plays, members of that sex are likely to be portrayed as utter strangers" (p. 43). The only other critic from the list above who makes any more than cursory mention of the women is Reese.

3. All citations are from *The Complete Signet Classic Shakespeare*, gen. ed. Sylvan Barnet (New York: Harcourt Brace Jovanovich, 1963, 1972).

4. Although this soliloquy has elicited comment from a wide range of critics, most of them appear oblivious to its misogynic thrust. Focusing upon Richard's statement that he is "determined to prove a villain," they ignore the motivation behind his determination. William B. Toole, for example, insists that we should *not* "seek a modern psychological explanation for Richard's behaviour on the basis of this passage. The main purpose of this part of the soliloquy [I.i.1–30] is to indicate that the protagonist has freely chosen to be a villain" ("The Motif of

Psychic Division in *Richard III*," *Shakespeare Survey*, 27 [1974], p. 25). A more interesting reading that appears closer to the text than Toole's, is Sigmund Freud's in "Some Character-Types Met with in Psycho Analytic Work," included in Faber, *The Design Within*. Freud explains that we accept Richard's articulation of his disadvantages in the soliloquy because we identity with him: "And now we feel that we ourselves might become like Richard. . . . Richard is an enormous magnification of something we find in ourselves as well. We all think we have reason to reproach Nature and our destiny for congenital and infantile disadvantages." (p. 345). Remaining true to both Freud and Richard, we might emend Freud's comment: "We all think we have reason to reproach women (the "Great Mothers") for our disadvantages."

    5.   See also Richard's soliloquy in *Henry VI*, Part 3, III.ii.124–95, in which the sexual opposition is more explicit.

    6.   Interestingly enough, although Shore may have a hand in Hastings's release, the evidence against Elizabeth's involvement in Clarence's imprisonment is such that we must dismiss all charges against her—but the probable guilt of one and the certain innocence of the other make no difference; when Richard requires a scapegoat, any woman will serve.

    7.   Again, although critical response to this scene has been abundant, it has also been very narrow in focus. Palmer, *Political Characters,* p. 81, maintains that the prime purpose of Richard's wooing "is to show Richard's insolent virtuosity in persuasion, his delight in the exercise of his mind and will, his pride in attempting the impossible and his triumph in its achievement." Palmer does not choose to see the sexual ramifications of the *contents* of Richard's virtuosity, delight, pride, and triumph. Similarly, Reese, *The Cease of Majesty,* pp. 217–18, notes that Shakespeare invents most of the first act in order to "show off [Richard's] powers," but does not comment on the fact that these powers are directed against women.

    8.   Claude Lévi-Strauss, *Structural Anthropology,* trans. Claire Jacobson and Brooke Grandfest Schoepf (New York: Basic Books, 1976), I, 46: "a man obtains a woman from another man who gives him a daughter or a sister."

    9.   See Otto Rank, *Das Inzest Motiv in Dichtung und Sage* (Leipzig: Franz Deuticke, 1926), pp. 211–12, for a more complete analysis of incest motifs in *Richard III*. Also see Charles A. Adler, "*Richard III*—His Significance as a Study in Criminal Life-Style," *International Journal of Individual Psychology*, 2. No. 3 [1936], 55–60, for a brief, and rather crude, commentary on the way Richard attempts to conquer his murdered opponents by "possessing their ladies" (p. 59).

    10.   Although guilty of several murders throughout the play, Richard never raises his sword against a woman; he does not need to; instead, he effectively disposes of women by disposing of the "primary terms" according to which they identify themselves. (Richard's wife Anne is the possible exception; it is questionable whether her death should be attributed to poison from the hand of Richard or to the equally lethal experience of marriage to him.)

    11.   Very few critics pay much attention to this scene. Fiedler provides an especially sympathetic reading of the way in which Margaret, "squatting on the ground with Queen Elizabeth and the Duchess of York . . . has helped project the image of the Triple Goddess in darkest form" (*The Stranger in Shakespeare*, p. 50). As Fiedler explains a while later, this Triple Goddess is comprised of "Hera, Aphrodite, Persephone: mother, mistress and queen of the underworld," but in Shakespeare, "the first two functions blur into the third [which is why] . . . in that terrible scene of *Richard III* in which Queen Margaret, Queen Elizabeth, and the Duchess of York gather together, the second two are portrayed as mere shadows of the first, who, we suspect, will disappear when she leaves the land which has never really been hers" (p. 73). Richard Wheeler, in "History, Character, and Conscience in *Richard III*," *Comparative Drama*, 5 (1971–72), 314, also takes note of the scene, observing that although Richard virtually makes a career out of killing men, "the real suffering of the play comes to be focused in the voices of widowed mothers." Reese, on the other hand, is completely unsympathetic. Although he believes scenes with the women are important ones—"They provide a formal setting for

Richard's crimes and epitomise the Elizabethan reading of history" (*The Cease of Majesty*, p. 209), he insists that the women's indifference to Richard's immortal soul "shows how low these women themselves have fallen. Except in an emptily rhetorical way, they are not touched by the finer issues" (p. 223). Finer issues?! Must such issues revolve around the eternal salvation of the male figure?

RICHARD III DECONSTRUCTED

◆

The following three extracts indicate current tendencies in the treatment of *Richard III*, both in the theater and in the study. The first recapitulates my work on the recent stage history of the play in the *Richard III* volume of the University of Manchester series on Shakespeare and performance and my association with the reconstruction of Shakespeare's first Globe Theatre near its original site in London. I also discuss the consequent interest in our recovery in some measure of the original conditions of Shakespearean performance. Jean Howard and Phyllis Rackin illustrate the modern subordination of texts to feminist preconceptions. Linda Charnes accommodates *Richard III* to the concept of Renaissance self-fashioning, showing how new historicists have subjected earlier concepts of Reformation subjectivity to Marxist determinism.

Postmodern Renderings of *Richard III*

HUGH MACRAE RICHMOND

The research and comment on *Richard III* reflected in the essays excerpted in the previous section of this book illustrate the culmination of a process of conscious recovery of the origin, nature, and circumstances of the play. After centuries of distortion in the text as performed (and therefore, to a degree, as discussed), scholars, critics, and performers found the restoration and explication of the *Richard III* of Shakespeare a worthy and challenging goal. However, the postmodernists of the later twentieth century, in both the theater and the study, have rebelled against the authority of the past as vigorously as did the reformers of the Puritan Commonwealth and Restoration periods, and such "improvers" have created no less bold mutations of the recovered Shakespearean scripts than did the neoclassical "correctors" of Shakespeare from Davenant and Dryden onward. Thus, the most recent critical fate of *Richard III* is once again to be dismantled, redesigned, rebuilt, and reinterpreted in the light of purely modern preferences, concerns, and theories. In many ways it is the performers who have led the way in this process of reinvention.

Some radical modernistic values can already be seen in the famous production of *Richard III,* directed by Bill Alexander and starring Antony Sher, at the Royal Shakespeare Company (RSC) in 1984. This production reflected the assumptions of postmodern multiculturalism to a remarkable degree, and its origins may stand as the precedent for postmodern revamping of the text, which has seen such recent transformations as Al Pacino's *Looking for Richard* and Ian McKellen's film version (following a stage version already set in the 1930s of a supposedly fascist England). The RSC program director who first solicited Sher's participation in 1984 was Ron Daniels, originally from Brazil; the program notes were written by a scholar from Canada; Lady Anne was an Australian who based the final phase of her interpretation on the psychological effects of Australian aboriginal witchcraft[1]; the lead was played by Sher, a South African, of Russian extraction, who used the German Reich (and Hitler in particular) as a model; and the interpretation of Richard was formulated by Sher's Freudian psychotherapist, Monty Berman, also a South African, "originally from good Communist Jewish stock" (Sher, 25).

The latter's advice about Richard simply involved treating him as if he came to Berman "as a patient." Berman supposed that he "would have to start with that mother," pointing out "that there isn't a single moment in the play when the Duchess of York talks of Richard without contempt and hatred. She shows no maternal instincts whatsoever. . . . the mother prevents the child from developing an accurate sense of self. She distorts his view of himself. . . . as Richard has not received love as a child, he won't be able to show any himself." After this discussion Sher concludes: "An absence of love. Caused by a hating mother. This is what I will base my performance on. But I will have to be quite secretive about it, because it sounds so corny—his mother didn't love him" (Sher, 129–30).

The RSC thoroughly researched the character of Richard from a historical perspective, and Sher discovered that "the real Richard was a good king, a gentle soul, not at all deformed, and didn't kill the princes in the Tower" (Sher, 131). In drawing these conclusions Sher was following the positive guidelines of the partisan Richard III Society, and he notes (131) Josephine Tey's equally committed defense of Richard in *The Daughter of Time,* which blames the princes' murders on Henry VII. Historical research into Yorkist ritual did suggest the addition of a nude coronation scene to the script. Sher found it all "an interesting read, but useless for my purposes. Except that in [Tey's] book a doctor studying the famous portrait diagnoses polio" (Sher, 131). In the event, Sher based his interpretation on the personal fact that he was himself using National Health Service crutches about this time because of damage to his Achilles tendon. These twentieth-century props were used in a classic gesture of postmodern defiance of historical consistency, despite the otherwise medieval sets and costumes.

Introduction of this biographical quirk may have been facilitated by the fact that the only Shakespearean drama that the production's director had handled previously was a minor tour version of *Henry IV,* and from this limited experience he had serious doubts about the fitness of native Anglo-Saxon talent for interpreting Shakespeare: "English actors," he once lamented in rehearsal, "English actors are so self-conscious. There'd be no problem with that scene if you had continental or American actors" (Sher, 183). At another time the director, Alexander, brooded about the difficulty of Shakespeare's blank verse: "It is our instrument and our challenge. It would be so easy if we were Russians and could have the verse roughly translated and then dazzle with the images. We've got to dazzle with Shakespeare's language" (Sher, 203). Not surprisingly, with this basic mistrust by the director of the essential element of Shakespearean scripts and performance, Antony Sher had a nightmare about the play's last scenes, in which "new material has been discovered about a Russian presence at Bosworth" (Sher, 230). The ghost of Stanislavsky haunted this Richard more compellingly than any other spirits, perhaps because of his own Russian antecedents. The whole production was conceived in the context of high—even envious—admiration of the *Richard III* presented during the recent visits to Britain of the Rustaveli company from then-communist Georgia to which Sher's book makes frequent and deferential references.

Both productions are truly representative of our own era's repudiation of the past, for the characteristic catalysts of their reinterpretation of *Richard III* are to be found in the distancing of performers and audiences from the essentials of the text and from the culture it exemplifies. The drama critic of the *Coventry Evening Telegraph* observed of the Sher production: "This is a bold and adventurous frontal assault on a literary figurehead. It rips apart the strands of a tradition by dictating a strong, irreverent approach and blows an invigorating wind of change across Bosworth Field."[2] The driving force behind this assault can be divined from Sher's remarks about English nostalgia for the past: "it doesn't actually relate to anything in my own past at all" (Sher, 43). And he later adds: "I find the classics difficult to watch and understand. So I like them done by Brook, or Adrian [Noble], or the Rustaveli Company" (Sher, 181). This condition of alienation and discontinuity means that there are no certain, instinctive, intuitive, or conditioned reflexes to inspire such actors as Sher and Downey of the kind that marked Olivier, or even Barton and Hall. As graduates from the Cambridge dominated by the confrontations of Tillyard and Leavis, Barton and Hall are products of a shared culture increasingly diluted for the English themselves by the "multicultural" character of their social values and culture in most major cities, with their influx of immigrants to whom (quite understandably and properly) the victories of a Henry V and the defeat of a Richard III are as remote as the enigmas of Elizabethan language and metrics seemed to be for Sher and Alexander.

Sher quotes approvingly Gielgud's self-betraying remark that "one of the pleasures of playing Shakespeare [is that] nobody understands what you are saying so you can make it up when you forget" (Sher, 207). Sher confesses to being "tripped up constantly" by Elizabethan usage: "Shakespeare's grammar is confounding me," and the metrics are also "a tricky area. It's my first big verse part" (Sher, 181). More broadly he says: "Reading Shakespeare is sometimes like looking through a window into a dark room. You don't see in. An unflattering image of yourself blind" (Sher, 36). For Sher the part of Richard was alien, and he even risked "irreparable damage" because of "the terrible physical strain," because "it is the play in which Shakespeare made all his mistakes. For a start he doesn't give Richard a rest" (Sher, 42).

What can be achieved in dealing with the classics to compensate for such a radical discontinuity with the past, which increasingly seems to be the characteristic of most modern mass societies? The handling of this factor in the Sher–Alexander production of *Richard III* makes it representative of our era's deliberate rejection of tradition—for it needed only a hint that Olivier had used a bit of business for Sher to reject it outright, as if the truly Shakespearean idea of art as an accumulation of insights from successful precedents were intolerable. Instead of adopting this view, intrinsic to his material, the South African Sher pursued the solution of American actors for their similar problem of dealing with alien masterpieces and unintelligible roles: the technique of method acting evolved by Lee Strasberg from actors' experiences at

Stanislavsky's Moscow Theatre to deal with such original scripts as the plays of Chekhov. In creating a crippled Richard, Sher drew on his own experience of dependence on crutches after straining an Achilles tendon while performing the Fool in *King Lear.* He also applied his own mother fixation to Richard's motivations following his psychoanalyst's interpretation. The added coronation scene derived from historical records, but ones ignored in Shakespeare's script, and the sets were based on the configuration of Worcester cathedral, but they bore no relation to any original Elizabethan stage, or to the Memorial Theatre's stage, which they filled with obstacles for the actors to dodge.

Such tangential, often subjective, input is the normal result of the method approach because, in the absence of accessible (or acceptable) tradition, the method pursues a combination of elaborate research, subjective projection, and realistic texture that proves ideally suited to film production, with its tendency to elaborately realistic sets (or shooting on plausible or even authentic locations) and to the exploitation of extreme close-up shots whose psychological scrutiny exacts the involuntary conviction best attainable by typecasting. Nothing could be further from the permanent stage sets of the Elizabethan theaters and the highly rhetorical style customary in addressing mass audiences of around 2,000 people in such open-air theaters as the Rose and its antecedents, for which *Richard III* was written. Whether because of the conscientious internationalism of Stratford's current recruitment of its actors or because of the general decline in historical education, the American method has increasingly dominated the procedures of actors at Stratford, as Bernard Beckerman observed them: "a preference for literal staging misnamed realism . . . carries over into our staging of Shakespeare, often trivializing situations and characters by making them 'real.' " Because of the loss of any sense of tradition in actors and audiences, "Producers . . . give reign to their natural predilection for treating the text as a play without history," and they therefore aim for novelty, of which Beckerman feels "the current spectacularly successful production of *Richard III* with Antony Sher is a case in point."[3]

What we know or can conjecture about the original production led by Richard Burbage must seem more relevant to the text than Sher's (or almost any other subsequent interpretation), because so few since the original performances have corresponded at all closely to a contemporary version of a Shakespearean script and hence to his implicit intentions. Yet the stage history of the play suggests that it includes many striking successes. These may require us to admit the propriety of almost any kind of theatrical adaptation if it satisfies audiences, as Sher's certainly did. Literary tradition must evolve, and even classics require revision to ensure a minimum of accessibility. Moreover, the radical restructuring of classic Shakespearean themes seems justified and rewarding in such examples as Shaw's plays, which often derive from Shakespearean precedents: *St. Joan* from *Henry VI, Part 1; Pygmalion* from *The Tam-*

ing of the Shrew; Caesar and Cleopatra from both *Julius Caesar* and *Antony and Cleopatra;* and so forth. No less rewarding are the many experiments of Stoppard using Shakespearean models, such as *Rosencrantz and Guildenstern Are Dead,* not to mention the reinvented Shakespearean plays of Charles Marowitz. Such drastic reconstructions have recently been directed to Shakespeare's script of *Richard III.*

When the RSC's director, Bill Alexander, regretfully wished that he could present *Richard III* in a coarse Russian translation with non-English actors, he was not speculating idly about an ideal situation but rather recalling enviously an actual production by the Rustaveli Company of Georgia (then still a province of the Soviet Union), which had been seen at the Edinburgh Festival in 1979, and the following year in London, to great acclaim. Antony Sher considers it to be "a stunning production." He comments on "how sexy" the lead role was, despite the fact that "Ramaz Chkhivadze plays Richard like a species of giant poisonous toad. And he touches people as if removing handfuls of flesh. I will never forget the moment of Accession. As the crown is landed on his head it seemed to squash the face beneath it like an animated cartoon." Sher's companion at the production, the actor and director Richard Wilson, "thought it was a definitive production" despite (or because of) the fact that it was in an unintelligible foreign language (Sher, 28, 158). On the other hand, Chris Hassell considers it to be the "most grotesque" of modern productions, filled with "gratuitous violence" by which "one was transported into a region of irredeemable degeneracy."[4]

The Georgians' widely accepted claims to do justice to the Shakespearean tradition were defended by the program notes of Michael Gearin-Tosh of St. Catherine's College, Oxford, who illustrates the desire to sophisticate critical awareness to match the new text. He wrote: "Shakespeare is second only to the great medieval poet Shota Rustaveli as the acknowledged inspiration of modern Georgian literature. Georgians readily argue that St. George's position as patron saint of both countries indicates the kinship of spirit whose articulation is Shakespeare. The terms of their argument are suggestive, as is the linking of Shakespeare with Rustaveli. For Georgian theatre has a living relationship with its medieval and ancient origins: a tradition of strolling players, circus and pageant, has endured throughout the violence of Georgian history. The Rustaveli Company use this tradition in presenting Shakespeare as much as they adapt Shakespeare to its idiom."

The argument of recovering the tradition in which Shakespeare wrote seems ingenious and even traditional, but it is frequently resorted to as a modern device for justifying a reversion from Shakespeare's subtle development of his sources to their more primitive (and thus supposedly more accessible) forms, which he seemingly overrefined. Good examples of this reductionist technique can be found in the reversion to the knockabout conventions of commedia dell'arte street theater in recent productions of *The Taming of the Shrew* by the Actors' Conservatory Theater of San Francisco, which was televised throughout the United States, and a similar adjustment of Clifford William's production of *The Comedy of Errors,* which has been frequently revived by the RSC since it first appeared in 1962. Both directors assumed their scripts were effectively insignificant examples of conventional farce using "the stock masks of the Italian comedy."[5] The revivification involved recourse to slapstick—in the former case with an injection of physical brutality that set back Shakespeare's reputation among feminists by its crude endorsement of male supremacy. This approach may have been characteristic of sixteenth-century misogynistic farce from which Shakespeare's play evolved but not of Shakespeare's *Taming* itself, as Germaine Greer has forcefully argued in *The Female Eunuch,*[6] nor of *The Comedy,* with Adriana's bitter censures of the sexual double standard.

We have seen the same attempt to return Shakespeare to the cruder tradition that he had transcended in Bill Alexander's desire to return *Richard III* to the format of a medieval drama set explicitly in a cathedral. Similarly, Michael Greenwald notes, the Rustaveli version "was pointedly theatrical in the morality play tradition."[7] Matching this concept, the set "was patterned after Bosch's painting of the Last Judgment" and the play finished with the "battle in cartoon style."

Such archaisms almost inevitably require adjustment of the Shakespearean text to accommodate the regression. The Rustaveli director, Robert Strurua, candidly avowed that he "approached *Richard III* not as an English tragedy, but as something [he could] manipulate to convey [his] own ideas" (Leiter, 617). The program notes assert that "the Georgian translation of *Richard III* stays very close to Shakespeare's original" but concede that "a number of details differ. Some minor characters have been eliminated or merged with others and greater prominence than usual is given to a number of roles." Perhaps we should feel that the omissions of Cibber are expiated in that "Principal among these [expanded roles] is Queen Margaret, widow of Henry VI who appears almost as a Greek chorus introducing scenes by reading the stage directions and commenting on the action." However, the notes add that "Richmond is also present as an observer at many stages of the play. In the third act there is a new character not found in Shakespeare—a cross between a court jester and the fool in *Lear*—who also comments on the action by quoting back to various characters things that they have said earlier in the play, pointing the contrasts between aspiration and reality." This again reminds us of the Restoration's need for explicit moral insistence. Interestingly, the actor who played the fool tripled as the archbishop of Canterbury and Edward IV. Moreover, in the Rustaveli version, Richard "divorces Lady Anne and marries his niece." The innovative confidence of Cibber has surely not been wholly exorcised.

For those not expert in Georgian (presumably almost all of the audiences in Britain), the program notes provided help with a translation of the more radical departures from Shakespeare. Two samples will indicate the boldness of the transpositions involved. The first is from the third act. In it there is much improvisation and reshuffling of lines: Richard's own confession of his methods is reattributed to the interpolated fool, while Richmond's final speech is given to Richard:

JESTER: The Life and Death of King Richard III.

Tut, I can counterfeit the deep tragedian

Speak and look back, and pry on every side,

Tremble and start at every straw,

Intending deep suspicion: ghastly looks

Are at my service, like enforcing smiles—

And both are ready in their offices,

At any time, to grace my stratagems.

RICHARD: England hath long been mad and scarred herself,

The brother blindly shed the brother's blood,

The father rashly slaughtered his own son,

The son, compelled, been butcher to the sire.

God, if Thy will be so, I shall

Enrich the time to come with smooth-faced peace,

With smiling plenty, and fair prosperous days!

But first I shall win our ancient right in France again.

DERBY: Hie thee Richmond! Towards the North

Gather an army and take command.

Make haste or else it will be late.

Fight the evil lest all of us

Fall victim to this blood-thirsty Richard.

RICHMOND: I will, father.

I shall do all in my power to destroy this monster

But am I powerful enough?

DERBY: If not, we are ruined.

Another cited passage is even more interesting. It comes from the revised script's recognition of Queen Margaret as Richard's ultimate alter ego, or conscience, which is achieved by the following reassignments of lines:

RICHARD: Is there a murderer here?

MARGARET: Yes, thou art! Fly!

RICHARD: What, from myself?

MARGARET: Lest thou revenge!

RICHARD:	Myself upon myself?
	Alack, I love myself. Wherefore? For any good
MARGARET:	That thou hast done thyself.
RICHARD:	Hush!
MARGARET:	There is no creature loves thee
	And if thou die no soul will pity thee. . . .

This revision explores the possibility of the speech being played, like *Everyman,* between allegorical characters making contrasting points rather than by the single virtuoso voice of Burbage evoking the inner dialogue of Richard's self-critique. Sher initially stumbled over just this challenge to his performance—"the nightmare speech is unfelt and technical. Different funny voices coming out" (Sher, 237)—and it is interesting that the Rustaveli company also balked at the same challenge of uniting the two personae of Richard in a single actor. The latter procedure involves a much subtler psychology—one nearer our modern sense of complex identity—and provides a richer option for the single actor replacing two. The Rustaveli text is made to revert to abstract identities in the medieval allegorical mode.

If Rustaveli freshens up supposedly stale material for the British by turning it into an unintelligible Russian dialect and reverting to a cruder theatrical convention, in 1985 the Berkeley Shakespeare Festival achieved a similar "renovation," but it justified many of the same effects by a sophisticated modern concept instead of recovery of an earlier mode. This innovation replaced the allegorical vision of medieval literature with something close to a Freudian review of the whole play as Richard's dream in his tent on the battlefield on the eve of the battle at Bosworth Field. The action began with Richard's retirement to sleep in that setting. Then it flashed back to the start of the play, whose eccentricities thus became parts of Richard's own extended, private nightmare, recapitulating his whole career in surrealistic terms, and governed by the ever-present spirit of Margaret. This resolved every bizarrerie—all were seen as the effects of Richard's own distorting imagination or conscience. And if Margaret was already dead by this point in history, she could certainly return as a ghost to haunt Richard, just as his other enemies finally do in recovering the dream's original ending. The most awkward consequence of this structure was that the performance required Richard to stay on stage throughout as the necessary spectator of his own dream, and Margaret also, as its stage manager. These exhausting requirements far exceeded even the protracted demands of the original script on the actors.

My point in briefly recapitulating these various modern productions of *Richard III* is to indicate how their fashionable postmodern approaches share a radical mistrust of Shakespeare's stagecraft and insight, adopted by repertory theaters that are utterly remote from each other. Whether in communist

Georgia, or suburban California, or rural Warwickshire, the text is no longer presented in Shakespeare's terms. The current tendency in interpretations of Shakespeare purports to update the original script by rejecting any expectation that we might properly attempt the best re-creation of the original performance effects that we can in modern terms, as William Poel once proposed, a goal the earlier critics in this anthology endorsed. This conscientiousness is often replaced by a radical but often unavowed reinterpretation and restructuring, far more drastic even than that of Colley Cibber. The assumption is that the conventions of Shakespeare and the Elizabethan stage are alien, irrelevant, and unreproduceable and that his plays should therefore be treated as expedient opportunities for innovative presentation rather than as scripts that provide exact specifications for staging. Thus Shakespeare's *Richard III* can now be recycled either by reversion to theatrical traditions even more archaic than those exploited in Olivier's film or as refracted through modern psychological theories yet more radical in application than Antony Sher's conscientious hospital visits for study of the physically and mentally handicapped before playing Richard. Behind such procedures lies a mistrust of Shakespeare's accessibility to modern audiences, which never occurred to most earlier critics and actors. Despite recent fear of archaism, in the late twentieth century modestly Elizabethan renderings of the script of *Richard III* have proved satisfying and intelligible to general audiences (as with the RSC productions in the 1950s and 1960s of Goring and Shaw, or Plummer and Gaskill).

However, directors and critics of *Richard III* will undoubtedly have to continue to confront this issue of whether radical reinterpretation is needed to appeal to supposedly not just alien but alienated modern audiences. Critical innovation at present closely matches the bizarre innovations of stage productions in the application of provocative concepts to update the script's sociological significance, reinforcing concerns antecedent to the examination of the script itself. Usually the principles of some commanding sociological authority, such as Claude Lévi-Strauss, Mikhail Bakhtin, Raymond Williams, or Michel Foucault, are invoked and then applied rigorously to dissection of a moribund text. This radical revisionism is reflected in many current studies. The two essays that conclude this volume seek to accommodate the text to various modern concerns, motivations, and ideologies—feminist, political, or sociological—that are supposedly latent in the original script but extrinsic to the literary or theatrical tradition. It is revealing to compare the traditional methodology of Nicholas Brooke (who invokes the Christian traditions of medieval drama) with the wholly modern and secular sociology of Linda Charnes as they develop analogous interpretations of Richard's tragically predetermined fate. In such work as Charnes's postmodern characterization of Richard's extreme self-consciousness as a role player, the resiting and reconstruction of *Richard III* in a new ideological context is once again reenacted.

Notes

1. Antony Sher, *Year of the King: An Actor's Diary and Sketchbook* (London: Chatto and Windus, 1985), 189. Hereafter cited in the text.

2. *Coventry Evening Telegraph,* 20 June 1984.

3. Bernard Beckerman, *Shakespeare Quarterly* 36 (1985): 589.

4. R. Chris Hassel Jr., *Songs of Death: Performance, Interpretation, and the Text of "Richard III"* (Lincoln: University of Nebraska Press, 1987), 9.

5. *The Comedy of Errors* (Program), Stratford-upon-Avon, Royal Shakespeare Company, 1972, 20.

6. Germaine Greer, *The Female Eunuch* (New York: Bantam, 1972), 220–21.

7. Samuel L. Leiter, *Shakespeare around the Globe: A Guide to Notable Postwar Revivals* (New York: Greenwood, 1986), 617. Hereafter cited in the text.

A Feminist Account of *Richard III*

JEAN E. HOWARD AND PHYLLIS RACKIN

Many of the female characters in Shakespeare's English history plays are distinguished by foreign nationality or low social origin. Joan of course has both, but it is worth remembering that all the female characters in *Henry VI, Part I* are French and that Margaret's French origins receive repeated emphasis in the subsequent Henry VI plays. In the second tetralogy, there will be the tavern women in the Henry IV plays, Mortimer's Welsh bride in *Henry IV, Part I,* and three more French women in *Henry V.* Many of these women are also distinguished from the English male protagonists by linguistic differences—in the first tetralogy by Joan's earthy, colloquial language and in the second by Mistress Quickly's malapropisms and the foreign languages spoken by the Welsh and French women (even when their male parents speak perfectly good English). These marks of national and class difference set these women apart from the noble English men who are the dramas' most privileged figures. In direct antithesis, all of the female characters in *Richard III* are highborn English women who speak in the undifferentiated, formal blank verse that constitutes the standard language of the playscript. Recruited to the service of the hegemonic project of the plot, the accession of Henry VII to the English throne, the women are also subsumed in its hegemonic discourse. As Nicholas Brooke has observed, "the flexibility of private speech" in this play is almost entirely "confined to Richard" (Brooke 1984:108). Even Margaret, the most powerful of Richard's female antagonists, speaks in the generalized rhetorical terms that constitute the normative language of the play.

Assuming their tragic roles as pitiable victims, female characters are no longer represented as dangerous, demonic Others. Instead, they conform to the stereotypical representation of female characters, especially bereaved mothers, in the drama of the period as "a symbolic focus of pity" rather than as individual figures "involved in an action through [their] own motive and volition" (McLuskie 1989: 136 and chapter 6 *passim*). The subversive theatrical energy of the peasant Joan is replaced by the pathos of suffering English queens. Margaret, the adulterous wife and bloodthirsty warrior of the Henry

From Jean E. Howard and Phyllis Rackin, *Engendering a Nation: A Feminist Account of Shakespeare's Histories* (London: Routledge, 1997). Reprinted with permission of the publisher.

267

VI plays, is transformed into a bereaved and suffering prophet of divine vengeance for the crimes of the past. In the Henry VI plays, the female characters are defined as opponents to the masculine project of English history-making. In *Richard III,* all of the women support the desired conclusion of the historical plot, the foundation of the Tudor dynasty.

Although the overarching goal of the dramatic action in *Richard III* (as in all of Shakespeare's English histories and a number of his tragedies as well) is the maintenance of a legitimate royal succession, in this play, unlike the earlier histories, it is the male protagonist who opposes the patriarchal project. The threats to patrilineal succession represented in the *Henry VI* plays by Joan's bastardy and sexual promiscuity and Margaret's adultery are replaced by Richard's murders and his deceitful effort to deny the legitimacy of his brother's innocent children, the rightful heirs to the throne he usurps, and even of Edward himself. In *Richard III,* the subversive power associated with female characters in the earlier plays is demystified, and all the power of agency and transgression is appropriated by the male protagonist. The threat of adultery is no longer real, and the character who threatens to displace legitimate heirs is not an adulterous woman, but the slanderous man, Richard, who brings the charge. Witchcraft, the quintessential representation of the dangerous power of women, is similarly reduced from a genuine threat to a transparent slander. Both Joan in *Henry VI, Part I* and Eleanor Cobham in *Henry VI, Part II* summon demons to the stage. In *Richard III,* however, there are only Richard's unsupported and obviously false charges against Queen Elizabeth and Jane Shore.

Joan in *Henry VI, Part I* is the prototype for the marginal and criminal status of the women in the Henry VI plays and also for their subversive, theatrical energy. Her inexplicable military power, first explained as deriving from the Blessed Virgin, is finally defined as witchcraft and punished with burning. Her very subversiveness, however, paradoxically authorizes her dramatic power. As both Catherine Belsey and Karen Newman have observed, the custom of requiring witches to confess from the scaffold "paradoxically also offered women a place from which to speak in public with a hitherto unimagined authority which was not diminished by the fact that it was demonic." These public occasions were also theatrical. As both critics note, "the crowds at trials and executions" were frequently described as "beholders" or "the audience," and "Pamphleteers often described[d] the scene of execution explicitly as a play" (Newman 1991: 67; Belsey 1985: 190–1).

Two episodes, one near the beginning of *Richard III* and one near its end, illustrate the way the powerful role of demonic other, occupied by women in the Henry VI plays, is now transferred to Richard. The longer of these is the second, the encounter near the end of Act IV between Richard and Queen Elizabeth, where Shakespeare altered his historical source in order to ennoble the character of the widowed queen. As Barbara Hodgdon observes, Shakespeare "displaces those attributes the chronicler ascribes to the Queen onto

Richard" (Hodgdon 1991: 109–10). In Hall's version, Queen Elizabeth exemplifies female "inconstancie," first promising her daughter Elizabeth (or, in the event of Elizabeth's death, her next daughter, the Lady Cecile) to Richmond (Hall 1548: 391), then, persuaded by promises of "promocions innumerable and benefites," agreeing to Richard's demands:

> putting in oblivion the murther of her innocent children, the infamy and dishonoure spoken by the kynge her husbande, the lyvynge in avoutrie leyed to her charge, the bastardyng of her daughters, forgettyng also ye feithfull promes & open othe made to the countesse of Richmond mother to ye erle Henry, blynded by avaricious affeccion and seduced by flatterynge wordes, first delivered into kyng Richards handes her. v. daughters as Lambes once agayne committed to the custody of the ravenous wolfe. (Hall 1548: 406)

Shakespeare's widowed queen, unlike Hall's, keeps faith with Richmond and adamantly refuses Richard's urgings to forget past wrongs. Insistently recalling the fate of her murdered children, she charges, "No doubt the murd'rous knife was dull and blunt/Till it was whetted on thy stone-hard heart/To revel in the entrails of my lambs" (IV.iv.227–9). Shakespeare thus appropriates for Elizabeth's use against Richard the very arguments, and even the terms, by which the authoritative narrative voice in Hall's chronicle condemns her action.

In Shakespeare's representation, it is Richard and not Elizabeth—or any of the women—who becomes the sole object of condemnation. The women are deprived of theatrical power and agency, both of which are appropriated by Richard, along with their demonic roles. The audience is never allowed to see Elizabeth deciding to bestow her daughter on Richmond. All we get is Stanley's laconic report that "the Queen hath heartily consented/He [Richmond] should espouse Elizabeth her daughter" (IV.v.7–8); and a number of critics have accepted Richard's judgment at the end of their encounter that the queen is a "relenting fool, and shallow, changing woman" (IV.iv.431; Hammond 1981: 296). Like the other women in *Richard III*, Elizabeth serves as a kind of ventriloquist's dummy. She gives forceful and eloquent voice to Richard's crimes, but her own motives can remain ambiguous because they are finally irrelevant to the outcome of the plot. What is important is that Richmond marries her daughter; whether or when the queen gives her consent is of so little consequence that it is never clearly specified in Shakespeare's script.

The earlier incident is much more brief, a telling moment in Act I when Richard literally appropriates the demonic power of a woman's voice. Margaret of Anjou, sent at the end of *Henry VI, Part III* back to France (where her historical prototype died in 1482), returns unhistorically in *Richard III* like a voice from the dead to recall the crimes of the past and pour out curses on her old enemies. In I.iii, she comes on stage as an eavesdropper who punctuates the dialogue with bitter comments delivered to the audience, unheard by the other characters. Finally, she moves forward to dominate the stage with a great outpouring of curses and denunciations, directed at each of the other characters in turn. When she comes to Richard, however, he interrupts the stream of malediction to turn Margaret's curses back upon herself. "O, let me make the period to my curse!" she complains. "'Tis done by me," he replies, "and ends in 'Margaret' " (I.iii.237–8).

This exchange dramatizes what will be a major source of Richard's theatrical power. Late in Act III, Buckingham advises Richard to "play the maid's part . . . and take" the crown (III.vii.51), but the woman's part has been included in the master showman's repertory from the very beginning. Characterized throughout in terms of warlike masculinity and aggressive misogyny, Richard also commands the female power of erotic seduction. It is interesting that Ian McKellen, who recently played the part of Richard to great acclaim, is openly gay. The dominant sexual ideology of our time equates masculinity with male heterosexuality, but McKellen's virtuoso performance in the part of Richard destabilizes this equation, bringing out what is implicit in Shakespeare's text, namely, that masculinity and femininity are performatively secured and are neither determined by a sexed body nor reducible to the performance of any particular sexual acts. In Shakespeare's play, Richard's monopoly of both male and female sexual energy is vividly portrayed in his seduction of Anne. The turning point comes when Richard lends her his sword and lays his breast "naked" for her penetration (I.ii.177). Overwhelmed by Richard's aggressive passivity, Anne's resistance quickly collapses, whereupon Richard seals his sexual conquest by enclosing her finger with his ring. "Look how my ring encompasseth thy finger," he says. "Even so thy breast encloseth my poor heart" (I.ii.203–4). Owner of both the sword and the naked breast, both penetrated ring and penetrating heart, Richard has become, as Rebecca Bushnell observes, "both the man who possesses and the woman who submits" (Bushnell 1990: 124).

The power that Richard takes from women to curse and seduce is not his only power. He is also able to transcend the frame of historical representation, to address the audience directly without the knowledge of the other characters, and to exude the theatrical energy that serves to monopolize the audience's attention. The structure of Richard's exchange with Margaret is also the structure of the early scenes in the play: it is always Richard who has the last word—along with the first. Each scene is punctuated by soliloquies in which Richard addresses the audience, predicting the action to come, responding to the action just past, flaunting his witty wickedness, gloating at the other characters' weakness and ignorance, and seducing the fascinated auditors into complicity with his diabolical schemes. It is a power we glimpsed in his father's soliloquies as early as *Henry VI, Part II.*

The female characters who do appear in the play are also recruited to Richmond's project; and like Elizabeth, they are also sacrificed to it. Richmond's victory, in fact, re-enacts in benevolent form Richard's earlier appropriation of the feminine. Just as the play begins with Richard's appropriation of Margaret's power of subversive speech, it ends with Richmond's appropriation of the moral authority of bereaved and suffering women to authorize his victory. To serve that purpose, the female characters must lose their individuality and become an undifferentiated chorus of ritual lamentation, curse, and prophecy that enunciates the play's providential agenda. Recounting the crimes of the past, they speak as "poor mortal-living ghost[s]" (IV.iv.26). Like the literal ghosts who appear on the night before the Battle of Bosworth Field, they announce the obliteration of patrilineal genealogy and invoke the higher authority of Divine Providence to validate Richmond's accession (Hodgdon 1991: 114).

In praying for Richmond's victory, the ghosts of Richard's victims speak for the entire nation, which is now identified as a helpless, suffering woman. This identification is reiterated in Richmond's final speech: "Abate the edge of traitors, gracious Lord," he prays, "That would reduce these bloody days again,/ And make poor England weep in streams of blood!" (V.v.35–7). The suffering victim of Richard's bloody tyranny, England is also the cherished object of Richmond's compassionate concern. Both here and in his oration before the battle, Richmond characterizes himself as a loving, protective paterfamilias, and he also promises his soldiers the rewards that go with that role:

> If you do fight in safeguard of your wives,
> Your wives shall welcome home the conquerors;
> If you do free your children from the sword,
> Your children's children quits it in your age.
> (V.iii.259–62)

Richard, by contrast, resorts to jingoistic appeals to masculine honor and misogynist charges that Richmond is a "milksop" (V.iii.325) and his soldiers "bastard Britains [i.e. Bretons], whom our fathers/ Have in their own land beaten, bobb'd, and thump'd." "If we be conquered," he says, "let men conquer us" (V.iii.333–4, 332).

Richard is still a powerfully seductive actor, but by this point in the play he is thoroughly discredited as a monarchial figure. The audience can now reject his aggressively masculine rhetoric and respond instead as Richmond's "loving countrymen" (V.iii.237) who desire to "sleep in peace" (V.iii.256). But although the audience is invited to accept Richmond's appeal to their "feminine" desires for peace and prosperity, the scene withholds actual images of female royal or theatrical authority. No women actors, of course, were on the stage, and no women characters appear in this scene. When Richmond invites the audience to join him in a prayer that the descendents of his union with Elizabeth will "Enrich the time to come with smooth-fac'd peace,/ With smiling plenty, and fair prosperous days" (V.v.33–4), he is invoking, as the descendent of this pair, the female monarch, Elizabeth I, who ruled England when Shakespeare was writing *Richard III,* and is praising the peace and prosperity she had brought to England. But just as the Elizabeth Richmond marries never appears on stage, the Elizabeth he foretells is never mentioned by name or even identified as a woman.

Assuming the role of benevolent paterfamilias, Richmond constructs himself in direct antithesis to the solitary individualism of the tragic hero he supplants, the murderer of the young princes, the character who defined himself from the beginning by his contempt for women and his separation from the loving bonds of kinship. Nonetheless, the play ends as it begins, with a male character speaking from the *platea* empowered by his appropriation of the woman's part and his performative self-construction as the object of a feminized audience's desire.

Texts Cited

Belsey, C. (1985) *The Subject of Tragedy: Identity and Difference in Renaissance Drama,* London: Methuen.

Brooke, Nicholas. (1984) "Reflecting Gems and Dead Bones: Tragedy Versus History in *Richard III* in *Shakespeare's Wide and Universal Stage,* ed. C. B. Cox and D. J. Palmer, Manchester: Manchester University Press 104–16.

Bushnell R.W. (1990) *Tragedies of Tyrants: Political Thought and Theater in the English Renaissance,* Ithaca: Cornell University Press.

Hall, E. (1548) *The Union of the Two Noble and Illustre Families of Lancatre & Yorke;* (1809) reprint. London: J. Johnson et al.

Hammond, A. (ed.) (1981) *King Richard III,* Arden edition. London: Methuen.

Hodgdon, B. (1991) *The End Crowns All: Closure and Contradiction in Shakespeare's History,* Princeton: Princeton University Press.

McLuskie, K. (1985) "The Patriarchal Band: Feminist Criticism and Shakespeare: *King Lear* and *Measure for Measure,*" in *Political Shakespeare: New Essays in Cultural Materialism,* ed. J. Dollimore and A. Sinfield, Ithaca: Cornell University Press, 88–108.

———. (1989) (*Renaissance Dramatists,* Atlantic Highlands, N.J.: Humanities Press International.

Newman, K. (1991) *Fashioning Femininity and English Renaissance Drama,* Chicago: University of Chicago Press.

The Monstrous Body in *King Richard III*

LINDA CHARNES

In Shakespeare's *Richard III,* as in the authorized Tudor histories, Richard's identity is inseparable from his physical "difference." So long as this identity is perceived by others within the play as corresponding to that of Tudor legend, so long as his body is regarded as "evidence" of his identity, he can have no "legitimate" authority. In order to acquire it, however briefly, Richard must combat the play's politics of vision with an alternative strategy, one that negates the ideology of the visual by realigning the significance of his body with an ideology of the *invisible* body. There are, both within the medieval setting of the play and in sixteenth-century England, ideological structures available that Richard (and Shakespeare) can appropriate to replace an *obvious* body with one that is implied, one not necessarily determined by physical characteristics. In seeking the crown, Richard seeks no less than a new body: the body implied by "the King's Body," which, according to medieval political theology, admits of no flaws and is the highest manifestation of God's grace on earth.[1]

Shakespeare's play diverges most clearly from its sources when it takes that most "sublime object of ideology," the English crown, and sublates it to another desire. For gaining the crown is not Richard's ultimate aim; his underlying aim is to use the King's Body to transform "handicaps" of his own. Gaining the crown will enable him to effect a kind of trade in which he imagines that he can exchange his misshapen, half made-up body for the "King's Body" and its divine perfections. With the success of this exchange, Richard will remove himself from the periphery (where his disharmonious parts place him) and relocate himself at the center.[2]

The fascination Richard holds for the audience lies in his attempts to resist and escape the deformed and deforming signification the play insists upon—his attempts to counteract the Richard of Tudor legend, which I will henceforth call "the play's Richard," with his own version, or Richard's Richard. The play's Richard is the figure inherited from John Rous, Morton, Polydore Vergil, More, Grafton, Halle, and Holinshed; his deformity was deployed as "evidence" of moral and political depravity. This identity is continually referred to by others, particularly the women, including Anne Neville, Margaret, Elizabeth, and his mother the duchess; and it is characterized by a language of dehumanization: he is a "bunch-backed" toad, a bottled spider, a mad dog, a devil, a foul stone, a lump of foul deformity. Since Richard's experience of himself is inseparable from how he "reads" the signs of his own body as a signifying text, his entire course of action can be seen as directed toward gaining control over the social construction, perception, and manipulation of bodily signifiers. Richard knows he cannot replace the perception of monstrosity with that of normalcy; but he can subrogate, by means of inversion, one ideology of exception with another. He can sublate his deformed body to the perfect "Body" of the king.

This is not to say that gaining the crown is a "psychological motivation" for Richard. At least, it's not psychological in the sense of individual pathology. Overdetermined by a habitus in which bodies *must* signify, Richard's "desire" for the crown is both an objective compulsion toward the only alternative structure available for him to inhabit that equals, in its own symbolically mandated weight, his portentous body; and a desire to replace stigma, and its shameful sense of social exclusion, with charisma—the symbolic value attributed to someone who is perceived as being "near the heart of things."[3] It is, as Bourdieu evocatively puts it, a desire to substitute one kind of "distinction" for another:

> Charm and charisma in fact designate the power, which certain people have, to impose their own self-image as the objective and collective image of their body and being; to persuade others, as in love or faith, to abdicate their generic power of objectification and delegate it to the person who should be its object, who thereby becomes an absolute subject, without an exterior (being his own Other), fully justified in existing, legitimated. The charismatic leader manages to be for the group what he is for himself, instead of being for himself, like those dominated in the symbolic struggle, what he is for others. He "makes" the opinion which makes him.[4]

It is just such a symbolic struggle that Shakespeare's Richard is engaged in: that of attempting to exchange status as the absolute object of Tudor historiography for that of the "absolute subject without an exterior," of his own making and regard. Richard's ontological project is to be for the group what he wishes to be for himself, rather than being for himself what the group always already knows that he is. This is how stigma operates: it deprives the subject of any inhabitable self-image that is not determined by others. The play, then, charts not so much Richard's "progress" toward the crown as his progress toward a fantasy of absolute subjecthood—a subjecthood that he will, paradoxically, lose *precisely by materializing it* when, like Bourdieu's charismatic charmer, he finally " 'makes' the opinion which makes him."

It is because subjects do not, strictly speaking, know what they are doing that what they are doing means more than they know.
—Pierre Bourdieu, *Outline of a Theory of Practice*

This, therefore, is the basic paradox we are aiming at: the subject is confronted with a scene from the past that he wants to change, to meddle with, to intervene in; he takes a journey into the past, intervenes in the scene, and it is not that he "cannot change anything"—quite the contrary, only through his intervention does the scene from the past *become what it always was:* his intervention was from the beginning comprised, included.
—Slavoj Žižek, *The Sublime Object of Ideology*

What we regard as "history" is always "mediated through subjectivity": it becomes history only by the process of repetitive inscription in and through the symbolic. Consequently its "Truth arises from misrecognition"—whatever it signifies in the social formation necessarily routes through the misrecognition of consciousness (what Žižek calls "the opinion of the people"—*Sublime Object*, p. 61). "If we want to spare ourselves the painful roundabout route through the misrecognition, we miss the Truth itself" (p. 63). And this Truth is that the significance of history is consolidated only retroactively, like the "truth" of the analysand who has come through psychoanalysis and assigned his symptomology its place in the narrative. The very grammar of history, therefore, is proleptic: it puts later things first (just as Shakespeare chronicles later historical events in the "first tetralogy"). In this way, what was once profoundly contingent is reconstituted as "inevitable." *Richard III* maps the function of repetition for the subject who wants to "spare himself the painful roundabout route," who will not know what he knows, who refuses to read the signs, as if they were external to him and he could choose *not* to read them. In the figure of Richard we see the subject who will not identify with the symptom, who does not "believe" in omens and therefore secures his function as the symptom and omen of others. By rejecting his own portentousness, Richard "intervenes" and in his illusion of contingency ends up confirming "providential" history. This illusion is figured in Richard's denial of the language of intertextuality, his mistaking of his existence as *a first time occurrence,* as if he had no prior textual existence which had already constituted his own "symbolic necessity." This in itself would not be remarkable if the habitus of the play (within the larger habitus of Elizabethan England) weren't structured around this "necessity," if it weren't full of other figures who continually speak Richard's deformed frame as the advertisement of an overdetermined historical frame.[5]

In his opening soliloquy Richard speaks of himself as the victim of a surround—alternately conceived as maternal, natural, social—that is assigned mysterious agency: he is "rudely stamp'd," "curtail'd" of fair proportion, "cheated of feature." Contrary to the rumors others have generated about his remaining too long in the womb and being born with teeth and hair, Richard claims to have been "sent before [his] time," "unfinish'd" and "scarce half made-up." The discrepancy of versions of Richard is apparent even here; and the emotional significance of his sense of being born before he was ready will permeate his relations with the play's female figures. Richard replaces a language of overgestation, of prodigious *belatedness,* with one of underdevelopment, of rude and untimely *prematurity,* and in doing so speaks a fantasy of preceding his own legend. By literally reconceiving himself, this time as "unfinish'd," "scarce half made-up," he speaks a fantasy of arriving early at the scene of his own story, with the possibility of "making up" the rest himself. However, Richard's fetal self-revisionism denies the conditions that compel the activity in the first place; and his efforts to reorganize the relationship between his body and the social becomes the driving impetus toward a status in which he will be not excluded (because he is not shaped for sportive tricks) but at the very center.

> I do mistake my person all this while!
> Upon my life, she finds—although I cannot—
> Myself to be a marvellous proper man.
> Richard III (1.2.252–254)[6]

After Richard's acknowledgment of his deformity in the first scene, it is others, and most notably the women, who repeatedly refer to his body in the most scornful and degrading terms. The project, then, of reorganizing the relations of social perception begins properly with Richard's courtship of Anne Neville. In this scene, and *apparently* against all odds, Richard produces himself as an object of libidinal attraction. I say "apparently" because however preposterous his success may seem, it reveals as much about the play's libidinal structures and affective investments as it does about Richard, and possibly more. Although critics diverge in their views of the courtship—its success, its apparent absurdity, its "psychological veracity" (or more commonly its lack thereof), most tend to fall into one of two camps. Either they find it unbelievable that Anne capitulates, or they see Richard's "genius" and his success as a function of rhetorical skill.[7] Although Richard must (and did) marry Anne as part of his progress toward the crown, this scene does far more than just establish the requisite "traffic in women" necessary for the disposition of property and lineage. The reach of its effectiveness, however—what Richard calls his "secret close intent" (1.1.158), cannot be understood by appealing to notions of psychosexual "health" or "normalcy." On the contrary. It is precisely its preposterousness that renders the scene dramatically successful, erotically convincing, and centrally revealing of the rest of the play's social and libidinal relations. The scene works by revealing the socially productive fascination that always underlies revulsion, and by demonstrating the discursive and libidinal identities between contempt and desire, revulsion and attraction, political obsession and sexual fixation. Richard's "genius" in this scene may be rhetorical; but its force issues from the way he both manipulates and sets in motion around himself the affective power of the object of sexual disgust.

Looking at the play retroactively, when Richard says at 1.1.30 that he is "determined to prove a villain," we know this to be true. But not because Richard wills it. In Richard's fantasy, to become England's king is not only to replace monstrous difference with royal difference; it is to rule others—those who have "rul'd" a deformed Richard (Nature, his mother, and by extension all women, all previous writers of Richard, and ultimately his coauthor, Shakespeare), and those who have ratified that ruling by reading his body as the expression of political disaster. Of course the play's ultimate structural irony is that Richard's declaration of "determination" leads him into actions that confirm his predetermination, his imprisonment in a body that is the spatial representation of already inscribed political and moral "perversion." With brilliant proleptic legerdemain, the play's ending sets up the play's beginning, repeating compulsively within its own parameters a history of Tudor writing about Richard Plantagenet that increasingly reifies him into a monster. Richard's determination of himself as villain is the literal realization of (and unwitting collusion in) the play's determination of Richard.

In his final soliloquy in 5.3.178–206, he faces the confusion, and final collapse, of the illusory distinction between the play's "two Richards," a distinction that achieving the King's Two Bodies will no longer sustain:

> What do I fear? Myself? There's none else by;
> Richard loves Richard, that is, I am I.
> Is there a murderer here? No, Yes, I am!
> Then fly. What, from myself? Great reason why,
> Lest I revenge? What, myself upon myself?
> Alack, I love myself. Wherefore? For any good
> That I myself have done unto myself?
> O no, alas, I rather hate myself
> For hateful deeds committed by myself.
> I am a villain—yet I lie, I am not!

Even the textual variations of the play contribute to the confusion regarding the doubling, and fusion, of the two Richards: the Quarto version of line 179 reads "Richard loves Richard, that is, I *and* I." I and I versus I am I: this is the conflict his notorious identity produces. In Richard's soliloquy we hear the confounding of "I"s and his disruptive confusion and doubt about his agency and status—no longer in relation to others, but in relation to himself. Richard is an agent. He knows this. But what emerges in these disturbing lines is

Richard's confrontation with the creature of Tudor legend he has simultaneously been delivering and disowning. Is the agency behind his actions his own? The play's answer is a structural one, and it is no. Richard has already revenged himself upon himself and has been doing it throughout the play. When he says "I am a villain—yet I lie, I am not!" he isn't denying his "hateful deeds." Rather, the statement is a last-ditch effort to retain the illusion of textual autonomy. In his disclaimer we see the realization break upon him that he has *been determined* to "prove a villain"; and that consequently, he has no "I" at all. Indeed, if "every tale condemns [him] for a villain" (5.3.195), he has determined nothing for himself.

At this crucial moment before the battle at Bosworth, Richard confronts the fact that he has lost what has always been the real battle—the battle against his own overdetermined textuality. The Richard of Tudor legend proves too weighty an opponent against which to sustain an alternative subjectivity.[8] By abortively invoking and then collapsing in these lines the distinction between "the same" and "the same as," Shakespeare's treatment of the Richard legend materializes at this moment a subject forced finally *to confront and to be identical to* his notorious identity; and furthermore, one that realizes it precisely by resisting it. Richard the actor confronts Richard the text; and in this, his only moment of genuine lucidity—the moment in which he confronts the real conditions of his intertextual existence—we see his subjectivity emerge as an effect of losing his battle with the books. The effect of this retroactive reconstruction of meaning is a kind of deconstruction of the play as a whole. By the end we must rethink, if not refute, our entire experience—for it has not been what it has seemed.

Throughout the play (or at least until Richard acquires the crown) the audience believes, with Richard, that it is watching him chart his own self-proclaimed course. We witness his fantasy of oppositional "self-fashioning" unfold, and we believe (in the sense I've outlined above, in which histrionic identification generates a belief effect, whether we "will" it or not), along with Richard, that he has managed to "see through" the play's didactic and prophetic elements. But by the time we reach the dream-vision sequence before Bosworth, we realize that the play has slowly been coopting "Richard's Richard," using his "revised" version of himself to *demonstrate* temporally and spatially the "authorized," accretive, and legendary text that the figure of Richard has, by the time Shakespeare takes him up, become. In this way, the play stages the question of what it is like to be cheated not by Nature but by textual history: what it is like for the subject who is barred from being anything other than a monster because his conception, gestation, birth, and body bear the mark of a villainy not only always-already accomplished but already written about repeatedly. Canceling the audience's *experience* of Richard as autonomous subject with its relentlessly "providential" logic, the play's structure subverts its content by insisting at the end that its content has always been (if one only goes back to the beginning again) its structure.

Notes

1. For the most complete exposition of the medieval legal and theological doctrine of the "King's Two Bodies," see Ernst H. Kantorowicz's seminal work *The King's Two Bodies: A Study in Medieval Political Theology* (Princeton: Princeton University Press, 1957). This powerful notion of the correspondence of the king's human body with its eternal, unimpeachable, and divine counterpart, the "King's" royal body, was still operative (although rapidly becoming demystified in post-Machiavellian England) in somewhat secularized form in Shakespeare's day; and thus would have been doubly appropriate in application to Richard. Since Richard III ruled in the Middle Ages, the doctrine can logically be considered a part of Richard's world within the play. And the secularizing of the doctrine under Elizabeth, as well as its increasingly obvious use as ideological mechanism, would have opened up for a playwright as astute as Shakespeare its histrionic possibilities. Shakespeare plays with the notion of the King's Two Bodies with the only other figure in English history who needed an "authoritative" king's body even more than Elizabeth: the "monstrous" Duke of Gloucester.

See also Clifford Geertz, "Centers, Kings, and Charisma: Reflections on the Symbolics of Power," in *Culture and Its Creators: Essays in Honor of Edward Shils,* ed. Joseph Ben David and Terry Nichols Clark (Chicago: University of Chicago Press, 1977). Geertz describes Elizabeth's appropriation of the doctrine of the King's Two Bodies, and the charisma she was able to fashion for herself out of the ingenious use of "rites and images" (p. 152): "[Britain's political imagination] was allegorical, Protestant, didactic and pictorial; it lived on moral abstractions cast into emblems. Elizabeth was Chastity, Wisdom, Peace, Perfect Beauty, and Pure Religion as well as queen . . . and being queen she was these things. Her whole public life—or, more exactly, the part of her life the public saw—was transformed into a kind of philosophical masque in which everything stood for some vast idea and nothing took place unburdened with parable" (p. 156).

And Leah Marcus discusses the ways Elizabeth manipulated both the discourses of gender and the ideology of the King's Body in her own self-staging and rhetorical self-references. By emphasizing Elizabeth's reliance on the doctrine of the King's Body, Marcus sublates the fact that Elizabeth's human body was a "weak woman's" body to the "fact" that she also possessed the symbolically masculine King's Body through her link to her father, Henry VIII. Marcus connects this practice to Shakespeare's representations of cross-dressed, rhetorically cross-gendered comic heroines such as Portia, Viola, and Rosalind. See "Shakespeare's Comic Heroines: The Political Uses of Androgyny," in *Women in the Middle Ages and the Renaissance: Literary and Historical Perspectives,* ed. Mary Beth Rose (Syracuse, N.Y.: Syracuse University Press, 1986), pp. 135–154.

2. My use of the terms "center" and "periphery" is influenced by but ultimately independent of the larger model Edward Shils constructs in his chapter "Center and Periphery," in *Essays in Macrosociology* (Chicago: University of Chicago Press, 1975), pp. 3–16. Some mention of that model is relevant here, however. One of Shils's defining characteristics of the "center" of a society is that its "central value system is constituted by the values which are pursued and affirmed by the elites of the constituent subsystems and of the organizations which are comprised in the subsystems. By their possession of authority, they attribute to themselves an essential affinity with the sacred elements of their society, of which they regard themselves as the custodians. . . . One of the major elements in any central value system is an affirmative attitude toward established authority. . . . Authority enjoys appreciation because it arouses sentiments of sacredness. Sacredness by its nature is authoritative. Those persons, offices, or symbols endowed with it, however indirectly and remotely, are therewith endowed with some measure of authoritativeness" (p. 5).

Shils's theory is germane in connection with my assertion that Richard's desire is to acquire the value attributed to the sacred perfection of the "King's body." If, as Shils claims, sacredness inheres within authoritativeness, and both together form the originary point from which all other values are derived, then we can regard Richard's desire to be king as his desire to make himself the *episteme* of all values (or, in other terms, the arbiter of all signification) in the play. This desire, however, must be pitted against the fact that Richard "recognizes" no sacred authority behind the kingship of others, notably Henry VI and his own brother Edward. In a classic circuit of willful misrecognition, he seeks to realize the symbolic capital that comes from being "round impaled with a glorious crown" (*King Henry VI, Part 3:* 3.2.171), capital that he scornfully denies to others. This is in keeping with his general attempt to render commutable the value of all signification only if it originates in his own person.

3.   Geertz, in "Centers, Kings, and Charisma," discusses Shils's conception of charisma as "the connection between the symbolic value individuals possess and their relation to the active centers of the social order" (p. 151).

4.   Pierre Bourdieu, *Distinction: A Social Critique of the Judgement of Taste,* trans. Richard Nice (Cambridge, Mass.: Harvard University Press, 1984), p. 208.

5.   Marjorie Garber's exploration, in *Shakespeare's Ghost Writers: Literature and the Uncanny Causality* (New York, Methuen, 1987), of the way Shakespeare uses the "historicity" of the figure of Richard pushes beyond the usual bounds of the Tudor-propaganda debate into the deconstructive politics of historiography. Garber argues that all history writing is essentially propagandistic insofar as it is "deformed" by the invested, "authorized" writing hand; and that the amplification of Richard's deformity over time signifies the inevitable deformations of history itself. Richard's character "marks the inevitability of deformation in the registers of the political and historiographical" (p. 33). Thus, the writing of history, like the writing of Richard, exemplifies "the dangers of re-membering, of history as an artifact of memory" (p. 44). Garber eloquently asserts that to remember is to re-member, to re-assemble, to assign new members to something; and that the figure of Richard is just such a "re-membering": "Richard is not only deformed, his deformity is itself a deformation. His twisted and misshapen body encodes the whole strategy of history as a necessary deforming and unforming—with the object of re-forming—the past" (p. 36). The suggestion here is that Richard *is* History: both are prodigious, both are untimely (in the sense of being constructed after the fact), both are misshapen by authorized and authorizing hands.

In what I take to be the central point of her argument, Garber asserts that, like history, and "created by a similar process of ideological and polemical distortion, Richard's deformity is a figment of rhetoric, a figure of abuse, a catachresis masquerading as a metaphor. In a viciously circular manifestation of neo-Platonic determinism, Richard is made villainous in appearance to match the desired villainy of his reputation, and then is given a personality warped and bent to compensate for his physical shape" (p. 36). While I agree with Garber's characterization of the vicious circle of historiography Richard finds himself in, and finds in himself, her exposition seems haunted by what it leaves out, forecloses on something about Richard that, however anamorphically, demands to be seen. As Garber herself points out early in her argument, "no account of Shakespeare's literary or political motivations in foregrounding his protagonist's deformity is adequate to explain the power and seductiveness of Richard's presence in the plays. Indeed, the very fascination exerted by the historical Richard III seems to grow in direct proportion to an increase in emphasis on his deformity" (p. 31). But emphasizing his deformity as standing solely for the process of writing a history play also seems inadequate "to explain the power and seductiveness of Richard's presence in the play." In her understandable concern not to essentialize "character," Garber ends an otherwise convincing discussion almost where one wants it to begin. Accepting the *play's* legerdemain by reinscribing the deformed figure of Richard as a "catachresis masquerading as metaphor," her account misses the way that Shakespeare is representing a *subjective identity between* metaphor and catachresis: the fact that anyone who is made to "stand for" him or herself will feel "incorrect" or warped, like a bad facsimile of some more "authentic" "original"—that the identity *coerced* by metaphor is always itself a "masquerade," always itself purchased *by* catachresis. In subsuming the figure of Richard under the larger conceptual carapace of "Shakespeare's ghost writers,"

Garber's account doesn't explain the "power and seductiveness of Richard's presence in the play" because it leaves out the ghost in the machine.

6. All citations from the play are taken from the Arden edition of *King Richard III,* ed. Antony Hammond (London: Methuen, 1981).

7. That the history of criticism of this scene is largely one of incredulity is evident in the vehemence of the criticism that argues for its psychological verisimilitude. Donald Shupe, in "The Wooing of Lady Anne: A Psychological Inquiry," *Shakespeare Quarterly* 29 (1978):28–36, argues that Richard's Machiavellian skill at manipulation makes the scene psychologically believable; and Denzell Smith, in "The Credibility of the Wooing of Anne in *Richard III,*" *Papers on Language and Literature* 7 (1971):199–202, argues for the psychological "realism" of the scene as well. However, for an interesting analysis of why the scene doesn't work for Richard precisely because he *does* accomplish his aim, see Marguerite Waller, "Usurpation, Seduction, and the Problematics of the Proper: A 'Deconstructive,' 'Feminist' Rereading of the Seductions of Richard and Anne in Shakespeare's *Richard III,*" in *Rewriting the Renaissance: The Discourses of Sexual Difference in Early Modern Europe,* ed. Margaret W. Ferguson, Maureen Quilligan, and Nancy J. Vickers (Chicago: University of Chicago Press, 1986), pp. 159–174. Dolores Burton, in "Discourse and Decorum in the First Act of *Richard III*" (*Shakespeare Studies* 14 [1981]:55–84), analyzes the wooing of Anne in terms of classical rhetoric, noting that Richard triumphs over Anne because of his skill with forensic or judicial oratory: "Because this oratory of the courtroom attempts to defend or to blame a person's behavior, it looks back to the past, develops arguments from the special topics of justice and injustice, and employs as its means accusation and defense" (p. 62). It is a rhetoric of disputation, and Richard wins because "despite [Anne's] ability to match Gloucester's language word for word and phrase for phrase, [she] is no match for his logic" (p. 65). Although Burton's interpretation is splendid in its attention to the details and nuances of the language, I don't agree with her sense of what is at stake in the scene. For Burton, the many references to eyes and sight must be understood in the sonnet tradition, the language of which Richard deploys against Anne. She makes no connection between Anne's plea for proper vision in this scene and the larger politics of visual evidence in the play.

8. This is not to say, however, that Richard is entirely deconstructed in this scene. On the contrary, he is consolidated into the reified text that has been the play's relentless ideological telos. Other critics disagree, however, about what this moment in the play achieves. Janet Adelman argues that "even while Shakespeare suggests the etiology of Richard's transformation into an actor, he participates in the erasure of Richard's intolerable selfhood: in *Richard III,* our attention is directed more to Richard's theatrical machinations than to any imagined subjectivity behind his roles; even in Richard's spectacular final soliloquy (5.3.178–204), the effect is less of a psyche than of diverse roles confronting themselves across the void where a self should be" (*Suffocating Mothers: Fantasies of Maternal Origin in Shakespeare's Plays "Hamlet" to "The Tempest"* [New York: Routledge, 1992] p. 9).

As I have argued earlier, it is precisely in those moments when the figure becomes aware of the gap between a notorious identity being foisted upon it and the possibility of or yearning for something "else" that subjectivity is represented; and it is precisely at this moment in the play when Richard materializes most fully as a subject. Not, to be sure, as a "psyche" (with its connotations of substantial inwardness and unity of self), but, rather, as an entity all of a sudden fully and horribly aware of the intolerable mandates of his social identity, a role that demands that he play the monster, a role that one finally senses, if only for a moment, he does not want to play. In this soliloquy Richard is not "the perfect actor who has no being except in the roles he plays" (p. 9) but the subject grown exhausted by the resistance these roles simultaneously require and break down. This scene doesn't "erase" Richard's "intolerable selfhood" (p. 9); it *produces* it in the face-off between the two versions of Richard the play has been advancing along convergent paths.

Notes on Contributors

◆

Peter Saccio completed a B.A. at Yale and a Ph.D. at Princeton before becoming a professor of English at Dartmouth College. He has also written *The Court Comedies of John Lyly.*

Geoffrey Bullough (1901–1982) was professor of English at King's College, University of London; in addition to his monumental survey of Shakespeare's sources and analogues, he also wrote about Milton, Fulke Greville, and the English lyric tradition generally.

Bernard Spivack, after research supported by Columbia University, became a faculty member of Fisk University.

Irving Ribner (1921–1972) was chairman of the English department at the State University of New York at Stony Brook. He edited volumes of the complete works of both Shakespeare and Marlowe and wrote the books *Patterns in Shakespearean Tragedy* and *Jacobean Tragedy.*

Wolfgang H. Clemen was a professor of English at the University of Munich. He has published widely on Shakespeare, including *The Development of Shakespeare's Imagery, Shakespeare's Dramatic Art,* and *Commentary on "Richard III."*

Scott Colley has written *John Marston's Theatrical Drama* and *Richard's Himself Again: A Stage History of Richard III,* from which is taken his review of Colley Cibber's version. He is dean of faculty at Hampden-Sidney College, Virginia.

Thomas Whately intended to write a broader study, titled *Remarks on Some of the Characters of Shakespeare,* but only the very long section on Richard III and Macbeth was published posthumously under this title in 1785. The comparison, favoring the greater humanity of Macbeth's character but stressing Richard's wit, verve, and ambition, provided the basis for much subsequent discussion. Brief representative sections have been excerpted from the much longer original.

Augustus William Schlegel, a leading romantic critic, translated 16 plays of Shakespeare into German. He was deeply opposed to the neoclassical aesthetics that dominated eighteenth-century literature, and he repudiated their often critical view of Shakespeare. Schlegel's published lectures, *über Dramatische Kunst und Literatur* (1811), were translated by John Black in 1815, and the extract comes from Lecture 12, principally devoted to Shakespeare.

William Hazlitt was a leading man of letters in the romantic period: journalist, essayist, and theater critic. Following Schlegel's lead in restoring *Richard III* to its historical context, and reacting against eighteenth-century modifications of scripts, Hazlitt published *Characters of Shakespeare's Plays* in 1817. He drew heavily on his experience as a reviewer of Shakespeare productions, stressing the subjective psychology of the roles as portrayed by such intense actors as Edmund Kean.

Nathan Drake was a physician but also a romantic literary critic; in 1817 he published *Shakespeare and His Times,* in which the section on *Richard III* places Milton's Satan in the literary tradition sustained by Richard. The comparison invited further correlation of this play with other texts, particularly ones favored by the romantics.

E. M. W. Tillyard was among the first students to graduate from the English faculty at Cambridge University, where he spent most of his career. His vast range of publications include many major studies of Shakespeare, Wyatt, and Milton. He writes in the tradition of literary history antecedent to the new criticism represented by his long-term adversary at Cambridge, F. R. Leavis.

A. P. Rossiter was a member of the English faculty at Cambridge University and published *English Drama from Early Times to the Elizabethans* and an edition of the anonymous play *Woodstock.*

Murray Krieger has been a professor of English at the University of California at Los Angeles and the University of California at Irvine, where he was director of the School of Criticism and Theory, and later directed the University of California Humanities Research Institute. He writes about literary theory and aesthetics.

Nicholas Brooke became a lecturer at the University of East Anglia, after graduating from Cambridge University. He edited Chapman's *Bussy d'Ambois* in the Revels series, *Macbeth* in the Oxford series, and studies of *Richard II* and *King Lear.*

Roy W. Battenhouse (1912–1995) was a professor of English at Indiana University and an Episcopalian minister. An expert theologian, he argued for a Christian interpretation of Shakespeare in numerous works, including *Shakespearean Tragedy*. He also wrote studies of Marlowe and St. Augustine.

Richard P. Wheeler, professor of English at the University of Illinois at Urbana, wrote *Shakespeare's Development and the Problem Comedies* and completed the last book of C. L. Barber.

Marjorie B. Garber has written numerous studies of Shakespeare, including *Coming of Age in Shakespeare* and *Shakespeare's Ghost Writers,* as well as *Creating Elizabethan Tragedy*. She is a professor of English at Harvard University.

Emrys Jones is professor of English at Oxford University and has written widely about Shakespeare and the performance of his plays. In addition to *The Origins of Shakespeare* he has written *Scenic Form in Shakespeare*.

M. M. Mahood has taught at Oxford and the University of Kent and has written *Poetry and Humanism* and *Shakespeare's Wordplay*.

Madonne M. Miner, professor of English at Texas Tech University, has published *Insatiable Appetites: Twentieth-Century American Women's Bestsellers*.

Jean Howard is a professor of English and comparative literature at Columbia University. She is a major participant in discussions of modern literary theory, including the new historicism, and has written *The Stage and Social Struggle in Early Modern England* and *Shakespeare's Art of Orchestration: Stage Technique and Audience Response*.

Phyllis Rackin, as a result of such works as her *Stages of English History: Shakespeare's English Chronicles,* was identified as a leading feminist critic by her election as president of the Shakespeare Association of America. She is a professor of English at the University of Pennsylvania.

Linda Charnes is an associate professor of English at Indiana University; she earned her doctorate in English at the University of California at Berkeley, in association with that institution's core of new historicists led by Stephen Greenblatt.

INDEX

♦

This anthology is oriented to Shakespeare's *Richard III*, so proper names appear in this index as they appear in the play, not according to any other historical criteria.

Actors' Conservatory Theatre, 261
Adelman, Janet, 281
Adler, Charles A., 253
adultery, 267–68
Aeschylus, *Oresteia*, 6, 7
Agincourt, 51
Alexander, Bill, 229, 257, 261
Alleyn, Edward, 8
Anne, Lady (Neville, later queen of Richard
    III), 8, 9, 11, 44, 168, 174–75; BBC,
    236; in Cibber, 77, 81–85; death,
    104–5, 134, 215; feminist views of,
    243–45, 270; ghost, 197; in history,
    17, 23, 25, 33; seduced by Richard of
    Gloucester (*R3*, I.ii), 46–47, 55–57,
    107, 125, 132, 148–51, 182–83,
    186–88, 203, 281; played with Kean,
    166; Rustaveli, 262, 281
Appius and Virginia, 57
Aquinas, Thomas, 175
Aristotle, 170–75, 226
Ashcroft, Peggy, 6
Augustine, Saint: *Confessions,* 173
Australia, 267

Barton, Anne. *See* Righter
Bayldon, Oliver, 235
Bakhtin, Michail, 265
Baker, Howard, 72

Baldwin, William, 38. *See also Mirror for
    Magistrates*
Bale, John, 72
Barber, C. L., 13, 176, 192
Barbu, Zevedi, 190–91, 193
Barclay, Sam, 236–37
Barnes, Barnabe, 1
Barnet, Battle of, 20, 38, 120
Battenhouse, Roy, 1, 115, 170–75, 285
Battle of Alcazar, 45, 70, 72
Baudelaire, 168
BBC *Richard III,* 7, 115, 232–40
Beaufort, Lady Margaret (mother of Henry
    VII, later wife of Lord Stanley), 32, 33
Beckerman, Bernard, 260, 266
Begg, Edleen, 63
Behn, Aphra: *Oroonoko,* 107
Belfast, 235
Belsey, Catherine, 268, 272
Benson, Frank, 91
Berkeley (in *Richard III*), 208
Berkeley Shakespeare Festival, 264–65
Berkeley, D. S., 71
Berman, Monty, 257
Berowne, 13
Berry, Ralph, 226, 231
Bethell, S. L., 72
bishops, the two, 223
Blakemore Evans, G., 14
Bolingbroke, 156
Bond, Edward, 13
Bond, James, 4
Booth, Edwin, 91, 94
Booth, Stephen, 12

The Volume Editor

◆

After completing a B.A. at Cambridge, a D.Phil. at Oxford, and studies at the Universities of Florence, Lyons, and Munich, Hugh Macrae Richmond became a professor of English at the University of California at Berkeley and developed the systemwide University of California Shakespeare Forum. He continues to direct the Shakespeare program there, as professor emeritus. Richmond has also served as education director for the Shakespeare Globe Centre U.S.A. and staged *Much Ado about Nothing* at the restored Globe. The University of California Shakespeare Program's educational videotapes in national distribution are *Shakespeare at the Globe* (Films for the Humanities) and *Shakespeare's Globe Theatre Restored* (TMW Media). Richmond's books include *Shakespeare's Political Plays* and *Shakespeare in Performance: "King Richard III."*

The General Editor

◆

Zack Bowen is professor of English at the University of Miami. He holds degrees from the University of Pennsylvania (B.A.), Temple University (M.A.), and the State University of New York at Buffalo (Ph.D.). In addition to being general editor of this G. K. Hall series, he is editor of the James Joyce series for the University of Florida Press and the *James Joyce Literary Supplement*. He is author and editor of numerous books on modern British, Irish, and American literature. He has also published more than 100 monographs, essays, scholarly reviews, and recordings related to literature. He is past president of the James Joyce Society (1977–1986), former chair of the Modern Language Association Lowell Prize Committee, and current president of the International James Joyce Foundation.